Anonymous

Bible Songs

Consisting of selections from the Psalms set to music; suitable for Sabbath schools,

prayer meetings, etc.

Anonymous

Bible Songs

Consisting of selections from the Psalms set to music; suitable for Sabbath schools, prayer meetings, etc.

ISBN/EAN: 9783744781732

Printed in Europe, USA, Canada, Australia, Japan

Cover: Foto ©Thomas Meinert / pixelio.de

More available books at **www.hansebooks.com**

THREE JOURNEYS

AROUND THE WORLD

OR

TRAVELS IN THE PACIFIC ISLANDS, NEW ZEALAND
AUSTRALIA, CEYLON, INDIA, EGYPT

AND OTHER

ORIENTAL COUNTRIES

IN ONE VOLUME

BY

J. M. PEEBLES, A.M., M.D., PH.D.

AUTHOR OF "SEERS OF THE AGES," " IMMORTALITY," " HOW TO LIVE A CENTURY
CAL REVIEW OF REV. DR. KIPP," " JESUS, MYTH, MAN OR GOD?" "THE
ITS PRE-EXISTENCE, " " DID JESUS CHRIST EXIST?" ETC., ETC.

" World-weary pilgrims, comfortless — forlorn ?
Up! Let us hence depart.
'Tis morning now. No longer let us stay
Where hope will wither, love and life decay:
Bright is the world to-day !
Let us on — on then and compass it."

BOSTON
BANNER OF LIGHT PUBLISHING CO
9 BOSWORTH STRE
1898
L.

PREFACE.

WHAT I saw in the Pacific Islands, New Zealand, Australia, Ceylon, India, Arabia and other Oriental Countries expresses in a few words the distinctive characteristics of this volume. It abounds in such facts about the people of far-away lands as all Americans and English-speaking citizens ought to know.

Owing to extensive travels and a well-trained eye, we were able to see phases of life, national characteristics and religious rites and ceremonies, especially among Brahmins, Buddhists and Parsees, usually denied the hasty traveler; these we propose to share with our readers.

The author has endeavored to describe what came under his personal observation in these so-called heathen lands with fairness and a true moral independence. Who and where are the heathen? are serious questions. Ceylon and India are both sending missionaries to America.

In this volume appear portions of my book on travels published nearly a quarter of a century since; and for the reason that truths never perish, and Oriental nations change slowly.

The natural tendency of travel is to give breadth to thought and a fresh impetus to the humanitarian sentiments of the soul.

"Over space the clear banner of mind is unfurled,
And the habits of God are the laws of the world."

THE PRELUDE.

"Pilgrim footsteps, whither bound ?
Pilgrim glances, whither bent ?

Sandal-shod and travel-gowned,
Lo, I seek the way they went."

LIFE is a divine gift — a pilgrimage with failures and victories — perils by sea and perils by land.

Travel is an educator, giving breadth to thought, depth to research, freedom to philosophy, strength to religion and a fresh, fiery impetus to the best humanitarian sentiments of the soul.

Seeing, in connection with consciousness, reason and the highest judgment, is knowing; and knowledge is the stepping-stone that leads up to the temple of wisdom.

STILL ON THE ROAD.

Since traveling and seeing are rungs in the ladder by which we climb, why not see the world we live in, traversing all lands, sailing o'er all seas, exploring all templed caves and studying all archaic ruins to further lift the veil from Isis ? Why not sink cables in all oceans and plant magnetic chain-links the world around? Are we not brothers all? The world has two classes : not the sheep and the goats of the parable, but the daring do-somethings, and those that do nothing except to eat, drink, doze, dream, read novels, paint the impossible and grumble that things were not done some other way. It tires the worker to drag such laggards along.

"Better see the wonders of the world abroad
Than, living dully sluggardized at home,
Wear out the soul in gruesome idleness."

CHAPTER I.

" Of the beginning that never began is life's tale,
And that never-finishing ending to which we all sail —
For the children of never and ever we are,
And our home is beyond, and our goal is afar."

CIRCUMNAVIGATING the globe several times is little more
than a matter of well-directed purpose and energy. The iron
will never hesitates. It delights to dare and to do. A firm
rational individuality is commendable. Every man of genius
has a way of his own. Let him have it. Help the world's
helpers, or stand aside, pout, and be forgotten.

Countries, like individuals, have their aural emanations —
their idiosyncracies. There is more soul-freedom and less
conventional restraint west than east of the Rocky Mountains. The climate uniform and bracing, thought free, the
intellect clear, liberalism fruits out spontaneously in California. Southern California is the Italy of America. Residing
anywhere in the stirring, pulsing West broadens the vision,
expands the emotional nature and inspires a most generous
and fraternal toleration.

The Orient with its treasures and the Occident with its
untold energies met upon the Pacific coast, and in its agone
years cities, cosmopolitan in character, sprung up as if by
some sorcerer's art. Old heads guided the feet that trod
these cities. Vigor, vigilance and public spiritedness consti-

tuted the red globules that flowed in the body politic.   And
to-day California is one of the grandest States in the American Union.

CALIFORNIA SCENERY.

Switzerland, with its mountain chains and towering Alps,
pales before the rich magnificent scenery of the Pacific States.
The mountain peaks are weird, grand, defiant; while the adjoining plateaus are covered with grass, sage-brush and pines.
The air is light, pure and bracing.   On the hilltops, in the
northern part of the State, white fleecy snow may sometimes
be seen; but in San Diego, where I reside, there is neither
snow nor ice nor frost, and, withal, it is the sunniest and most
equable climate in the world.

FRUITS AND VINES.

Piled-up tons of melons, peaches, pears, figs, apricots and
semi-tropical fruits literally blockade the wharves and front
streets of the California cities during the autumn and winter
seasons.   Though oranges, lemons and pineapples grow luxuriantly and ripen in any yard and garden, only sixty miles
away up on the highlands at Julian very choice apples are
grown.

Passing up and down the coast railways, walnut-groves and
apricot-orchards literally reel under their fruitage, while vineyards everywhere shook their purple clusters.   Swiftly whirling by lemon and orange plantations, loaded and golden, they
weave and sway like waving forests.   Delicious things for the
palate, beauty for the eye, lands for the toiler, minerals for
the miner, health for the invalid, wealth for the industrious,
books for the student, friends for the worthy, and religious
toleration for all regardless of ancestral clime or color — *these*
are among the charms of the sunset States.

Life and activity flame everywhere.   The universe is God's
habitation; this earth, one of the smaller apartments! enter-

ing it some seventy-six years ago, I found it already furnished. What a carpet! — the emerald grass. What a ceiling! — the frescoed sky. What tapestried pillars! — the
granite rocks. What a front! — the flaming sunrise. What
a rear-door! — the sunset, through which the day goes down
into shadow-lands. What a chandelier! — the sun and fiery
stars. What fields for future explorations! — the interstellar
spaces of infinity. Surely, God is infinitely great and good.

REQUIRED IMPROVEMENTS.

Arise, O land of the west winds — cities encircled with the
lemon, the orange and the pomegranate — and deck yourselves in more beautiful garments! Your gardens and your
highways even, so far away from the snows of the north
land, might be made to bloom like the rose.

A house devoid of shade-trees and flowers reminds one of
a salesroom for caskets, with an accompanying perpetual
funeral. What opportunities we have in California for landscape artists! Transformations and suburban decorations pay
even property-holders. If there's a praiseworthy *mania*, it is
the laying out of beautiful gardens, noble avenues, and mammoth parks. Inspired we feel to preach a sermon to the citizens of California upon the importance of putting shade-trees
around their houses, and books into them. Home presup-
poses a library, a cabinet, a conservatory, an orchard, and a
grove with weird, winding paths for walking and meditation.

> " Who loves a library, still his Eden keeps ;
> Perennial pleasures plants, and wholesome harvests reaps."

How easily the interior towns of this thrifty State might
be made to rival the villages in the Atlantic States, by putting out ornamental shrubbery! In a hot, dusty summer's
day, what is more inviting than the cooling shadows of graceful evergreens, or the serried lines of maples and elms that
interlace and arch public highways? And then, why not

plant fruit-trees all along the wayside? Why not have the
gardens of the Hesperides in our midst to-day? Why not
have a heaven on earth, with the divine will fully done?
When half-dreaming of heaven, with its homes of love,
dreaming of the spirit-gardens that hang and float in ether
spaces above us, our brain throbs and brims in ecstasy. Let
us, then, make real to-day our divinest ideals.

CHAPTER II.

MY THIRD VOYAGE.

"I cannot rest from Travel: I will drink
Life to its lees."—TENNYSON.

IT was on September the 11th, 1872, that I embarked, under an Australian engagement, upon the steamer "Idaho" for a voyage around the world, not alone to see, but to teach as I traveled.

Five years later I again girdled the globe, *via* Australia, India, Madagascar, Natal and South Africa, teaching and lecturing as I went upon the great moral reform subjects of the age.

And again moved by the missionary spirit, I sailed from San Francisco for a third voyage around the world Dec. 5, 1896. Friends, relatives pleaded with me not to undertake such a perilous journey at my age. Age! I spurned the thought. The soul knows nothing of age. The eternal years past and future are hers. The clay, the shell, the house that the man lives in is not the man himself. I am rollicking, glorying in the gorgeous morning of abiding youth.

True, there is a momentary sadness in the parting good-byes:

"But this I've seen, and many a pang
Has pressed it on my mind,—
The one who goes is happier
Than those he leaves behind.
God wills it so, and so it is:
The pilgrim on his way.

> Though weak and worn, more cheerful is
>   Then all the rest who stay.
> And when, at last, poor man, subdued,
>   Lies down, to death resigned,
> May he not still be happier far
>   Than those he leaves behind ? "

The past conspired to mold the present. It was the yesterdays that fashioned the to-days. Let us not too rudely crush the rock from whence we were hewn. The old moon is not lost though invisible. It is the invisible helpers that often help the ideal to become the real, and faith to become fruition.

The universe is infinite. The wisest have not so much as entered the portal of her temple. The atom no eye hath seen. On — onward, then, oh my soul, like the sandal-footed Solon of Grecian memory! Why not travel? Why not lift old manuscripts from their moldy recesses? Why not find and read the historic stories of half-forgotten ages? Why not · unearth the once proud Nippurs that were gray with antiquity when ancient Babylon was in her earliest mornings of prosperity?

Courageous energy with rich linguistic culture behind the spade, pushing aside the babyish biblical chronology of Archbishop Usher — has revealed a very polished civilization existing several thousands of years B. C., in the valleys of the Tigris and the Euphrates.

Diving deeper, and going still farther in the line of the Babylonian excavation down to the deeply-buried Assyrian city, Nippur, authentic inscriptions — authentic history written upon bricks, cylinders, tablets and vases, push the existence of a grand civilization back on Time's dial to 7000 years B. C. And there must have been millenniums of preceding years to have coined such a mighty civilization. Wisely, Lord Kelvin, recently at the annual meeting of the Victoria Institute, London, of which I have the honor of being a member, said: "The earth could not have been a habitable globe for more than 30,000,000 of years."

Sailing, gazing on the blue depths below and now on the bright skies above, I further philosophize. If the universe is one, as Monism affirms, infilled and governed by infinite spirit-causation — if matter is the vestured clothing of this causation — if the spiritual is the one great reality, and all else is illusion, as the higher philosophy teaches, then Spiritualism is the one true religion — the wisdom religion of the ages.

Spirit, whether incarnate or discarnate, responds to spirit by the law of vibration as music responds to music. Life is everywhere. Consciousness and love are universal; and accordingly all nations, races, tribes necessarily sympathize. There's but one pulse-beat, one heart-throb in the universe. My birds, trees, flowers know me — know and love me. . . .

December 9th. — Four days out on the tremulous ocean. Our steamer, though the waters are rough, wriggles along like a revolving auger. Our crew, a nautical commonwealth, is getting social. Games are instituted for the day and a programme for evening literary exercises.

December 11th. — How calm the sea is to-day! What a relief. No calls, no correspondence to answer, no diseases to diagnose! What a quiet life, reading by day, and gazing at the glittering stars by night — those shining altar-lamps set in the heavens by the finger of the Eternal! A sudden change this evening, — rough and rolling, the ocean! Would you escape seasickness, diet; walk the deck in defiance of dashing waves. Exercise a plucky will-power — no compromise. Grace aside, it is grit that leads to glory on the ocean.

Up higher in thought for a moment! Afloat on the ocean of boundless being, uncontrollable circumstances affect us, unseen powers influence us. None of us are wholly our own. We did not choose our birth-land, its locality, or climate ; neither did we select the time of coming into this objective existence ; nor the government under which we would live, nor the color of the skin that should cover us. And yet, deeper, diviner — regardless of circumstance, clime or color, humanity senses, *weeps* the same tears over human suffering. India's late famine was in a measure America's famine ; and so she sent to the far-off Orient her cargoes of wheat. Humanity, be it to the utmost limits of East or West, has one common heart centre, one common aspiration for immortality, one common desire for angel ministries, one God, one law, one origin, one brotherhood, and one grand destiny, ultimately awaiting all human intelligences — such is the interpretation of the vision.

As polished mirrors reflect and reveal; so seers and mystics, standing upon the mountains of the beautiful, wrapped in the seamless mantles of prophecy, reflect and largely outline the future. Neither God nor his prophets are dead. There are prophets of to-day of which the world is not worthy. The worldly proud, the mole-eyed miser cannot see them; the deaf plutocrat cannot hear their voices; and our millionaires, dumb save to talking of dollars and dimes, never deign to sing their praises. Those selfish, encrusted money-makers, such as Jay Gould, Astor, Vanderbilt, Crocker and that morally gangrened gang of Wall-Street gamblers long ago dug their own graves — graves over which willows refuse to weep, or respectable owls to hoot. Pity and pass on, oh, fellow mortals.

A scroll is unrolling, a prophecy fulfilling. Thrice or more said the oracle was he to magnetically enzone the world — thrice or more was he to sow the seeds of spiritual truth in all lands and under all skies. What shall the harvest be?

CHAPTER III.

THE SANDWICH ISLANDS.

"My spirit to yours dear brother,
Do not mind because many sounding your name do not understand you,
I do not sound your name, but I understand you,
I specify you with joy O my comrade to salute you, and to salute those who
are with you, before and since, and those to come also,
That we all labor together transmitting the same charge and succession,
We few equals indifferent of lands, indifferent of times,
We, enclosers of all continents, all castles, allowers of all theologies,
Compassionaters, perceivers, rapport of men,
We walk silent among disputes and assertions, but reject not the disputers
nor anything that is asserted,
We hear the bawling and din, we are reach'd at by divisions, jealousies,
recriminations on every side,
They close peremptorily upon us to surround us, my comrade,
Yet we walk unheld, free, the whole earth over, journeying up and down till
we make our ineffable mark upon time and the diverse eras.
Till we saturate time and eras, that the men and women of races, ages to
come, may prove brethren and lovers as we are." — WALT WHITMAN.

IT was good to know the good gray poet, nature's seer.
It was in Washington, D. C., that I first met him, being the
bearer of a friendly note to him from Emerson, whom I had
just visited in his Concord home. At this time Whitman
was a Government employee, yet a poet by nature and a
practical interpreter of the ideal as revealed in nature. In
later years I frequently met him in his pamphlet-pressed,
book-crowded study room in Camden, N. J., a very Mecca for
his literary admirers.

A class of cheap critics pronounced his " Leaves of Grass "
immoral. They were immoral, perhaps, to the immoral — immoral to the prude and the crone. Men and women generally. find what they hunt for. They see in others what is

most active and seething in themselves. There are those altogether too pure and sweet to attend properly and promptly to the demands of nature, medically speaking. Such die early — die from the transgression of law. Nature is God's divine garment — and glittering with sunshine and gold and silver and crystal, and tropical foliage, is unsullied only when contaminated and misdirected by human passions. The good, the cleanly, have no need to personally prate of their cleanliness. Never lived there a cleaner, purer-minded man than Whitman, the peer of Whittier, Holmes and other distinguished American poets. . . .

But let us on with our travels. It is December, 1896. Our outward-bound steamer is the " Alameda." "All aboard!" shouted the gruffy Dutch captain. The editor of the Philosophical Journal and other friends accompany me to the steamer, tendering fraternal hand-shakes and good-wishes as heartfelt send-offs. It is well to have many acquaintances — and but few friends. Unselfish friendship is immortal — pure love undying.

Three days of ocean calm! Most of the passengers have now settled down into little sympathetic knots: smokers and gamblers in the smoke-room, topers in the bar-room; the thinking and the cultured to the music saloon, or the library, which, I am sorry to say, is constituted mostly of novels and old antiquated volumes, dry as a Calvinistic sermon of the seventeenth century.

Five days on the way and stormy. The steamer is crowded. Several are seasick, and thinking temporarily that life is not worth living. Living and existing are utterly unlike. The stupid oyster exists, men and angels live. I am never lonely when alone: the thronging multitude makes me lonesome.

We may touch people mechanically; but if there's no soul fellowship, there will be an impregnable, impassable gulf between us. We cannot go to them. They cannot as they are come to us. There's no vibrating chain of sympathy between us. They have no balm that heals, no soft, sunny aura that soothes. Have you not been hand-touched when you felt no thrill of ecstasy? No rivulets of life leaping down from the ever-green mountains of the soul? The nearest in body may be the farthest off in soul. One may live in a palace gilded with gold and ivory and mother-of-pearl, and yet be in a social and spiritual dungeon amid the flapping of leprous wings. There are men occupying structures plain to severity, free from frescoes and exquisite carvings, and yet, spiritually, they are living in Alhambra palaces and banqueting with the gods of science and literature. There are flowers so sensitive to the approaching signs and sounds of storm that they close their petals; so there are mortals that close their delicate natures to the tread and touch of the rough and the selfishly depraved. They are called unsocial. This is injustice. They simply occupy a gentler, higher plane of life attainable by all. As musical notes respond to music in the same key, so these souls, afire with love, respond to the touch of the pure in heart — to the thoughts of the good, the beautiful and the true everywhere.

SENATOR STANFORD AND PRESIDENT LINCOLN, SPIRITUALISTS.

Comfortably settled in my cabin and well on the way to Honolulu and Apia, I renewed acquaintance with Mr. Clark, the chief steward, born in Vermont near my own birth-place.

The chief stewardess, Mrs. Graham, a woman of great energy, of culture and of English birth, is exceedingly well liked for her good qualities and many personal kindnesses to the ladies. She was a personal friend of Ex-Governor and Senator Stanford. These Stanfords, eminent and very excellent people, moving in what is denominated the highest circles of American social life, were avowed Spiritualists. Often did Mrs. Graham meet them at Mr. Slater's seances. Conversing of Spiritualism, she remarked to me — " I have heard the Stanfords say more than once, 'Had it not have been for our son's passing into spirit life and the messages

from him and from other spirits, the Palo Alto University,
called the *Stanford University*, would not have been built.' "

It was Spiritualism, too, that inspired Abraham Lincoln
to issue that magnificent proclamation of emancipation that
struck the chains from the limbs of four millions of slaves.

Often when in Washington, D. C., many years ago, did I
attend seances at the residence of the Lauries, where President Lincoln, listening to teachings and trance utterances
from the fathers of our Republic, through the inspired lips
of Nettie Colburn, became so fired with justice and the spirit
of freedom that the strokes of his pen broke the shackles of
millions, and made of slaves, that were being bought and sold,
men, with the inalienable right to "life, liberty and the pursuit
of happiness."

SOUL DREAMS AND HOPES.

Half-dreaming, pondering, let us philosophize. Conscious
of a conscious existence, I fancy myself a sort of a moral
equation. Consciousness and aspiration are the algebraic
equals ; and eternity is the unknown quantity. Laws are
not creative, but methods, — Deific methods of procedure.
Mathematical laws are universal. Every atom, every parti-
cle of iron circulating in my body, follows the law of its
strongest attraction, — follows it mathematically. Results
are true to their producing causes. Moral equations, because
relating to moral actions and to the moral possibilities of the
soul, admit of self-solution only. Personally, I am the problem ; and I, too, must solve myself.

As between nations, arbitration is the great word. The
genius of this intellectual age requires the abolition of wars,
of the crimson flag and cannon ; of school-boy whip and a
personal devil — aye, more, the gradual yet almost complete reconstruction of jurisprudence, theology and governments. Politicians ! We've had enough of them. Oh, for
the coming man, for the constructor ! Oh, for self-denial
and moral heroism ! Why cringe and cower ? Why toddle
like babes, and lean like half-dipped candles ? Cautiously

inquiring for the winning. Alone,— alone with the truth, is a majority!

WHEN DOES THE SOUL BEGIN TO EXIST?

"I looked, and, behold, a door was opened in heaven," exclaimed the Revelator John. The harmonial philosophy recognizes this open door, —those golden gates ajar.

Sitting with a distinguished medium, he was immediately entranced, and the conversation turning upon pre-existence, the controlling spirit said, that, "While making no pretensions to infallibility, still I must say that I consider the theory of 're-incarnation,' that is, the re-incarnating of resurrected and immortalized souls back into the uterine receptacle, into childhood with no memory of a past life in mortal form, and on up into gross earthly bodies with embittering experiences, as neither necessary in the divine economy nor correct in fact. Over two hundred years have I traversed the regions that you call spirit and I have no desire for a re-conception or a re-birth into mortality. I have heard fraternal spirit intelligences teach this theory, but have never witnessed a practical illustration of it. If necessary there will doubtless be facilities provided to produce the result. But the soul's eternal pre-existence is to me true — an intuitive truth of my inmost being. It is no more true that a *this* implies a *that* than that a beginning implies an ending."

WHAT IS THE SOUL, SPIRIT KNIGHT?

This spirit replied: "The soul is a potentialized portion of God, the divine principle —the spirit *esse*, the keystone that crowns man with a fadeless immortality. This original soul, commencing to accrete spiritual substance and physical matter, takes the human form germinally from the sacred moment of embryonic conception." . . .

"Our astronomers," said I to Parisi, an Italian spirit, "pronounce the moon uninhabited, having no atmosphere."

It matters little to me what your astronomers in their

earthly blindness, may or may not say. There is an atmosphere pertaining to your earth, to the moon, to the planets, to every orb, every object, and entity in nature. The most refined atmosphere relating to any star in the range of your telescopic system is one of the Pleiades, third of the series. There are other planets in interstellar realms far in advance of this, however. Earthly astronomers know nothing of them; nor very little, as yet, of their neighbor the moon, with its atmospheric strata, and swarming inhabitants. The science of astronomy among mortals is yet in its swaddling-clothes. They should talk with becoming modesty. . . .

" Most certainly. There are old Oriental cities, precious stones, treasures and statuary, buried in deltas, and imbedded under mountains of sands. These, by the aid of clairvoyance, and the citizens of the heavens who lived in remote antiquity, might and *will* be unearthed when mortals become unselfish enough to wisely appropriate such immense treasures."

Aaron Knight, influencing, said, "Spirits have infinitely better facilities for moral progress than mortals; but as to how they use them is a matter of choice. I am no fatalist. Neither men nor spirits are mere things, but moral actors. . . . Certainly, there are planets whose surfaces are so refined, fruits so sublimated, and atmospheres so ethereal, that the inhabitants peopling them, though having an outer envelope comparable to the physical body, do not die as the term 'death' is understood by you. They gradually throw off the external vesture in particled emanations, but do not for a moment cease to be conscious. . . . Spirits are, of course, fallible. Many of them do not understand either the laws or the effects of psychological control as they should. Mediums are both benefited and injured by magnetic influences. This depends upon the wisdom and motives of the intelligences. . . . The guardian, other things being equal, can the most effectually impress a medium. All mediums should have in attendance organized circles of spirits. This is a shield and a safeguard. No effective medium is ever left entirely alone. Some member of the sympathizing circle continues with him, to minister as necessity demands. . . .

" No : none retrograde as a whole. There is no law of absolute retrogression. While mortal or spirit may retrograde morally, they may at the same time be advancing intellectually ; a man, while declining physically, may be progressing spiritually. Action must ultimate in progress in some direction. Upward, as one of your poets wrote, ' all things tend.' "

THE SANDWICH–ISLAND GROUP.

This ocean-embosomed cluster of isles, nine in number, has some hundred thousand inhabitants. When discovered by Capt. Cook, the group was supposed to contain full four hundred thousand. Remnants of mounds, temples, and ruins indicate it. During the second voyage of this navigator, a difficulty arising, a high chief was killed by one of the captain's party. The slain chief's brother swore revenge. In the midst of the fray, Capt. Cook himself shot a man. The natives, who had previously supposed him a god, found him decidedly human. Though finally killing him through retaliation, they dissected his body for anatomical purposes. History and legend agree that these natives were never cannibals.

The entrance to the harbor is through a passage in the coral reefs that girdle the island of Oahu. Seen from the harbor, Honolulu is exceedingly beautiful. The city, embowered in fresh green foliage, numbers six thousand ; the district, twelve thousand, only about two thousand of whom are white. The Hawaiian Hotel, and the public buildings generally, would do honor to any larger city. The gardens are decidedly tropical. They are irrigated from mountain streams. Fruit clogs the market. Sugar-plantations and pulu-fields plead for more workmen. The " labor-question "·

here, as elsewhere, awaits solution. All men are about as lazy as they can afford to be.

It is very common to see native women trooping along the streets horseback. Some were richly though quaintly attired in long riding-habits. They all, like the Turkish and Arab women of the East, ride astride their poor-bred horses; and some deck themselves in ribbons and othelo flowers. Their dresses are entirely loose and flowing, *all* the weight coming upon the shoulders.

On the outskirts of the city, 'mid tropical shrubbery and graceful palms, I saw taro growing, the original Hawaiian food of the natives. It thrives on soil that can be flooded. Exceedingly nutritious, it not only tastes, but, when steamed in their stone ovens, looks, very much like huge, rough Irish potatoes.

From this taro, they make their *poi* by pounding it into a semi-fluid consistency, and then storing it in gourds and calabashes. It is eaten by dipping one — if very thin, two — fingers into the pot of *poi*, and thrusting them quickly into the mouth.

THE MORALS OF THE ISLANDS.

These Hawaiians are considered by some ethnologists as vestiges of the Semitic stock. Others think to the contrary. It is certain that the primitive poetry of these natives bears a striking resemblance in style to the Hebraic. They practiced, when discovered, circumcision, and had what corresponded to the Israelitish " house of refuge." They had three orders of priests, — Kaula, prophets; Kilo, magicians or ghost-seers; and Kahunas, the teachers. They have a tradition among themselves, that they came from Tahita. Europeans brought among them liquors and syphilis, and taught them war upon the principles of Christian civilization. As a people, these aborigines are rapidly dying off from the island. Civilization, such as it is, hastens their inevitable doom. In twenty years there will probably be no Kanackas, pure-blooded natives, left upon the Hawaiian Islands. Their moral degeneracy has kept pace with their physical. Though nominally Christianized, their "easy virtue" is patent in the flocks of half-castes that throng the city and mountain districts. If missionaries have not filled the brains of these poor heathen with intelligence, and exalted moral principles, they have managed to fill their own purses.

Morals are at a low ebb. Many white men — Germans, French, Portuguese, and some Americans — live with native women unmarried. This is considered no social disgrace, since commenced many years ago by distinguished officials. Color is no bar to office or position.

The government of these islands was a constitutional monarchy. Queen Emma, who traveled through Europe and our country a few years since, became queen by marriage.

The Sandwich Islands have now become a republic, and desire annexation to the United States. The natives oppose it.

Though belief or unbelief in no way affects the truth, still the belief of a man, if held in earnest, and woven into the spiritual frame of mind, must necessarily exert a controlling influence upon the springs of action, and leave its impress upon the life. The natives originally believed in good and bad spirits, in a future life, and the return of their departed from the land of shades. Their idols were the images of deified mortals. Dr. Damon, a resident of Honolulu, or some of the Polynesian groups, for thirty years, assured us that these aborigines all believed in a future existence when first visited by missionaries. The belief bubbles up spontaneously in the souls of all tribes and races.

HAWAIIAN SPIRITISM.

Candid research will ultimately force the concession that the lowest and most degraded tribes have deep-rooted ideas of gods, spirits, and a future existence. Otherwise, they are not men, but monkeys, apes, baboons, chimpanzees, gorillas! Man devoid the cranial organs of hope, veneration, conscientiousness, ideality, and spirituality, is not a wholeness, — is *not* man. With these organs, he necessarily conceives of another and superior state of existence. His notions may be rude ; still they are germinally bedded in truth. Under all skies, man naturally believes in the superhuman, in the return of departed ancestors, and the care of guardian spirits. This is pre-eminently true of this Hawaiian branch of the Polynesians. Faith of this kind is so rooted in their souls' soil, that thirty years' missionary drillings have in no way eradicated it.

Bennett, after describing, in his historic sketches, their mythology, and the "*tabu* imposed by the chiefs," says there was always a " class among them who practiced sorcery and conjuration, and offered prayers to the spirits." Richardson assures us, that, in all past times, " they dealt in divination, calling upon the spirits of their dead to assist them in war, and bless them in peace. Their gods were the spirits of departed heroes."

A strong effort was early made to convert Kamehameha I. to the Christian religion. The purpose signally failed. He listened, however, with great gravity to the churchal argument for the "necessity of faith in Christ;" and then, says Jarvis, he coolly replied, —

"By faith in your God, you say any thing can be accomplished, and the Christian will be preserved from all harm. If so, cast yourself down from yonder precipice ; and, if *you* are preserved, I will believe."

It was a clincher !

SINGULAR SOCIAL CUSTOMS.

Naturally trusting and affectionate, Hawaiian men, when meeting in their more primitive times, embraced and, kissed, as do women in civic life. Missionaries, forgetting Paul's injunction, "Salute the brethren with a holy kiss," have taught them a different way of salutation. Their priesthood was hereditary. Each chief, before the consolidation in a

kingdom, had his family priest, who accompanied him to battle. In Christian countries this class of men is called chap-
lains, praying for victory through war, in the name of the
Prince of peace !

In the better period of these islanders, a falsehood was
considered a fearful offense, and fœticide was unknown.
The male child then born, and now also, takes the preference. This is the case in the Christian kingdoms of Europe.
Lunatics were supposed by these Sandwich Island people to
be obsessed by angry spirits.

In their old traditionary ages, the man had but one wife.
Marriage ceremonies, as such, were unknown. Wooing for
a season, the parties commenced living together, and, if
reciprocally pleasant, the union was understood to be permanent ; if unhappy, however, they mutually agreed to separate.
If children were born into their rude homes, it was then
considered disgraceful to annul the marital relation. They
are exceedingly fond of their children, and in every department of life are naturally kind and generous.

INTELLECTUAL DECLINE.

Though doubtless true,

" That through the ages one unceasing purpose runs,"

still there are lost Edens of civilization and culture. If literature and art, like the nationalities they crowned, have had
their ebb and flow, so civilized countries and island tribes
have had their golden ages now dead and buried. Extant
monuments, mammoth ruins, and exhumed scrolls, substan-
tiate the position.

Who has not been charmed while reading, in Baldwin's
" Pre-Historic America," of that ancient Peruvian road extending over marshes, ravines, rocky precipices, and the great
chain of the Sierras, — strongly walled on each side, and
quite as long as the two Pacific railroads ? These macad-
amized roads were constructed, according to Gomara, long

before the reigns of the Incas.   Humboldt, examining them,
writes, —

"Our eyes rested continually on superb remains of a paved road of the
Incas.   The roadway, paved with well-cut dark porphyritic stone, was
twenty feet wide, and rested on deep foundations.   This road was marvelous.   None of the Roman roads I have seen in Italy, in the South of
France, or in Spain, appeared to me more imposing than this work of the
ancient Peruvians."

So there are remnants of a magnificently paved road
around the Isle of Maui, one of the Hawaiian group.   It
was constructed long ages ago by a king of the island, named
Kahihapilani, who was expecting his sister from the island of
Hawaii.   This masonry, as well as templed ruins, point to a
once high, but now entombed civilization.

And, what is equally interesting, the native poets of the
Hawaiian Islands were an order by themselves, something
like the Druidic bards of Briton.   These were called Kàhu-
meles (poet-bards) in ancient times, and were not unlike the
Homeric balladists, and Grecian rhapsodists.   Their chant-
like poems were handed down from father to son; and they
proudly sung that in the halcyon ages their ancestors came
from Asia.   Their poems, drawn from natural scenery, were
weird and musical, but neither measured nor rhythmical.
This is true of those old compositions of the Vedic ages.

Declining and degenerate, the Hawaiians have no genuine
poets now.   Some, however, excel in music and mathematics.
Natives constitute the missionaries' choirs.   Many of the old
Hawaiian chants in praise of their chiefs and their gods have
been committed to writing by Judge Fanander, for the purpose of publication.   Fortunately, while attending a natives'
"hula-hula" dance in the queen's gardens, I listened to
some of these meles, or ballad-songs.

RECENT PHENOMENA.

The apostolic "discerning of spirits" is a gift as common
in "heathen" as Christian lands.   The Sandwich Islanders,

though frequently seeing and conversing with departed
spirit friends, speak of their manifestations with great reserve ; because the missionaries have assured them that all
such phenomena were the " devices of the Devil."

The gentlemanly editor of a prominent daily, and an old
resident of Honolulu, Mr. Prescott, narrated to us several
interesting incidents relating to Spiritism in his own family,
and others among the natives of the islands.

My visit to the Leper Hospital, in the suburbs of Honolulu,
was deeply interesting.   For this disease no specific has been
found. . . .   Among volcanos, Kilauea is thousands of times
larger than Vesuvius.   It is seldom quiet, being an overflowing, ever-bubbling lake of fire, with an area of nearly
twenty acres. . . .

Called Dec. 17 to see Bishop Willis — a long-bearded
English ecclesiastic, wearing long, tight stockings, a sort of
knee-buckles and a very long coat — a quaint sixteenth-
century figure.   He belongs to the past.

The present Hawaiian Government, with the wealthy missionaries, desires annexation to the United States of America.
But the masses, especially the natives, are opposed to it.   A
vote relative to annexation has never been submitted to the
people.

To-morrow we sail for New Zealand by way of Samoa.

CHAPTER IV.

THE PACIFIC-ISLAND RACES.

> " The two kinds of people on earth that I mean,
> Are the people who lift and the people who lean."

How true of this human hive, humanity — the workers and the drones, the toiling lifters and the lazy, dragging leaners! I hate laziness.

What a day of bustle, — coaling, loading, transferring, packing! The beeves have been driven in from the mountains by the natives. Panting, frightened, and fevery with heat and rage, they are roped on the wharf by the sailors, beaten, thrown to the ground, and tied with strong hempen cords. Then while bellowing, struggling, and frothing at the mouth with very madness, they are dragged by marine tackling up into the vessel to be killed and eaten by passengers on the voyage. And the crew — sadly do we say it — greedily ate the fevered bodies of those poor, bruised, dead animals! In the year 2000, meat-eating will be considered a monstrous practice, only paralleled by the cannibalism of the South Seas.

THE DAILY OUTLOOK.

Sunny are these days, sailing 'mong the Pacific Islands, decked in the rich and gorgeous drapery of the tropics.

> " Oh! soft are the breezes that wave the tall cocoa,
> And sweet are the odors that breathe on the gale ;
> Fair sparkles the wave as it breaks on the coral,
> Or wafts to the white beach the mariner's sail."

The Bishop of Oxford describes the inhabitants of Polynesia as " children of nature, children of the air, children of light, children of the sun, children of beauty, taking their greatest pleasure in the dance." Though these paradisaical isles sparkle like gems in the Pacific, the origin of the races peopling them is a study. Ethnology and comparative philology can at most but point to the quarries whence nationalities and tribes were hewn. From the rich table-lands of India, and the undulating valleys of Iran, came those primeval emigrants that gave to the West culture and intellectual activity. But the extreme East, the Micronesians and the Polynesians of the Pacific, whence these intertropical races? During our week's stay on the Hawaiian group of islands, and others since, the natives, their customs, laws, languages, and religious ideas, have been a constant theme of thought and study.

It is generally conceded that the languages spoken by the millions of Polynesians have the same common structure, with such differences as may be resolved into dialects resulting from long non-intercourse.

When a native New Zealander and Hawaiian meet, though more than four thousand miles apart, they are so closely connected lingually, that they very soon engage in a free interchange of ideas. This, in some degree, is true of the Marquesan, Tahitan, Samoan, and others of the Polynesian stocks. The system of " taboos " in some form runs through all the Southern Polynesian families.

THE MICRONESIANS.

Glance at the location of your island neighbors in Oceanica. Have we not all one father? Are we not brothers all? The numerous Caroline, Ascension, Gilbert Islands, and others adjacent, evidently belong to the Micronesian division, and were peopled either by the Indo-Chinese, or Northern Malayan races. The ruins on Ponapi, one of the Caroline group, built entirely of basaltic prisms, indicate a marvelous civilization in the past. The present natives have no conception why nor by whom such massive walls, parapets and vaults were constructed. The present race upon the Gilbert Islands has stout physical developments, high cheek-bones, fine straight hair, black and glossy. The aquiline nose is the rule, and the cerebrum is largely developed. They are less savage than some of their trafficking visitors.

Swarms of children, innocent of any clothing, flock to the harbor upon each landing. So prolific are they yet, on the greater number of these islands, and so uncontaminated with the diseases of foreign civilizations, that their population is deliberately limited by practicing abortion to prevent too great a number of hungry mouths. They should study the Malthusian method of depopulation, or welcome to their sea-girt shores Shaker missionaries to initiate celibate communities.

THE MARSHALL ISLES.

These are a large group of the Micronesian family, ranging from 4½° to 12° north latitude. They were first discovered by the Spaniards in 1529, and called by them the "good gardens." The inhabitants were straight, light-colored, and strangely tattooed. Their dress was decidedly Adamic, — fig-leaves and mats about their loins! At present the men wear full beards, are energetic, and very hospitable. The women are dressed in fine matting, have long black hair, and decorate themselves profusely in shell-jewelry. Ocean travelers consider them beautiful, though minus corset and waterfall, pannier and paint.

They traverse the seas with large retinues, are eminently clannish, and count nobility of descent on the mother's side. While worshiping deities, they hold the spirits of their ancestors in great reverence. They are skilled, say European residents in their midst, in every kind of "incantation and necromancy." They consult their mediums when in a state of ecstasy, and heal by beating and striking the diseased part. Consecrated groves, and sacred spots, are common among them. Their desolate cemeteries are in waving groves of cocoanut trees; and weird-shaped paddles lift their blades for tombstones. They are evidently of Japanese extraction.

THE SAMOANS, OR NAVIGATORS.

These very important islands, a sort of half-way steamship house in the Pacific, for recruiting, repairing, and re-provisioning, lie between latitudes $13\frac{1}{2}°$ and $14\frac{1}{2}°$ south, and about 170° west longitude. Our captain made a short call at this group, — nine in number, — too short for our individual purpose. They are volcanic in origin, safe to approach, and partially belted with coral reefs. Pago-Pago is a deep, land-locked harbor on the south side of Tutuila. Upolu is the most thickly populated, containing twenty thousand inhabitants. Our gentlemanly commander, of the steamer had permitted us to study his maps and charts of this densely-wooded group of isles — gems of the ocean — before reaching them. The afternoon approach was too grand and gorgeous for the pen to paint. The sea was a polished mirror; the sky, glass; the sun, well adown the western spaces, gold; and the scattering clouds, crimson and purple, were chariots of fire.

The steam checked, and the vessel at rest, the natives flocked to us like birds to a banquet. Physically, they are a splendidly-made race, with full, high foreheads, wavy beards, and white, exquisitely-set teeth. They are light in color, and quick in motion. They have dark-brown hair, eyes black and expressive. The occasional reddish hair seen had been bleached. Honest and trusting, they are evidently of Indo-Malayan origin.

The women are well-formed, healthy, handsome, and, what is more, are famed for their chastity. Both men and women go as naked as new-born babes, except weirdly-woven leaves and sea-grass aprons around their loins. Our passengers bought of them war-clubs, fans, fruits, head-gearings, birds, baskets, spears, and shells. Missionaries are among them. Already they exhibit hopeful signs of civilization in wishing to barter for tobacco, whiskey, fancy-colored clothing, and lime preparations for bleaching their hair. Some of these natives bleach or color the hair red; Americans, black: tastes differ.

The scenery upon these islands is transcendently beautiful. Cascades are numerous, the valleys fertile, and vegetation varied and luxuriant. Tropical fruits, cocoanuts, pine-apples, bananas, citrons, bread-fruit, oranges, limes, sugar-cane, coffee, taro and dye-wood trees abound in rich profusion. The largest portion of Upolo has a fine garden soil, where large springs of pure water bubble up, and flow in thousands of little streams toward the sea. The whole group is ex-ceedingly valuable. Action has already been taken by the United States toward annexation.

Among the code of laws drawn by these native chiefs, to be recognized in commercial relations between the United States and the Samoan Islands, are the following : —

" 5th. All trading in distilled or spirituous liquors, or any kind of in- . toxicating drink, is absolutely prohibited. Any person so offending shall be fined one hundred dollars on conviction before a mixed court. All such liquors found on shore, and kept for sale or barter, shall be seized and destroyed. If any native is found intoxicated, the individual who has supplied him with drink shall pay a fine of ten dollars. If any for-eigner be found drunk or riotous, he shall pay a fine of ten dollars.

" 6th. Any person found guilty of offering inducement to a native female to prostitute herself to a foreigner, to pay a fine of ten dollars; and any native female found guilty of prostituting herself to a foreigner, to pay a fine of twenty dollars."

And these Samoan chiefs are called " savages," " degraded heathen," to whom tobacco-using, wine-drinking Christian missionaries must be sent to save them from hell !

I can but deplore that conceited ignorance which charac-terizes two classes of Americans, — radical rationalists who crankly assert that there " are islanders in the Pacific, and ferocious tribes in Africa, that have not the faintest idea of God or another state of existence ; " and pompous clergymen who everlastingly prate about the " polluted and fiendish *heathen* " of Oceanica. We spent Christmas at Apia.

THE FEEJEES.

Islands, like individuals, have their reputations. Those dotting an ocean which covers one-third of the entire surface of the globe should be more thoroughly surveyed and explored. The Feejees, constituting quite an archipelago, contain one hundred and fifty-four islands, seventy of which are inhabited. They are governed by chiefs. The natives, though dark-hued, are noble in mien, shrewd, and enterprising. Missionaries have given them a hard name. Bear in mind the Feejean side of the story has neither been heard nor published. They stoutly deny having been aggressors, yet admit themselves good at retaliation. A. G. Findlay, F. R. G. S., says, —

" These islanders have been misrepresented. Late visitors speak very highly of their honesty, cleanliness, refinement, and virtue."

The men have heavy, bushy heads of hair, and wear full beards. When discovered by the navigator Tasman, they knew nothing of the venereal diseases that accompany Christian civilization. The taint of syphilis is not yet common among them. They had, when first visited, no idols. They believed in transmigration and immortality. They worshiped in caves and groves. They also had their mediums, who, when in ecstatic states, foamed at the mouth ; but every utterance breathed in this rude trance-condition was carefully noted as the voice of a god.

They build their houses in cocoanut groves. Often they are umbrella-shaped, and rudely thatched. It requires little or no labor to sustain life. Enterprise is little more than a dream all through these equatorial regions. The English are aiming to get full control of the Feejee group for cotton-growing, and. a military basis.

HOW WERE THESE ISLANDS PEOPLED ?

What the camel is to the Arab, the horse to the Asian Mongul, the canoe is to these islanders. In the construction of their *proas*, — sea-crafts made of bread-fruit wood, — they display great talent. The better class of them will carry a hundred men in the open sea. The sails and rigging are managed with great dexterity. They provision these *proas* with cocoanuts, taro, preserved bread-fruit, &c. ; which, with their skill in fishing, enables them to sustain voyages for several months. This partially explains the method by which the different and widely separate Pacific isles may have been peopled. The Malay race — nomads of the sea — whether for adventure, commerce, or plunder, had but to put their wives and utensils into their canoes, and, drifting with the prevailing trade-winds, were sure to reach some island, intermingling with the inhabitants ; or, if uninhabited, establishing a new race.

Not only have these Polynesian natives swift-sailing canoes, but they have rudely-constructed maps of their own invention, made of large tropical leaves, and sticks, tied in straight and curved lines, indicating ocean winds and currents. And, further, Japanese and Chinese junks have been blown to sea, performing long voyages, and finally stranding, with their occupants, upon distant islands. Bancroft tell us that these have even reached the continent of America.

In December, 1832, one of these junks was wrecked on Oahu, near Honolulu, after having been tempest-tossed eleven months. Only four, out of a crew of nine, survived. The population of Lord North's Island must have originated in some way similar to this, as it is over a thousand miles distant from any other land.

Furthermore, the mariner's compass is not new. Navigation is old as tradition. China was known to Egypt more than three thousand years before the Christian era, and a commercial intercourse maintained between the countries.

Africa was circumnavigated by ancient Egyptian mariners; and among the relics of that old civilization may be traced indications of an acquaintance with the American coast. In that period the geography of the world was well understood. Ancient spirits inform me that many of these Pacific islands are the unburied prominences of a submerged Polynesian continent having an immense antiquity. The speech of this great oceanic nation, derived from the primitive Sanscrit of say fifteen thousand years since, tinged with the Indo-Malay, lies at the base of the present Polynesian languages. Remnants of the ancient Sanscrit have been discovered in the highlands of Central Africa.

Our captain, unrolling his Pacific charts one day, directed my attention to the locations of over sixty islands, definitely marked by the old navigators, that have entirely disappeared, sunk in fathomless depths. In consonance with these cataclysmic changes, Mr. Brace, in his " Races of the World," assures us that both Dana and Hale notice evidences of a gradual subsidence of islands even within the historic period; the ruins of temples on Bānabē, for instance, being found partly submerged by the sea. Biblical dogmatists have sought to trace relations, and draw parallels, between the Israelitish " lost tribes " and the Polynesians. This theory vanishes like mist, however, when it is considered that the Hebrews themselves were derivatives, — the refuse and clannish outlaws sloughed off from the mature civilization of Egypt. Burrowing with, these Hebrews borrowed their religious notions from, the lower castes of the Egyptians. They were afterwards modified into Mosaic theology. And Egypt, be it remembered, received her religious doctrines largely from India.

CIVILIZED TREATMENT OF THE ISLANDERS.

The testimony of missionaries and explorers is alike uniform, that Pacific traders have, with few exceptions, exhibited the worst traits of meanness, injustice, and rank dishonesty.

Dr. Damon of Honolulu said a certain shipmaster, dealing with the Marshall Islanders, agreed to pay for cocoanut-oil a fixed amount of tobacco; but, in place, delivered "boxes filled with pieces of old tarred ropes cut up to correspond in length with tobacco-plugs." This was civilization! Another merchant trader, dealing with them, sold them for "stipulated brandies, kegs filled with salt water."

Two captains of whalers from Massachusetts under friendly pretenses coaxed several chiefs aboard; then, moving out into the harbor, demanded a heavy ransom for their delivery. Others, aflame with passion, have with basest motives induced the native women to come upon their vessels. And, when these poor natives have retaliated, the cry has been "savages," "cannibals," "fiendish heathen!"

When the New-Zealand aborigines were at war, a few years since, with the English for the illegal seizure of their lands, the unsuspecting Maoris were unprepared for an attack, because it was the Christian sabbath. They had been taught that Christian soldiers would neither attack nor fight on the Lord's Day. And yet, on this sacred day, they rushed out well-prepared, attacking and butchering hundreds of the trusting heathen. The wrongs, deceptions, and diseases of civilization have been so burnt into the bodies and souls of these aborigines, that they distrust everybody with a white skin. Are they blamable?

The distinguished Rosser sadly says, —

"It is painful to be obliged to report that disease is now being rapidly introduced even among the Ralik Islanders by whale-ships passing the islands, and which now permit natives with females on board their vessels. How sad that the safe residences of missionaries among them should be the causes of attracting physical and moral death to their shores! With but few exceptions, the contact with the representatives of civilization serves to render their diseases more deadly, and their vices more vicious."

So far as missionaries have taught these islanders to read and write, taught them the industries of civilization, they have done a good work. On the other hand, their shrewd, selfish conduct, and theological dogmas, have proven a curse to the native mind. To get a correct opinion of the millions peopling the Pacific islands, their manners, habits, purposes, laws, and religious convictions, one must see and converse with *them*, with old voyagers, explorers, and non-sectarian residents.

. . . To thoroughly know the Samoan natives is to love them. They are naturally honest, peaceful, affectionate and hospitable. What a pity to have them Christianized! They have a soft, warm, brown skin. Their hair is bushy and black unless bleached with lime. They wear mulberry-bark cloth about their loins. The men are generally tattooed. They go through with the process about the time that the youth reaches "pubic virility" — assuming the *toga virilis*.

The distinguished writer, Robert Louis Stevenson, was buried up near the summit of an evergreen mountain over-looking Apia. He loved the native Samoans, and dying, wished his mortal remains buried upon one of Samoa's sunny isles.

CHAPTER V.

" Over space the clear banner of mind is unfurled
And the habits of God are the laws of the world."

OWING to the dictates of latitute and longitude to-day, we dropped a day — going to our berths Tuesday night and waking up Thursday morning. This comes from sailing westward.

The sunsets are gorgeous. It is a fitful season for meditation. Some poet thus sings of man's origin: —

" Heaven's exile, straying from the orb of light."

Who at times does not feel himself an exile, a prisoner? The world is a hotel. The soul is imprisoned in the body; and a fashionable conservatism would make us all moral prisoners by compelling conformity to the shams of society. Why not sleep each alone, as did Pythagoras? Why not wear linen only, as did Apollonius? Why not wear the hair and beard long, as did sage and *savant* in the palmy period of the lost arts? If shaving at all, why not be consistent, shaving away the eyebrows, and even the hair, as do the Chinese?

Louis XII. ascended the French throne at the age of nine, beardless. His courtiers, famous for their cringing servility, rushed to the barbers, and came away clean-faced. That stern old state counselor, Sully, refused to shave, as he had previously done under the reign of King Henry IV. These vain, face-scraped courtiers often made merry at the attorney's odd appearance. Sully, hearing their jests for a

time, said to the king, "Sire, when your father of glorious memory consulted me upon important affairs, the first
move he made was to turn away all apes and buffoons from
his court!" This silenced the French dandies.

Our floating institution darts like an arrow from crest to
crest. The passengers are jolly in defiance of the discomforts. Why not make the best of every thing? Why peddle
pains and aches to excite and elicit sympathy? Any thing
but a peevish, fault-finding disposition. John the Revelator heard "music," not complaining, in heaven. The
wise patiently submit to life's destiny, having learned to
"labor and to wait." All this mental unrest, this hot seething, this stern struggling, this toiling up the steeps, this
magnetic fire that comes pouring down from the higher
realms, is only

> "The spirit of the years to come,
> Yearning to mix itself with life."

Watching the tremulous waves, this morning, while baptized by a dripping shower, I yearned to stand upon their
white crests, and have all the world's dust washed away from
my garments, making my heart so warm, so sunny, so like a
bank of fresh, fragrant flowers, that the careworn and weary
earth would delight to thereon rest, in faith and trust.

My fellow-passengers have engaged to-day in all kinds of
amusements, — sleight-of-hand, trickery, story-telling, and
ventriloquizing in imitation of pigs and puppies; any thing
to be heroes. My *mania* for books makes me an odd one.
The pleasure is exquisite. Blessings on book-makers! . Oh
that men would think more, write more, converse more, and
talk less!

Blab and witty words are cheap. Books all âfire with the
personalities of their authors nourish the soul. Pythagoras
enjoined not only purity and patience, but seven years'
silence, upon certain of his students, as preparatory steps to
wisdom. This way, this way, O Samian!

Public speaking on the ocean is more novel than pleasant. Invited by a committee, through the purser, a nice fellow, to address the officers and passengers upon the divine principles of the spiritual philosophy in their relation to immortality, we so did, Dr. —— following in a most interesting manner. In accordance with an arrangement between the doctor, his attending spirit-guides, and ourself, previous to sailing, we held semi-weekly séances for spirit-communications. In answer to several inquiries, Mr. Knight said, —

" We can not well draw the line of demarkation between physical matter and spirit-substance, they so interblend and over-lap. There are atoms, and molecular particles of physical matter, in their highly sublimated state, more ethereal perhaps than some portions of spirit-substance. This unsteady upward-reaching is seen in every direction. There possibly may be gorillas with reason flaming up to a higher point than in some of the lowest tribes of men. But mark, *they*, the gorillas, have reached their acme ; while these lower tribes have but just started in the line of human possibilities.

" All insects, all venomous reptiles, and brutes, are tottering and imperfect structures ; and it is illogical to predicate immortality of imperfection. The arch can not stand without the keystone. . . .

" By your request, I have inquired of John who was meant by the ' elect lady,' in his second epistle ; and the gist of the response was, the phrase *elect lady*, a symbolical expression, referred to the Christian religion in its purity. This lady elect was the lady of his faith, the most spiritual religion of that age. Spirituality pertains to the feminine, intellectuality to the masculine."

A strange controlling intelligence now comes, making the medium exceedingly spasmodic. Listen! It is a weird, unknown tongue. What does it mean? . . . He has gone, and Mr. Knight comes to explain : —

" This spirit was a chief of the Oahu Island, who lived in a mortal body over a century since. He desired to inform you that himself and his people believed in spirit-intercourse when on earth, though it was connected with much superstition. Since his transition, he has progressed rapidly ; and still he cherishes a deep interest in the remnants of his race. He is very desirous to have you remain on the islands you have left, and preach true doctrines, in contradistinction from the false and gloomy theology that is being taught by missionaries."

Another change. Swailbach, a German spirit, comes. The accent is unmistakable.

"I have just taken possession to say that I had visited these natives as a spirit many times in the past. They are Aryanic rather than Semitic in origin. In a very remote period, this root-race moved south-easterly from the high plateaus of India, through Malayan lands, towards the Pacific islands."

Do you understand the language of these natives?

"Not as they speak it in their mortal bodies ; and yet I can converse freely with them when disrobed of mortality. Ours is largely soul language. The movement of a muscle, throbbing of a nerve, or slightest facial expression even, of a spirit, is language, and self-interpreting. Study of many earthly languages, unless for the purpose of teaching, is time unwisely spent. Languages, earthly in origin, like nationalities, gradually fade away as spirits ascend and unfold interiorily, the tendency being from the special to the universal."

Aaron Knight, again controlling, said, —

"Those failing to make the right marks along the pathway of human life have to retrace their steps after entering spirit-life. There is a band of explorers with us. They are properly naturalists. Some of them are very ancient spirits. . . . We are now passing over the ruins of a grand old city, which had vast surburban forests. The petrified remnants indicate a likeness to the mammoth trees of California. They were an enlightened race. The people lived in stone houses, and were engaged in mechanical and pastoral pursuits. They were the progenitors of your American mound-builders. Were your clairvoyant eyes opened, you would this moment see under *débris*, sands, and sea-plants, the scattered remnants of a long-forgotten civilization. As volcanic isles and lofty mountains have been thrust up from the ocean's depths, so islands and continents have sunk 'mid commotions unknown to earthly history. The sinking of the new Atlantis continent some nine thousand years before the Platonian period, as mentioned by Plato, Solon, and the Egyptian priests, is no myth."

USES AND ABUSES OF SPIRITUAL SÉANCES.

" *You*, and multitudes of others," exclaimed the spirit Knight, "should never sit in circles. Many of the best mediums on earth have never even attended a séance. And yet for scientific observations, or for obtaining physical manifestations, circles help to more readily concentrate the magnetic forces. But to see clairvoyants, to see the impressional, or the truly inspired, sitting in promiscuous circles, holding hands, and imbibing diverse aural exhalations, is to us mentally painful.

"Morbid and nervously sensitive natures require, or think they require, a constant change. They have a *mania* for the stimulus of séances, not understanding that promiscuous magnetic blendings are as injurious to the soul as sexual promiscuity is to the body. These, *all* these practices opposed to the natural laws of life, yield but thorns for the flesh, and obsessions for the spirit. . . . Every mortal has a guardian, and often this guardian spirit does not wish the individual to become a medium. Spiritualists seem to greatly lack wisdom relating to the nature and mission of mediumship. Only the few are fitted for it."

HATS AND BALD HEADS.

Overboard went a hat. It broke the lull of the hour. Did the winds reason? What do men wear hats for, — those tall, silken, stove-pipe, cylinder-shaped hats?

Indians in the West, and Polynesians in the Pacific, have no bald heads. These natives, taught by Nature, let God's sunshine and cooling breezes fan their bare heads. Is there not much to be learned of "savages"?

In Christ's Hospital, the "Blue-Coat School," London, founded by Edward VI., the boys, even the seniors, all go bareheaded. This was a condition of the endowment. And, though they thread city streets in the hottest weather, there has never a case of sunstroke been known among them.

THE ITALIAN TEACHER.

To-day Parisi Lendanta controlled the medium again. He is an Italian spirit, profound and peerless. Among other things he said, —

"We are now passing over mountain ranges towering up from the bottom of the ocean. These lofty rocky eminences serve somewhat to hold the waters in check, and render them 'Pacific.' This ocean has no such raised plateau across the bed-surface as has the Atlantic. Owing to its uneven depths, and rough volcanic ridges, it would be difficult to cable."

His elucidation of the atmospheric and electric stratifications above us was singularly philosophical. It is impossible to fully report him. He flourished near the close of the Middle Ages, — that period which elapsed between the decline of ancient learning, and the revival. The Dark Ages are said to have ceased about the year 1400. They terminated, however, at various times in the different countries of Europe. The destruction of feudalism, the invention of printing, and the discovery of America by Columbus, mark the general period of resurrection from the darkness of the mediæval ages.

I find this spirit, Parisi, perfectly familiar with the histories of Petrarch, Tasso, Dante, Ariosto, and other Italian *littérateurs*. Dante's ideal of the old Latin poets was Virgil, much of whose fame was owing to the Fourth Eclogue, interpreted by churchal fathers as a prophecy of Jesus Christ. Virgil quoted Livy and Lucan to prove that gods and angels had wrought spiritual marvels through mortals during all the ages of antiquity. The sibylline oracles should be extensively read by scholars.

ONE OF THE SOUTH-SEA ISLANDS.

January 1, 1897. — Safely in Auckland, New Zealand, distant from New York nearly nine thousand miles. The city, built upon high land, looks fresh and vigorous. The gardens come down close to the sea. Inclusive of suburbs, it numbers fifty-five thousand. Natives in the province of Auckland, divided into five tribes, number some twenty thousand. June and July are the coldest months of the year; and January and February, corresponding to July and August in England and America, are the warmest. Neither serpents nor noxious reptiles of any species have been found upon the New-Zealand islands. Toads and frogs are also unknown. Has some

Saint Patrick here lifted his magic wand? The original inhabitants call themselves Maoris. They are a dark race, but athletic, brave, ingenious, and intelligent. Efforts to Christianize them have not been very successful. In the New Zealand group they number forty or fifty thousand. Racially they belong to that branch of the Polynesians that are of Indo-Malayan origin. They have handsome black hair, straight or aquiline noses, and well-balanced brains. They tattoo themselves.

Auckland remained the capital of New Zealand till 1864, when it was removed to Wellington. The great attraction of Auckland, like San Diego, California, is its harbor. This is simply magnificent, being fringed with evergreen hills and dotted with verdure-clad islands. Its museum abounding in Polynesian curios, its art gallery rich in paintings, and its large free public library unique in manuscripts and rare old books, all combine to present a panorama of the good and the beautiful. An excursion out and up on to Mount Eden, an extinct volcano, was exceedingly enjoyable. All around may be seen the craters of other volcanoes. In some far-away historic period this must have been a *Gehenna* corner of the world.

Only three or four hours by steamer from this city are the famous Waimera Hot Springs, situated in a most charming spot, with inviting scenery in every direction, hot swimming-baths, thickly-wooded hills and lovely evergreen lawns.

CHAPTER VI.

NEW ZEALAND.

> " I have come from a mystical land of Light
> To a strange country ;
> This morn I came, I must go to-night —
> But others are coming, women and men, Eternally."

CERTAINLY — coming and going, moving in cycles ! This is the divine method. If essential spirit, as the sages of the past and the seers to-day teach, is substance — if the spiritual is the real, and if this objective life is but the shadow-world of effects, then, that parliaments of angels should conceive plans above to be executed on earth is both possible and natural. All conscious intelligences, from archangel down to man, must necessarily sympathize. None of us are wholly our own ; uncontrollable circumstances affect and unseen helpers influence us. And so I am in New Zealand, north and south at different times.

The mental atmosphere of Auckland is unlike that of Sydney and Otago. Its aural emanations differ materially from that of Victoria. It is more Scottish. It is stiffer, sterner, and not so flexible. One breathes equally free in Melbourne and America.

Constantly summering, and wintering too, under the Southern Cross, the evergreen foliage of New Zealand—the Britain of the South — literally charms one. The scenery seems a blending of Swiss with the Scottish Highlands. As I see the clear waters and the fern-clad hillsides from the windows of "mine host" — Mr. Redmayne — this sunny February morning, they remind me not a little of deeply wooded isles reposing under Ionian skies, rough, rugged, and yet inviting, in some respects, as the gardens of the Hesperides. God be praised for every hill and valley, and tree and flower!

In these islands the indigenous trees, whether ornamental or valuable for building purposes, retain their native verdure throughout the year. When these islands were discovered by the Dutch navigator, Tasman, 1642, they were inhabited by a bold, athletic, dark-skinned race, supposed, while closely related to the Hawaiians, to have descended from the Malays; others say from the Central Americans. They are called *Maoris;* the word meaning "primitive inhabitants." In Capt. Cook's time, and after, some of the tribes were cannibals. These natives, though superior, on the whole, to most aborigines, are fading away. They understand their destiny. There have been at times some of these *Maoris* in the General Assembly. Britain has set Columbia a good example in this matter. May we not hope to see, at no distant day, both Indians and women in our American Congress?

New Zealand is nearly on the opposite side of the globe from Great Britain, the precise antipodes being a small island seven hundred miles to the southeast. The two islands designated as the North and the Middle, separated by Cook's Straits, are over a thousand miles in length, volcanic in formation, and contain about sixty million acres. Seen from the ocean, the land is rough and barren; and yet the country has fine plains, open valleys, beautiful springs and rivers, and is unsurpassed in value for agricultural purposes. I have met wool-buyers here from New York and the New England States. Having a seaboard extent of some four thousand miles, with several splendid harbors, this country is destined to occupy a very important position in trade and commerce, in fact it does already.

CLIMATE OF NEW ZEALAND.

Though one of the finest in the world, the climate is far warmer and more genial on the western than on the eastern coast of this group. The average rainfall is twenty-nine inches. The atmosphere is light and buoyant, while the winds are continually freshened by traversing an immense expanse of ocean. Not a flake of snow is seen in the northern island of this group, save in the highlands. At an elevation of six thousand feet, however, the snow is perpetual.

These islands unlike many in the South Pacific, are emi-

A Tattooed New Zealander.

nently adapted for agricultural and pastoral pursuits. The sunny valley of the Taieri, the undulating plains, the neatly tilled fields in the rural districts, with millions of choice yet unoccupied acres, incline one to ask, "Why do tens of thousands remain in Britain to beg or starve? England has colonies and provinces enough to supply multitudes with homes, thus feeding her over-crowded population. Why do they not emigrate?" And so of New York and other great American cities; millions prefer to stay in them and half-starve rather than to go out on the great prairies of the West and till the soil.

BOTANIZING IN FERN-FIELDS.

While in Australia and New Zealand, I went out several times with botanizing parties. Though fatiguing, it was thrillingly interesting; and the more so, because — as in Ireland — there are in New Zealand neither frogs, toads, nor serpents. How is this, since no St. Patrick banished them? Fuchser was a German botanist; and the small, yet beautiful flowering plant in America, named after him, is a native tree in these islands, with a trunk from a few to eighteen inches in diameter. Tramping over the hills, one is continually reminded of extinct volcanoes and the carbonaceous period. Some of the tree-ferns are over one foot in diameter. They grow straight and erect as chiseled pillars, while their long, arching, thick-ribbed leaves spread out like roofs of daintiest beauty, through which sun-rays can scarcely gleam. The birds we saw on the mountains were few, but exceedingly tame. These natives, the *Maoris*, neither shoot nor otherwise harm them. What a lesson to Christian sportsmen! The kiwi is the last living representative of the New Zealand wingless birds. These wild birds, so called, will sometimes take crumbs from the hand, and peck at the nails in your boot-heels when sitting down to rest in a thicket. The moa, a gigantic wingless bird, corresponding to the giraffe in the animal kingdom, has long been extinct. The bones are valuable to naturalists. Several skeletons of this bird may be seen in the Christchurch Museum, nine, ten, and even twelve feet high. The flesh was eaten by the Maoris; the feathers were used as ornaments, and their skulls for holding tattooing-powders.

MAGNIFICENT SCENERY AND MINERAL SPRINGS.

Among the natural wonders of this island group, are the geysers, or boiling lakes. They are said to far surpass those of Iceland. Columns of steam, rising from these volcano-heated springs, may be seen above the white cliffs while sailing along the coast. Approaching them, the roar seems like mighty engines madly working in the bowels of the earth. And, what is singular, no two throw up water of exactly the same character. Some are clear as crystal, others are dark-hued and muddy; some are impregnated with acids, some taste of soda, many contain sulphur, and one is salt as the briny ocean; but they are all intensely hot and boiling. The natives make use of them for all kinds of skin diseases and rheumatic complaints. Not far distant from these springs, on the North Island, are the Tarata Falls, fringed with weird shrubbery and incrusted boughs. The sprays and glassy sheets, pouring over molded alabaster, are strikingly beautiful. Below are delightful baths of different temperatures. The baths of the ancient Romans, so famous in history, could not have surpassed these adjacent to the boiling lakes. The crystallized terraces are absolutely magnificent. Te Roto Wanapanapa is a strange-looking greasy lake of yellowish-green water, clear, cold, and deep. There are hot, muddy springs close by, throwing up a gray-colored, greasy clay, which the roaming Maoris call *Kaikai*, and eat with avidity. The prettiest hot spring is Nawharua, called the Moss Spring. It is used for cooking purposes. The quantity of sulphur around some of these lakes is enormous; and the mineral impregnations give the waters all kinds of colors. Some of the terraces are pink, some purple, and others white or orange, caused by crystallizations. Names written on them are soon coated over, becoming permanent; while fern-leaves, flowers, and the fine swinging twigs, seem to have been converted into stalactite-shaped crystals of silver and gold. No painter can put this scenery upon canvas. A Walter Scott or Bulwer-Lytton could hardly do the subject justice. The prince of all romancers, Dumas, would fail.

WINES AT FUNERALS.

Officiating once at a funeral in Dunedin, New Zealand, there were wines put upon the same table with the uncoffined corpse. After I had spoken the words of consolation, the sectarian neighbors present, and a portion of the mourners, " imbibed." This is quite common, I am told, at Christian burials.

Think of it, — wines at births and wines at funerals. Think of it, O ye priests! who, guzzling wines, beers, and brandies, solemnly preach that "no drunkard can enter the kingdom of heaven!" Is it not to the silly and stupid custom of " entertaining" by drink that Hamlet alludes, when he says to Horatio, " It is a custom more honored in the breach than the observance " ? The peerless Shakspeare makes Cassio to say, " Oh, that men should put an enemy in their mouths to steal away their brains! that we should with joy, pleasure, revel, and applause, transform ourselves into *beasts !* "

During an English election overthrowing the reigning Gladstone party, both the Scriptures and liquors were used at public gatherings for political purposes. Flags and banners bore this inscription : " *Beer and the Bible — a national beverage and a national Church !* " Chinese, Persians, Arabs, " heathens of the East," often taunt and scourge Christians for their habitual drunkenness. One of Buddha's commandments was, " Drink no liquors, neither wines ; but walk steadily in the path of purity." Mohammed said, " O true believers! surely wines and games are an abomination, a snare of Satan." The heathen (so called) of Asia, have wines neither upon their sideboards, nor even at their funerals.

CANNIBALISM.

As one stimulus leads to another, why should not meat-eating open the way to cannibalism? If, according to the unphilosophical epicure, flesh is a better food than vegetables, grains, and fruits, and higher, too, in the scale of sustenance, why not subsist upon it altogether? And so, if *human* flesh is still higher, more readily assimilating with the juices and forces of the system, because magnetically humanized, why not eat *that* also? The Maori cannibals of New Zealand did *this* very thing. When the giant-like moa-birds failed to supply necessary meat, the natives resorted to cannibalism; eating, first, enemies slain in battle. *Animal food* they must and *would* have.

One old Maori told me that he had helped eat eighteen human beings. He declared that baked man and baked pig tasted very much alike. Horse flesh is eaten in London and Paris; and snakes are eaten by certain African tribes.

The Rev. Mr. Baker said to me, while at a dinner-party given by the Rev. Dr. Lang, Sydney, "I have visited one hundred and ten of the South-Sea Islands, and am perfectly acquainted with their manners, customs, regulations, and religious notions. They believe in one or more gods, and in an existence hereafter. Those on the Isle of Lifu, Loyalty Group, Western Polynesia, believe that the good spirits of their ancestors — whom they sometimes see as apparitions — dwell on the sunny side of the island, and the bad spirits among the lagoons on the other. They are dark complexioned, and capable of a high civilization. Some of these islanders yet continue their cannibal practices." This clergyman personally knew one old chief who had helped to eat and digest thirty human beings. They generally bake them. It is considered an honor to drink the blood, and feast upon certain parts of the bodies, of those slain on their battlefields. They believe the silly adage that every part strengthens the part allied to the animal — or to the man-corpse being eaten.

MAN-EATING UNNATURAL.

Animals, only in exceptional cases, devour each other. It was not innate barbarism, nor a monstrous heathenism, that drove the South-Sea Islanders to eat their fellows. It may be accounted for in the extermination of the moa-birds and the native rats, depriving them of flesh-food. Europeans, when shipwrecked and at the point of starvation, have laid hold of and greedily devoured their companions. History relates many occurrences of this kind. Before casting too many stones at those "vile savages," it were well to glance at antiquity. Donovan, in Lardner's Cyclopedia, assures us that "our own ancestors were of the number of these cannibal epicures." Diodorus Siculus charges the Britons with being *anthropophagi;* and St. Jerome, living in the fifth century of the Christian era, accuses the British tribes, not only of a partiality for human flesh, but a "fastidious taste for certain delicate parts of it." Gibbon brings the same accusation against the Caledonians. Allied by a common bond of sympathy, war in Christian nations, and cannibalism among the native islanders of the Pacific, must perish together.

THEOLOGICAL CANNIBALISM.

Did you ever attend the Sunday services of the Ritualists? What a display of millinery! — the alb, girdle, stole, maniple, and chasuble; referring, it is said, to the trial and death-scene of Jesus! After the waving of the incense, comes the administration of the eucharist, which eucharistic elements are declared to be the "veritable flesh and blood of Jesus Christ."

The Rev. Mr. Bailey, the English clergyman of Christchurch, New Zealand, says that the "priests of a certain order offer the sacrifice; and such mysterious authority do they wield, that the *real body and blood* become infused into the bread and wine upon the altar." These are the teachings of the "Prayer-Book." At the words; "THIS IS MY

BODY, THIS IS MY BLOOD," you must believe that the bread and wine become the real body and blood, with the soul and the Godhead, of Jesus Christ. . . . Except " ye eat my *flesh*, and drink my *blood*, there is no life in you." 'Mid gorgeous vestments, bursts of music, and clouds of incense curling above the altar, the priest asks the members of the church present to eat the *miracle-made flesh*, and drink the *blood* of Jesus the son of Joseph, called, in his time, Joshua the Galilean. If this bread *is* made "flesh," as the clergy affirm, eating is cannibalism! There are few churchal practices more opposed to the genius of the nineteenth century, than these little select Sunday parties denominated the "Lord's Supper." Open wide your church-doors, O Christians! and spreading out, with liberal hands, good coarse unleavened bread, fresh fruits, and pure cold water, invite in " the poor, the halt, and the blind; " and then converse of the Nazarene, his benevolence, his self-denial, his devotion to principle, and his martyrdom upon Calvary!

THE MAORI RACES.

The original inhabitants of an island or country must naturally interest all thoughtful persons given to ethnological studies. According to Tasman, Cook, D'Surville, and other navigators, New Zealand, when discovered, was thickly inhabited by a most interesting people, — one hundred thousand or more in number. In color they were of a yellow brown or olive. Those that I have seen on camp-grounds, or strolling along the streets, were of a light copper hue. Blood, in many of them, is strangely mixed with that of Europeans. In hight they are above middle stature, erect, well proportioned, and muscular. Their countenances are open, eyes dark, foreheads finely developed, noses large, broad at the base, and often aquiline, and their hair black, waving, and often inclined to curl. Some of them have as fine, heavy beards as Americans. Their hair never falls off from their heads, but gradually turns gray. The old natives affirm that their ancestors lived to be very aged, and then died by slowly wasting away, as a lamp goes out for lack of oil.

These Maoris, as relics demonstrate, were certainly, in the past, more than semi-civilized. Those yet living are the degenerate specimens of a nobler ancestry. In social life they were industrious, good-natured, temperate, and cleanly. They dwelt together in large fenced villages. Rising early, the men went to their land-cultivations or sea-fishing, and the women to cooking or basket-making. Their house-building, and architectural conceptions generally, were infinitely superior to those of the Australian aborigines. They excelled in some few manufactures, especially in weaving mats and garments from *phormium,* — New-Zealand flax. This plant, growing spontaneous, reminds one of the wide green flag-leaves seen in American marshes. The fiber is wonderfully tough ; and the mats and rude dresses, made from it by the natives, were both useful and ornamental. This flax is now being utilized for the English market.

Iron was unknown to the New-Zealanders when Capt. Cook landed upon the island. Their stone axes of various sizes, used for felling trees, were made of green jade, basalt, or hard gray stone. For water-vessels, they used the ripened rinds of gourds. Oil they kept in calabashes similar to those we saw in the Sandwich Islands. Their musical instruments, such as the flute, were made from human bones, or the hollow stems of wood. They did not buy and sell, but dealt in exchanges and gifts. Priests generally named the children. They practiced polygamy. As a religious animal, man is polygamic and promiscuous ; as a spiritual being, he is monogamic in marriage, and chaste in marital conduct ; and as an angel he is a celibate. The embryo angel is within. Men may become angelic on earth. This is the resurrection with God's " will done on earth as in heaven."

The chiefs of these tribes were known by their tattooing, dress, insignia, and ornaments. The eldest child was the favorite one, ruling the others. A species of slavery existed among them. Slaves could never reach the rank of patricians. When these Maoris met, they did not shake hands, but affectionately rubbed their noses together. This is their present practice. While some American women carry poodles for pets, these natives carry little pigs. They are very hospitable to strangers. Cannibalism was unknown in their earlier traditionary times. Their decline commenced with the advent of the missionaries. The " Wanganui Herald," in an able editorial upon the " decline of the native race," says, —

" Let one get into conversation with any of the old settlers, principally whalers, whose recollections date back some forty years, and he will be astonished to learn how these tribes have disappeared off the face of the earth, and how the present representatives of these departed races, noble specimens of civilized savages as some of them are, bear comparison in stature, appearance, mental qualifications, or social influence among their respective tribes, with their departed ancestors. It is almost saddening to watch the gradual though certain diminution among those once powerful *hapus ;* and it is no less humiliating to have to acknowledge, that, in the majority of instances, death and disease can be unerringly traced to their intercourse with the less civilized *pakeha,* the white man. In Otaki, the centre of missionary influence on this part of the coast, will be found the greatest immorality, the most degraded mental and physical condition, and consequently the most rapid and certain decline, among the natives as a people. . . . Yearly statistics unerringly state, that, so far from the natives being benefited by their religious, political, and social intercourse with ourselves, the reverse is the case. Disease and death are on the increase ; and crimes, often of a heinous nature, are committed more frequently in proportion to the progress of their acquaintance with our manners and our customs, our habits and our views, our treachery and our falsehood. This seems an appalling picture, but nevertheless it is a true bill."

TATTOOING.

The term " tattoo," of Oceanic origin, relates to those indelible devices pricked into the skins of natives. The

New-Zealanders used originally the wing-bone of a bird,
sharpened to a point. This they dip into the juice of a tree,
producing the desired color. The tattoo-artists hold a high
social position. The process is painful and tedious. Chiefs
are very thoroughly as well as weirdly tattooed. Besides
being ornamental, the operation is regarded with religious
veneration; the one thus decorated being placed under the
protecting care of some spirit. The god of the tattoo is
called Tiki. The practice is ancient. Herodotus informs us
that "both in Thrace and Lybia the natives were accustomed to puncture and color their faces, and various parts of
their bodies."

WHENCE CAME THESE MAORIS?

The native population may be classed into several divisions, distinguishable by peculiarities of dialect, physiognomy,
and disposition. These divisions are dimly traceable to the
crews of different canoes finding their way to these islands.
Evidently they came from different Polynesian groups.
They certainly did not come from Australia, as their color, ·
habits, religion, and language demonstrate; neither are they
the descendants of the Sandwich Islanders, as some have
contended. Among substantial reasons to the contrary, the
following may be mentioned: The New-Zealanders carry
their burdens on their backs, much like our North-American Indians; while the Sandwich-Islanders carry theirs on
a balance-pole, something like the Chinese. Further, these
New-Zealand Maoris have no words for swearing, no temples for religious worship, no idols, no refuge-cities; nor did
they ever practice circumcision. Many of their taboos, *tabu*,
were utterly unlike those of the Hawaiians. But, affirma-
tively, the carvings of the Maoris agree wonderfully with
those of the ancient inhabitants of Central America. Like
those Central-Americans, these aborigines obtain fire by friction; they steep kernels of *Karaka* for food; and have religious as well as many other customs resembling those remote

nations, as late discoveries at Uxmel and Palenque plainly show.

THE MAORIS' RELIGION.

Men, civilized and savage alike, are naturally religious. The principle is God-implanted. These New-Zealand Maoris believed in a plurality of invisible gods, and a future existence, although the *tapu* took the place of religious observances. They had priests and "sorcerers," and held intercourse with their "ancestral dead." They were troubled with demons. The heads of the chiefs were tabooed (*tapu*), no one being allowed to touch them, or hardly allude to them, under fearful penalties. They believed in charms, and wore them. Death, to them, was the passage to the *Reinga*, the unseen world, or the place of departed spirits. They prayed to their gods for aid and direction. They did not fear to die, yet preferred living in their mortal bodies. They believed that individuals occupied different apartments in *Reinga*, according as their earthly lives had been good or ill. Messages were frequently given to dying persons to bear away to deceased relatives in this shadow-land of souls. All of their funeral wails over their recent dead ended with, " Go, go, dear one, away to thy people!" It is a singular coincidence that the Fijians, Tahitians, Tongans, and Samoans, as well as the New-Zealanders, considered the place of departure of the spirits, on their journey to the unseen world, as the western extremities of their islands.

Burning *Kauri* gum for a kind of incense at funerals and festivals, they considered the trees pointing skyward as symbolizing life in a higher, better state of existence. This resinous substance, *Kauri*, — imported for making varnish, — is not obtained in the present living *Kauri* pine-forests, but only in the Auckland province of the north island, where such trees originally grew ; yet of such ancient forests no other trace remains than the resin now found deep in the soil.

MAORI SPIRITUALISM.

Relation to, and communion with, a world of spirits are beliefs almost, if not completely universal. The native tribes and clans of these islands are not only aware of holding intercourse with the so-called dead, but they understand the abuse, often using their mediumistic privileges for selfish ends. During their wars with the English, they were uniformly made acquainted by vision, clairvoyance, or clairaudience, with the movements of the British troops, before action in battle. Not a plan of her Majesty's officers could be kept from them. The leading chief of the *Han Hans* was a noted medium and medicine-man. He distinctly said that the " spirits of the dead " guided him to his victories. The Maoris in the north island still own much territory, have their king, believe in communicating spirit intelligences, and hold but little intercourse with *pakeha*, the white man.

The medium-priest in a tribe is called *Tohunga*. They meet in close apartments, and chant their songs till the flickering fire fades away, when the *Tohunga* goes into his ecstatic state, and the spirit controlling tenders counsel, describes his new habitation in spirit-life, gives the names of those whom he has met, and bears messages in return to kindred in the higher life. That these *Maoris* of New Zealand talk with immortals, no intelligent man having lived among them disputes. Are they Spiritualists, then, or *Spiritists?* Spiritualism is the synonym of the harmonial philosophy. Spiritism is the bare *fact* of spirit-converse.

TOHUNGA, AND VOICES OF THE DEAD.

The racy writer of " Old New Zealand," * treating of spiritual experiences among the Maoris, says in substance, " A popular young chief, something of a scholar, and register of births and deaths, had been killed in battle ; and, at the request of friends, the *Tohunga* had promised to evoke,

---

* Old New Zealand, by the Pakeha, p. 157–161.

on a certain night, his spirit. The appointed time came. Fires were lit. The *Tohunga* repaired to the darkest corner of the room. All was silence, save the sobbing of the sisters of the deceased warrior-chief. There were thirty of us, sitting on the rush-strewn floor, the door shut, and the fire now burning down to embers. Suddenly there came a voice out from the partial darkness, '*Salutation, salutation to my family, to my tribe, to you, pakeha, my friend!*' Our feelings were taken by storm. The oldest sister screamed, and rushed with extended arms in the direction from whence the voice came. Her brother, seizing, restrained her by main force. Others exclaimed, 'Is it you? is it you? *truly* it is you! *aue! aue!*' and fell quite insensible upon the floor. The older women, and some of the aged men, were not moved in the slightest degree, though believing it to be the spirit of the chief.

"Reflecting upon the novelty of the scene, the 'darkness visible,' and the deep interest manifest, the spirit spoke again, 'Speak to me, my family; speak to me, my tribe; speak to me, the pakeha!' At last the silence gave way, and the brother spoke: 'How is it with you? is it well with you in *that* country?' The answer came, though not in the voice of the Tohunga-medium, but in strange, sepulchral sounds: "*It is well with me: my place is a good place. I have seen our friends: they are all with me!*" A woman from another part of the room now anxiously cried out, 'Have you seen my sister?' — 'Yes, I have seen her: she is happy in our beautiful country.' — 'Tell her my love so great for her will never cease.' — 'Yes, I will bear the message.' Here the native woman burst into tears, and my own bosom swelled in sympathy.

"The spirit speaking again, giving directions about property and keepsakes, I thought I would more thoroughly test the genuineness of all this; and I said, 'We can not find your book with the registered names; where have you concealed it?' The answer came instantly, 'I concealed it between the *tahuhu* of my house, and the thatch ; straight over you, as you go in at the door.' The brother rushed out to see. All was silence. In five minutes he came hurriedly back, with the *book in his hand!* It astonished me.

" It was now late ; and the spirit suddenly said, ' *Farewell, my family, farewell, my tribe: I go.*' Those present breathed an impressive farewell ; when the spirit cried out again, from high in the air, ' Farewell ! '

" This, though seemingly tragical, is in every respect literally true. But what was it ? ventriloquism, the Devil, or what ? "

This last paragraph is simply a sop thrown out to please the orthodox. It might be paralleled thus: Peter, James, and John heard the spirits of Moses and Elias " talking with Jesus" upon the Mount of Transfiguration. " But what was it ? — ventriloquism, the Devil, or what ? "

Spiritualism is as common in the isles of the ocean to-day as it was in Palestine when the Nazarene there lived, eighteen centuries since. Dillon, commanding the East India Company's surveying ship " Research," visited the island of Vanikovo, — lat. 11° 40' south, long. 166° 40' east, — for the purpose of inquiring into the fate of the French expedition under La Pérouse. At this island Dillon tells us there were *large houses set apart for the use of disembodied spirits.* Markham, in " The Cruise of ' The Rosario ' in the South Seas in 1871," refers to the fact as related by Dillon.

The New Zealand mind is naturally skeptical ; and some of the Spiritualists tread upon the very border-lands of materialism. As did the ancient Jews, they continually ask for a " sign " — some astounding spiritual wonder. Many new-fledged Spiritualists prefer a combative, frisky sensationalism to the historic, philosophic, and pathetic style of lectures. The two methods of public utterance are the solid and the sensational: the one is enduring, the other ephemeral. Straws flash and flame ; but the clear, glistening anthracite warms the apartment, and gives permanent comfort.

NEW ZEALAND'S PROSPERITY.

While India suffering from the plague and famine was the poorest country I saw during my third tour around the world, New Zealand was the most prosperous, and among the reasons are the following :

The government controls the post-offices and the post-office savings bank. Postage is cheap. The government also owns and manages the telegraph system ; and a ten-word message anywhere upon the islands costs but a sixpence.

The government owns and operates the telephone system which is excellent, and the charges are more than one-third less than they are in America.

The government gives State or mutual life insurance, and the premium rates are considerably lower than the average rates charged by the private companies. Accordingly, every government policy-holder feels that he has the whole country as a guarantee behind him.

Eight hours constitute a legal day's work. The schools are free. The government has expended nearly $2,000,000 in establishing special and technical schools.

The government has established a government bank, thus making deposits safe as the government itself. Victoria and South Australia have done the same.

The law imposes a tax upon incomes, and an ordinary tax upon land and mortgages, the amount of which is fixed annually by a " rating act," and also an additional graduated tax upon the unimproved value of land held in large blocks or tracts.

The government, through parliamentary law, administers and is responsible for all estates, thus insuring justice and safety to the widow and the orphan.

The government owns and operates the railroads, and the passenger and freight rates are such as give about three and one-half per cent. interest on the capital invested. Traveling railroad rates are considerably less than in my native country.

Conciliatory boards have been established by the government in every city and town where disputes are likely to arise between labor and capital. Each board is comprised of three representative business men of capital and three representatives from the labor organizations and the district judge — a veritable board of equity ; hence a strike is next to impossible in New Zealand.

New Zealand has also woman's suffrage. Bishop Cowie of these islands, my traveling companion by steamer from Auckland to Sydney, was a devoted advocate of extending full and free suffrage to women. " It had already," he said, " raised the standard of politics, and elected a higher class of officials." Those who most violently opposed the woman's suffrage movement were gamblers, liquor dealers, and the men that owned or patronized houses of ill-fame. Our sainted mothers, wives, sisters, daughters — in a word, women, being the subjects of law, and punishable if violating law, it is but the simplest act of justice that they have a direct voice in the making of law.

We had the pleasure of meeting in London one of New Zealand's most worthy citizens, the Hon. Mr. McLean, ex-member of Parliament. A gentlemen by nature, he is a stanch Spiritualist in theory and practice. Pleasant are our many memories of him. Our friend of old sunny recollections in Dunedin, Robert Stout, the erudite lawyer, is now Sir Robert Stout, a member of Parliament, residing in Wellington. Whatever position he may occupy relative to either religious or political measures, he is not, neither can he be, a bigot. And, further, he is honest and conscientious. Parliaments and Congresses need just such statesmen as McLean and Stout.

CHAPTER VII.

MELBOURNE, AUSTRALIA.

" But all through life I see a cross;
There is no gain except by loss,
There is no life except by death,
There is no vision but by faith,
Nor glory but by bearing shame
Nor justice but by taking blame —
So, the Eternal Father saith. '

LOCKED up in a floating prison a month or more over 10,000 miles of sea, it was refreshing to reach Sydney, noted for its handsome harbor, magnificent scenery, parks, recreation grounds and gardens dotted with plants and flowers from every known part of the world.

At the steamer's landing I was met by several friends. The welcome was most cordial. Several of their faces were familiar, and their hands just as friendly as when a score of years previous I was lecturing for them upon the phenomena and philosophy of Spiritualism.

Disorganized as the Spiritualists of the city are they gave me a most hearty public reception. The hall was filled to overflowing; but before the exercises ended the demon of discord stepped in, and a number of supposed Spiritualists proved themselves to be only spiritists devoid of that forgiveness, that charity, that fraternity and that tender sympathy and forbearance that become those who have drank from the fountain of angel communion; for many Spiritists are quite as human as the orthodox that they condemn.

Preferring the solid land to water, I journeyed by railway from Sydney to Melbourne; observing, as I dashed along, a very superior country for grazing, for farming, as well as vast forests of eucalyptus trees. This is a sort of a national tree, tall, unique, medical. New South Wales is free trade; Victoria is tariff, and so my luggage had to be overhauled and examined at the dividing-line between these two non-federated provinces.

REACHING MELBOURNE.

Sunny was the morning that I reached this stirring, bustling business city. Mr. W. H. Terry, upon whose forehead

W. H. Terry.

the angels wrote long ago in letters of gold the word " FAITH-FUL," was at the station to meet me. I was soon taken to his country residence, surrounded by fruit-trees, waving pines, ornamental shrubbery and a great variety of flowers.

It is several miles out, but of easy access by railway to the city.

Melbourne, the capital of Victoria, and the finest city in the Southern Hemisphere, has a population approaching five hundred thousand. It stretches along, dotting and fringing both banks of the Yarra to within a few miles of its mouth. Though quite English in architectural appearance, Melbourne, considering its age, is a most magnificent city. Its climate and geographical situation, as well as its extensive suburban parks, lawns and gardens, can elicit only profuse praise and commendation from travelers.

CHANGING WITH THE PASSING YEARS.

What changes! was my common exclamation. There had been so many changes in the city since my first visit to the city, and for the better, that I hardly knew some portions of it. The then suburban fields are now studded with neat cottages — the buildings in some localities have grown up more towering — the tramways now dash along the streets, and thrift marks lawn, garden and grove.

The principal streets are wide, well-paved, and brilliantly lighted in evening-time with gas. Along the curb-stones, in some of the streets, run rippling streams of pure water. There is no doubt of its being a decidedly healthy city. Epidemics are almost unknown. It is said that the first case of hydrophobia has yet to occur. Could dogs, pleading, ask for a healthier, better paradise? Nothing surprises me so much in this country as the museums, fine public libraries, and free reading-rooms. The city library contains over five hundred and fifty thousand volumes. Others, connected with the university, or other public institutions, are nearly as large, and accessible daily, free of charge. This is a blessing to the poor. The parliament "Education Bill," making education secular and compulsory, was bitterly opposed a few years ago by bishops, priests, and aristocrats. This was to have been expected. The priesthood in all

lands aims to keep the people in ignorance, or to so monopo-
lize their education as to turn it into sectarian channels. Education is the key-word of the age. Schools should be *free*, and
education compulsory, under all skies. In the ratio that mental and moral instruction is enforced, crime diminishes. To
this end Barlow says, " It may be safely pronounced that a
State has *no right to punish a man* to whom it has given *no
previous instruction*." Sir Thomas More writes to this effect
in his " Utopia " : " If you suffer your people to be *ill-edu-
cated*, and their manners to be corrupted from their infancy,
and then *punish* them for those crimes to which their first
education *disposes* them, what else is to be concluded from
this but that you *make* thieves, and then *punish* them ? "

PARKS AND FLOWER GARDENS.

If flowers are the alphabets of angels, gardens are the
delight of gods and good men. The Melbourne Botanic
Gardens, beautifully situated on the south bank of the flowing Yarra, some half a mile from the city, cover an area of a
hundred and fourteen acres, and abound in almost an innumerable number of trees, shrubs, plants, and ornamental flowers, snowy, crimson, and golden. The palms and ferns are
exceedingly fine ; and the deep emerald of the tropical foliage is, on this January day, absolutely magnificent.

The city and suburbs comprise in the aggregate not less
than three thousand five hundred acres. These reserves are
not mere enclosures, but most of them are laid out, planted,
and ornamented in the most approved style.

The eucalyptus abounds everywhere. It is said there are
some fifty species, the wood being excellent for ship-building
and railroad-ties. The foliage is beautiful ; some are clothed
in beautiful blossoms and the leaves are said to have a thera-
peutic value. These eucalyptus back in the gullies and
mountains rival, if not excel, the renowned forest-giants of
California. Through the kindness and financial courtesy of
Vice-Consul Stanford, brother of the late Senator Stanford of

California, I journeyed with Mr. Ross up among the eucalyptus forests and fern gullies of the mountains. The accommodations were excellent, the scenery indescribably grand, and the whole trip was sure to linger in the memory. Mr. Klein measuring a eucalyptus on the Black Spur, found it four hundred and eighty feet high. The minster spire of Strasbourg has been pronounced the highest of any cathedral on the globe, sending its pinnacle to the height of four hundred and sixty-six feet; the great Pyramid of Cheops is four hundred and eighty feet in height; and yet these eucalyptus trees would completely overshadow spire and pyramid.

AMUSEMENTS AND MORALS.

Cricket, football, shooting, bay-fishing and boating on the Yarra have their daily devotees. Holidays are frequent. At these seasons, arcades, stores, offices are closed, business put aside, and the old become young again. Horse-racing in Melbourne has become a craze. Somewhere in the vicinity of the city there is a horse-race every day of the week except Sunday. I wonder what race-horses themselves think of the business.

Amusements at proper seasons and places are both right and pleasing. It is well for even the old to unbend, doff their dignity at times and be boys again. It smooths away the wrinkles, sets the blood to bounding and relieves the mind of cankering cares. But amusements should be harmless. They should be strengthening to the muscular system and exhilarating to the mind. There is everywhere in social life the sunny side and the shady side. That only is sin that injures. The long, sanctimonious face is a certain symbol of hypocrisy, and prudish social sin-hunters see in others what is most prominent, though veiled, in themselves. Morality is based upon justice and right — and right is that which benefits self and others.

The causes of a morally cancerous condition of society in Melbourne or any other city is largely owing to the prevalence, and practical influences of Orthodox theology. If these sinning parties believed in the certainty of retribution, and the abiding presence of ministering spirits, they would immediately turn from the error of their ways. In Spiritulism, as a Christ-baptism, is the world's hope.

AUSTRALIA CLIMATE.

Pale and low in the south-west of clear New England skies swings the sun these wintry days of January. Here, in Victoria, it is nearly vertical, and the heat quite oppressive; while the maddened dust-clouds that whirl and waltz along the streets of Melbourne are fearful to encounter. The interior of Australia is pronounced largely a desert. The rains extend back only some forty or fifty miles from the coast. When it rains in these regions it pours.

Considering the latitude and marine position, Victoria can but enjoy a climate quite genial to Europeans and Americans. Approximating the trophical, it constantly reminds me of New Orleans, and the Gulf States generally. The weather is excessively warm only during the prevalence of the hot northerly winds. They are something like the California winds in the valleys of the interior, only more scorchingly withering. The hottest of all the months is January, the coldest, July. A thin ice, and occasionally frosts, are seen during the winter months June, July, and August. These frosts vary in different portions of the country, depending upon the elevation above the level of the sea. The haying season is over in January, immediately after which the farmers commence harvesting their wheat. Quite a number of Americans have become permanent residents in Melbourne.

A BROAD AUSTRALIAN OUTLOOK.

Though an immense island, Australia may reasonably be considered a continent. It length, from east to west, is over two thousand five hundred miles, and its breadth nearly two thousand; the northern part, approaching the equator, being about four thousand miles to the south-east of India, and four thousand to the south of China. It is estimated to contain three million square miles; fifty times the size of England, and one hundred that of Scotland. It is divided into Victoria, — Melbourne, the capital; New South Wales, Queensland, South Australia, and Western Australia. Each of these colonies is governed by councils, — legislative bodies something like the houses of Parliament, — under the superintendence of a governor appointed by the Queen of England. Victoria has an area of 86,831 square miles. It is very nearly as large as all of Great Britain, exclusive of her islands in the sea. A chain of hills traverses the whole colony, called the Dividing Range. The snowy Alps form the boundary between Victoria and New South Wales. They range from five thousand to six thousand feet above the level of the sea. The rivers of Victoria are neither serviceable for steamers nor magnificent in appearance. Many of them dry up during the summer months. To this the Yarra, on the banks of which the metropolis is situated, is an exception. The country back in the distance contains numerous salt and fresh water lakes and lagoons. They are generally shallow, except when happening to be the craters of extinct volcanoes.

The country is subject to great droughts. Irrigation is required to make the country blossom as the rose.

RECEPTION AND LECTURE-WORK.

Soon after my arrival, the Victorian Association of Spiritualists, of which Mr. Terry is President, gave me a most cordial reception. The room was filled to its utmost capacity. There were present such old pioneers as Ross, McIlwraith, Terry, Carson and others that greeted me on my first visit to this country. The world needed and still needs such moral heroes. After the music, the speeches and responses, tea was served with choicest foods and fruits — a most enjoyable occasion.

THE PROGRESSIVE LYCEUM.

A few days later the Children's Progressive Lyceum, under the conductorship of Mr. Elliot, gave me a reception all afire with enthusiasm. The music, the gymnastic exercises, the recitations and the addresses were most interesting — an evening never to be forgotten!

It was on my first tour to this country that I aided in organizing this Lyceum and be it said in praise its flags have never ceased to float nor has its light been dimmed or gone out in indifference. The Lyceum is a royal institute for the young.

Children are comparable to sensitive buds and blossoms. Their minds are something like sheets of white paper awaiting impressions; hence it is morally cruel to send them to sectarian Sunday-schools to be taught theological dogmas that may blight their normal aspirations, or drive them into the maddening whirlpools of insanity or atheism. The Melbourne Lyceum is doing most excellent work. Mr. George Spriggs, so well and so favorably known for his mediumistic gifts in both England and Australia, is now conductor.

THE HEAD-CENTER.

A circumference necessarily implies a center; and the objective head-center of Spiritualism in Australia is in the " Harbinger of Light " and bookstore office, Austral Building, Collins Street, Melbourne.

It was as early as 1861 that Mr. Terry began to investigate the Spiritual phenomena. Tests unexpected and convincing were received. Evidences accumulating from time, he was mentally forced to believe that the dark gulf had been spanned, the Lethean River between the two worlds bridged, and that though a man die, he dies to *live* again, and is capable of demonstrating his future existence. Oh, grand fact, blessed truth! Now, hope and belief become knowledge — and faith fruition. Mr. Terry walked in new-

ness of life — a life meaning immortality. Soon becoming
mediumistic, he developed fine healing gifts. Diagnosing
impressionally, he still treats the sick, using botanic remedies
which he imports from Boston. He uses no poisonous, dras-
tic drugs.

The "Glow-Worm," conducted by the venerable Mr. Nay-
lor, was at an early date succeeded by the "Harbinger of
Light," owned and ably edited by its present proprietor, and
which, by the way, was, and continues to be, one of the most
excellent and scholarly journals published in defence of Spiritualism. Among its corps of contributors is James Smith,
whose cultured essays, articles and critical reviews long
graced the columns of the Melbourne "Daily Argus." The
writings of John Ross and Mr. Wilton conspire to make the
"Harbinger" an honor to the cause it represents.

MEDIUMS IN AUSTRALIA — GEORGE SPRIGGS.

"O for the touch of a vanished hand,
Or a sound of the voice that is still!"

Multitudes in all ages re-echoed these words. Human life
is brief — the future endless! And which is it to be, a dreamless annihilation, or a conscious, progressive existence in a
better, higher land of immortality? How are definite answers to these all-important inquiries to be obtained? — Answer — through mediumship, and mediumship only! These
psychic sensitives alone can roll the stone away from the
mouth of the sepulchre.

A writer in the Melbourne "Daily Herald" said there
were five hundred mediums in the city. This was as right-
fully as seriously questioned. It was my privilege, however,
to meet several, and among them Mr. George Spriggs, with
whom I was privileged to have regular sittings each week,
witnessing the trance, and listening to the independent, clear-
ringing voice of the Indian Skiwauki. I was acquainted

with Mr. Spriggs' honorable record in England before meeting him in Australia.

It was in Cardiff, England, that this gentleman began his sittings for mediumistic development. And they were not in vain, as the future revealed. Much of his original success must be credited first to the guardian influences of wise spirits, seconded by the rigid discipline of Mr. Rees Lewis, a solid, substantial, old-time Spiritualist. His conditions, seemingly severe, were sustained by the controlling intelligences. All the members of this séance were compelled to strictly abstain not only from wine and from beer, but from all liquors, all tobacco, and all animal food. They were to be, and *were* during the period of all their sittings, straightout vegetarians. And upon séance days they were required to fast from after breakfast till after the evening's séance. And, further, frequent bathing and cleanliness were demanded. Each person was required to take a bath before going into the séance room. These regulations and conditions were prescribed by the spirits themselves; and they were as rigid as they were righteous. These conditions being complied with, in connection with calm, aspirational and reverential minds, the finest, perhaps the grandest, manifestations were obtained that have gladdened the earth during this century. The materialization of spirits was seemingly perfect, and other phases of manifestations were equally wonderful.

Upright in his daily walk, and conscientious, never did the breath of scandal or fraud or trickery touch Mr. Spriggs' garments. He ever considered mediumship sacred; and felt that its instruments should be consecrated to the upbuilding of the good and the true.

The above conditions instituted by Mr. Lewis were not unlike those of the old prophet Daniel before one of his great visions. These were his words: "I ate no pleasant bread, neither came there flesh nor wine into my mouth"; and he "fasted for three full weeks."

How many séances are held in ill-ventilated rooms, by people with unbathed bodies, swine-stuffed stomachs, beer-soaked visceras, and tobacco-scented breaths — a very pool-room of physical and moral stench; and, then, ask the beautiful angels to come with loving messages. Heavens ! Why, you give just the conditions for demons to come — demons and pretentious spirits, with lying lips and great swelling words of flattery.   Such séances are the hotbeds and nurseries of obsession.

A séance room should be a consecrated room, and those entering should be clean and sweet, calm and spiritually-minded — consecrated to a conscientious search for that truth and wisdom which cometh down from above.   It is with these conditions only that the best results can be secured.   If we would have our loved in heaven—if we would have angels in all their spotless brightness and loveliness come into our conscious presence, we must give them the loveliest and purest conditions possible.

> " How pure in heart and sound in head,
>   With what divine affections bold
>   Should be the man whose thought would hold
> An hour's communion with the dead."

The Cardiff " Circle of Light," with which Mr. Spriggs was connected as medium, became in England historic ; and the similar manifestations through him in Melbourne will not be forgotten by those who witnessed them.   But the materializing phase of mediumship drew so much vital substance from his organization that he abandoned it for the impressional, for the trance and for diagnosing and prescribing for the sick.   In this he is eminently successful.   Occasionally he gives old-time sittings, to special friends.   Upon one of these most interesting occasions, the light in the room slightly subdued, I heard the independent voices of Ski, Stainton Moses, Frederic W. Evans, the Shaker elder; all as natural as though in their own mortal bodies.   Surely Spiritualism is the light not alone of America, Europe and Australia, but of the world.

THE MASONIC HALL MEETINGS.

" And as ye go, teach ! " was the ancient command. Our public meetings in Masonic Hall under the auspices of the Victorian Association of Spiritualists, Mr. Terry, the president, proved a very great success. The audiences were overflowingly large and exceptionally quiet and receptive. Evidently the people were hungering for the truth. Sectarian creeds no longer satisfy the souls of thinkers. Manna may have fattened the Israelites ; Nebuchadnezzar may have feasted upon grass, and Calvinists upon the fiery confessions of the murderer of Servetus ; but those babyhood periods are past. The present clamors for living bread — for science, for a rational religion and for demonstrations of immortality.

The music at these meetings, vocal and instrumental, was most excellent. At the conclusion of each lecture the opportunity was given for asking questions, some of which if not knotty were amusing. My lectures, too, in the Lyceum Hall in the Unitarian pulpit and in the hall of the Australian Presbyterian Church and the Church of our Father were all equally well attended ; and be it said in praise of the press it reported me fairly ; especially was this true of the " Daily Herald."

PROGRESS OF PUBLIC SENTIMENT.

Absolute retrogradation is as impossible as for the sun to rise and set. The setting is in the seeming. No truth ever dies. The prodigal son of the parable, though wandering from home temporarily, was wandering into such retributive experiences of hunger and raggedness as would enable him to the better appreciate the comforts and happiness of a loving father's home. Upward all things — all true things tend. The progress of Spiritualism in Australia is not so vividly manifest in the addition of newly-organized societies and lyceums, as in the increasing liberality of opinion and breadth of thought. Spiritualism made the Rev. Mr. Strong's church possible. Spiritualism is a divine force — a diffusive power, crushing creeds and leavening the whole theological lump. Spiritualism and primitive Christianity with its visions, trances, healings and gift of tongues are in perfect accord.

The progress of liberalism and Spiritualism were especially noticeable in the general tone of the city press, which was courteous and fraternal, presenting a most marked contrast with that of my first visit. As a matter of history I republish the two succeeding paragraphs from the "Daily Telegraph" — organ of the clergy, and theological kin to the clergy of the past, whose hands closed dungeon doors, whose lily-white fingers tightened the thumb-screws, whose voices kindled the fires of martyrdom, and whose churchal tongues delighted to lap the blood of heretics — and all, *all* for Jesus' sake !

But here are the paragraphs appearing in the "Telegraph" nearly a quarter of a century since.

"If the 'Seer of the Ages' get your length in earth-life, you had better treat him well; for I can assure you, you will seldom find his equal. If his spirit should get the length of 'Arabula' before his body reaches N. Z., — I don't know the latitude of this place, viz., '*Arabula*,' but I refer you for information to 'The Arabian Nights,' you should get *his hide stuffed*, and preserve him to posterity; the 'ages' I fear, shall nevermore look on his like again. I cannot better begin to describe him than by giving a few of the delicate epithets bestowed on this Mr. Peebles in all the newspapers, town and country : an 'impudent American,' an 'impious pretender,' a 'long-haired apostate,' a 'specious humbug,' a 'rabid lunatic,' an 'uncouth revivalist,' a 'vulgar blasphemer,' a 'long-haired apostate !' These figures of speech might be indefinitely multiplied, and yet half the truth would not be told. This 'great and good man ' (Peebles) in speaking works himself up to a frenzy, while with bloodshot eyes, and rolling tongue, and foaming mouth, he tells the opinion that some 'heathen Chinee' had formed of Christianity away somewhere in the Far West. He then maudles over a Yankee story about some poor youth mourning for his granny, whom he had never seen, and who came from 'Arabula,' to pat him on the head. . . . On every occasion of his public appearance, the same hysterical

females, the same half-crazed, wild-looking men, are to be seen ready to
swallow any thing and every thing; the more absurd the better. They cry,
'The new and beautiful faith!' 'There is no God, but Peebles is a
prophet.'"

The distinguished late William Howitt, Spiritualist and
author, it is said, of seventy volumes, never wrote a pithier
paragraph than this: —

"Many persons who have attended *Spiritual séances* of various kinds,
and satisfied themselves of their *reality*, express their surprise that the
press, as a body, remain doggedly *unconvinced*. Why should they be surprised? It is simply an affair of Hodge's *razors*. Journals, whether of
news or literature, like those celebrated razors, *are made to sell*. So long
as the press thinks it will *pay better* to abuse Spiritism than to profess it, it
will continue to do so; but should the writers for the press hear to-day, or
any day, that the public is gone over to Spiritism, they will, all to a man, be
zealous Spiritists the next morning. Then, and not a day earlier, nor a day
later, will the press be *convinced*. Their logic all lies in the three celebrated words, pounds, shillings, pence."

CHRISTIANITY AND BIGOTRY.

Bigotry has no head and cannot think, no heart and can-
not feel. Her prayers are curses, her communion is death.
Before me lies an evangelical work with the following title:
"A Declaration for Maintaining the True Faith, held by all
Christians, concerning the Trinity of Persons in one only
God, by John Calvin, against the Detestable Errors of
Michael Servetus, a Spaniard; in which it is also proved
that it is *lawful to punish Heretics, as this Wretch was justly
executed in the City of Geneva.* Printed at Geneva, 1554."
In a letter dated February, 1546, Calvin says, "If Servetus
come to Geneva, I will exercise my authority in such a manner as not to allow him to depart alive." In another of
Sept. 30, 1561, he writes, "Do not fail to rid the country of
such zealous scoundrels, who stir up the people to revolt
against us. Such monsters should be exterminated, as I
have exterminated Michael Servetus, the Spaniard." This
is the real genius of Evangelical Christianity in Melbourne.

THE SPIRIT OF THE CHURCH.

Read the history of Queen Elizabeth. Study the horrible secrets of that English Inquisition known as the High Commission Court and the Star Chamber. Through it heretics and scholarly free-thinkers were brought to the block. In after years John Bunyan was imprisoned, George Fox hunted and vilified, and Ann Lee banished. Persecutions, fetters, dungeons, fires, swords and inhuman butcheries have ever been the attendants of Christianity. And, what is more, these red-handed Christians have justified their murderous proceedings by quoting the commands of Scripture, " If thy brother, thy son, or the wife of thy bosom . . . say, Let us go and serve other gods, . . . thou shalt surely kill him. . . . thou shalt stone him with stones that he die " (Deut. xiii. 6, 10).

"If any man or woman be a wizard or witch, that is, consult ' familiar spirits,' they shall surely be put to death " (Exod. xxii. 18; Lev. xx. 27).

" If any child or children, above sixteen years old, and of sufficient understanding, shall curse or smite their natural father or mother, he or they shall be put to death " (Exod. xxi. 15, 17; Lev. xx.). Also, " A stubborn and rebellious son, above sixteen years of age, which will not obey the voice of his father, or the voice of his mother, . . . such son shall be put to death " (Deut. xxi. 18, 21).

That reigning Protestant Christian, Henry VIII., issued, in harmony with Bible commands, this edict : —

"If any person, by word, writing, &c., do preach, teach, or hold opinions, that in the blessed sacrament of the altar, under form of bread and wine, after the consecration thereof, there is not present, *really*, the *natural body and blood of our Saviour Jesus Christ*, or that *in the flesh, under form of bread, is not the very blood of Christ*, or that *with the blood, under the form of wine, is not the very flesh of Christ*, as well apart as if they were both together, then he shall be adjudged a heretic, and *suffer death by burning*." *

* Pickering's Statutes, vol. iv., p. 471.

When persecuting "Bloody Mary" — a devoted Christian by profession — was reproved for those merciless butcheries perpetrated for Christ's sake, she replied, "As the souls of heretics are hereafter to be eternally burning in hell, there can be nothing more proper than for me to imitate the divine vengeance by burning them on earth."

Wherever a purse-proud Christianity has gained the most power, it has most obstructed the march of civilization, as in Spain and Italy. Guizot, the great historian of civilization in France, tells us that "when any war arose between power and liberty, the Christian Church always planted itself on the side of power, against liberty." This churchal Christianity in our midst is the importation of the dark ages, the horrid nightmare of the world. It is immoral in its tendency; for it sends good moral men to hell, and the lifelong wicked to heaven, if soundly orthodox. According to the sectarist's belief, a man may commit all manner of crimes, — lie, swear, cheat, steal, and murder, — then comply with the "conditions of salvation," and swing from the gallows to glory!

Consult the records of capital punishment. Nearly every victim attended, during the last weeks of imprisonment, by the clergy, makes full confession, repents, believes, and with a spasm leaps from hemp to heaven. For proof, we are referred to the repentant "thief upon the cross," and all closing up with the hymn, —

> " While the lamp holds out to burn,
> The vilest sinner may return."

Some of the most distinguished scientists and learned jurists in England are deists, — disbelieving in immortality, revelation, and the miraculous conception. This, on churchal grounds, seals their damnation. There are many good men in churches, however, — good and excellent in spite of the demoralizing tendencies of their creeds.

The immortal fathers of American independence were theists. Abraham Lincoln was an " infidel." He made no profession of Christianity. He had no " saving faith in the atoning blood of the Lord Jesus." He was neither converted, " born again," nor baptized. He joined no Christian church, and yet was hurled, with a "fell shot," from a theater into eternity ! And, if the orthodox creed be true, Lincoln, the martyred president, is in hell, — wailing this moment with the *damned in hell!* If so, let it be my doom. I would prefer hell — whatever it may be — with Lincoln, Franklin, Jefferson, Adams, Madison, Washington, Shakspeare, Byron, Burns, Shelley, Edgar A. Poe, Dickens, Humboldt, and the whole galaxy of political, intellectual, and moral lights of the world, to that little jasper-walled heaven of the sectarian Christian, where a few lonesome, long-visaged saints, saved through another's merits, wave palms and serenade the Jewish Jehovah for ever ! Orthodox Christianity, with its fanaticism, superstition, and cramping creeds, is rapidly sinking, in enlightened countries, into hopeless decrepitude and remediless decay. It has failed to save the world. Professing Jesus, it has practiced Moses. Its sun is setting, its corpse awaiting burial.

Quietly drinking the cup, patiently receiving the poisoned arrows of secular and sectarian spite, I forwarded to the Victoria press in those days of journalistic persecution no retaliatory replies ; neither did I correct the purposed misrepresentations of press reporters. Sitting at the feet of the persecuted and martyred Nazarene, I had learned to return good for evil and blessing for cursing. In the economy of the universe I knew that thorns precede moral victories, and Calvarys ascensions into the Heavens.

CHAPTER VIII.

AUSTRALIA.

... " A continent of beauty sleeping, on a summer sea,
Lying all at rest and silent, never dreaming what should be, . . .
Rich with stores of mineral wealth,
And flocks and herds by land and sea. . . .
Here through veins with young life swelling, rolls the blood that rules the world;
Here as hers, and dear as honor, England's banner floats unfurled.
Oh, Australia! fair and lovely, empress of the Southern Sea,
What a glorious fame awaits thee in the future's history.
Land of wealth and land of beauty, tropic suns and arctic snows,
Where the splendid noontide blazes, where the raging storm-wind blows ;
Be thou proud, and be thou daring, ever true to God and man ;
In all evil be to rearward, in all good take thou the van!
Only let thy hands be stainless, let thy life be pure and true,
And a destiny awaits thee, such as nations never knew."— AGNES LEANE.

DEEP is the bond of sympathy existing between Australians and Americans. Both are English-speaking swarms from the same old hive.

The entire population of Australia at the close of 1896 was estimated by census to have been 4,325,151. When the census was taken in 1891, the population of the seven colonies was 3,809,895. Sometimes New Zealand and Tasmania are included in the phrase, " the colonies." The above figures show that the increase during the past five years has been much less rapid than formerly.

The home-born are considered more desirable citizens than immigrants. By the time of the next census Australia will doubtless number over five million.

Australians are rather an uneasy and nomadic-inclined people. Last year 210,000 left Victoria — a few for South Africa, but the most of them for the gold-fields of Western Australia. Many have returned to Victoria, and more will. These gold-fields are doubtless very rich ; but it requires a mint of capital to successfully work them. The principal city is Coolgardie. It numbers about 30,000. This Western Colony has drawn largely from all of the other colonies. Tasmania, famous for its fine climate, is fast increasing in numbers. Its last native died a generation ago. Of the colonies, all considered, New South Wales has excelled Victoria in the increase of population. Why, is not clear to me. Americans universally prefer Melbourne to Sydney for residence or business. The latter is more conservative. New South Wales is the oldest of the colonies. It has free trade.

The Kangaroo at Home.

It lost 842 more people last year than it gained. It is given to boasting.

A general land boom occurred several years ago, and after collapse, with the failure of banks in Melbourne, detrimentally affected the whole country. Now, the people are regaining their normal condition of prosperity and the country its consequent attractiveness. Booms are curses, and land speculators are the bane of society. American cities have had, and still have, their fill of them. They are moral pests, heartless and seemingly soulless. Better be a beggar, considering the long stretch of years here and hereafter, than a clutching money-loaner or a city-lot speculator. If for no other reason, hell is a necessity to adjudicate and equalize the inequalities of this life : it is the invisible realm of discipline, the realm of revealings, where preys the undying worm of remorse.

AUSTRALIAN FEDERATION.

This great island continent is just now in the throes of a new birth — a union birth — a federation birth of all the colonies into one, constituting the United States of Australia. Such federation is considered indispensable for self-protection and internal improvement alike. A single stick, as is said, is easily broken; a compact bundle of them defies the giant. These colonies now have each its governor, sent from England; each, too, has its imposing House of Parliament, and each makes its own local laws. New South Wales, as aforesaid, is free-trade; while Victoria has a protective tariff. Each is a trifle jealous of the other.

When I visited Adelaide, March 24, 1897, on my way to Ceylon, the recently elected Federators were in session at Adelaide, the capital of the South Australian colony. Stepping into their Parliament building, I had the pleasure of seeing this august body in council and of hearing the address of the Hon. Mr. Barton. The resolutions commenced as follows : —

1. That in order to enlarge the powers of self-government of the people of Australia, it is desirable to create a Federal Government which shall exercise authority throughout the federated colonies, subject to the following principal conditions : . . .

Among this body of men elected by the popular vote was the tall manly form of Alfred Deakin, M. P., formerly so well known in the Spiritualistic circles of Melbourne. His soul at present is re-incarnated into politics — a pursuit that God knows needs just such honest and honorable men.

Though generally very low and inferior, some of the aborigines in Western Australia have Jewish features, and follow the circumcising laws of Moses. Professor Holmes, an explorer, says: "Many of the natives have broad, and in some instances, high foreheads, indicating intellectual faculties, which, however, it seems in most cases, are more difficult to cultivate than the appearance of the head would

Australian Native.

lead one to expect. Among the Fraser Range blacks I found one who had a moderately aquiline nose and a decidedly Jewish appearance."

At a station not far distant from Melbourne I witnessed them hurling the boomerang, saw them kindle fires with sticks of dry wood and go through with a sort of wild, worshipful dance, not wholly unlike the dances of our North American Indians.

THE AUSTRALIAN NATIVES.

The aboriginal inhabitants of Australia are called "black men." They are not black, only dark olive complexioned, bearing no real resemblance to African negroes. Seen walking from you, their physical appearance is rather commanding. They are straight as arrows, and flexible in their motions. The skin is brown and smooth, and the hair straight, black, and glossy. Their foreheads are low, eyes full and far apart, nose broad, mouth wide, and filled with large, white teeth. When sporting, using the boomerang, or throwing the spear, their attitudes are exceedingly graceful. Many of the men not only have sinewy and finely-chiseled limbs, but long beards that would naturally excite the envy of smirking aristocrats.

Sir Thomas L. Mitchell says, " They are a fine race of men. Their bodies individually, as well as the groups which they formed, would have delighted the eye of an artist. Is it fancy? but I am far more pleased in seeing the naked body of the black fellow than that of the white man. When I was in Paris, I was often in the public baths, and how few well-made men did I see ! "

Dr. Leichhardt, when visiting Australia, gave this description : " The proportions of the body in the women and the men are as perfect as those of the Caucasian race ; and the artist would find an inexhaustible source of observation and study among the black tribes."

These aborigines, residue of a very ancient race, number little over a thousand now in the colony of Victoria, and probably not many over a hundred thousand in the entire country. The fittest survives. Such is the logic of law.

THEOLOGICAL AND SOCIAL CHARACTERISTICS.

Religion is innate, and in some form universal. Theology is man-made, stinging the bosom that hugs it. Belief affects the moral conduct.

Ethnologists and Australian residents differ in their estimates of the native character. Certain missionaries, pronouncing them the lowest specimens of humanity, declare that they have " no conception of Jehovah, innate depravity, justification by faith, nor pardon through a sacrificial redemption." This is quite likely ; all of which, putting the evangelical construction upon these terms, is quite to the credit of these " heathen " aborigines.

It is the united testimony of thoughtful, honorable men, however, that aboriginal children are noted for retention of memory, quickness of perception, and readiness to acquire the usual elements of education. This was demonstrated by the experimental school at the Merri-Merri. And, a few years since, an aboriginal boy in the Normal School of Sydney carried off the prize from all his white companions. They are trusting and affectionate among themselves. Respect to age is rigidly enforced. Without the hollow fashions and jealousies, without the conventional decorum and restraints, of civilized society, they sing and gambol in the evening-time as though life were a continuous carnival. Suicide is unknown among them. Some of them tattoo themselves. The women use ochre, and other colored ingredients, to paint their faces. What of it ? English, French, and American women quite generally paint and powder. What a merciless tyrant is fashion !

TESTIMONIES IN FAVOR OF THE WILD AUSTRALIANS.

These inhabitants, evidently a cross between the African and the Malay, exhibit some excellent traits of character. Archbishop Polding, of New South Wales, said to the Sydney Legislature, " I have no reason to think that the primitive natives, uncontaminated with modern civilizations, are much lower than ourselves, in many respects. The missionary Ridley, noted for his candor, declared that in mental acumen, and in quickness of sight and hearing, they surpass most white people."

Mr. Batman, not inaptly denominated the William Penn of the colony, finished an interesting account of the original inhabitants, many years since, in these words: "They certainly appear to me to be the most superior race of natives which I have ever seen." This is an extreme view: the Maoris of New Zealand, and certain other races in the Pacific islands, are vastly their superiors. European interference here, as elsewhere, has proved a destructive curse to the original inhabitants.

Essayists of materialistic tendencies have strangely, though doubtless undesignedly, underrated the intelligence, the moral and religious position, of the Australian tribes. Mr. Whitman, writing in "The Boston Radical" upon ideas relating to immortality, says, —

"The intellectual plane of the Hottentots, Andamanas, *many* of the Australians and Tasmanians, and some of the Esquimaux, is but little, if any, better than that of the ape-like Bushmen just described. It has been said that the Australian savages can not count their own fingers, not even those of one hand."

If this writer had ever conversed with old colonial residents, and read the carefully-written works of Mitchell, Sturt, Leichhardt, and Gov. Gray; or if he were conversant with the history of William Buckley, who lived with the Australian natives thirty-two years, never seeing, during this time, a white man's face, — he would not have written thus disparagingly, and unjustly too, of these aborigines. Long acquaintance and study led Sir Thomas Mitchell to exclaim, "They are as apt and intelligent as any other race of men I am acquainted with." Mr. Burke bears this testimony before the Committee of Council in 1858: "I believe," says he, "the intelligence of the aborigines has been much misunderstood. The introduction of civilization has not tended to develop their character advantageously; but, on the contrary, they have suffered a moral and physical degradation, which has re-acted upon their intellectual powers."

CLOTHING. — COOKING. — HOMES.

Tacitus informs us that the ancient Germanic tribes spent "whole days before the fire altogether naked." The old Caledonians of Scotland were described by the Romans on this wise: "They live in tents, without shoes, and naked." Gov. Hunter thus mentions his glance at the natives of Jervis Bay, New South Wales, Australia, in 1789: "They were all perfectly naked, except one young fellow, who had a bunch of grass fastened round his waist, which came up behind like the tail of a kangaroo."

The climate being temperate or tropical, they require but little clothing. In the colder portion of the season, they wear rugs made of opossum and kangaroo skins. They are not given to finery. The feathers of the emu, swan, cockatoo, &c., are their ornaments upon important occasions. Some tattoo themselves. This custom, prevailing quite generally among uncivilized nations inhabiting warm countries, owes its origin probably to a want of mental resources, and more attractive employment of time, together with a love of ornament. They bore the cartilage of the nose to suspend bones and shells. American ladies prefer having the ears bored. The Chinese compress their feet, French women their waists.

Nutrition was abundant till the invasions of the Europeans. They pitched their kangaroo meat upon live coals, steamed their fish, and baked their turtles in the shell. Hunting wild honey was a favorite pursuit. The mysnong-root, the ends of tender grass-bulbs, the tops of certain palms, and various wild berries, also constituted articles of diet. Their dwelling-places, though unsubstantial, were sufficiently comfortable for such a fine, warm climate. Sticks, reeds, boughs, and blankets, by the side of a rock or tree, with opossum rugs for breakwinds, were about all they desired. These homes, though comparatively transient, were made musical and happy in early night-time with the relation of droll stories, the appearance of weird apparitions, the song, and the dance. The learned Dr. Lamlie, visiting and spending a long time either with, or in the vicinity of, the natives, gives this interesting description: "In some places, large, well-constructed habitations, shaped in the form of a span-roof, thatched with reeds, pleasantly situated on the verge of a lake, though quite unique, were highly creditable to their industry and skill." They are very warm-hearted in their natures, and kind to their aged; they seldom have but one wife at the same time; they will always generously divide with each other, and especially with Europeans who visit them. "These Australians drank only water," says Mr. Thomas, "till white men introduced their poisonous liquors; and imported private diseases also, that are now rapidly sweeping them off from the face of the earth." Mr. Protector Robinson reported officially, that "nine-tenths of the mischief charged to the aborigines is the result of the white men's interference with the native women."

RELIGIOUS NOTIONS AND CUSTOMS.

Worship is natural to all grades of humanity. There have been found, among the aborigines in portions of Australia, remnants of ancient faiths and traditional mythologies. Caves have been opened along the coast, on the walls of which were drawn unique and telling figures. The bottoms were handsomely paved. Mystic circles have been noticed on the tops of hills, the stones of which were arranged after the Druidical fashion. Enough has been discovered to indicate their connection with the civilizations of the most early Asiatic races.

Though probably dimly conscious of an indivisible deific Presence, they evidently adored the starry hosts, — believed in a multiplicity of gods, and in some sort of a future existence. " Go down, black fellow; come up, white man ! " is at present a common saying among them. That critical ethnologist, Strzelecki, says in his exhaustive volume, " The native Australians, recognizing a God, whose duty it is to supply them with all the necessaries of life, regard themselves as his servants. They believe in immortality, and locate their heaven in the stars : they do not dread God, but reserve all their fears for the evil spirit. To this spirit, the ' Debble,' they render a sort of worship."

Upon each returning November, the Australian spring-time, these natives hold the grand festival of the Pleiades, called the "Corroboree." It was a matter of individual regret that I could not have personally witnessed this native anniversary. Those in Northern and North-eastern Australia are far the most interesting. These "corroborees," cele-brated only in the spring, when this cluster of stars shines the most brilliantly, are evidently a kind of worship paid to the Pleiades "as a constellation announcing the spring season." Their monthly festivals and dances are in honor of the moon. An intelligent native said to me in Sandhurst, "The Pleiades are the children of the moon, and very good to us black people." The remark reminded me of a line in that Biblical drama, the Book of Job, —

" The sweet influences of the Pleiades."

These, called by the Romans " Vergiliæ," the stars of spring, appear above the horizon at evening-time in November, and are visible in these regions all night. The prophets of the tribes believe that these stars rule natural causes. Some of their festivals are connected with the worship of their dead ancestors. These last three days.

FROM WHENCE THESE NATIVES?

Their origin is involved in impenetrable obscurity ; and those who have attempted to trace their migrations, or detect the links which connect them to the primitive races, have failed of satisfying even themselves. The structure of the language is said to be the most nearly identified with the

Sanscrit ; others choose to connect it with the nomad c Tartars. In physical type they resemble the Malays, and yet there is not a Malay word in their language. They have religious mysteries, and a fearful method of initiation. Some of the tribes practice, like Jews and Mohammedans, the rite of circumcision. They wear charms upon their persons ; and certain of the old chiefs, looking into rock-crystals, profess to see the future. They find the bodies of murdered men by watching the trail of beetles. Mourning paint to be used for the face is invariably white. Young mothers used to very frequently name their children after flowers. A surname was sometimes added, descriptive of personal peculiarities. When a child is named after another person, and this person dies, the name dies also. The dead are never spoken of by name, nor referred to only by implication. They refrain from touching a dead body, as did the Jews and ancient Phœnicians. That a bond of brotherhood exists among the dark races of Australia and the Indian seas, is indisputable ; but whence they originally sprang, and by what circumstances they became scattered over thousands of miles, through seventy degrees of latitude, remains a problem to be solved. Doubtless the Australian country was peopled long before Abraham went down into Egypt, or before the walls of ancient Nineveh and Thebes were raised to their proud position.

THE NATIVE'S BELIEF IN SPIRITS.

Spirit is the underlying cause of all motion, energy, and moral activity. In the aboriginal " ceremonies, superstitions, and beliefs, there may be traced," says Mr. Parker, " relics of sun-worship, serpent-worship, and the worship of ancestral spirits whom they profess to frequently see." They believe that one class of spirits dwell in the air, another in the mountain, and others still wander about among the tall trees. These natives seldom quit a camp-fire at night, for fear of encountering malignant spirits. Mr. Benwick, among other marvels, writes this: "A spirit appeared to a *lubra*, — black woman, — announcing her speedy death. She related the occurrence the next day, with serious forebodings. Two days after seeing the apparition she died. Believing in demoniacal possession, the mediumistic 'medicine-men' of the tribe 'exorcise the evil spirits,' something as did Jesus and the apostles in New-Testament times. This class of men also alleviate pain, remove disease, and heal the sick, by charms and magnetic manipulations. They dance within the inclosures of mystic rings, fall in the trance, and describe the marvelous visions beheld." The Rev. Mr. Ridley gives the following account of a "corroboree:" "At Burndtha, on the Barwon, I met a company of forty blacks engaging in a ceremony of some mystical purpose. A chorus of twenty, old and young, were singing, and beating time with boomerangs. A dozen or more were looking on. Suddenly, from under a sheet of bark, darted a man, with his body whitened by pipe-clay, his face painted yellow, and a tuft of feathers fastened upon the top of his head. He stood twenty minutes gazing upwards. One of the aborigines, who stood by, said he was looking for the spirits of dead men. At length they came, proving to be evil spirits, and a brisk conflict followed. Others of the party joined in this warfare with the 'powers in the air,' driving the ghosts away." They have a singular ceremony, called *Ye pene amie gai*, or dance of separate spirits. Holding branches in their hands, they dance in measured tread, and sing, till they fall prostrate in a sort of ecstatic trance. While in this condition, they hold converse with spirits, and utter prophecies.

DECLINE AND DESTINY.

Nominally the aged men are their chiefs, exercising the principal influence in the tribes. "Civilization" is a very indefinite term. Australian aborigines, believing it to consist in being and doing like white men, engage in smoking, swearing, tricking, drinking, and gambling. The Rev. J.

C. S. Handt, Lutheran missionary, bears this testimony : " A principal cause of their decrease is the prostitution of their wives to the Europeans. This base intercourse not only retards the procreation of their own race, but almost always tends to the destruction of the offspring brought into existence by its means." Mr. Cunningham, well known in England and the English colonies of the Pacific, wrote thus: " Personal prostitution, among those associating with the whites, is carried on to a great extent, the husbands disposing of the favor of their wives to the convict servants, for a slice of bread, or a pipe of tobacco. The children produced by this intercourse are generally sacrificed."

Infanticide is very prevalent. Tradition says it did *not* exist in the past. At present half-caste infants appear to be the most exposed to this fate. Chiefs living and roaming back in the mountains, or interior districts, acknowledge that they cannot stop the murderous practice. When the parties are reproved for the unnatural crime, they at once respond, " We have no country now, no good children now, and nothing to keep them on." A glance at the journals reveals the fact that infanticide is not uncommon in Victoria; while fœticide is a quite common practice in the most aristocratic families. It is *murder* nevertheless.

Without hope, without seeming ambition, the remaining Australian natives have sunk down into a state of stupid listlessness. They know they are declining, and are conscious of their destiny. It seems an inflexible law of nature, that aboriginal races must, in every instance, either perish, or be amalgamated with the general population of the country. In Tasmania, originally known as Van Diemen's Land, there is not a native left. The bell of fate has tolled ; and the last man of his race, putting down his rude pilgrim staff, has gone on to the shadowy land of immortality.

CHAPTER IX.

FROM NEW ZEALAND ONWARD.

"There's a wideness in God's mercy
Like the wideness of the sea;
There's a kindness in His justice
Which is more than Liberty.

"For the love of God is broader
Than the measure of man's mind,
And the heart of the Eternal
Is most wonderfully kind."

NONE choose the land of their birth; and none can fully fathom the finer forces connected with racial influences. If deer and foxes leave the scent or aura of their footsteps along their beaten paths, why should not aboriginal men impart a characteristic emanation to the soil their feet pressed and to the atmosphere they breathed? They certainly do. Seemingly minute causes produce mighty effects. People born in the western portion of America naturally grow tall, and become wiry, angular and active, like our nearly extinct Indians. In South Africa children born of European parents are not only more rounded in features and sluggishly heavy, but they are inclined to be indolent like the Hottentots. The theory is not without confirmation.

Sailing — we are still thinking, reasoning, reflecting. No library, no daily journals: time drags. And what *is* time? A series of conscious impressions daguerreotyped upon the spiritual sensorium. And, considered with reference to the primal God-principle, *all* are equally aged. Each is pivoted in the centre of eternity. Causes are before effects; so are souls before bodies. To affirm that bodies make souls, is only paralleled by the position that ignorance is the source of knowledge; that matter may produce spirit, and nonentity reality. In dream and trance, memory sometimes sc dispels slumber that the conscious soul recovers recollections of pre-existence, of its descent and destiny,

TOO TRUSTING, OR NOT?

If, as Lord Bacon said, "reading makes the full man, talking the ready man, and writing the exact man," travel makes the *doubting* man. The past eight months' experiences in the colonies and islands of the Pacific have cooled my ardor as to the immediate approach of any world's millenium. I can but think of these lines in the "Songs of the Sierras:" —

> "For I am older, by a score,
> Than many born long, long before,
> If sorrows be the sum of life."

The play of Hector and Achilles is being constantly re-acted in my presence. Though there are tropical sunsets, and gorgeous skies, seen on this sapphire-crowned ocean, "my" and "mine" are the rallying-words. Men are exceedingly intriguing and scheming. Why, there are men mean enough, on this Polynesian part of the globe, to steal cocoanuts from a blind savage, or the sandals from the feet of Jesus. It saddens my soul.

Reviewing the fading years of half a century, I am certain of having believed too much, trusted too much, and confided too much in others. And yet is it noble or wise to write upon every human forehead, " *Cave hominem*," — beware of man? Is there not a golden mean? Are not the extremes of distrust and suspicion a long way from a just estimate of human nature? And may not the constant exercise of harrowing fears and doubts be hindrances, rather than helps to the soul's unfoldment?

MEN IN AND OF THE WORLD.

It quite shocked me, a few hours since, to hear a man say, " Well, the only two principles insuring success in this age are, to look out for one's *self* first, and, secondly, to consider every man a rogue till proved honest." Are not such words revelators, — voiced echoes out of a grasping, cankering selfishness? Is not a man-distruster a bad man-helper? Did ever a libertine believe in the virtue of woman? Or did ever a thief like Ahab fail to keep his locks and keys bright? The sordid, selfish man, the petty village lawyer, knows no other text than this : " To them that are under the law I became as under the law, and to them that are without law, as without law ; " adding, not as Paul did, " that I might gain *them*," but, " that I might gain their *fees*." In this money-worshiping, transition state of society, men seem to be drifting into a set of repulsive atoms, each seeking his own gain and welfare to the neglect of the common weal. This " getting-on system, " with the " survival of the fittest " and the " Devil take the hindmost," is well expressed in the abominable lines, —

" As I walked by myself, I said to myself,
And the selfsame self said to me,
Look out for thyself : take care of thyself,
For nobody cares for thee."

Let us deepen the thought, and widen the vision, of existence ! Essential spirit infills and spans all space. The " image of God " — the divine spark — is within ; and human nature, therefore, sounded to its depths, is good. If there is not a charity that " believeth all things," there *is* a charity that " hopeth all things ; " and, further, there is in the world tender sympathy, genuine friendship, manly honesty, generous benevolence, unselfish love ; and there are beautiful characters too : the angels affirm it. Cunning, shrewd, and selfish men, who can not discover it, are comparable to blind men who can not see the sun. Be it mine still to seek the good of *others* first, and to believe every man *honest* till proven to the contrary. If the practice of such principles produce failure, let "*failure*" be carved on my tombstone.

TRUCKLING TRIMMERS.

He who removes a thorn, and plants a rose, who brushes away a falling tear, plucks a scale from a theologian's eye, or transforms a bit of chaos into *kosmos*, is a benefactor of his race. Turn over the picture. Do not the angels weep o'er the platitudes of truckling, two-faced, many-sided hypocrites, standing in market-places, in pulpits, and upon public rostrums, with no higher aims than gold, or a stamping, sensational applause? Oh for men of principle! Policy-men fatten to-day, to faint in the to-morrow of eternity. It was a childish weakness in Peter to deny " knowing the man." Erasmus was too much of a trimmer. Luther was a reformer that made Rome tremble. The waters of a dashing cascade are sweet and fresh. A good, screaming fanatic, with sling and stone, will always floor the greatest giants, though armed with the newest devices of controversy. I sympathize deeply with fanatics. They generally have something to say, and are brave enough to say it. They keep the mental world in motion. John the Baptist was a fanatic. Fanaticism is not coarse, brawling, blatant, overbearing egotism, but earnest enthusiasm, steady, stirring self-denial, coupled with a conviction of some living truth as a potent spiritual force. These fanatics, these resurrected souls, preach of heaven on earth, sing of Utopia to-day, and often die early, as did Keats.

" Thy leaf has perished in the green."

CANNIBALISM AND COMMUNISM.

Passing an art-gallery in Dunedin, a friend pointed me to a photograph of an old, tattooed Maori, who had assisted in baking and eating seventeen human bodies since his remembrance. Cannibal eats cannibal, and clinging, parasitic souls feast upon the magnetic life of other souls. Such is selfishness, — the devouring, corroding selfishness of the world And yet who has not pictured and prayed for the prophets realization of " Zion " ? or who has not dreamed of that golden age where love shall be law, where the only rivalry shall be in doing the most good to others, where harmonial souls shall breathe benedictions of peace and good-will, and where a competitive, clutching self-appropriativeness shall have become a half-forgotten tradition ? May we not still hope that, before the sunset of this century, co-operative leagues, and communistic fraternities, may dot the land, as cities of light set upon a thousand hills.

PLATO'S REPUBLIC.

The most eminent philosophers and sages of antiquity, when mediumistically illumined by heavenly wisdom, either conceived or wrote of a coming communism, — a state of society where every one would be respected according to his worth, where individual happiness would be sought in seeking the happiness of all, and where the isolated family would widen out into co-operative combinations, and these into spiritual families, with wisdom and love the governing powers.

Among the more prominent of this school was the Grecian Plato. This prince of philosophers, flourishing some time before the Christian era, defined a well-ordered, if not an ideally *perfect* state of social life, to be known as a " republic." Though treating largely of justice and charity, he considered absolute " communism of property " an indispensable condition. He lived unmarried, had no children, died a *celibate!*

SIR THOMAS MORE'S UTOPIA.

Looseness in the use of phraseology causes many fruitless discussions. " Socialism " and " communism " are not inter-

changeable terms.   Communism proper should never be con-
founded with " Red Republicanism," the " Paris Commune,"
or any form of " loose socialism."   They are as unlike as
Christ and Belial.   Socialism implies co-operation, or any
form of association which does not involve the abolition of
private property ; while communism in the absolute is that
unselfish apostolic system which " *holds all things in common*."

Sir T. More, at one time privy councilor to Henry VIII.,
and afterwards lord high chancelor, published his Utopian
theories in 1516, creating a deal of excitement because of
his scholarship and high social position.   This distinguished
personage painted his conceptions of a commonwealth, or
true state of society, as a " *Happy Island*," based socially
upon the Utopian idea of equality of rights and the communism of property.   He says, —

" Thus have I described to you, as particularly as I could, the constitution of that commonwealth, Utopia, which I do not only think to be
the best in the world, but to be, indeed, the only commonwealth that truly
deserves the name.   In all other places it is visible, that, whereas people
talk of a *commonwealth*, every man only seeks his *own* wealth; but in
Utopia, where no man has any property, all men do zealously pursue the
good of the public, . . . for every man has a right to every thing.
There is no unequal distribution; no man is poor, nor in any necessity;
and, though no man has any thing, yet they are all rich; for what can
make a man so rich as to lead a serene and cheerful life, free from anxie-
ties, neither apprehending want himself, nor vexed with the endless complaints of others ? "   ,

Respecting labor, he speaks as follows : —

" They do not wear themselves out with perpetual toil from morning
till night, as if they were beasts of burden; which, as it is indeed a heavy
slavery, so it is the common course of life of all tradesmen everywhere
except among the Utopians; but they, dividing the day and night into
twenty-four hours, appoint eight hours of these for work, and the remainder for rest and individual improvement.   Each seeks another's
good; and, as to the studies and employments of women, all living in
Utopia learn some trade.   Industry is honorable: men and women go in
large numbers to hear lectures of one sort or another, according to the
variety of their inclinations.   Women are sometimes made priests, . . .

and a peace that the world knows not of crowns the days of the happy dwellers upon this island."

ST. SIMON AND FOURIER.

No man could be a socialist or communist, without being moved by a welfare for his fellow-men. It was to Horace Greeley's credit that he took such a deep interest in the North American phalanx. Socialism in Europe, promoted not *by* the poor, but *for* the poor, has generally been espoused by men of generous impulses and honorable enthusiasm. Fourier's great idea was to make labor attractive. He thought, that, by rightly grouping people together for work, all the natural passions would fall into harmony, and become utilized for human good. The movement gained but little footing in France. St. Simon, dying in 1825 at the age of sixty-five, had already become quite an author. He contended in his books that all social institutions ought to aim at the amelioration, physical, mental, and moral, of the poorer classes; that privileges of birth should be abolished, and the state be the ultimate owner of all lands, all public works, and all realized property. Associative effort was to be among the prominent teachings of science, the Church, and the State; while the natural inequalities of men, as primal gradations, were to be made basic pillars in this Simonian order of social life. St. Simon was eccentric, and aflame with humanitarian sentiments. He was far more imaginative than practical. Suffice it, that, while many of the ideas put forth were rational, the plan, though eagerly seized by a few trusting disciples, proved a speedy failure.

ROBERT OWEN.

This philanthropist and great social reformer, while showing at New Lanark, Scotland, that he was a clear-headed business-man, proved himself at the same time a genuine humanitarian. If a dreamer, he dreamed grand and golden dreams; and, what was more praiseworthy, sought to realize

them.   As the friend of man, he frequently said to English
society, " If you want the poorer classes to become better
men, place them in better circumstances ; raise the wages
of laborers, diminish their hours of hard work, increase their
food, improve their dwellings, expand their range of thought ;
let science serve them, culture refine them ; and, above *all*,
help them to help themselves."   Though emperors and kings
had listened to Mr. Owen, and though distinguished statesmen had been his associates, he never forgot the crowning
ideal principle of his life, — *communism !*

Rising from the miry plains of selfishness, to the mountain-
tops of equality and "good-will to men," it may be clearly
seen that communism is the voice of God through Nature.
Light and air, rain and sunshine, are common.   The prince
and the pauper child, at the hour of birth, are equal and
common.   Death is common to king and subject.   And the
laws of the universe are common.

A disorderly, anti-law, anti-marriage "Paris *commune*"
aside, Mr. Owen meant by communism that state of society
in which the common fruits of industry, and the common
results of science, intellect, and a sincere benevolence, should
be so diffused that poverty would be unknown, and crime
quite impossible.   Though a theist, contending that "theology was a mental disease," though loathing pious cant and
churchal superstitions, he was nevertheless a religious man
in the best sense of the term.   Non-immortality did not satisfy the wants of his great, manly soul.   Investigating the
Spiritual manifestations, in the later years of his life, he
became a believer in a future existence.   He died, or, rather,
went up one step higher, a Spiritualist.   Robert Dale Owen
is the worthy son of such a sire.

Many are the pleasant hours that I've whiled away listening
to Elder Frederic W. Evans's descriptions of memorable
occurrences transpiring in the life of the large-hearted Robert
Owen.   It may not be generally known that Elder Frederic,
one of the prominent Shaker elders at Mount Lebanon,

N.Y., was one of the Harmonial brotherhood, settling with Mr. Owen upon the thirty thousand acres purchased of the Rappites in New Harmony, Ind. This great and good man, a communist and Spiritualist to the last, passed to the world of spirits Nov. 17, 1858.

> " They made him a grave too cold and damp
> For a soul so warm and true."

Looking with thoughtful, cosmopolitan eye at the state of society in different countries ; considering the poverty of Pekin, the beggary in Constantinople, the infanticide in Paris, the political corruption in New York, and the fifty thousand thieves, one hundred thousand prostitutes, and one hundred and sixty-five thousand paupers, of London, — is it strange that noble souls in all lands yearn for social reconstruction ? Are not mediæval methods already dead ? Are not present political and social systems falling to pieces? What mean these panics, strikes, internationales, trades'-unions, and co-operative fraternities ? Does not Whittier, writing of recurring cycles, say, —

> " The new is old, the old is new " ?

JESUS THE SYRIAN COMMUNIST.

Oh, the moral altitudes attained by those great practical communists of the past, Jesus and the apostles! The Nazarene, gifted with the intellect of man, and the love of woman, loathed that reform which talked platitudes of well-meaning, and did no work. His promise was " to him that *doeth* the will of my Father." The present " landshark " talk about the sacredness of private property constituted no part of Jesus' teaching. The apostles, imbibing his spirit, pronounced woes upon the selfishly rich. " Go to, now," says St. James, " ye rich men, weep and howl for your miseries that shall come upon you ; . . . your gold and silver is cankered, and the rust of them shall be a witness against you." Few need to be reminded of the " gift of tongues," and the other rich spiritual gifts showered upon trusting hearts on the " Day of Pentecost." The power was so marvelous that " three thousand souls " were moved to repentance. And of these it is recorded, " All that believed were together, and had all things in common, and sold their possessions and goods, and parted them to all men, as every man had need." On this auspicious day the Jewish Apostolic Church, or genuine Christian church, under the inspiration and baptism of the *Christ-spirit*, began to exist. The communism was absolute. These newly baptized souls, full of fervor, were willing to surrender selfish ownership for the common good. Their principles were peace, purity, and " all things in common," constituting the millennial church, the church of the ages. " *Ekklesia*," translated " *church*," means, literally, " assembly." As understood apostolically, it implied a sympathizing assembly, convened and welded for a heavenly purpose. " Now there were in the church (*ekklesia*, assembly) that was at Antioch certain prophets " (Acts xiii. 1). These prophets, apostles, " women of Samaria," and believers generally, quickened by the Christ-principle, constituted themselves into spiritual families, brotherhoods, and communities holding " all things in common." " But," says one, " men naturally like to have their own." Granted ; and so *some* men naturally like to have their neighbors' ! Thieves are of this kind. But it is no more natural for thieves on a low physical plane to steal, and misers to clutch and hoard, than for the philanthropic and spiritually-minded to adopt a broad, fraternal communism. The angelic in the heavens are certainly communists. And I have yet to learn that spirits put patches of the summer-land into market, loan money, or speculate in corner-lots. When men pray, " Thy will be done on earth," why do they not go to work, and *do* it? Jesus came centuries ago. When is salvation coming ?

THE CHINESE PRAYING FOR WIND.

Our crew of Chinamen is a source of fruitful study. They have books aboard, and read them, when not playing at chance-games. Their heads are all shaven, save the pig-tail tuft. Rising in the morning, they clean their tongues by scraping them, and then sip their black tea.

In the latitude of the trade-winds, we were sorely vexed with calms. It had been a dead calm under a scorching sun for five days. As Nature hates a vacuum, so do sailors a calm. Was there a remedy? On the sixth day, Sunday morning, at sunrise, there came on deck a dozen or more serious-visaged China passengers, with dishes of rice, bowls of tea, different colored paper, slim, dry incense-reeds, slender, red-topped wax-candles, and matches. "What's up?" inquired several. Just informed by the "mate," our reply was, "The Chinamen are going to pray for wind." Among the number who had come forward, was the Chinese doctor, and another grave-looking, shaven-headed individual, evidently endowed with some priestly function. Putting themselves in position, they touched matches to the paper, throwing it overboard while in flames; then, lighting their reeds and candles, they went through with certain pantomimic incantations, becoming their method of prayer, ending by throwing the rice and tea into the ocean. Result, a fine breeze soon from the right quarter. "There!" exclaimed our exultant Celestials, "the wind-god has heard us!" Why not just as rational for Chinamen to thus pray for wind, as for Christians bowing over cushioned pulpits to pray in their way for "rain," for the "staying of the grasshopper devastation," or the "recovery of the Prince of Wales"? True prayer is not lip-pleading, but silent aspiration. It affects suppliants, and inclines angels to listen, but does not change the deific laws of the universe.

THE SCIENCE OF SAILING.

Navigation has reached a wonderful degree of perfection
How soon will aëronauts sail through the atmosphere in
safety? Air-ships are sure to prove successes. The principle is perfectly understood in spirit-life.

Our captain brings out his "sea-Bibles" each day, — the
sextant, quadrant, and chronometer, for observations; the
thermometer, indicating the temperature; the hygrometer, to
show the degree of moisture in the air; and the barometer, to
mark its weight. *These*, locating positions, foretell approaching weather with great exactness. What a perfect system
of circulation!— the aërial wind-currents, and the briny currents of the ocean. It is thrillingly interesting to watch
storms at sea. By the way, the typhoons of the China Seas
and the cyclones of the Indian Ocean have their fixed laws.
When courses of steady winds are obstructed by islands,
towering mountains, or other causes, producing whirling
tempests termed typhoons, the wind takes a rotary motion,
while the storm itself has a progressive motion. These
spiral storms, following the law of gyration, sometimes move
at the rate of fifty miles per hour. The typhoons prevail in
the China Seas from June to October. Sailors dread these
storms, and also the "pirate-junks" of Chinamen. The
approach of a typhoon is indicated by rolling, uneven swells,
the rapid sinking of the barometer, and reddish, hazy clouds
deepening into purple and black. "No rules can be relied
upon," says Capt. R. Mailler, "for the management of a
vessel during these terrific tempests." "Give us sea-room,"
however, is the sailor's cry.

THE NORTH STAR AND SOUTHERN CROSS.

We are nearly under the equator.

The stars, luminous lamps of heaven, are out each evening
on parade. The nights are gorgeous. I sometimes picture
the constellations as star-ships sailing on the ether-ocean of

infinity. The clouds, white and crimson, are the coral-reefs, and the winds the breathings of God.

Nearing the equator, on the voyage to Australia, I was thrilled with delight when catching the first glimpse of the Southern Cross glittering, in a peerless beauty all its own, just above the horizon in the south-west path of the Milky Way. Seeing churchmen thought of Calvary ; while scholars, more conversant with antiquity, talked of Oriental phallism. Getting near the equatorial circle again from the south, on this route northward to China, the cross was seen to be nightly receding ; and, at the same time, the Great Dipper was looming up from nearly the opposite direction. Two of its stars point to the North Star, not yet in sight. Most gladly shall I welcome the appearance again of the " pole-star," as it points in the direction of home and friends.

I never tire, in these clear, tropical regions, of gazing at those mighty orbs, sailing through the ether-ocean of space, shedding their tremulous beams upon the restless waters.

> " I sit on the deck, and watch the light fade
> Still fainter and fainter away in the west,
> And dream I can catch, through the mantling shade,
> A glimpse of the beautiful isles of the blest."

See! there is Orion, there Andromeda, there Sirius, brightest of the so-called fixed stars; and there are the Pleiades, Alcyon excelling in magnificence, and of which Homer sung nine hundred years B. C. Turn back in thought to the Chaldean shepherds who watched the waning moon from the plains of Shinar; study the astronomical observations recorded in the East three thousand years ago, — and ask yourself, O modern! how much the intervening decades have added to the literature or general knowledge of the ancients.

THE LOST DAY.

Since sailing upon the Pacific westward, the question has been sprung, " Where does day begin? " The general answer was, "Here, there, or at that place where the sun-beams first strike the earth during the twenty-four hours." The geographical and nautical answer is, "Day begins at the degree of longitude 180 east or west." Every school-boy knows, that, traveling round the world from east to west, a day is literally lost, and for the reason that there is a difference of one hour for every fifteen degrees of longitude in each day. Accordingly, journeying westward, a certain length of time is added to each day; and, making the world's circuit, — as many are doing at present, — would amount to an entire day. This is a puzzler to strict observers of "sabbath days." When crossing the meridian 180°, before reaching Auckland, New Zealand, our captain dropped from his reckonings the day we had lost; and Sunday was this *very* lost day! How queer, going to bed Saturday night, and getting up on Monday morning! Invited by our fellow-passengers on "The Nevada," I lectured upon Spiritualism.

But what a babyish notion, — this stress laid upon Sunday, or Saturday, or any day, as especially "holy"! Considering the revolutions of our earth upon its axis, it is absolutely impossible for all its inhabitants to keep the "Christian sabbath" at the same time. If a party of Second Adventists, Seventh-Day Baptists, and Israelites should sail from San Francisco on Friday (the Mohammedan's sacred day of rest), circling the world, they would all be converts, willing or not, when reaching New York, keeping or observing the Christian's Sunday! To a Spiritualist, all lands are equally holy, and all days are equally sacred. The observance, however, of one day in the seven for rest, recreation, and spiritual improvement, is eminently profitable.

SPIRITUALISM IN THE FIJIS.

This group of Pacific islands, numbering over two hundred, sighted by Capt. Cook, and discovered by the navigator Tasman, has recently become somewhat famous with

Englishmen, because of its cotton-planting advantages. The climate is tropical. Naviti Levu is the most populous of the isles; and Thakombau, a native six feet high, and kingly in bearing, is the most influential of the chiefs. Levuka, though having few natural advantages, is the principal commercial mart. Cotton, sugar, and coffee planters do well. Cocoanuts are abundant, and some wool is exported. The ramie plant, or China-grass, samples of which I remember to have seen in New Orleans, grows finely in these islands. Cannibalism was practiced here till 1854. What Americans there are here, were originally from the Southern States. White men are in possession of three hundred and fifty thousand acres of these cotton and coffee growing lands.

In a recent copy of " The Fiji Times," I find a labored article under this heading : " *Spiritualism in Fiji.*" The writer, after speaking of the natives as " low and depraved in the moral scale," assures us that, "low and brutal " as they are, they " believe in a future state of existence, in apparitions, and the efficacy of charms ; " their " prophets profess to talk with the dead; and they cure by striking the diseased part with the hand." This writer, treating of Spiritualism among the European residents, says, " There is a deep interest, among the more thoughtful of our citizens, upon this important subject. . . . Those who believe, affirm that the phenomena throw new light upon the Scriptures, as well as demonstrate immortality." There is a " want among us," he further says, " of a good test medium."

The Fijis may soon fall into the hands of the English.

LONGINGS FOR THE LAND.

And still a prisoner on this ocean clipper, — a vault, a charnel-house ; oh, how monotonous! Nearly two months now at sea, utterly oblivious to all the doings and rushing activities of land-life ; and yet a long distance from Hong Kong! Each returning day brings fair skies or dripping clouds, surging waves or dead calms, finny tribes, sailing sea-birds, chattering Chinamen, and stale, ship-scented food. Sea-birds, weary with flight, light in the rigging. The sailors pet them. Oh for the wings of — well, any thing that would drop me down upon *terra firma!* I term this, cabalistically, " concession " route. The luckless position is not without rich lessons; the blue, unfathomed depths beneath, and the infinite expanse above, kindling the fires of the ideal, incite me to self-examination, to meditation, and hopeful conceptions of a social state to be ultimately realized by all nations, — a peaceful state rivaling in moral excellence the Eden of the poets, and the Zion of the prophets. But to contemplation.

CHAPTER X.

AMONG the beautiful thoughts of that celebrated German philosopher, Kant, are these : —

" The day will come when it will be proved that the human soul is already, during its life on earth, in a close and indissoluble connection with a world of spirits; *that their world influences ours, and impresses it profoundly ;* and that we often remain unconscious of it as long as every thing goes right with us."

Mediums, necessarily sensitive, are as well aware of this connection referred to by Kant, as thinkers are conscious that sound, healthy bodies, and clear, well-balanced minds, are requisites for the reception of high spiritual inspirations. Mediumship, a powerful mental stimulant, is largely fashioned by the controlling spirit-intelligences. Therefore, studying a medium's tastes and tendencies, through a term of years, is comprehending the characteristics and purposes of such spirits as influence and minister to the medium, or psychological subject.

DELICACY OF CONDITIONS.

It is becoming definitely understood that Spiritualism in its phenomenal aspects is a science controlled by laws as fixed and absolute as those that govern the motions of physical bodies. All of Nature's forces are exceedingly subtle. Therefore, in every branch of research, compliance with conditions is indispensable ; and these conditions must be

thought out and experimented upon, until they can be for
mulated. Then they are ready for future service.

Physicists understand the delicacy of the conditions they
impose. It is said that Dr. Kane, while wintering in the
extreme polar regions, discovered that three thermometers,
agreeing at medium temperatures, disagreed materially at
very *low* temperatures, though suspended near together.
Approaching them suddenly from the windward side
affected them. Also a breath, and even the electric emanations of the body, would cause fluctuations, and accordingly
incorrect readings. The common surveyor, using a delicately balanced compass, need not be informed that bodies
of iron and steel affect his needle. The presence of a
pocket-knife sometimes vitiates results. Sea-captains, using
mercury for an artificial horizon in sextant observations,
know that a footfall, a loud word, or a quick motion of the
body, causes an oscillation of the quicksilver, and necessarily incorrect calculations. Alpine travelers tell us, that, on
ascending Mont Blanc, strata of snow are held in such wonderful poise that a violent exclamation would precipitate
a thousand tons down the declivity. Returning, a few years
since, from Pompeii and Herculaneum to the Museum in
Naples, I there saw vast rolls of calcined papyri covered with legible writing, though nearly two thousand
years buried; and a quiet gentleman, with repressed
breath and dexterous fingers, identifying, lifting, or unrolling those long-interred evidences of literary wealth
and historic record. A breath might have reduced these
charred leaflets to an impalpable powder. Success lay only
in the most delicate manipulations. If compliance with conditions are so indispensable, then, in dealing with physical
bodies, with *known* phenomena, — how much more so when
investigating partially unknown phenomena, involving the
laws of psychic force, and the momentous subject of spiritual manifestations! Mediums, sensitive and highly impressional, are in circles infinitely more susceptible than Kane's

thermometers. A harsh word, a disagreeable odor, the sudden opening of a door, the introduction of a certain individual into the séance, — *these*, and other disturbing causes. may destroy all the conditions necessary for the influx of thoughts and ideas from that ethereal world of spirits.

TEACHINGS OF SPIRITS.

The following communications, and many others through the unconscious mediumship of Dr. E. C. Dunn, were received during four-o'clock sittings in our stateroom when the conditions of the treacherous ocean would permit. They were generally given in answer to questions; though, for want of space, the inquiries are usually omitted.

The spirit Aaron Knight, controlling one afternoon, coolly remarked, " I see that my years of labor with you have not produced a very luxuriant harvest."

" How so, Mr. Knight ? "

" Well, approaching your sphere a while since, I heard you remark that you had only a slight, or, rather, no positive knowledge, of spirit-life and its peculiar conditions."

" True ; but I referred to daily objective knowledge."

" Metaphysical terms are of little avail. You have heard my voice frequently for years. You have felt our magnetism upon your brain. You have inhaled the fragrance of spirit-flowers. You have had things borne to you through the atmosphere. You have been made spasmodic when alone, by our electric touch. You have seen spirit-forms improvised, and then vanish from sight. *These*, with such confirmatory witnesses as consciousness, intuition, and reason, ought to have given you *positive knowledge*."

" Well, let *that* pass. Do you hear all I say ? "

" No, not necessarily ; but then I could, if desirable, know all you said ; and, further, could know your very thoughts, inasmuch as they produce a reflex action readable by your attending circle. And, what is still more recondite, the effects of your thoughts, aims, and plans are spiritually photographed in the sphere you will inhabit when released from mortality. You have no secrets. It would be well if all men thoroughly understood this."

" Are you now within this stateroom ? "

" I am, and others also. We have so fixed the atmosphere, that, if not congenial, it is endurable."

But some clairvoyants tell us that spirits seldom return to earth, to dwell in our midst even for a moment.

" Can you conceive or imagine any thing that clairvoyants and psychological sensitives have not taught? The truth is, millions of spirits have never got away from the earth, spiritually speaking. Their past tendencies, present desires, and undone work, chain, mentally hold them near to your earth. Those more advanced, who have passed to the heavenly abodes of the divine life, can return at will ; while very ancient spirits seldom visit earth, and then only for the holiest purposes."

SÉANCE II.

How long a time has man inhabited the earth ?

" Time — indefinite term ! Nations of antiquity reckoned time by the revolutions of constellations, by the disappearance and return of comets, by the sun and moon ; and others less ancient by kingly dynasties. It is difficult to even approximate the period when man first appeared on earth. The most ancient spirits with whom I have conversed upon the subject tell me it was millions of years in the past. Three times, at least, the earth has been nearly submerged in water, destroying the people. The whole surface has been repeatedly changed and modified by fire and flood, heat and cold. Fossilized elephants and other tropical animals are often unearthed in the frigid zones, proving that those ice-belted regions were once tropical and even equatorial in temperature.

" *Present man*, with the shattered remnants of his primeval civilization, originated in the southern zones more than fifty thousand years since. There are traditions and legends extending back full forty thousand years. Types are permanent. Vegetation there was perennial. Fruits grew spontaneous. Tilling the earth was unnecessary. To reach up, pluck, and eat, was the only requisite. From Southern Asia there were radiations east, west, and north, peopling foreign lands. After a series of centuries, the Northmen, increased in numbers, and warlike, swept down into Central and Southern Asia. Wars crimsoned hills and mountains. The conquerors drove their vanquished foes into that country now known as Hindostan. They were hunters and herdsmen, leading roving lives. Peoples making a second descent from the rich table-lands of Asia into India gathered into communities, establishing petty kingly governments. These were denominated Aryans."

SÉANCE III.

. . . " Be punctual to the appointed time of meeting us. Remember that our avocations and appointments are quite as important as yours. . . . Prophecies are often fulfilled by the prophets. I remember of saying to you, in my earliest conversations, that the medium and yourself would be mutual helps, traveling together, even to making the circuit of the globe. . . . Preceding him to spirit-life, you will impress and entrance him with perfect ease because of your earthly associations social and spiritual." . . .

Could you go directly through our globe?

" Possibly; although, from having no desire, I have never made the attempt."

If you were to go, when leaving the medium, to my home in Hammonton, America, would you take the short cut straight through the earth?

"No: I should pass above the surface of sea and land. This would be the more feasible route. Solid matter, so called, forms little or no obstruction to the movements of spirits. But gross matter, remember, is interpermeated with

etherealized spirit-substance; and then, there might be
emanations from spirit-strata and various entities, prevent-
ing or at least impeding the passage. The walls of a room
may be so surcharged with magnetism and spirit-auras that
a spirit can not pass them. There are gradations of spirit-
substance as of matter. When you are in your library-room,
we fix an atmosphere about you, and so infill the walls of
your study-room with our positive magnetic spheres that
intruding spirits can not enter."

SÉANCE IV.

. . . " If angel lips are portals to the palace of wisdom,
angelic beings are modest and unassuming. Whenever you
hear a spirit talk about himself, — what mighty things he did
on earth, and what he has done in the supernal spheres, —
put it down that the brother is but a pupil in the primary
department of immortality. High and pure spirits are dis-
inclined to even give their names. And there is nothing
more repellant to an exalted spirit, than to refer to himself.
In a congress of spirits, I once heard a spirit of sage-like
appearance say he had sometimes thought that loss of
memory would be a great blessing, thus forgetting *self*.
Selfishness is the root of all the cankering vices of the age.
. . . A mortal, reaching the better land of immortality,
gravitates, or seeks the plane of his choice, something as the
immigrant in a new country looks for highlands or lowlands, cultivated fields or heavy-timbered forests; but a
spirit, owing to the condition of the spiritual body and other
considerations, can not become a permanent resident of a
higher plane than he is spiritually prepared for. . . . The
desires, or, rather, the demands of the carnal nature, such as
gluttony, and sexual intercourse, do not obtain in the spiritual world. These fleshly and animal appetites are laid aside
at death. And yet low, undeveloped spirits, from force of
habit, vividness of memory, or downward tendencies acquired on earth, may enjoy the sight of lasciviousness ; or,

for some scheming wicked purpose, may psychologically
lead mediums into debauchery and the 'unfruitful works
of darkness.' Low, selfish, disorderly spirits are at the
bottom of the 'free-lust movement,' known by the n ore
attractive term, 'social freedom.' This scum, now floating
upon the peaceful stream of spirit-communion, will ere long
settle away into merited oblivion."

SÉANCE V.

You speak of conditions and employments in the spirit-
world: I wish you would be more minute in your descriptions.

" Hoping to enlighten, I will try. The spirit-world, real
and substantial, is the counterpart of your world. The
earthly life is rudimentary and preparatory. The wise of
earth ripen up, while in their bodies, for higher planes of
existence. As to 'discreet degrees,' referred to by the
admirers of the Swedish seer, they do not exist *per se.* The
phrase 'discreet degrees' should give place to 'states' and
'conditions' of being. Logically understood, the spirit-
world is *all* space, because essential spirit fills all immensity.
Inhabitants leaving your earth by death occupy the atmosphere immediately surrounding it, — *many* of them, at least,
for ages. They can in time occupy other places and spheres.
The difficulty in passing to remote spaces and regions is at
the medial points of conjunction between different planets
and systems. Each planet, and system of planets, have their
physical, gaseous, ethereal, electrical, and spiritual atmospheres. In these atmospheres abound the centripetal and
centrifugal forces; and these forces hold a similar relation
to spiritual beings that the physical forces do to human
beings. Therefore they encounter kindred difficulties in
passing and repassing the aural atmospheres, and different
strata, of the interstellar spaces, that mortals do in exploring
pathless oceans, or aëronauts in their air-ship expeditions.

" In the belts that encircle your earth, the grosser lie the

nearest to it. The more refined extend outward into the
ethereal regions. Coarse spiritual natures inhabit the outer
surfaces of the inner belts; while the more refined and spiritual of earth pass on, by virtue of their refinement and
purity, to remote and those more beautiful belts in astral
spaces. The lower spheral belts, partaking of the earthli-
ness of the earth, and embodying the grosser of the spiritual
elements, abound in things similar to earth-life, such as lawns
and lowlands, fields and swamps, insects and animals. The
inhabitants are likened unto these conditions. Here the
worldly and the sordid have taken up their abodes. Awakening to consciousness, from the event termed death, they
found they had entered the new plane of existence mentally
and morally as they had left mortality. This realization was
at first exceedingly gratifying. Activity is natural to all
spheres. In this first spheral zone, the selfish find a satisfaction in the gratification of their desires and tendencies.
Those who loved sport, and low theatrical amusements, here
find means for their enjoyment. Misers seek and clutch
money. Greedy landholders find broad acres. Speculators
traffic in spiritual estates. Gamblers engage in games of
chance; and here, too, deceivers and tricksters ply their wily
arts during long periods of time. It is their choice. They
prefer these groveling planes, because satisfying their desires in connection with the influences they are able to exert
over the mediumistic of earth. . . . It should be remembered, then, that shrewd, scheming spirits of the lower
spheres cast a powerful psychological influence upon earth's
inhabitants; and that miserly fathers, influencing, often
intensify the selfishness of their sons by pointing out rich
mineral beds, and otherwise aiding them in earthly specula-
tions, which, eventually culminating in hoarded wealth, must
be followed ultimately by remorse and deepest suffering. "

SÉANCE VI.

What have you been doing in spirit-life to-day, friend Knight?

"Accompanied by a sympathizing band of philanthropists, I have been teaching the truly repentant how to make reparation for wrongs done on earth; the ignorant and superstitious, how to rise out of their darkened spiritual conditions. . . . There are no arbitrary barriers to coarser, undeveloped spirits passing to the outer and higher zones of perpetual joy. It is only a law of adaptation that attracts, *chains*, them to the plane of their own preferences. Clairvoyants who speak of a summer-land only in spirit-existence, convey an erroneous idea. There are summer-land surfaces on the outer belts, freighted and dotted with magnificent forests, fountains, fields, fruits, gardens, and flowers, of the exquisite beauty of which mortals have no conception; and there are dark winter-lands too, corresponding to the cold, selfish, and perverted natures of those dwelling on earth.

"The lower, grosser planes of spirit-existence necessitate animal life; not the individualized spirits of *your* animals, but the legitimate productions of the sphere in which they exist; something as the birds and animals of your physical earth are *its* natural productions. As you pass outward and upward through almost measureless spaces, you find less of animal life, till in the celestial spheres there are no animal forms whatever. This might suggest a question relating to the unhappiness of certain spirits if deprived of pet animals. If unhappy for this reason, it would only prove that they were yet clogged and tainted with earthly tastes and tendencies. Angelic affections do not flow out to animals. This explanation harmonizes the seemingly different statements of clairvoyants; and, more particularly, those who pass out of their bodies, traversing spirit-spheres. Some while thus disinthralled, save by the silken cord of magnetic life, beheld animals of a low type, others of a high type,

and others still none whatever.   Briefly stated, they described such conditions and localities as they had explored.
In all the planes and states of infinity, there's a marvelous
adaptation of means to ends.   If discord is the child of the
hells, order reigns in the heavens. . . . Grossness of condition, referring not alone to the spiritual body, holds a
direct relation to the mind, *alias*, the inner spiritual nature,
and the influences proceeding therefrom.   Coarse, selfish
organizations in spirit-life eliminate coarse auras and influences, tending to deception and vice; while those in high
celestial spheres, having more refined spiritual bodies, and
more intellectual and spiritual natures, generate conditions
of harmony and purity.   These revel in the golden sunlight
of perpetual love and happiness.   The life that each leads
on earth prepares him for the sphere of his own moral likeness.   These spheres — heavens and hells — were vaguely
described by the seers of antiquity.   All modern theological
doctrines are but the shadows that the ancient cast."

   " These spheres, or zoe-ether zones, related to, sail *with*, the
earth in her revolutions through space.   Some spirits take
up their immediate abode just above their former homes,
casting upon them a powerful psychological influence.
Miserly spirits linger about their vaults; and others, disorderly, and maliciously inclined, cling to their previous localities, producing magnetic conditions suitable for haunting
houses, for producing obsessions, insanity, and nervous diseases."

SÉANCE VII.

   " Remember that in the lower spheres are found the counterparts of your earth, — its follies and vices, its labors and
pursuits, prompted by natural desires; and spirits here, as
mortals with you, are subject to disappointments and failures; while in the heavens love, — *love* devoid of all selfish·
ness, is the motive that inspires action.   Here harmonial
spirits reap a rich reward in leading the aspirational into the

paths of purity, in laboring unselfishly for the good of others and in pointing those who will listen to the "tree of life," that ever buds, blossoms, and bears immortal fruitage. *This* is to them satisfaction, true rest, heaven! Considering the condition of those in the lower spheres of moral darkness, you see that it is infinitely preferable for mortals to prepare, while on earth, for the higher life, that at death, so called, they may avoid the planes of pride, passion, and perversions, that, with their seeming gains and joys, bring to their possessors, in the end, mental grief and deepest despair.

" Passing from this first spheral belt outward, we pass different gradations of indulgence, vice, and discontent, — outward and upward, till we reach etherealized planes of spirituality, where resurrected souls have no desire to engage in activities beneath themselves. These heavenly inhabitants have become baptized into a celestial life of love, with desires only for the cultivation of the spiritual ; quite forgetting the things beneath, and seeking the ideal of perfection, which must ever lie in the infinite beyond.

" The intermediate spheres between the two just described abound in all the employments and associations conceivable. There is the scholarly plane, where all else is sacrificed to intellectual research ; the musical, and the poetic ; and the inventive, where all things are made subservient to the genius of mechanism, thus sacrificing much that is higher and more divinely beautiful. And there, too, is the domestic plane, where abound the attractions of family and family associations, with the narrow and selfish love for one's own offspring. Family love, as opposed to universal love, is a serious impediment to unfoldment of the soul. 'Complete happiness is attained by sacrificing present ease, by forgetfulness of self, in labor for others' good. Those thus toiling mold angels from their own forms.

" In the more exalted states of existence, it is considered that an equalizing and harmonizing of the mental and moral faculties indicate an approach to the Christ-sphere of immortality, where we have the highest form of the perfected spiritual being. In advancing from this high moral stand- point to diviner altitudes, extending above and still beyond, souls are intromitted into the sphere of virgin purity and love ; the sphere of spiritual balance, properly denominated the holy ; the Christ-sphere of angelic purity, where the spiritual brain-organs, subjecting and over-arching, crown all the others with a matchless glory."

CHAPTER XI.

" When thou haply seest
Some rare, noteworthy object in thy travels,
Wish me partaker of thy happiness."— SHAKSPEARE.

ALL nations are brothers. Hong Kong, a rough border-island of the Flowery Land, has been under British control since 1842. It is properly an English colony, though the people are mostly Chinamen. The sweeping distance we traversed from the southern portion of New Zealand to China was nearly seven thousand miles, meeting necessarily with islands, coral shoals, calms, tempests, burning equatorial suns, — *many* bitter experiences! The passage occupied over two months.

I became heart-sick of hearing the guttural gabble, and of looking at our China passengers, with their inevitable cues dangling from their crowns, their shaven heads, almond-shaped eyes, flat noses, high cheek-bones, saffron-colored complexions, and sack-like clothing loosely, awkwardly hung around them. Being from different portions of China, they had among themselves one serious fight, using clubs, bits of wood, and marline-pins, the blood flowing freely for a few moments. While censuring, I must not forget that these are *coolies*, — the poorer classes.

Steaming up the harbor, and landing at Hong Kong, we leaped into a " sam-pan," — a small Chinese skiff, partially roofed with bamboo. There were seven residents in this

junk-shaped boat, — the youngest, a child, strapped to the
mother's back, Indian fashion. Both grandmother and
mother aided in rowing the "sam-pan." These families
know no other homes.

Hong Kong, in the Chinese language, means "Incense
Harbor;" referring to the junks and proas, that here dis-
charge their cargoes of fragrant spices.

THE FIRST OUTLOOK.

The city is crowded. The country presents every conceivable shade of landscape, — rich valleys, alluvial plains,
high table-lands, and magnificent mountains. Stretching
along the coast-cities, canals, to quite an extent, take the
place of roads. Instead of locks, they have what are termed
"mud-slides," using cables of bamboo, and windlasses.
Men, instead of machinery, turn them. Multitudes are
born, eat, sleep, live, and *die* in these boats. Every thing
looks un-American. The people are mainly agricultural,
cultivating almost every available foot of the soil. Every
object seen indicates an overburdened population. The
canals swarm with boats, the shops with artisans, the roads
with pedestrians, and the fields with hard-toiling workmen.
It is work or starve in China.

The empire proper has eighteen provinces, each of which
is divided into about ten divisions called *Fu;* and these are
still further divided into *Hien.* Politically speaking, these
correspond somewhat to our districts, counties, towns, only
they are much larger than with us in America. The empire
contains five millions of square miles. Each provincial capital averages about one million of inhabitants. The great
Chinese Empire numbers nearly five hundred millions, — *one-
third* of the whole human race. It has one thousand **seven**
hundred walled cities.

CHINA'S PAST HISTORY.

Humiliating as it may be to Europe, it is true, that, for a period of nearly three thousand years, China existed in almost complete isolation from other portions of the globe. This made her arrogant and egotistic. During those mediæval times known as the "dark ages," the very existence of China was unknown to Europeans. The Chinese themselves knew nothing of the term "China." Speaking of their country, they denominated it *Chung Kwoh*, the Middle Kingdom, or *Chung-Hwo-Kwoh*, the Middle Flowery Kingdom; because they consider themselves as occupying the middle of the globe, and as being the centers of civilization and intelligence. They further believe that their empire, once proud and world-commanding, was established by the "law of Heaven" over forty thousand years ago, and is destined to stand for ever. Owing to national conceit, Western nations call them "Celestials."

The almost measureless antiquity of China is not denied. The point in dispute is as to the boundary-line between the genuinely historic and the mythological. Of this, Chinese scholars are certainly the best judges. Meadows, in his elaborate work upon the Chinese, puts the reign of Fuh-hi B. C. 3327. The reign of the *Chow* dynasties began about one thousand years before Christ, during which Lau-tsze and Confucius lived. Though Lau-tsze was the oldest, born B. C. 604, they were cotemporaries. Both of these philosophers, referring to the wise who lived before them, term them "the ancients."

Herodotus and Ptolemy, treating of this quite unknown country, referred to these isolated people living in the northeast of Asia as "inventive and prosperous." Marcellinus the Roman writer, Virgil, Pliny, Tacitus, and other historians, mention these olive-colored people under the name of Seres, dwelling in the land of Serica. They speak of them as "rich in silks" and the "luxuries of life," besides being cumbered with "much useless lore."

The " Chinese annals" give their nationality an antiquity
so marvelously vast, that sectarists sneer.   This is a too
common argument with the ignorant and the impudent.   A
learned Chinaman, *Le Can*, assured me that Confucian
scholars put their reliable historic records relating to the
creation back full forty-four thousand years ago.   The candid and scholarly John Williams, in his " Observations on
Comets," admits the accuracy of the Chinese chronological
computations.   In his investigations he shows, from the
" records in the Shu-King, one of the oldest historical documents of the empire, that the star *Cor Hydrœ* culminating
at sunset on the day of the vernal equinox, in the time of
Tau, the sun must have been in Taurus, then the equinoctial
point.   By a simple calculation, *Tau* can be shown to have
lived four thousand one hundred and seventy-six years ago,
or two thousand three hundred B. C. ; just after the disper-
sion from Babel, according to the common chronology." . . .
Dr. Hales long ago pointed out the agreements of the Egyptians and Chinese with the Babylonian or Chaldean astronomical observations.

THE ANCIENT NAMES OF CHINA.

The primitive inhabitants of Southern Asia, speaking of
the people now known as the Chinese, used the terms, Jin,
Chin, Sin, and Sinistæ; referring, evidently, to the Tsin dynasty, which took absolute control of the northern portion
of the country about 770 B.C.   Being ambitious and powerful, this Tsin family wielded the scepter over the whole
empire as early as 250 B.C.   This period, and several hundred years previous, was famed for its literary men.   The
prominence of Tsin, and the dimmed records of travelers,
confirm the view taken by learned commentators, that the
Chinese were referred to in the forty-ninth chapter of Isaiah,
— " Behold, thou shalt come from afar, . . . and those from
the land of *Sinim*."   Classic writers described the country
under the names, Sinæ, Seres, Serica.   An Alexandrine

monk, writing in the sixth century, called it Tzinistæ, which much resembles the Persian appellation, Chinistan. The Turks and Russians knew it as Khitai. The Khitans were of Nanchu lineage, and related to the present imperial family. In the tenth century they completely conquered the adjoining provinces. From about this period, or before, strange as it may seem, Europe became utterly oblivious of any such great civilized nation in the East. But in the year 1245, John of Plano Carpini, a native of Umbria, and another Franciscan monk, wandering along the Mongolian desert, found their way into Eastern Asia; and, returning from their mission, told of a highly-civilized people living in the extreme East, upon the shores of the ocean. To this country, so unexpectedly found, they gave the name of Cathay. One of these monks describes them thus : —

"The Cathayans are a Pagan people, who have a written character of their own. They are learned in many things. They worship the one God, and have sacred scriptures. . . . They have no beard, and in their features are very much like the Mongols, but not so broad in the face. They have a peculiar language. Better craftsmen, in all the arts practiced by mankind, are not to be found on the face of the earth. Their country, also, is very rich in corn, in wine, gold, silver, and in silk, and in all other things that tend to human maintenance."

EARLY EFFORTS TO CHRISTIANIZE THE CHINESE.

Portuguese missionaries reaching China by doubling the Cape of Good Hope, near the close of the fifteenth century, despaired of converting self-willed Chinamen to Christianity; because, said these Romish zealots, "They have a God of their own. Burning incense, they worship their ancestors. They also hold converse with spirits, using the black art, and think that the original tendency of man's heart is to do right."

De Rubruquis, an intelligent monk, was the first to identify, in 1253, Cathay with the ancient *Seres* or *Sinim*. In 1295 Friar John went on a mission to China. Writing to Rome, he says, —

"I have bought gradually one hundred and fifty boys, the children of Pagan parents, who had never learned any religion. These I have baptized, and taught Greek and Latin after our manner; also I have written out psalters for them, with thirty hymnaries and two breviaries. . . . And I have a place in court, and a regular entrance, and seat assigned me as legate of our Lord the Pope; and the Cham honors me above all other prelates, whatever be their titles."

All early travelers to this Asian country were stars of the second magnitude, however, compared to the Venetian, Marco Polo; and yet for a long time he was counted a romancer. This injustice ultimately died away; and this gentleman's veracity, and correctness of observation, shine brilliantly to-day under the recovery of much lost and forgotten knowledge. His descriptions of cities, libraries, civilization, and the general refinement of the people, read to Western nations like fairy-tales. He was the great traveler of his age.

Hon. Anson Burlingame, head of the Chinese embassy to our and other countries, said, in his speech delivered in New York, June, 1868, —

"China is a land of scholars and of schools; a land of books, from the smallest pamphlet up to voluminous encyclopedias. It is a land where privileges are common. It is a land without caste; for they destroyed their feudal system over two thousand years ago, and they built up their grand structure of civilization on the great idea that the people are the source of power. This idea was uttered by Mencius between two and three thousand years since, and it was old when he uttered it. . . . They make scholarship a test of merit."

HONG KONG TO CANTON.

If not original, the Chinese are certainly unique. Hong Kong has a population of one hundred and twenty-five thousand, about four thousand of whom are Europeans and Americans. The buildings are roofed with tiles. The streets, narrow and dirty, swarm like beehives. All nationalities dress to suit themselves. Nearly every Chinaman has an umbrella over his head, and a fan in his hand. They are compelled by law to carry a hand-lamp, if traversing the streets after seven o'clock. Only a portion of the women — the better classes — have small feet. These, in walking, simply waddle as though lame. They think it graceful.

After visiting the Chinese temples, hospitals, foundling institutions, and riding upon men's shoulders in sedan-chairs, — a method of locomotion to us as distasteful as unnatural, — we took the steamer for Canton. The native name is *Yang-Ching*, meaning "the city of rams;" but from subsequent mythological circumstances connected with the wise men of the past, and their communion with the gods, it now signifies "the city of genii." Thronging with a population of over a million, it numbers less than two hundred foreigners. The city is situated on the Pearl River, up the country some ninety miles from Hong Kong. The river, wide, muddy, and moderate, reminding one of the lazy Missouri, flows into the bay at Hong Kong, just under the shadow of Victoria Peak, a mountainous point, towering up nearly two thousand feet above the level of the sea. The flat lands all along this river were covered with rice-fields, banana plantations, ly-chee trees laden with ripening fruit, peach-orchards full of promise, and banyan shrubbery, more ornamental in this latitude than useful. Odd-looking villages, lying a little distance away, dotted the river valley. These are more noted for compactness and bustle, than cultivation or beauty. The most important of these minor cities, commercially considered, is *Whampoa*, — virtually the port of Canton, — being just at the head of navigation for heavily-laden vessels. Seen from the steamer, agriculture and architecture seemed decidedly primitive. The buildings were generally one story high, and covered with tiles, — no glass in the windows, nor gardens in front of them. Back in the fields, men and women were plowing their half-submerged rice-lands with water-buffaloes. These huge, hairless creatures are considerably larger than our wild droves of the West. Butter made from their milk is white as lard. These buffalo-cows, with others, and goats also, are driven to the door to be milked, thus avoiding the city pests of impure milk.

CANTON WITHIN THE WALLS.

Approach to this, the wealthiest and most elegant city of China, seemed almost impossible, from the wilderness of skiffs, "sam-pans," and junks plying the muddy waters. These junks, clumsily modeled, yet richly decorated, have bamboo sails, and are better adapted to inland harbor and river purposes than European-rigged vessels. Full two hundred thousand Cantonese live, traffic, eat, sleep, and die on these river-boats. Their sam-pans, though floating property, are their real estate. The smallest children have bamboo-blocks tied to their bodies, so that, should they tumble overboard, they could be easily rescued. Landing, and presenting letters of introduction from the Rev. Dr. Eitel, and our gentlemanly and kind-hearted consul Mr. Bailey, appointed to Hong Kong from Cincinnati, and, by the way, a distant relation, his maternal grandparent being a Peebles, we were made the recipients of the Rev. Dr. Kerr's hospitalities.

The streets of Canton, irregularly laid out, are from five to seven and ten feet wide, and generally covered in with fluttering matting and bamboo-reeds, giving them a dull, shadowy appearance. Broad avenues are yet to be dreamed of by Chinamen. Wheeled carriages out of the question, sedanchairs carried by coolies are the only means of transportation. It pained me to see that the shoulders of some of these poor burden-bearers were calloused and scarred. The principal streets, with such lofty names as " Pure Pearl," " Just Balance," " Unblemished Rectitude Street," &c., have banners and gaudily painted signs dangling in front of their bazaars, presenting an aspect at once gay and gorgeous. China has a million of temples. The emperor's temple is magnificent. Only imperial buildings have yellow tiles. Canton's guardian god sits majestically in the city temple. The Confucian temples have images of Confucius. There are few places more frequented that the Temple of the Five Genii. In this, and the Temple of Horrors, daily congregate magicians, diviners, and fortune-tellers, spiritual quacks. Sam-un-Kung is a Tauist temple; while Hok-hoi-tong is a hall to encourage literary men by granting prizes for the best compositions. There are a hundred and twenty-five temples in Canton.

The viceroy, the highest civil officer, is appointed from Pekin for the term of three years. Chinese lawyers have no fees; and yet, when gaining the suit through marked ability, they accept presents.

The native dispensary, located in the eighteenth ward, employs three Chinese physicians, besides providing support for widows, coffins for the poor, and funds for the support of free schools. Penalties for treason are rigidly severe. During nine months of the provincial rebellion, in 1855, fifty thousand rebels were beheaded on the "execution-grounds," in the southern suburbs of Canton.

China had homes for the aged, asylums for the blind, foundling hospitals, and retreats for lame and worn-out animals, long before missionary feet touched their soil. Streets leading from the city of Canton into the country should, after a few miles out, be called paths. Poorly paved, if at all, they range from three to seven feet wide. Canals are really the thoroughfares of the country.

CHINESE AS THEY WERE AND ARE.

Cycles are certainties, pertaining alike to individuals and nations. China had her noonday of prosperity many thousands of years ago. To-day, and for centuries, she has been in a galloping decline. In that indefinite period known as antiquity, she rightly considered herself the superior race, the center of civilization and learning. It must not be forgotten by Americans that the Chinese were adepts in astronomy and medicine over two thousand years since; that they employed the magnetic needle when Europe was smothering under the pall of the dark ages ; that printing, originating with, was used by them for centuries before known in the West; that they discovered electro-magnetism, the curse gunpowder, and that they have excelled in silks, china-wares, and porcelains from time immemorial.   It should be further borne in mind that the Chinese inoculated for the small-pox nearly three thousand years before the Christian era, putting the virus in the nostril instead of the arm ; and that a medical work published prior to Christ's time, during the Hau dynasty, treats in part of the circulation of the blood.

Chinese scholars are proud of their past.   They admit that " Western barbarians " excel them, at present, in science and the mechanical arts; but they claim the pre-eminence in literature, metaphysics, and the mysterious sciences, such as ontology, geomancy, physiognomy, divination, and necromancy, or methods of conversing with the dead.

During the tedious voyage from New Zealand with a crew of Chinese, I was surprised one day to see a young coolie perusing a fine old Chinese volume, thickly embellished with pictures and plates of the human form, the human brain laid open, the curves and facial features indicating character delicately marked, and the fortune-lines of the hand clearly traced.   Inquiring through the interpreter when written, and by whom, I ascertained that it was one of a series of volumes by an ancient sage, treating of reading character by the brain-organs, the facial angles, and the general contour of the person, *alias* a volume upon phrenology and physiognomy.

It can not be consistently alleged that Christian missionaries would be partial to, or inclined to overrate, the virtues and intellectual altitudes of the " heathen " they were sent to save.   And yet the Rev. J. L. Nevius, ten years a missionary in China, says in his work entitled " China and the Chinese," " China may well point with pride to her authentic history, reaching back through more than thirty centuries; to her extensive literature, containing many works of sterling and permanent value; to her thoroughly elaborated language, possessed of a remarkable power of expression; to her list of scholars, and her proficiency in belles-lettres.

" If these," says Dr. Nevius, "do not constitute evidences of intellectuality, it would be difficult to say where such evidences might be found." Further, China has given a literature to nearly forty millions of Japanese, and also to the inhabitants of Corea and Manchuria. If the Japanese surpass the Chinese in skill and impulsive action, the Chinese excel them in intellectuality and morality. The better classes of Japan use the Chinese classics, much as we do, in our collegiate courses, those of Greece and Rome.

For centuries the Chinese have been traversing the downward segment of their national cycle. Compared with Americans, they seem dull and phlegmatic. Though their bodies are healthy, they lack energy, muscular force, and mental activity. To see a Chinaman in a hurry would be a marvel. They walk their narrow streets moderately, seldom getting excited about any thing. Gymnasiums, and vigorous athletic exercises, are quite unknown among them. They have the appearance of being timid; and yet they are persistent in accomplishing what they undertake. Most of these Chinese labor sixteen hours a day. Their industry is proverbial.

THE CHINESE COOLIE TRADE.

Portugal and Spain, Christian (?) nations, commenced the coolie traffic some forty years since. Labor in China was exceedingly cheap. Europeans were quick to discover this. Accordingly, a Spaniard from Peru, while at Macao, China, seeking a cargo, conceived the idea of securing under some pretense a crew of coolies to work in Peru. This he did under the false promise of conveying them to the island of Java, to return in a few years well paid for their services. But they were landed in Callao, South America, never again

to see their native land. They complained bitterly of the
deception; but no number of Chinese complaints could
avail in court against a Spaniard's oath. The reported industry of these Chinamen reaching the ears of Cuban planters,
ships were sent out bringing cargoes of them to labor
on their plantations. But when those who first went out
with the Spanish captain on the "Don Pedro," and those who
afterwards sailed for Cuba, and other islands in the west, did
not return to their homes and families; and when rumors
returned that these Chinese labor-emigrants had been
enslaved, or slain for insubordination, — no more would ship
for that land afar over the waters. Then commenced that
wretched system of buying, kidnapping, and chaining, which
disgraced our common civilization. Ship-owners and traders,
sailing into Chinese ports, organized bands of thieves to
steal and kidnap coolies by thousands. And these poor
Chinamen seized in rice-fields, and boys in schoolrooms, were
gagged, and dragged by force down into the ill-aired holds
of vessels, to be borne away, the veriest slaves, to toil in the
guano-islands, or other portions of the distant West. And
all this under the flag of European civilization! Guilty of
theft, and red-handed, wholesale murder, these Christian
nations have the cool impudence to send missionaries to
heathen Chinamen!

Kidnapping is still quite a business in the South-Sea Islands. A little prior to our reaching Australia, the brig
"Carl," owned by Dr. J. P. Murray, sailed under the British
flag from Melbourne towards Fiji, for the ostensible purpose
of pearl-fishing; but really engaged in man-stealing in the
southern sea. This was afterwards proved in the court of
justice that arraigned Mr. Mount. Dr. Murray, now professedly pious and prayerful, was guilty of deception, of
stealing natives, and downright murder. Some of the
wounded Bougainville natives were *thrown overboard alive.*
Is it strange that missionaries find it so difficult to convert
South-Sea Islanders to Christianity?

AMERICA LONG KNOWN TO THE CHINESE.

A scholarly writer in the "North China Herald" assures us that a "superstition" in the provinces of Honan and Hupee declares that America and China are to be sympathetically, if not politically and religiously united. This is based upon the testimony of Chinese visionists, who in their ecstatic state see "an immense bridge over to the United States." These clairvoyant visionists further teach that the "Chinese and American nations were once brothers." The mandarins say they have books under the name of *Fusang*, written long ago, that describe America and Occidental scenery with a marvelous precision. Chinamen returning from California tell their relatives that they found races in America — the Indians — who could talk some of their own language. These notions, with the admiration that China had for Mr. Burlingame, give them a strong predilection in favor of America, as well as constitute the *animus* of their emigration to our shores.

The French ethnologist Baillet, in a letter to the Royal Society of Antiquarians, makes certain statements, current among the Ting-chause scholars of China, of which the following is the substance : —

"There was a great family, called Tooloong, which lived in the land of Fukien, and became rich. When a mighty conqueror came from the north, and the emperor Hia was not able to protect his children, Tooloong and his family joined themselves with some barbarians, — Assyrians from the west, — and abandoned their homes in grief. They gave themselves into the hands of the gods. The great dragon watched them by night, and Su-wang-Shangty by day. For more than a thousand days, Tooloong wandered northward and eastward until the icicles grew on the skirts of his garments; still the gods said, 'Go on,' and Tooloong's heart was stout. Then they found a great bridge as white as the summer's cloud, and very strong. The barbarians hesitated, but Tooloong was brave. They all crossed over. On the other side was a new China, where no one lived. The trees were beautiful, and the beasts kind. Tooloong wondered. But they kept on till a land of flowers was seen in the distance. The barbarians said, ' Let us not go farther : it will burn us.' But Tooloong said, ' I stop not till the dragon-god stops.' So they entered the land of flowers. Here they were blessed. The gods were very kind. Toolong wanted dwellings and a pagoda. He built great cities in the flower country, and died. After a long period, some of his children tried to come back to China. But the great bridge was gone. So they all, with the exception of *Nung-yang*, were sent back to the flower-country by the gods. He, becoming immortal by death, flew over on a cloud, and told his kindred of the great things Tooloong had done."

The Americans, whom the Chinese hear of as living in a great country to the north and east, are believed, says M. Baillet, to be the descendants of Tooloong and the Assyrians that accompanied him.

And Mr. Conwell, a Chinese traveler and author, suggests that the "north and east" would very naturally refer to the direction of Behring's Straits ; that the " bridge " might have been ice, or an isthmus covered with snow, since submerged ; that the "flower-country " might be the land of Mexico ; that the " pagoda, and blocks of stone dwellings," might relate to those wonderful structures, the ruins of which, at Palenque and Uxmal, astonish the antiquarian, as well as favorably compare with those of Upper Egypt and Syria. And what, if possible, is more singular, the images of gods manufactured at Bohea, near Ting-Chan, are the exact counterparts of the idol-gods found in Southern California and Mexico. A striking corroboration of the above hypothesis is furnished by Gen. Crook, in his discovery of ruins, while operating against the Apaches. And Capt. Manning, of the regular army, writes from New Mexico under date of July 14, 1874, touching the discovery of ancient ruins, and the remnants of a fading race, "This once walled, but now city of ruins, was originally discovered by a Spanish Jesuit, who published his wanderings in America in 1529. His account is quite correct. The demolished structures symbolize, in conception, those of the East. The language of the remnant of this people, so says an eminent archæologist visiting them last season, resembles the Chinese. And so do some of their minor customs; such as their reverence for the aged, and devotion to ancestors. The women are of the Celestial type, — almond eyes, protuberant bodies, and small feet. They dress much in Chinese fashion. Their religious ceremonials are formal, the priests wearing embroidered robes." Were not the Aztecs the racial link, connecting this fading race in New Mexico with the migrating Chinese and Assyrians of the Tooloong era?

COOLIES IN CALIFORNIA. — WHY THEY COME.

The first Chinamen reaching California in 1849 were not gold-hunters, but fugitives from Peruvian masters, hiding in ships *en route* from New York to San Francisco, *via* Callao. Others came, ere long, from China in vessels, as Chinese cooks and servants. Hearing of the gold-diggings, these, with those from Peru, hurried to the mining districts. Purses soon filled with the precious metal, they returned to their native country, *prodigies*, painting the Pacific coast a very paradise. The news flew. The lower classes, listening, became uneasy. While mandarins and Confucian scholars live in palatial buildings, rich in furniture, sofas, mirrors, and china dishes, the coolies live in houses built of bamboo-matting and mortar, with sliding doors for windows, and no chimneys, neither pulu upon which they may pillow their heads. Often a room in which a family lives is not over ten feet square. Their fires are kindled and kept burning outside their miserable dwellings. In this one room may be found scraps of red paper, as "tablets" to some guardian spirit, a kitchen god, a few stools, and burning joss-

sticks.   Their daily dish is rice, pork, paste rolls, and pulse.
Rice the great staple, they cook by steaming.

Most of the coolies come from the Canton district.   Ship-
owners and brokers in Hong Kong send circulars up into the
provinces, describing our country in glowing terms.   And
further, they urge coolies to arrange their affairs, social and
financial, preparatory to embarking for America, where they
may soon acquire fortunes, becoming rich as the mandarins.

CONSULTING KITCHEN-GODS AND SPIRITS.

The Chinese have been educated to believe that communications can be received from the inhabitants of the heavens
and the hells, after complying with certain conditions.
Dreams and visions are carefully noted.   Trance is common
in the higher circles of Chinese society.   Considering it
sacred, and connecting it with their ancestors in heaven, they
conceal it, so far as is possible, from the searching, critical
eyes of foreigners.   A recent writer [*] says, " I wonder if the
Spiritualists of this day in New England ever think that their
belief is nothing new in theory or practice, or that it has
been known and believed in China for more than twenty-
three hundred years.   Not only do the Chinese Spiritualists
believe in the same agencies and same results which distinguish Spiritualists here, but they also practice all the methods
adopted in this for spiritual manifestions, and a hundred
others that do not seem to be known here. . . . During the
stay of spirits in that nether world, the lower spheres, they
can rap on furniture, pull the garments of the living, make
noises in the air, play on musical instruments, show their
footprints in the sand, and, taking possession of human
beings, talk through them.   In a thousand other ways they
manifest their presence."

It is very common for coolies to consult trance-mediums
of the cash-taking kind, touching the wish and will of their
ancestors, before deciding to sail for the western world.

[*] R. H. Conwell's Travels in China, pp. 163, 164.

They also sacrifice to Buddha, and petition the attendance of guardian spirits during their absence from China.

THEIR HOME IDEALS.

These are, good health; happy families, several living contentedly under the same roof; gardens and fish-ponds, well stocked; tea fragrant, and grain abundant; the young Confucius of the family preparing for competitive examinations; ancestral tablets recording honored names; gilded halls for the wise elders; violin-shaped instruments with but a single string; plenty of holiday festivals, cheerful with music, showy silks, savory dishes, flowers, and hanging creepers; city walls and store-fronts glittering with quotations from favorite authors; the conscious presence of spirits; sacred books, treating of old sages, reverentially read: *all* these, with residences near Confucian, Buddhist, and Tauist temples, and Chinamen are supremely happy.

CHINESE CEMETERIES.

When approaching Whampoa, we had a fair view of a Chinese cemetery, the tombs in which were constructed much in the shape of the Greek Omega. They are built upon hillsides, and terraced up to the very summit. It is believed that tutelary gods protect the graves, and guide the spirits of the dead back at certain seasons to their earthly homes and ancestral altars. The captain of our steamer, pointing to this hill of bones and ashes, said, "I have seen on festal days, crowding about those graves, fifty thousand people." At the time of burial, they usually make an offering to hungry and unhappy spirits, believed to haunt burial-places. They clothe their dead bodies in several suits of garments for burial. Fashion demands this, which, if neglected by the children, is construed as a want of filial piety. White is the proper emblem of sorrow and mourning, — red of joy and gladness. Widows are required to wear mourning three years; while the widower is expected to mourn but one year, wearing a white girdle. The Chinese have not the least fear of death, and really mourn deeper and wail louder at their weddings than at their funerals. The aged procure their coffins before they die, decorating them with red silk and other costly material, keeping them in their houses as ornamental furniture. One monument in this cemetery, towering above the others, was erected to the memory of a " *literary man.*" Money, oftener than merit, puts up marble shafts in both Europe and America. They are useless expenditures in any country.

PAGODAS.

Who built them ? and what the original purpose ? There are several within the walls of Canton, and we passed a number crowning the hill-tops on the way up the Pearl River. These graceful towers, three, five, and nine storied, are built of brick or stone. The walls are some ten feet thick. . Perfect in proportion, they range from seventy to two hundred feet high. Difficult of ascension, terraced with vines, and capped with verdure and tropical foliage, they constitute an interesting feature in Chinese landscapes. The one near Whampoa is only about six hundred years old. Many of them, however, are very ancient, antedating the introduction of Buddhism into China from India, 250 B.C. They originally symbolized aspiration, pointing toward the great Ruler of heaven. At the base, and up their rising stairways, the wise sat for meditation and self-examination. They were also used as outlooks in time of danger, and places of rest for traveling pilgrims. After the visits of Buddhist missionaries, they became the repositories of the ashes of Buddha and various relics. In some localities they are now falling into ruin. Everywhere and in every thing there seems a lack of enterprise.

CHAPTER XII.

CHINESE RELIGIONS AND INSTITUTIONS.

"Chariots are vanity, horses are vanity : the thing remains, the man departs : a shadow leaves no trace behind.

"Station is vanity, office is vanity : when the tide of fortune is spent, the retributions of justice begin, and remorse is without bounds.

"It may be said of every thing in earth which affords happiness, after a little time the gratification passes away, and it is, after all, but emptiness.

"The conclusion of all is, that only one thing is real, and that is the effect of virtuous deeds leaving their lasting impress on our individual being."

Chinese Essay.

CONFUCIAN TEMPLES.

CONFUCIANISM is not a religion, but rather a system of morals. The best scholars of China to-day are the Confucians and Tauists. Mandarins never attend services in missionary chapels : it is beneath their dignity to listen to the theological religions of Christian nations. They have no objections to Jesus, the Syrian sage, and would willingly give him a niche in the temples of their gods ; but hypocritical, money-making, warlike Christians they despise. Visiting a Confucian temple, I saw a costly image of Confucius. There were also tablets of his most distinguished disciples and commentators. Students occupied rooms in rear of the building. The Chinese no more worship Confucius and hero-gods, than do Americans George Washington and Thomas Jefferson, or High-Churchmen the Bible and prayer-book.

Walking up the Highway of Science with Dr. J. G. Kerr,
Secretary of the Medical Hospital in Canton, to the " Examination Hall," I was filled with wonder and admiration.
The hall itself is about fourteen hundred feet in length, by
six hundred and fifty wide. The principal entrance is at the
" Gate of Equity ; " and the first inscription over the avenue
reads, " The opening heavens circulate literature." The
examination of candidates for the Kü-yan, or second literary
degree, is here held triennially. Connected with this mammoth hall are nine thousand five hundred and thirty-seven
stalls, or rooms for the students on trial ; and in rear of these
rooms are other apartments for three thousand officials, —
copyists, servants, policemen. Each candidate for a degree
is put into a stall, with only pen, ink, and paper, and
required to write an essay from a given text in the classics.
One day and one night only are allowed for the production
of the thesis. There is great competition ; and there are
thousands of strangers in the city during these examinations. ˙ The third degree is conferred only in Pekin.

WALLS IN THE EMPIRE.

In the declining years of the Mongolians and Chinese,
man losing faith in man, reigning dynasties conceived the
notion of constructing gigantic walls. For over three thousand years, therefore, the Chinese have been a wall-making
people. Those around the old city of Canton, as they now
stand, were built in 1380 A.D. The one inclosing the new
city dates to A.D. 1568. The oldest of the walls surrounding Canton is thirty feet thick at the base, about thirty feet
high, nearly seven miles in length, and four horses may
travel upon the top abreast. A recent writer says; " It
would bankrupt New York or Paris to build the walls of the
city of Pekin. The great wall of China, the wall of the
world, is forty feet high. The lower thirty feet are of
granite or hewn limestone ; and two modern carriages may
pass each other on the summit. It has parapets the whole

length, and frequent garrisons along the way, whether running through valleys, or over the crests of mountains. It would probably cost more now to build the great wall of China, through its extent of a thousand miles, than to build the sixty thousand miles of railroads in the United States. This wall, so effectual several thousand years since, is now an incumbrance." Borne in a sedan-chair, one hardly observes, the gate that lets pilgrims inside the Canton walls. A sort of a cross-wall surrounds *Shameen*, the chief residence of foreign merchants. This wall was finished in 1862.

SIGHTS AND SCENES IN THE CITY.

Traversing the streets, the olfactories suffering more or less from contiguous meat-markets, gaping crowds would gather around us, commenting upon our dress, beard, and unshaven head, calling us in Chinese " red-haired men from the west." It is reported that they shout, " *Fan Kwai*," — foreign devils. Though this were true once, it is not now. They treated us with perfect respect.

Do they eat " rats, cats, and puppies," as the old geography-makers said ? If so, it is an exceptional custom practiced by paupers. I saw no cats, but did see a few dressed rats and dogs in the Canton markets. Missionaries are very apt to see in " heathen lands " what they search for. Dr. Kerr informed us that a very small portion of the poorer classes probably ate them, superstitiously connecting them with certain medical effects, upon the principle that " every part strengthens a part." The unjust reports that Chinamen ate " cats and puppies," put in circulation by sensationalists, were keenly parried by the fact that Europeans ate swine, shrimps, snails, frogs, horses, and water-serpents!

The Chinese are naturally a rice-eating people ; and in the palmy ages of their old seers they subsisted entirely upon vegetables, grains, and fruit. Meat-eating, and the shaving of their heads, are modern customs ; the one indicating the moral degeneracy, and the other subserviency to a foreign

power.   When the Tartars poured down from the north,
conquering China, the shaving of the head, except the cue,
was imposed as a token of subserviency to the new dynasty.
It is now fashionable ; the more foppish adding black silken
braids to make their long, glossy cues more conspicuous.
The women dress their heads doubtless, as they imagine, very
artistically, combing the hair straight back, and then putting
into it a profusion of tinselings, ornaments, and artificial
flowers.   The Chinese are naturally polite, the mandarins
haughty.   The women paint and powder much as they do in
America.

The two sexes occupy different rooms at night, and also
eat separately : chop-sticks take the place of knives and
forks.   During the first day after reaching Canton, we visited
Buddhist temples, a Confucian temple, the Examination Hall,
Chinese printing-offices, china-ware manufactories, embroid-
ery shops, native schools, the execution grounds, and the
" Temple of Horrors," where are exhibited the pictorial pre-
sentations of the ten punishments in hell.   This temple is
much frequented by tricksters and fortune-tellers.   The
schools half deafened us, because the scholars all study aloud
at the same time ; some literally screaming from behind their
desks.   It was Babel.   Education in these primary schools
consists principally of committing to memory things worth
knowing in books; when well committed, the teacher
explains the meaning, and the application to life.

In surgery Chinese physicians are far behind European ;
and for the reason they do not believe in amputations, or the
use of the knife.   They diagnose disease by touching the
pulse.   Some heal by " the laying-on of hands."   They permit their patients the use of little or no water.   Much sleep
is among their recommendations.   They use a vast number
of remedies, some ridiculously superstitious and useless.
They rely much upon diet, charms, faith, and the driving
away of evil spirits.   Some consider these Chinese physicians
exceedingly skilful : others do not.   They certainly are not

scientific in the Western sense of the term.   But *is* medicine
a science ?   Dr. Kerr is doing an excellent work, and Chinamen have in him great faith.   Speaking, at the breakfast-
table, of the general intelligence of the Chinese, Mrs. Kerr
remarked, " These Chinese are in some respects in advance
of the Europeans and Americans: *all* they need is the
Christian religion."

It must be remembered that Chinese literature is not only
extensive, but absolutely *massive*.   The Chinese dictionary
is a work of one hundred and fifty volumes ; the history of
China is a work of three hundred and sixty volumes ; while
there are one hundred and twenty volumes in just the cata-
logue of the imperial library at Pekin.   The learned Lew
Heang (120 B.C.) wrote several voluminous works entitled,
" The Biography of Famous Women."   Two thousand, and
even one thousand years previous to Heang's time, women
in the Mongolian countries were considered the equals of
men.   The greatest of these nations was governed by a
queen, with a liberal sprinkling of mothers and sisters for
officials.   No traveler reading ancient literature, and studying old ruins, can deny the " fall of man."

When the French and English, under their national banners, entered the gates of Pekin in 1860, be it said to the
lasting shame of that portion of the " allied army," the
French, that they burned a very valuable library connected
with the summer-palace of the emperor ; and these French-
men are called Christians, and the Chinese "heathen."

Not only is Chinese literature, extensive as it is, free from
all obscene allusions, but most of it is eminently suggestive
and moral.

In one of their odes treating of " discontent," the voyage
of life is graphically traced from babyish longings to youth,
then to ambitious schemes, thence to family associations,
to the possession of horses and vehicles, to thousands of
fertile acres, to official stations, and finally to positions of
rank. · Still discontented, he aspires to be prime minister,

then emperor; and then he calls for exemption from death, that he may rule empires and worlds. The following are the closing lines of this ethical ode : —

> " His numerous and foolish longings know no stopping-place;
> At last a coffin for ever hides him,
> And he passes away, still hugging his discontent."

In a Tauist work, treating of " rewards and punishments," I find these Emersonian teachings : —

" When you see the way of truth, enter it. What is not truth, avoid it. Watch not in false ways. Do not deceive yourself in committing sins in secret. Add to the store of your virtues, and thus increase your merits. Let your compassion extend to every object. Be loyal, dutiful, and affectionate. Reform yourself that you may reform others. Pity the desolate, compassionate the distressed. Honor the aged, be kind to the young. Have a care not to harm either plants or reptiles. Sympathize with the unfortunate, rejoice over the virtuous. Help those who are in difficulty, save those who are in distress. Regard the good fortune and losses of others as if they were your own. Do not make a display either of the faults of others, or of your own excellences. Suppress what is evil, give currency to what is good. Receive abuse without resentment ; receive favors, as it were, with trembling. Dispense favors without asking a return. Give to others without after-regrets. There is no peace in wrong-doing. The effect follows the producing cause. If a person has been guilty of wicked deeds, and afterwards repents, receive him into confidence. Forget the past. To appropriate to one's self ill-gotten gains, is like allaying hunger with poisoned food. If desires to do right arise in the mind, divinities are present to aid and bless.

" As regards the virtuous man, all men honor him, Heaven protects him, happiness and fortune follow him, evil influences flee far from him, divine spirits attend him ; whatever he does will prove successful, and he may aspire to being one of the genii of heaven."

LAU-TSZE, THE GREAT MAN

Circumstances, rather than merit, often weave the crown of fame. Confucius is often termed the sage of China. That he was treasury-keeper to the court of Chow, a gatherer of ancient wisdom, and a wise man, is admitted : but he was not original, as was the old philosopher Lau-tsze.

who founded the Tauist sect or school of thinkers. Tauism is literally rationalism. Confucius spoke as a schoolmaster, quoting the ancients of almost forgotten dynasties as authority.

Lau-tsze, born 604 B.C., was a radical intuitionist. His great work is called the *Tau-teh-king.* " Tau " means " truth," or " doctrinal discourse." Most of his works are abstruse and metaphysical. He is represented to have descended from heaven, being begotten in a miraculous manner, as were Pythagoras and Jesus. At birth his hair was already white with age ; and accordingly he was named what the word " Lau-tsze " implies, — " the immortal boy." In a poem aflame with rhapsody, addressed to this personage, these lines occur : —

> " Great and most excellent Tau,
> Thou who gavest instruction to Confucius in the east,
> And called into existence Buddha in the west,
> Director of kings, and parent of all sages,
> Originator of all religions, *mystery* of mysteries! "

Confucius, once visiting him, did not seem to comprehend his transcendental philosophy. Confucius's brain was a cistern ; Lau-tsze's a living fountain. Seeing the hollowness of education, government, and society, he condemned it ; and then, soaring into the regions of thought, he uttered truths, and lived them.

It is a matter of no little surprise to us that friend Stebbins, in his excellent compilation, " The Bible of the Ages," made no selections from the venerable philosopher Lau-tsze, who, though preceding Confucius by a few years, lived in the sixth century before Christ.

The following are gems gathered at random from the volume entitled " Tau-Teh-King : " —

" The wise produce without holding possession ; act without presuming on the result ; complete their work without assuming any position for themselves ; and, since they assume no position, they never lose any.'

" The sage has no special love. He puts himself last, and yet is first; he abandons himself, and yet is preserved. Is not this through his having no selfishness? When a work of merit is done, and reputation is coming, he gets out of the way. To produce, and have not; to act, and expect not, — this is sublime virtue."

" A man on tiptoe can not stand still ; astride his neighbor he can not walk on. He who is self-displaying does not shine; he who is self-praising has no real merit. The unwise are full of ambitious desires, lusting for the stalled ox, or for sexual enjoyment. The wise conquer themselves, putting away all impurity, all excess, and all gayety."

" The sage, timid and reserved, blends in sympathy with all, for he thinks of them as his children. There is no greater misery than discontent; no greater sin than giving rein to lust. Tau, the spirit, is permanent, yet undefinable. Spirits, but from some source of spirituality, would be in danger of annihilation."

" The sage wears a coarse garment, and hides his jewels in his bosom. He grasps nothing, and therefore loses nothing. He does not copy others. He recompenses injury with kindness, and excels in forgetting himself."

After a long conference between Lau-tsze and Confucius, the latter said to his disciples, " I can tell how the runner may be snared, the swimmer may be hooked, and the flyer shot by the arrow. But there is the dragon : I can not tell how he mounts on the wing through the clouds, and rises to heaven. To-day I have seen Lau-tsze, and can only compare him to the dragon."

RECKONING TIME.

The Chinese profess to trace mystical relations between time and certain inherent principles in nature. Their year is composed of lunar months, beginning with the new-moon, that is, the first new-moon after the sun enters Aquarius, which occurs between the 21st of January and the 19th of February. This period marks the returning spring ; and the first day of the new year is a universal holiday throughout China. In reckoning their time, especially if it relates to astrology, they use a sexagenary cycle, which confers meaning names upon years, months, days, and hours. The Swedenborgian theory of correspondences takes a wide range with Chinese scholars. They insist that the earth in organization bears a striking resemblance to man ; having veins, arteries, magnetic currents, and a principle of life infilling the whole, which principle is denominated *fung-shwuy*.

CHINA-WOMEN AND SERVITUDE.

Women, though occupying a better position than in Mohammedan lands, are held in a sort of semi-subjection. Their often-expressed desire to be born men in the next state of existence, reveals their real condition. They paint excessively, are exceedingly polite, and desire to become the mothers of *male* children. In some localities women are virtually sold. And yet Chinese slavery is much less irksome than was African slavery in our country, inasmuch as it is not hereditary. When a coolie sells a daughter, he is supposed to convey no right to the services of unborn grandchildren.

Nearly all Europeans and Americans doing business in the cities and treaty-ports buy each a China girl as a " mistress," for from three to five hundred dollars, keeping the same till returning to their native country. This, though considered no disgrace by Europeans residing in China, gives the Chinese a bad opinion of " Christian " morals in the West. Leaving for their homes, some of these men make provision for their "kept women " and their children; others sell them ; and others still turn them off upon the world's cold charities.

Matches being made by the parents, the luxury of courting or love-making is not among the fine arts of the Flowery Land. Betrothals take place at a very early age, and frequently the parties do not see each other till the day of marriage. Living together, they generally learn to love as husband and wife.

Though polygamy is permitted, the rule is one wife Taking other wives, though not highly reputable, is excused when the first proves unfruitful. Ancestral worship is fundamental in the Chinese mind. Nothing can exceed their desire to have male children to visit their graves, and venerate their memories. Parents in some of the provinces have the power of life and death over their children. Sons obey their parents the same after as before their marriage. Children by the second, third, and other wives are legal, and have the same rights as those by the first. Sons, marrying, bring their wives to the father's house, having different rooms, yet forming one household. The first wife, queen of the shanty, may not only control, but legally beat the others to produce obedience. They are, in fact, her servants ; and she claims the ownership and jurisdiction of their children.

The Rev. Dr. Eitel, of Hong Kong, gave us an interesting account of a childless couple connected with his church, who came to him begging consent for the husband to take a second wife, hoping to raise a son. The wife was far the most anxious of the two for this consummation. During the importuning, she quoted the Bible case of Abraham and Sarah. The doctor, after advising them to " submit to the will of God," suggested, that if they must have a son, looking forward to ancestral worship, they adopt some outcast child. The Christian woman replied, " This was not Abraham's course ; and then, such children usually inherit bad temperaments and dispositions."

BUDDHIST TEMPLES AND BUDDHISM.

Buddha means the " enlightened ; " as *Christos*, Christ, signifies " anointed."

Having read for years of Buddhism, and the older religions of Asia, my first visit to a Buddhist monastery, to witness the temple-services of the priests, was thrillingly interesting.

Stepping inside, and glancing at the brazen trinity of the " three precious ones," the lighted tapers and burning incense, the priests with shaven heads, long robes, — gray, black, and yellow, according to the order, — bowing their heads to the floor, then rising and re-bowing before their images, I mentally said, " Who are the thieves ? " Nothing can be more patent than that Roman ritualism is stolen from the Buddhists, or that Buddhism is borrowed bodily from Roman Catholicism. Unfortunately for churchmen, *Saka-muni*, Gautama Buddha, the original founder of Buddhism, died in the year 543 B.C. One of the earlier Catholic missionaries, traveling in China, wrote and published that " there was no country where the Devil had so successfully counterfeited the true worship of the Holy Church as in China. . . . These Buddhist priests burn incense, hear confessions, and wear long, loose gowns resembling some of the fathers. They live in temples like so many monasteries, and they chant in the same manner as with us." The vesper services in this temple were conducted in the following order : the striking of a tom-tom, ringing of bells, intoning, chanting, genuflections, and marching up and down the gorgeously decorated edifice. The chanting was not only in good time, but really melodious. We had a social chat with these priests, Dr. Kerr interpreting. The abbot who led the service had a solemn visage, and finger-nails nearly an inch in length. Taking our departure, these priests joined each his *own* hands, and shook them vigorously, instead of shaking *ours*, — the sweaty, clammy, unclean hands of flesh-eating Christians (?)

The appearance of a superior Buddhist temple, exhibiting considerable architectural skill, is to an externalist truly grand and imposing. Symmetrical and well-proportioned, these structures, with their adjoining gardens, are admirably calculated to excite wonder and reverence. The tiled roofs are decorated with fretted-work, — unique figures of dragons, elephants, war-horses, and historical dramas ; while their interiors are ornamented with Oriental carving-work, weird scrolls, mysterious inscriptions, and gilt sentences written over the heads of their divinities. Lotus-flowers adorn most of their altars. This lotus symbol is not understood.

however, by the more ignorant of Buddhist worshipers.

Passing the gates of this temple, we saw on our right a
number of pigs wallowing in the choicest food. An inscription upon the block by the inclosure read, " *Save life*." All
life, in the eyes of Buddhists, is sacred ; one of their chief
commandments being, " Thou shalt not take life." And
yet travelers, — and among them a member of the " American Expedition to China and Japan," — after describing what
they term their " sacred pigs," speak of the worship paid to
this " sanctified pork." Saying nothing of the injustice
done, such a blunder is almost unpardonable. The Rev. Dr.
Eitel, a German clergyman of Hong Kong, in publishing a
correction of this mistake, adds, " There is not a trace of
porcine-worship to be found among Buddhists." Modern
Buddhism, bearing but little relation to its ancient grandeur,
exists to-day in a degenerate and dying state. This missionary, the Rev. Dr. Eitel, treating of ancient Buddhism in his
" Three Lectures " delivered and published in Hong Kong,
says (p. 37) : —

" Ancient Buddhism knows of no sin-atoning power. It holds out to
the troubled, guilty conscience no chance of obtaining forgiveness. A
Buddha is *not* a Saviour. The only thing he can do for others is to show
them the way of doing good and overcoming evil; to point out the path
to Nirvana by his example ; and to encourage others, by means of teaching and exhortation and warning, to follow his footsteps. *Do good*,
and you will be saved: this is the long and short of the Buddhist
religion."

CHINAMEN AS EMIGRANTS.

The written language of this vast empire, understood by
the learned of Japan, Loo-Choo, Corea, Manchuria, and
Cochin China, reaches and may influence more of the human
race than any other in the world. The genius of emigration
has touched, and become a kind of inspiration with, a portion
of these Asiatics. Ubiquitous by nature, these Chinese are
literally the Yankees of the East. For a long period, ingress

and egress from the empire were governmental regulations. The policy was eventually changed; and Chinamen are now everywhere in the great cities of the world, and the out-of-the-way islands of the Pacific,—servants, agriculturists, artisans, as circumstances demand.

Every Chinese dealer, buyer and seller, has his own scales. They can not trust to others. They live cheap, except on feast-days, and keep their valuables in tall stone buildings called by Englishmen "pawn-shops." In detecting counterfeit coin they are experts, depending entirely upon the touch and the ring of the metal. While canals are very common, they have no railways, no telegraphic lines, and no insurance-offices. In money-making they excel, and yet they are not considered miserly.

It matters little what rival Irish laborers in America may say or do: Chinamen are certain to flock westward in increasing crowds. Competition in many directions, and ultimately an intermingling of blood, an intermixture of the whitish-pink and the olive-brown races, — beneficial perhaps to both the Orient and the Occident, — will be the result. There are no white men on earth. The three original colors were pink, copper, and black, corresponding to the equator, the tropics, and temperate zones. Already in Australia and the Pacific islands marriages are not uncommon between Englishwomen and wealthy Chinamen. This cross of blood and temperament produces handsome as well as very intelligent children. Is it a foreshadowing of their future social life in America?

MURDER OF THE INNOCENTS.

China is packed with people. Though ambitious crowds emigrate, the old hive continues crammed. The Tai-Ping war took off infatuated multitudes; and provincial rebellions result not uncommonly in a wholesale slaughter. Still the country swarms with over-population. This *fact* is father to much of the *infanticide*. Is there as rational an excuse for the prevailing fœticide of America? That infanticide prevails to an alarming extent in some of the poorer local:ties, is beyond dispute, while in others it is entirely unknown. Major Studer, our American consul in Singapore, though residing in this city of sixty thousand Chinamen, says there has not been a case of infanticide before the courts, nor has he as yet even heard of a child's being killed by the parents. Chinese women, like other mothers, naturally love their children; but the family is large, the means of support limited, and the country deluged with population. What must be done? A check of some kind seems indispensable. They do not destroy the first female infant. If the second born is a female, there comes a struggle between natural affection, and the nuisance of two female children, with no son to bear the name down to posterity, securing ancestral worship. If the third is a daughter, it seldom escapes strangling by the "woman-nurse" in attendance. There is a tacit understanding between the parties to this effect. The method of destruction is either by strangulation or drowning. True, there is a well-defined law against this crime; and the public sentiment of China is decidedly opposed to it. And what is equally encouraging Chinese scholars write essays and books against the criminal practice. A popular tract has this heading: "*An Appeal to dissuade from drowning Female Children.*" In it I find these teachings: —

"Virtue and vice are connected with their appropriate results as the shadow follows the substance. The offending man meets with innumerable troubles and distresses. Suffering follows him. . . . Suppress what is evil. . . . Avoid displaying the faults of others, doing things in an underhanded manner, and *destroying children before or after birth.*"

Not mentioning other authorities, the Rev. Dr. Eitel, the German missionary in Hong Kong, assured us that the morals of Chinamen would compare very favorably with those of Europeans; that they were far more chaste, and upright every way, in the country than in the cities; and that, just so far as traders and foreigners generally exercised any influence, it was in tendency demoralizing.

CHINESE BENEVOLENT INSTITUTIONS.

Churchmen are inclined to boast of their charitable asylums and reform-institutions as proofs of the divinity of the Christian religion. When premises are assumed, erroneous conclusions quite naturally follow. Many hundreds certainly, and in all probability thousands, of years before the Christian era, China not only had her universities of learning, but her public charities and extensive benevolent institutions. And though China is, intellectually and nationally, in her dotage now, *these* have not ceased to exist. Not only every city, but every country village of any importance, has its free school and orphan-asylum. Some wealthy citizen leading the enterprise, others unite in raising funds, which are often increased from the government treasury.

"In Hang Chow," says the Rev. Mr. Nevius, "I found, in connection with a variety of benevolent institutions, an asylum for old men, which had about five hundred members." It was my good fortune to visit *one* foundling-hospital. By diligent inquiry I learned that there were many societies for the relief of aged widows, and also for cripples, but none for the insane, and for the plausible reason that it is among the marvels of the country to see or hear of an insane person.

Charity-schools are very common in China. And then there are numerous medical hospitals, where medicines are administered to the poor gratuitously. "There is a society in Suchow," writes the missionary Nevius, "for the suppression of the publication and sale of immoral books." The mandarins contributed largely to this establishment.

I was repeatedly informed by hunters and travelers that in the interior of the country the people were exceedingly hospitable, bringing tea and rice to the roadside to refresh

the wanderer.   Turanians and Semitics are proverbially less
acquisitive than Europeans.   Just in proportion, however,
as they mingle with the Western civilizations, do they become
scheming and mercenary.   Heaven knows, I despise a grasping selfishness!   There are individuals of Aryan descent
mean and selfish enough to suck the moon from the sky, bag
the golden sun, and, pocketing the stars, wait for a rise in
fire-mist matter, hoping for a "bargain" at world-building.
Selfishness breeds devils.

THE MOSAIC OF GIVE AND TAKE.

Scholastic Chinamen, given to egotism, think meaner of us
than we possibly *can* of them.   Their map of the world puts
China in the center, and America in a small compass adrift on
the border-lands of the globe.   If we laugh at their shaven
heads, thick-soled shoes, and sack trousers, they sneeringly
smile at our shaven faces, short-cropped hair, stovepipe hats,
gloved hands in summer-time, and tight-fitting pants half
revealing the anatomy of the organism.   If we refer to
the small feet of women among the Chinese nobility, they
sarcastically point to the wasp-like waists, swinging hoops,
uncouth chignons, and tawdry manners, of the Americans.
And then, to walk arm in arm, man and woman, is considered
by them exceedingly vulgar.   Lecture the more intellectual
upon the subject of morals, and they will push in your faces
an old copy of "The New-York Herald," with flaring sub-
headings of *poisonings, forgeries, murders, drunkenness, thiev-
ing, suicide, divorces, adulteries, fœticide*, &c.   Chinamen and
Japanese, attending school or traveling through America, see
in the city hotels printed cards of warning, "*Valuables
must be handed to the clerk to be locked in the safe.*"   Sallying
out into the streets, they see club-bearing policemen arrest-
ing disorderly and drunken men, and occasionally a drunken
woman.   These vices, and others so common in Christendom,
they report to their countrymen when returning, and then
make merry over the mock civilization of Christian nations

Cool and reflective, these Asiatic Chinese are not slow to forget that foreign Christian nations introduced opium into their empire, against the positive remonstrances of the Pekin government. Out of this opium-trade business, grew the first war, with a great slaughter of life. They also well understand that their countrymen have not been allowed to testify in the civil and criminal courts of America only under certain crippled conditions ; and, further, they take a sort of demoniac satisfaction in reminding Western nations of their frequent drunkenness, their houses of prostitution, their city dancing-dens, their immodest pictures, and their publication of obscene books. On the whole, they think Christian nations not only terribly immoral, but downright hypocrites. Sir John Davis sensibly wrote thus to Englishmen : " The most commendable portion of the Chinese system is the general diffusion of elementary *moral education*, among even the lower classes. It is in the preference of moral to physical instruction that we might perhaps wisely take a leaf out of the Chinese books, and do something to reform this most immoral age of ours."

THE MANDARINS AND SCHOOLS.

Those known as mandarins are all scholars, having passed the prescribed examinations. The important offices of the empire are filled with mandarins only. They may be recognized by their costly costume, insignia, and train of attendants. Money does not, as in America, buy "honorable" positions. Bating the "blue-button" mandarins, — those who, because of some signal service rendered, have received a sort of "side honor," — the others, the genuine, are often popular in consideration of their scholarly attainments and munificent gifts.

The court language is mandarin, being spoken by *all* officials ; and although it is important as a written language, being spoken all over Northern China, it is nevertheless but one of the dialects of the empire. As the Latin may be read and spoken by the very learned of universities in all lands, so the written language of China may be understood by the *literati* of North-eastern Asia.

As a nation, China is eminently literary. The first degree conferred upon the scholar is A. B., "beautiful ability;" the second is A. M., literally "the advanced man;" while it is only after the most critical and rigid examination that students receive the crowning degree at the capital. Free "day-schools" for boys are common. Girls are neglected; and yet in some of the provinces there are free schools established for them also, with female teachers. Nearly *all* of even the poorer classes in this vast empire are versed, to some degree, in writing, reading, arithmetic, and memorized passages from the classics. Japan has a compulsory system of education, equally binding upon the children of both sexes. Religion in these lands is free. Church and State are unmeaning terms. Their great teachers, such as Lau-tsze, Confucius, and others, were moralists rather than religionists. Thousands of the truly learned are pantheists. Many of their statements are as transcendental as Emerson's. They believe in *Tau*, — the absolute Unity, manifest as duality in the positive and negative forces of the universe. There are three great systems of morals and religions in the country. Tauism savors of metaphysical pantheism; Confucianism, of practical morals; and Buddhism, of the old religions of India; and yet these different religionists frequently worship in the same temples. And why not? Is not this a lesson of tolerance to Christendom? "Heathen" may well say of Christians, "Behold how they love one another!"

GOD-WORSHIP AND GENERAL WARD.

Nearly every office and shop in China-lands has its image, its sacred altar, and its smoking incense as a "sweet-smelling savor." Rightly understood, however, worship in all Mongolian countries implies little more than respect paid to superiors. Besides ancestors, whose spirit-presences China-

men evoke, scholars worship the god of letters, soldiers the
god of war, business-men the god of wealth, medical men
some Chinese Esculapius ; and even gamblers have their altars
and their gods, to whom they appeal, pleading for good luck.
Lau-tsze and Confucius rank highest among their gods.
The latter, generally called by them *the Ancient Teacher*, *the
Perfect Sage*, is the most popular.

All these gods whom they worship were once men, famous
and renowned as heroes or sages.

It will be remembered by Americans that John Ward,
originally a Massachusetts sailor, and afterwards in league
with Walker in the wild undertaking of conquering Nicaragua for slavery-extension purposes, took an active part in
the Tai-ping rebellion, fighting on the side of the emperor,
rather than in behalf of a more democratic government.
The rebellion, calling to its aid many scholars, soon assumed
gigantic proportions. These Tai-pings in their manifestoes
indorsed the Christian religion, abolished slavery, encouraged
education, and cautioned their soldiers against the inhuman
treatment of prisoners. Victories attended them.

But the American Ward, introducing into the emperor's
army European discipline and tactics, proved a martial
success, and a help to the imperial cause. Still the
rebellion continued. At first the French and English sym-
pathized with the Tai-pings. But when the emperor, trembling for his throne, invited foreign assistance, the French
and English, in consideration of *more* open ports, and other
mammon-like interests in the line of finances, turned at once
against the " Christianity " and promised constitutional
government of the Tai-pings, in favor of the imperial reign,
and co-operated with the Chinese army in the capture of
cities held by the Tai-pings. Blood flowed in torrents.

During this Titanic struggle, in which a religio-spiritualism
formed a powerful element, Ward married a mandarin's
daughter, became immensely rich, and was promoted to the
army position of general. But, while reconnoitering a rebel

fort, a bullet from the enemy proved fatal. He closed his mortal career a few days thereafter, at Ningpo, and was interred in accordance with the Chinese method of burial. His body was afterwards removed to Soong-Kong, and then to the inclosure near the Confucian temple, where there is a tablet erected to his honor. Now deified, he is one of the warrior-gods of China. His widow and three children reside in a palatial mansion at Shanghai.

THE SPIRITUAL ASPECT OF THE TAI-PING REBELLION.

This daring movement originated with Hung-sew-tswen, born near Canton, — a clairvoyant seer from infancy. When a lad, he was considered strange and eccentric. Returning to his home, when a young man, from an unsuccessful examination, he was attacked with a severe sickness, during which he declared that he had been favored with supernatural manifestations and revelations. He felt that he had been washed from the impurities of his nature, and introduced into the presence of an august being, who exhorted him to live a virtuous life, and exterminate demons. This immortalized man, whom he often saw, of middle age and dignified mien, further instructed him how to act. Hung called this visitant his " elder brother." About this time he read the New Testament, and declared immediately thereafter that this imposing personage seen in his visions was Jesus Christ, the Sent-of-God. A scholarly friend of his, named *Le*, uniting with him, they commenced preaching, baptizing, and making converts. During their inflammatory discourses, persons would fall into the trance, speak in strange tongues, and utter alleged revelations and prophecies. They organized to protect themselves, and punish their persecutors. This led to war : the insurrection became formidable, and for a time successful. Multitudes perished by sword and famine ; vacated fields, and burned cities yet in ruins, remain to tell the tale of war. The primal purpose was to overthrow the reigning dynasty, destroy the idols of the land, and establish a *quasi*-Christianity.

Hurg-sew-tswen, now putting himself at the head of the new kingdom, was styled *Tai-ping tien Kwoh*, assuming the title, "Son of Heaven." He professed to have direct communications from God, and spoke very familiarly of Jesus as his brother. He continually read the Old Testament, and observed religious worship in his camp. He assured missionaries that his revelations were as authoritative as those of the Bible, and he could prove it by his divine gifts. He further declared that spirits aided him in his victories. Loyal Chinamen called him and his soldiers, "long-haired rebels." Successes corrupting his leading officers, with envies and jealousies in different camps, the emperor's armies aided by Gen. Ward and the English and French in combination, the Tai-ping rebellion was put down. The struggle continued fourteen years. The leading spirit of the rebellious host committed suicide. Those caught by the government officials were tortured and massacred. Hung-sew-tswen's teachings continued to produce their legitimate results. His admirers believed him to have been God-inspired for a purpose, as was Moses of Hebrew memory.

TEA.

Of tea-cultivation and the tea-districts I have little to say, and because everybody *does* who is privileged to put a foot down in China. Suffice it that the Chinese themselves, though great tea-drinkers, do not drink "*green tea.*" Further, in preparing tea, they steam it a long time, in preference to boiling. There is a delicious, invigorating freshness to the black tea, when thus prepared by the people who cultivate the shrub. They use their best teas themselves.

Stepping into their silk-shops, or bazaars of any kind, they present you a cup of tea instead of a glass of intoxicating liquor. Why should *Americans* drink tea? Why should so much pure crystal water be spoiled by putting into it tea, coffee, and other Eastern drugs? Why import either Asiatic herbs or religions?

The spirit of progress, which flashes up in the political heavens of the West, has touched with intellectual intensity our antipodal kinsmen of the East. Commerce, whitening all seas, is a great civilizer. "Transition" is the great word now in China and Japan. Europeans and Americans are not only flocking into the original "five treaty-ports" of China, but are exploring the interior and the highlands of the Mongolian regions. The central government, in admitting foreign ministers to Pekin, in sending an embassy to Western nations, in establishing a university and schools with European teachers, and treating other nations with the respect becoming the fraternity of humanity, is taking a step in the right direction. Bating a national egotism, and a certain innate reserve, I place a much higher estimate upon the China races, intellectual and moral, since seeing the better classes in their native country.

Mandarins and officials, so far as I heard, spoke in great commendation of the Hon. Mr. Burlingame, our former minister to the capital. It may not be generally known, even in America, that he was a Spiritualist. This writer in the Atlantic Monthly, however, must have known it : —

"As an example of the influence of a single man, attained over an alien race, whose civilization is widely different, whose religious belief is totally opposite, whose language he could not read nor write nor speak, Mr. Burlingame's career in China will always be regarded as an extraordinary event, not to be accounted for except by conceding to him a peculiar power of influencing those with whom he came in contact; a power growing out of a mysterious gift, partly intellectual, partly spiritual, largely physical ; a power whose laws are unknown, whose origin can not be traced, and whose limits can not be assigned ; a power which we designate as magnetism."

When the Chinese government received official notice of Minister Burlingame's death, they gave him a tablet in a Pekin temple, thus preparing the way to deification.

CHINESE SPIRITUALISM.

Conversing with consuls, missionaries, the older European residents, and the Chinese themselves, concerning their belief about gods and demons, genii and spirits, with the relations they sustain to mortals, the inquiry arises, " Where shall I commence? what say first? " The Rev. Dr. Mac-Gowan, returning to America, said when lecturing in Chicago, " China is a nation of Spiritists." Dr. Damon reiterated the same thing to me in Honolulu. Mr. Bailey, our Hong-Kong consul, assured me that the lower classes were very superstitious; that the *Fung-shwuy* was a mystery; and that they all believed in the presence of their ancestors, and their power to hold converse with them." A delineation of the *Fung-shwuy* in its relations to the selection of burial-places, to the ethereal principles of the universe, to atmospheres, emanations, and vitalizing forces under the influence of gods and spirits, would require a chapter rather than a passing paragraph. When foreigners look at the sky, or at a beautiful landscape in the distance, Chinese bystanders are sure to remark, " They are looking at the *Fung-shwuy*."

These Orientals have their trance mediums, mostly females, their writing mediums, using a pointed, pen-like stick, and a table sprinkled with white sand; their personating mediums, giving excellent tests; their seers, who professedly reveal the future; and their clairvoyants, who, to express their meaning in English, " see in the dark." It may be affirmed without dispute, that Spiritism in some form is an almost *universal belief* throughout the Chinese Empire. It seems natural to the Turanian and Semitic races. In making this broad affirmation, I use the term " Spiritism " in preference to " Spiritualism," because the latter implies not only phenomena, but philosophy, religion, and the practice of true living.

WHAT MISSIONARIES SAY OF THEIR SPIRIT-INTERCOURSE.

Hear their testimonies: —

" There is no driving out of these Chinese," says Father Gonzalo, " the cursed belief that the spirits of their ancestors are about them, availing themselves of every opportunity to give advice and counsel."

" They burn incense, beat a drum to call the attention of the desired spirit," writes Padra De Mae, " and then, by idolatrous methods, one of which is a spasmodic ecstasy, they get responses from the dead. . . . They have great fear of the evil spirits that inhabit forests."

In two volumes entitled " Social Life Among the Chinese," by the Rev. J. Doolittle, the author informs us that " they have invented several ways by which they find out the pleasure of gods and spirits. One of the most common of their utensils is the *Ka-pue*, a piece of bamboo-root, bean-shaped, and divided in the center, to indicate the positive and the negative. The incense lighted, the *Ka-pue* properly manipulated before the symbol-god, the pieces are tossed from the medium's hand, indicating the will of the spirit by the way they fall." . . . The following manifestation is more mental: " The professional takes in the hand a stick of lighted incense to expel all defiling influences; prayers of some kind are repeated, the fingers are interlaced, and the medium's eyes are shut, giving unmistakable evidence of being possessed by some supernatural and spiritual power. The body sways back and forward; the incense falls, and the person begins to step about, assuming the walk and peculiar attitude of the spirit. This is considered infallible proof that the divinity has entered the body of the medium. Sometimes the god, using the mouth of the medium, gives the supplicant a sound scolding for invoking his aid to obtain unlawful or unworthy ends." . . . Another " method of obtaining communications, is for the applicant to make his wishes known to a person belonging to a society or company established for facilitating such consultations. Upon these occasions, the means employed consist in the use of a willow or bamboo pen, placed upon the top of the hand over a table of white sand ; the arm becomes tremulous, and the writing is produced. And still another course is " for the female medium to sit by a table on which are two lighted candles, and three sticks of burning incense. After inquiring the names of the deceased, and the time of their death, she bows her head upon the table with the face concealed. Soon lifting it, the eyes closed, the countenance changed, the silence profound, she is supposed to be possessed by the spirit of the dead individual, and begins to address the applicant; in other words, the dead has come into her body, using her organs of speech to communicate with the living. . . . Sometimes these mediums profess to be possessed by some specified god of great healing powers, and in this condition they prescribe for the sick. It is believed that the god or spirit invoked actually casts himself into the medium, and dictates the medicine."

Rev. Mr. Nevius in his work, " China and the Chinese," declares that " volumes might be written upon the gods, genii, and familiar spirits supposed to be continually in communication with the people. The Chinese have a large number of books upon this subject, among the most noted of which is the *Liau-chai-che-i*, a large work of sixteen volumes. . . . Tu Sien signifies a spirit in the body. And there are a class of familiar spirits supposed to dwell in the bodies of certain Chinese who became the mediums of communication with the unseen world. Individuals said to be possessed by these spirits are visited by multitudes, particularly those who have recently lost relatives by death, and wish to converse with them. . . . Remarkable disclosures and revelations are believed to be made by the involuntary movements of a bamboo pencil, and through those that claim to see in the dark. Persons considering themselves endowed with superior intelligence are firm believers in those and other modes of consulting spirits."

It was my privilege to see these coolie Chinamen conversing with their spirit-ancestors in several temples. Their methods are numerous; and the prevalence of this belief among them astonished me. It is almost universal; and yet with the lower classes it has degenerated into absurd superstitions.

" The practice of divination," writes Sir John Barrows, " with many strange methods of summoning the dead to instruct the living, and reveal the future, is of very ancient origin, as is proven by Chinese manuscripts antedating the revelations of Scripture." The " eight diagrams, with directions for devination, were invented," says the Rev. Mr. Nevius, " by the Emperor *Fuhi*, probably nearly 3000 B.C. About 1100 B.C., Wen-Wang, the Literary Prince, and his son *Chow-Kung*, further developed the system with explanations." The Yih-King is a sort of an encyclopedia of spiritual marvels and manifestations. It was denominated in the time of Confucius, the " Book of Changes."

Gliddon writes, " The emperor of China, Yao, who reigned about 2337 years B.C., in order to suppress false prophecies, miracles, magic, and revelation, commanded his two ministers of astronomy and religion to cut asunder all communications between sky and earth, so that, as the chronicle expresses it, ·there should be no more of what is called 'this lifting up and coming down.'"

This missionary, Mr. Nevius, further assures us that in the "latter part of the *Chan* dynasty, which continued to 249 B.C., *Kwei-Kuh-Sien-sz* applied the Yih-King to the use of soothsaying, and is regarded as among the fathers of *augurs*. During the past and the preceding dynasty, many books have been written upon this subject, among the most noted of which is the *Poh-shi-ching-tsung*, a work of six volumes on

the " Source of True Divination."   Here are a few passages
from the preface : —

" The secret of augury consists in communication with the gods.   The
interpretations of the transformations are deep and mysterious.   The
theory of the science is most intricate, the practice of it most important.
The sacred classic says, 'That which is true gives indications of the future.'
To know the condition of the dead, and hold with them intelligent intercourse as did the ancients, produces a most salutary influence upon the
parties. . . . But when from intoxication or feasting or licentious pleasures they proceed to invoke the gods, what infatuation to suppose that
their prayers will move them!   Often when no response is given, or the
interpretation is not verified, they lay the blame at the door of the augur,
forgetting that their failure is due to their *want of sincerity*. . . . It is
the great fault of augurs, too, that, from a desire of gain, they use the art
of divination as a trap to insnare the people," &c.

Naturally undemonstrative and secretive, the higher classes
of Chinamen seek to conceal their full knowledge of spirit
intercourse from foreigners, and from the inferior castes of
their own countrymen, thinking them not sufficiently intelligent to rightly use it.   The lower orders, superstitious and
money-grasping, often prostitute their mediumistic gifts to
gain and fortune-telling.   These clairvoyant fortune-tellers,
surpassing wandering gypsies in " hitting " the *past*, infest
the temples, streets, and roadsides, promising to find lost
property, discover precious metals, and reveal the hidden
future.   What good thing is not abused?   Liberty lives,
though license prowls abroad in night-time.   Christianity
wore the laurels it wove, though Peter denied and Judas
betrayed.   Spirit-communion is a reality, and, wisely used, a
mighty redemptive power, as well as a positive demonstration of a future existence.

Though wars are to be deprecated, and the war-spirit made
subject to arbitration, it must nevertheless be admitted that
the recent war between China and Japan had a very salutary
effect upon the Chinese.   It cooled their self-esteem and
humbled their pride.   They already begin to have a higher
appreciation of Western civilization.

CHAPTER XIII.

COCHIN CHINA TO SINGAPORE.

ABOARD " The Irrawaddy," a magnificent French steamer the sea, calm and smooth as polished glass, richly did I enjoy sailing down the coast of Cochin China to Anam.

THE ANAMITES.

Though the French are wretched colonists, they have made a success at Saigon, Anam, the southern part of Cochin China. The city, numbering several thousand inhabitants, has a naval station, situated up the lazy, serpentine Saigon River, some fifty miles from the beautiful bay.

Three miles from this French town, where we land facing bristling soldiery, is the old China city itself, claiming from seventy to a hundred thousand. During the latter part of the Bourbon reign, the Jesuit missionaries from France had difficulty with the Anamites in this portion of Cochin China, whose king resides up the River Hue, in an old walled city. France, in accordance with her usual policy, sided with the priests, sending a fleet to adjust a settlement, and enforce claims. The king was frightened. Demands were made, and a fine slice of territory was ceded to the French. This occurred during the reign of Louis XVI., noblest of all the Bourbon rulers.

The Anamites — evidently a mixture, afar in the past, of Malays and Chinese — are small in stature, and slovenly in appearance; chewing the betel-nut, which colors their lips, teeth, and tongue a dark, inky brown. Women are more excessive chewers than the men. Though a subject of discussion by our party, it was decided by a slight majority that their sooty, shriveled mouths excelled American tobacco-chewers in *nastiness !*

These women wear rings on their toes, ankles, wrists, and generally one in the nose. They sling the nude young child astride the hip, throwing the right arm around it as a protection. Their complexion is a dark olive or copper. Those residing back on the highlands, and in the interior, away from French civilization, are not only physically larger, but superior mentally and morally. History writes these people down as the original Chinese, — bold, brave, and unconquered by the Tartars. They do not shave their heads, nor wear clothing save around their loins.

The principal language spoken is French. The religion of the natives is Buddhism. The Bonzes are very courteous, allowing foreigners to inspect every thing in their temples. We are only a few degrees north of the equator. Intensely hot, it is the paradise of gnats and mosquitoes. Fahrenheit, 88°.

The country along the Saigon River is low, flat, and densely wooded, but excellent for rice-culture, the gum of lacquer, cinnamon, and many of the precious woods. The highlands afar back from the valley abound in fertile fields. Tropical fruits burden the markets. The city and valley-lands are unhealthy. This is acknowledged by the French. On account of the heat, business is suspended in the French part of the city from ten o'clock, A.M., till five o'clock, P.M.

FRENCH FASHION AND AMERICAN INDEPENDENCE.

The French are reported polite and fashionable. But what *is* fashion ? How far is it authoritative ? and who are subjects of the fickle goddess ? Sitting at the table aboard our steamer, the doctor was reminded, and I was twice asked, by the *garçon*, to appear in certain suits at certain times of

the day, — say the *dinner*-hour. It was a piece of impertinence ; and I sent the following note to the navy officer in
command of the steamer : —

COMMANDER OF "IRRAWADDY." *Sir*, — It is, in my estimation, nobler
to be a man, maintaining true moral independence, than to be a French-
man or an American. And as the two legitimate purposes of clothing
are to cover the body, and conduce to its comfort, will you have the
kindness to instruct your servants to give neither myself nor Dr. Dunn
further annoyance by suggesting what hour we dress for the day, or in
what style of dress we appear at the dining-table? *Fashion*, a heartless
tyrant, has no international standard ; and, if it had, I should be guided
entirely by my own judgment and good sense of propriety.
Respectfully thine,
J. M. PEEBLES.

The reply, prompt and gentlemanly, saved us from future
annoyances.

Society is like a light honeycomb, pretty but empty,
while fashion is the ruling queen of the nations. Rich and
poor, the stupid and the intelligent alike, fawn around, and
bow down to this stupid goddess. And if any individual,
man or woman, conscious of that moral independence inherent in the God-given nature, refuses allegiance to, or rises
to overthrow the mandates of fashion, a pig-headed public
raises the cry at once, " He's eccentric ! " " He does it to
attract attention ! " And the poor soul, finding no moral
support, is often whipped back into the popular rut, to
sheepishly trot along with the dawdling multitude. Down
in my soul's depths I detest, despise, loathe, and *hate* this
cringing worship paid at the shrine of fashion ; and be it
known to France in particular, that I will shave or not, wear
my hair long or short, and dress precisely as I please,
regardless of fashionable dandies or dictatorial aristocrats.

SINGAPORE.

Sing of Cuba, queen of the Antilles, if you choose; but
I'll sing of Singapore and its spice-fields, Singapore and its

waters of crystal and sapphire. The word, literally *Singa-pura*, from the Sanscrit *singa*, touching, and *pura*, city, implies the ancient " touching-city " for commercial traders between China and the countries west.

Nestling down to within some seventy miles of the equator, one would naturally suppose, though imbosomed in flowers and fadeless foliage, that Americans from the Northern States could not here live ; and yet they do. The green isles, the sea-breezes, the atmospheric moisture from frequent showers, and the financial facilities for traffic, reveal the reasons. There are really no seasons here, — not even the wet and dry of California and Asia Minor ; but a perpetual summer, with a remarkable equableness of temperature, crowns the year. All this said, nevertheless the climate must be enervating.

Just before reaching this unique city of 150,000, made up of Chinamen, indigenous Malays, Klings from Madras, Burmese, Siamese, Parsees, and Arabs, we crossed the 180th meridian west from New York, being almost directly opposite our home in New Jersey ; and yet, though feet to feet with Americans, we did not fall off into space, nor did the law of gravitation cease to fasten us to Mother Earth. Making into the harbor, the steamer passed between a large island covered with palms, and a cluster of little islets putting up from coral depths. At the feet of these were glittering white sands, while their summits were crowned with rich green jungles. Others had been cleared, their sides serried something like potato-fields, and planted with pine-apples.

The isle of Singapore is owned by the English. While there are about five hundred Europeans in the city, mostly English, it seems a general landing-place for the waifs of the world. Races are terribly mixed. This is a famous mart for articles in the line of jewelry. Their coral, sea-shells, precious stones, tiger's claws, birds-of-paradise, Chinese porcelain, and carvings in sandal-wood, are exceedingly beau tiful. Many Oriental imitations are sold by these natives for the genuine. A daily-expected steamer, bound for India in the opium-trade, detained us over two weeks. It is at present (June 22) the season of the monsoons in this latitude. Junks are turning Chinaward.

NATURAL BEAUTY OF THE MALAY LANDS.

In these Eastern archipelagoes and oceans, Nature puts human language to shame when it attempts a description of her luxuriance. These islands of loveliness, comparable to emeralds set in seas of silver, or gems glittering upon the bosom of hushed waters, their foliage reaching to the shimmering edge, where they dip their broad leaves in heaving waves; *these Indies*, the lotus-lands of the East, considering the geological formations, the Oriental vegetation, the magnificent forests musical with birds of gaudiest plumage, the cocoanut-palm (prince of palms for beauty and nobility), the groves of spices, where one eternal summer gilds hill and dale, — *all* these conspire to constitute the loveliest region on earth. It is not strange that certain theologians, ethnologically inclined, have fixed the Adamic paradise in the Malay Archipelago. Other islands have their charms, but these bear away the palm. Perfumed isles and aromatic airs are no fabled dreams. Stepping out under brilliant skies in evening-time, when the land-breezes were coming in, I have been literally fanned by soft winds laden with most delicious perfumes.

The Malays proper inhabit the Malay Peninsula and nearly all the coast-regions of Borneo, Sumatra, Celebes, and many of the smaller islands.

In this equatorial latitude, and the islands adjoining it, Alfred R. Russell, the distinguished naturalist and Spiritualist, spent eight years collecting an immense cabinet of plants, insects, birds, and animals.

Though the Malay Peninsula abounds in bananas, mangoes, mangosteens, gambier, nutmeg, pepper, bamboo-groves, gutta-percha forests, pine-apple plantations, tapioca uplands, clove and cinnamon gardens, it has its drawbacks in the way of insects, lizards, serpents, and tigers. Mosquitoes sing the same bloodthirsty tunes as in America. Though tarrying at the best hotel, our rooms are infested with flies, beetles, fleas, and slimy lizards, crawling upon the walls and ceiling. The other morning, upon rising, and lifting my pillow, out darted from under it a wretchedly ugly lizard! All poesy lands have their prose sides.

THE MALAYS AN OLD RACE.

Though the Malay Peninsula was unknown to Europeans till the arrival of the Portuguese in India about the year 1500, the race for weary ages possessed the knowledge of letters, worked metals, domesticated and utilized animals, cultivated fields, and led the commerce of the Pacific Ocean. Their language crops out not only in very remote islands to the east, but according to the English ethnologist, Mr. Brace, " in Madagascar, three thousand miles distant, the Malay words form one-seventh of the vocabulary of the islanders."

Dr. Prichard regarded it as settled that there was a Malay-Polynesian race, which, at a period before the influx of Hindooism, existed nearly in the state of the present New Zealanders.

Marsden declares that the main portion of the old " Malay is original, and not traceable to any foreign source." *Humboldt* considered the Malay-Polynesian languages to have been " primitively monosyllabic, with marked resemblances to the Chinese."

Crawford, who has made the Malays a study, says, after speaking of the "immemorial antiquity of their language," that the art of converting iron into steel has been immemorially known to the more civilized nations of the Malay Archipelago. There are Sanscrit inscriptions in Java, and some of the other Malay-peopled islands. The Malay annals, a blending of fact and fable, date back nominally to the reign of Alexander the Great. Among relics found, while excavating in some of these islands, are very ancient Chinese coins.

MALAY FEATURES, DRESS, AND DISPOSITION.

Standing upon the steamer before landing in Singapore, you see a motley crowd dressed in every possible costume, from the simple white hip-rag of the nearly naked Kling, the silken attire of the well-to-do Malay, and the everlasting blue of Chinamen, to the flowing dress of the Mohammedan Hadjee. Wealthy Chinamen dress, however, in fine style, having on these islands their carriages, and scores of servants.

The Chinese coolies carry every thing, from pails of water to cook-shops, on balancing shoulder-sticks; while the Klings, from Madras and the Coromandel coast, and the Malays also, carry their cakes, fruits, and wares in trays upon their heads.

The Chinese in these islands are not permitted to be policemen because of their belonging to secret societies among themselves. These coolies are frequently brought into the criminal courts; but a Malay seldom appears as a culprit. The Malayan costume consists of a *baju*, or jacket, a pair of short trousers, with a *sarong*, i.e., a piece of silk, wide at the top as at the bottom, gathered close around the waist. In addition to the *sarong*, the women wear a loose, sash-like garment thrown over the shoulders, called a *kabia*, which, to say the least, is cool and comfortable.

In complexion they are fairer than the men, — a handsome light olive. In married life they are noted for chastity, and the love of family. Owing to the comeliness of their features, their delicate hands, drooping lashes, fair faces, lustrous eyes, and ruby lips, many Europeans are charmed with them; and who, if they do not, *ought*, by every principle of justice, to marry them.

Though a degenerate race at present, they are naturally

proud, frank, generous, true to their friends, and affectionate in disposition. In *physique* they are well-proportioned. They step with an independent gait. They are *not* industrious. They have no acquisitiveness. In an ungenial clime, among selfish worldlings, they would starve. They exemplify the command, " Take no thought for the morrow." Some of them are endowed with rather a high order of intellect. Their foreheads, though full, are larger in the perceptive than the reflective range.

The Malay nobility, usually exceedingly wealthy, are called *Rajahs*. These, with the *Maha Rajahs*, a rank higher, are now educating their children in Europe. The Rajah of Johore has eighty thousand subjects. His position is nearly equal to that of a petty king in Continental Europe.

WHENCE THE MALAY RACE?

America, young and ambitious, is not *all* of the world. Who were the mound-builders of the West? From whence the aboriginal red Indians? Before the American Continent had been pressed by human feet, Asian civilizations had flourished and died. Saying nothing of theories pre-historic, there are solid reasons for believing that the Malays were originally a composite of Central Africans and Mongolians. In fact, both tradition and inscription unite in teaching, that, long ere the Pyramids reared their mighty forms, the Malays were conquered by powerful kings from the north. Twice brought under the yoke of foreign rulers from the north and north-east, they inherited from that nationality now known as the Chinese. Each invasion necessarily left the racial effect upon the posterity.

Do not shrug the shoulders at the mention of Africa. Neither Congo nor Congo negroes constitute *all* of Africa. And, further, all Ethiopians did not originally have thick lips, a flat nose, and short, knotty hair. Cushite history proves this. The color, however, was always dark, or jet black.   There is a lingering Aryan element in Central Africa. The New Guineans, set down by all ethnological writers as Malayans, have curly, crispy hair; it is also long and bushy, and of it they are very proud.   Whenever the negro element comes in collision with the Mongolian or Malay race, in its advanced stages, as in Asia, and more recently some of the Philippine Islands, it melts away much as do wild animals before civilization.

HOW CAME THE MALAYS INTO NATIONAL POSITION?

Subjective thinkers, as well as geologists, care little for Jewish records, Usher's, or any other theologian's calculations.   Ruins, monuments, inscriptions, and lingual roots, — these determine eras of civilization and the colonization of races.

Eastern traditions state that many, *very* many thousands of years since, when a traveler entered a distant country, having a different colored skin, he was supposed by the more superstitious to have been dropped from a star, to people a new portion of the earth; and accordingly the tribe that he visited gave him several wives, and sent him adrift to replenish and populate.   But to approach the historical, with inferences from monumental ruins, inscriptions, and suggestions from attending unseen intelligences, some eight thousand years since the Malay Peninsula, and a vast tract of country north of it, was the great half-way halting-ground between the Central Africans of the west, and the Chinese or more northern Mongolians of the east.   On these rich table-lands, abounding in wild grasses, grains, and fruits, intercrossing caravans with their merchandise rested and recruited.   Settlements commenced, intermarriages followed, villages, then cities; and finally an opulent kingdom was the result.   Becoming proud and depredatory, this kingdom warred with, and was conquered by, Tartar hordes and Mongolians; getting, among other consequences, a fervid infusion of Northern blood through the lax social relations then prevailing.

After the lapse of a few hundred years, they were again conquered by the Chinese and their allies, the conquerors in considerable numbers remaining in the country, softening the skin to a light copper, and straightening the hair, through intermixture in their social relationships. These causes, with various climatic conditions, constituted the Malay race, which about six thousand years ago were in their palmy periods. Their language, ever flexible, shows plainly that it has been acted upon both by the monosyllabic Chinese and the Sanscrit. The very word " Malay " is Sanscrit.

Inheriting Mongolian energy, and naturally sailors, these Malayans began at a very early period to emigrate, and colonize islands to the south and east. The north-east monsoons would take them first to Sumatra ; and then, considering the oceanic currents and prevailing winds, they would gradually drift southward and to the east. Evidently the mound-builders, and the descendants of *these*, the North-American Indians, were largely Malayan in origin. This long-unsolved problem admits of ethnic demonstration.

THE MALAYANS AMERICA-WARD.

While cruising across the Pacific, Capt. Blythen pointed out to us, on his North and South Pacific charts, *sixty islands* reported and located by navigators some two hundred years since, that have sunk from human sight. Some of these were said to have been inhabited. Cataclysms and convulsions were ever common along the volcanic zones of the tropics. A vast continent, something like the New Atlantis spoken of by Plato, was submerged in the Pacific, save the mountainous peaks, several thousands of years ago. Such of the aborigines as survived, upon the mountain-summits and high lands, intermingled maritally with roving, eastward-bound Malays. They crossed from island to island in crafts corresponding somewhat to their present *prahus*. Traversing the island-dotted waters through Polynesia, they reached the western coast of South America. Their conti·

nental course during the succeeding centuries was northward, through Mexico, to the great chain of northern lakes.
Ruins, symbols, and the crumbling pottery of the last of the
mound-builders and Mexicans, are almost identical with
ruins, carvings, and old roads in Malay-peopled lands.

The acute ethnological writer, D'Eichtal, declares that
"the Polynesian is an original civilization, and apparently
the earliest in the world; that it spread to the east and the
west from its focus in Polynesia, *or in a continent situated in
the same region, but now submerged;* that it reached America
on the one side, and Africa on the other, where it embraced
the Fulahs and Copts." He further suggests "that a germ
from the Polynesian cradle, falling into the valley of the
Nile, originated the ancient Egyptian civilization."

CUSTOMS COMMON TO MALAYS AND INDIANS.

The Rev. Mr. Keasbury, thirty years in the East, and one
of the best Malay scholars in the world, has, in keeping with
another gentleman, a list of words found both in the Malay
and the original dialects of the American continent. But
we have no space to adduce the argument from the similarity of language. Since starting upon this tour, I have seen
no Pacific Islanders, no people anywhere, that in general
features, color of skin and hair, carriage in walking, method
in sitting, and government by chiefs and sub-chiefs, so
closely resembled our better Indian tribes of the West and
South-west.

Traveling out into the country from Johore, and also up
the Peninsula (starting in at the Wellsley Province, opposite Penang), where monkeys and the ruder of the Malays
inhabit alike fields and forests, I either observed, or learned
from others, that these degenerate Malays, instead of shaving
the beard, pluck it out, as do the Indians of America.

Walking in streets and forest-paths, the woman strides
along in advance, the man following to ward off beasts of
prey. So with the Indians. In this country, by the way,

tigers, stealing up behind, pounce upon the victim, the fore-paw striking the back of the neck. Deaths by tigers are frequent.

The Malays generally bury their dead in a sitting position, interring with them implements of war, and food, as do some of our Indian tribes.

The Malay women, back in the mountainous districts, per-form all the hard labor, while the men hunt and fish. So with our Indians.

The Malayan-dyaks of Borneo, and others of the more warlike tribes, put showy feathers in their hair, and take a portion of the scalp from the head of the slain enemy as a trophy; and so with our Indians.

They wear their black hair loose and long, paint their faces in war-time, use the bow and arrow, are fond of tinsel jewelry, and never forget an injury, — *all* of which traits characterize American Indians. The above comparisons refer to the rustic tribes, however, rather than the higher classes of Malays.

THE " FALL OF MAN."

Under the droll drapery of Æsop's Fables nestle lessons sunny with moral beauty; so concealed in the Mosaic myth, " Adam's fall," there is a germ of truth. All through the East are moss-wreathed ruins, telling of golden ages and higher civilizations.

" In the province of Kedu," writes A. R. Wallace, " is the great temple of Borobodo. It is built upon a hill, and con-sists of a central dome, and seven ranges of terraced walls covering the slopes of the hills, forming open galleries. Around the magnificent central dome is a triple circle of seventy-two towers; and the whole building is six hundred and twenty feet square, and about one hundred feet high. In the terraced walls are niches containing four hundred fig-ures larger than life; and both sides of all the terraced walls are covered with bas-reliefs carved in hard stone, occupying an extent of nearly three miles in length. The Great Pyramid of Egypt sinks into insignificance," says Mr. Wallace, "when compared with this sculptured hill-temple in the interior of Java." There are other templed ruins and inscriptions, remember, in Malay-peopled countries and islands, long antedating this. Who were the projectors? — who the constructors? Ask the Malays: echo! Appeal to history: it is silent as the chambers of death.

THE RELIGION OF THE MALAYS.

In the thirteenth century, Mohammedan missionaries converted the Malays in the Straits of Malacca to Islamism, using persuasion instead of the sword. Their original religion, however, was entirely different. John Cameron, F.R. G.S., assures us that "such Malays as have embraced none of the more modern religions believe in some divine personality, corresponding to God; and a future life, where good men enjoy ecstatic bliss, and the wicked suffer purgatorial punishments." But "their religion," he adds, "is strangely mixed up with *demonology*. They believe that every person is attended by a good and a bad angel; the latter leading to sickness, danger, and sin, while the good angel seeks the individual's health and happiness." In their "lives, they are influenced more by fear than hope." They propitiate the wicked angel and the evil spirits. It is only at death that they ask the especial care of their good angel. They stand in no fear of the transition. Some of their ruins indicate a relationship theologically to the sun and serpent worshipers.

MALAY HOSPITALITY. — THE "ORANG-UTAN."

"The higher classes of Malays," writes Mr. Wallace, "are exceedingly polite, and have all the quiet ease of the best-bred Europeans." To this I will add, they are very kind, warm-hearted, and hospitable. Calling at a Malacca-Malay's palm-thatched dwelling, we were at once treated to tea, fruit, cocoanut-milk, and durians. This latter fruit is quite generally considered the choicest and most luscious fruit in the world ; and yet, like tomatoes, one must cultivate a taste for it. The odor of the shell is truly disgusting. The eatable substance is of a yellowish creamy consistence, tasting like a mixture of mashed beech-nuts, bananas, onions, strawberries, pumpkin-seeds, and sweet apples.

The children three, five, and seven years of age, playing about, perfectly nude, were quite shy of us. Though absolute nakedness in this climate is comfortable, the custom is quite too Adamic. These Mohammedan Malays circumcise between the years of eleven and fifteen ; and old and young strictly abstain from opium and liquors of all kinds. Mr. Hewick, Chief of Police in the Wellsley Provinces, accompanying us into the country to see Malay life, amused us, when returning, by sending a baboon species of the monkey up a smooth, limbless cocoanut-tree to pick some fruit. The ingenious method the cunning brute devised to twist the nuts from the tree showed a striking intelligence.

In the Malay language " *muniet* " is the term for monkey, " *karra* " for baboon, and " *orang* " for man. " *Orang-laut* " implies sea-people, or seafaring men ; " *orang-gunung* " is defined mountaineer, or a rustic, uncultivated man ; while " *orang-utan* " signifies literally a man of the forest, or the aboriginal people. The famous " man-like ape," to which Darwinian sympathizers give this name, is never so called by the natives, but is known among all Malay-speaking races under the name of " *mias.*" How easily words mislead, especially when an extreme theory is to be maintained !

Evolution — the great doctrine of evolution is true. But Darwin's straight-jacket method of interpreting it was not true. Man's inmost Spirit did not originate in, or spring up, from the monkey. Alfred R. Wallace is right — follow him — not Darwin.

CHAPTER XIV

THE little kingdom of Johore lies just across the straits from the isle of Singapore. Accompanied by our American Consul, Major Studer, a gentleman ever alive to the commercial relations of America, we called to see his majesty, the Maha-Rajah; who, if he does not sit

> "High on a throne of royal state, which far
> Outshone the wealth of Ormus and of Ind,"

has a fine palatial mansion, constructed in truly Oriental style. His "royalty" was absent, which left the secretary to do the etiquette of the palace. The drive across the island of Singapore, with the exception of the poor, vicious horses, was richly enjoyable. The Britains are famous in all foreign lands for excellent thoroughfares and an effective police. The Dutch are too rigid in their measures.

This excellent road above referred to is dotted and lined with bungalows, plantations laid out in exquisite taste, bamboo-hedges, and fan-palms, quite as useful as ornamental, called "the traveler's fountain." The out-jutting stems of these broad palm-leaves, collecting the night-dews, tender their cups of crystal water the following day to the weary, thirsting traveler. Surely God's living providence is everywhere manifest.

JOHORE.

Reaching this unique city of five thousand, we became the guests of James Meldrum, many years in the country, and owner of the largest steam saw-mills in Asia, employing five hundred men. His *bungalow*, situated upon a shady eminence, spans an extensive arc of enchanting scenery. "Bungalows," by the way, a *term* applied to all kinds of Eastern dwelling-houses having lofty ceilings and broad verandas, are built with reference to ventilation and coolness.

Mr. Meldrum saws the famous *teak*, as well as cedars, mahoganies, maraboos, kranjees, chungals, rosewood, sandalwoods, camphor-woods, &c. A report before me says, —

"The Johore forests cover an extent of about ten thousand square miles, and contain upwards of one hundred different kinds of timber-trees. These forests are being opened up by his highness the Maha-Rajah of Johore, K.C.S.I., K.C.C.I., &c., who is constructing a wooden railway into the interior. It will pass through dense virgin forests abounding in all the various kinds of timber-trees known in the Straits."

The Malay *Maha-Rajah* of Johore, being a strict Mohammedan, uses no wines, no liquors of any kind; and, further, he will permit the existence of no "house of ill-fame" in his dominion. Just previous to our arrival, he had broken up a den of prostitution established in New Johore by some Catholic Chinamen. Jesuit missionaries had converted these Chinese from Confucianism to Christianity! Is it strange that Mohammedans think Christians very immoral?

The Malays of these regions never, — no, *never*, drink intoxicating liquors of any kind. Such practices are forbidden by the Koran. Would not an infusion of Islamism into Christianity improve it, at least practically? The Arabian prophet taught no scape-goat atonement, no salvation through another's merits. Neither do Mohammedans in their mosques have "infidels" to *fan* them while they worship. Not so with Christians. In the Singapore English Church, built by convict-labor, sixteen "heathen" natives stand out under a scorching noonday sun on the "Lord's Day," pulling *punkas* to fan these ritualistic English Christians, while they drawlingly "worship God," saying, very sensibly, "*Have mercy upon us miserable sinners.*"

During this trip over to Johore, we saw monkeys leaping on trees, birds of rich plumage, a young elephant, a huge, slimy boa-constrictor just killed by the wayside, and the fresh skin of a tiger, which, while covering the ravenous brute, had concealed the remnants of many a man. In his stomach was found part of a breastbone, and several human hands. Government pays a handsome bounty upon tiger-killing.

A JUNGLE. — TIGERS.

What American has not read of the East-India jungles? Permit the pen to paint one. A jungle is a heavy forest of gigantic trees with a compact foliage of dark-green leaves. Under these grow up another tribe of trees, shorter, more umbrageous, and loaded with such wild fruit as mangosteens, mangoes, and jumbus. Beneath and around these again, there's a prolific growth never seen outside the tropics, — palms, rattans, ferns, and indescribable plants, literally woven together, like the "lawyer-hedges" of New Zealand, by a net-work of creepers and parasites. Such a forest is a jungle, the home of the tiger. I never passed one without thinking of tigers and boa-constrictors. Serpents — cold, slimy, treacherous, and poisonous — I loathe and despise. Eden's fable has nothing to do with this inborn dislike to crawling things. Men that tame and handle serpents, and women that pet poodle-dogs, reveal what they might as well conceal!

It was estimated, a few years since, that one man a day fell a victim to the crushing stroke of the tiger in Singapore, an island of about two hundred square miles. These tigers swim across the straits from Johore to the island. The distance is about two miles. The tiger stealthily strikes, and seizes the person by the back of the neck. Like other wild beasts, he is too cowardly to face a man. The Malays have the saying, "If you will only speak to a tiger, and tell him he can get better food in the jungle, he will spare you."

SPICY GROVES. — BEGGARS UNKNOWN.

Descriptions of cinnamon-trees, clove-trees, and others of this nature, might be interesting. Let a brief sketch of the nutmeg-tree suffice. Handsomely formed, and beautiful in proportion, it grows from twenty-five to thirty feet high, and is thickly covered with polished dark-green leaves, which continue fresh the year round. The fragrant blossoms are thick, wavy bells, resembling the hyacinth or lily-of-the-valley. When the fruit is ripening, it might be mistaken, say the old cultivators, for the peach, bating the pink or yellow cheek. When the nut inside is ripe, the fruit splits down, remaining half open. If not now picked, it soon falls. On the same branch — as with the orange — may be seen the bud, blossom, and the ripening fruitage. Nutting-fields in the Singapore region have nearly gone to decay. A cureless blight has rendered their spice-gardens unprofitable.

Want of energy in the Malay Islands, and other portions of the East, has become a proverb. There is little inducement to labor where Nature is so unsparing. All individuals are about as lazy as they can afford to be! Two hours of daylight in the Malay Peninsula is enough for a native to build a decent "shanty," and thatch it. Beggars are unknown away from seaports and cities. They have but to lift the hand, to pluck plenty of fruit. Most delicious pine-apples sell for fifty cents a hundred in the Singapore market.

VOLCANIC BELTS, AND MINERALS.

One of the great volcanic belts of the globe stretches along across these Malayan Islands. The breadth of the belt

is about fifty miles. Java alone has over forty active volcanoes. Borneo and New Guinea are just outside of the
volcanic zone. Peru and South-American coasts faintly compare with these islands in terrible lava upheavals. The
Javanese eruption occurring at Mount Galunggong, in 1822,
destroyed twenty thousand inhabitants. A gentleman just
from Batavia informs me that there has recently been
another serious convulsion upon the island. Instead of liquid
lava, as at Vesuvius, heated sands, stones, and red-hot ashes
were thrown up with great violence. "Why," is it asked,
"do Europeans live upon these islands?" The love of
money, is the only answer. Gold in this century is god.

A granitic mountain-chain runs the whole length of the
Malay peninsula. It has thermal springs, but no active
volcanoes. The mountains are not over a third as high as
those in Sumatra and Java. This region is famous for minerals, — iron, copper, tin, and gold. Malacca and Siam are
said to be the greatest tin countries in the world.

I met several times "Charlie Allen," the young man
who accompanied Mr. Wallace during his prolonged explorations in the East Indies. He had just come down from the
Chindrass gold-mines in Malacca. These are forty-five miles
from the old city of Malacca, and fifteen from Mount Ophir.
They promise "rich," as Californians say. "Oh for American energy to work them!" exclaimed Mr. Allen.

What interested me more than the quartz specimen he
exhibited, was the description of an ancient, yet substantially built road during some important excavations. It lies
embedded deep under a modern thoroughfare, yet revealing
an entirely different kind of constructive conception. Who,
what people, built it? Echoing ages are dumb.

BIRD'S-NEST SOUPS.

As turtle-soup is a great dainty with English epicures, so
are bird's-nest soups among Chinamen at Singapore and
elsewhere. The Indian Archipelago, and adjacent rocky

isles, are the harvest-fields for these delicacies. The nests, a sort of gluey, gelatinous substance, seen in China markets, are found along the rocks, in deep and damp caves, and are the choicest if gathered before the birds have laid the eggs. The nests resemble in shape those of the chimney-swallows in America. The finest qualities of nests are when they are clean and white as wax: the poorest are those gathered after the young birds have flown away.

THE UPAS.

That terrible *Gueva Upas*, — the valley of poison, — written about many years ago by a Dutch surgeon at Batavia, and afterwards by others, without inspecting the locality, proved to be a hoax. True, there is a valley, grim, bare, and as destitute of vegetable as animal life, caused by the deadly nature of the carbonic and sulphurous acid gases that continually escape from the crevices and soils in this volcanic region. There are numerous plants and shrubs more poisonous than the Upas. Geographies, as well as Bibles, need revising.

BETEL-NUT. — GUTTA-PERCHA. — COCOANUT-GROVES.

The bewitching betel-nut, used by and so staining the lips and teeth of the natives, is common in Cochin China, Sumatra, Java, and tropical Indies. Its exhilarating fascination is said to excel even tobacco. Penang is the more common name of the nut; accordingly Pulo-Penang signifies betel-nut island. While growing on the graceful and slightly tapering trees, they look something like nutmegs. When ripe, and broken into small pieces, the natives prepare them with the siri-leaf and the unslacked lime of shells. Though producing a dreamy, stimulating effect, it must necessarily injure the membranous surfaces of the mouth.

Gutta-percha abounds in both Singapore and Penang. The Malays term the tree *tuban*. It grows large, has a smooth bark and wide-spreading branches. The tree is not only tapped to get the juice, but often literally girdled, destroying the tree itself. This forest vandalism is now forbidden. The juice — life-blood of the tree — is caught in cocoanut-shells, poured into pitchers made from the joints of large bamboos, and then conveyed to caldrons for boiling and the further preparations for sale.

Cocoanut-groves, being planted in horizontal lines, present a most beautiful appearance. These trees, running up some forty feet, unbroken by leaf or branch, are roofed with deep green foliage. The nuts grow in clusters between the roots of the leaves and branches at the top. If not picked when ripe, they drop, and are broken. Planters of large groves tell me that the noise of falling nuts in night-time breaks the silence with sounds " weird and ghostly." Falling upon the skulls of the natives, they sometimes break them. When the oil is sought, they are allowed to ripen. The nuts sell for a penny each. The watery milk within them is considered as cooling and healthy as nutritious.

FIRE-FLY JEWELRY.

Lower races and tribes in all lands are fond of pearls, precious stones, jewelry; — *display* of all kinds. The Malays, unable to purchase diamonds, have a little cage-like fixture, in which they imprison a fire-fly. This, excited, continues to give out perpetual flashes, quite excelling in brilliancy the diamond itself. The natives are sufficiently humane to set them free when the evening party is over. The poor things are not, as some writers have said, impaled on golden needles, that, by increasing the agony, the glitter of the flash may be intensified. The flash has more the appearance of electricity than phosphorescence. But what an idea ! — imprisoning harmless insects to attract attention, and minister to human vaɪ ity !

OFF TO CALCUTTA, VIA PENANG.

Left Singapore, June 27, on the steamer, "The States-man," under the command of Capt. Valiant. This line — running between China and Calcutta — is engaged in the opium-trade. The accommodations are excellent; both the captain and his interesting lady, Mrs. Valiant, striving to their utmost to make the voyage pleasant and homelike.

Penang, a nearly circular island, off from the Malacca coast, contains some seventy thousand acres; and its history is the history of the "British East India Company" in its efforts to get a foothold in the Malay Peninsula. The island, laying high claims to beauty of scenery, seems a mass of hills, rising like cones from the water's edge, near the sum-mits of which are the neat, tasty bungalows of the residents, surrounded by palms, pepper-vines, fruit-trees, and cocoanut-groves. In the harbor hardly a ripple dances upon the glassy waters. Crossing it to visit Mr. Hewick, an official over in the Wellsley Province of Malacca, the phosphores-cent flames (when returning) flashing up at the dipping of the natives' oars, gave it the seeming of sailing through a sea of fire. Penang, like all the Oriental cities in these lati-tudes, is peopled with Malays, Chinese, Klings, and other Hindoo derivatives. The town covers about one square mile. The approach to it, through emerald isles, was magnificent.

MOUNT OPHIR.

Rounding the most southern point of land in Asia, and hugging the Malacca coast toward Burmah and India, we had a fine view of Mount Ophir, four thousand feet high. Whether this be the biblical Ophir, or not, is unimportant; but who honeycombed the mountain with shafts? who here searched for gold in the distant past? This is an interesting inquiry. Of the location of the scriptural Ophir, nothing is known that will positively fix the geographical position. It was a place with which the Jews and Tyrians carried on a

lucrative trade in the time of Solomon, twenty-eight hundred years since. At this period the Jews were unacquainted
with iron, knowing only bronze, silver, and gold. Their
bronze they received from the Tyrians. Half barbarous, they
had no commerce till David conquered Edom (or Idumea),
giving them some coast on the Red Sea. The Jewish crafts
that traded with Ophir may have been the "navy of Tarshish;" and this Tarshish may have been a Tyrian port on
the Red Sea, — the part known, perhaps, as the Gulf of Suez.

The celebrated German Orientalist, Lassen, places Ophir
somewhere about the debouchement of the river Indus.
His theory is founded upon resemblances between the Hebrew and Sanscrit names of the commodities brought from
Ophir. There is no resemblance, however, between the
ancient method of working the Ophir mines, and the copper
mines bordering Lake Superior — worked by whom? The
mound-builders. But who were the mound-builders?

When — who by — and how were the Pacific Islands
peopled, are still unsettled questions. It was my privilege
to meet on this last voyage Hon. S. W. Baker, late Premier
of Tonga, whose brain was an encyclopædia of knowledge
relating to the customs of the Malays and the Pacific Islanders generally. He is now a resident of Auckland, New Zeal-
and. His description of seeing the formation of a volcano
near Tongatuba was thrillingly interesting. It was preceded
by an earthquake shock. The volcano opened up from the
ocean, and volumes of steam, of carbonic and sulphurous gas
shot up in fiery jets over a thousand feet. Immense quantities of matter were thrown up. The crater soon became two
miles in circumference. Volcanos and islands are ever rising
and sinking in the ocean.

CHAPTER XV.

SPIRITUAL SÉANCES ON THE INDIAN OCEAN.

OUT on the waters restless and sea-tossed, deprived of daily journals and libraries, how naturally the mind turns to that inexhaustible field of research, spirit-communion!

Dr. Willis, a medical spirit, controlling the medium, said in his off-hand, epigrammatic manner: —

"Disease is obstruction. Vital phenomena are profound studies. The human system is interpermeated by a very complex network of nerves. The brain, comparable to a sounding-bell, echoes through these nerves the condition of every portion of the physical organism. This is why I touch the head in diagnosing disease through the Doctor. Certain nerves allied to the *medulla oblongata* throw their sensitive branches across the back of the neck. A current of air striking this part is quite certain to produce colds, catarrhs, and serious neuralgic affections. Wearing long hair, therefore, is a preventive. The ancients in Oriental countries understood this. . . . I see no deleterious effects in your abstinence from meat-eating. And yet considering the formation of the teeth, with the make-up of the whole organic structure, I favor it; that is, considering humanity as it is. The system requires oils, as well as materials for muscle. But animal oils are more clogging to the brain than vegetable. . . . Color affects the health. Red should never predominate in the sick-room, especially if the patient is nervously sensitive. It is an excitant. Pale blue and

cream colors are quieting. Sunlight is a natural stimulant
Pure air is indispensable. Diet, and the right use of water,
are helps. The ancient Romans indulged in tepid baths,
followed by sun-baths. The will-power is a wonderful
restorative. Our treatment, including the above, is, you know,
magnetic and medicinal. Chronic complaints require medicines : *these* we magnetize and vitalize. Nervous affections
readily yield to magnetic treatment, providing mediums are
healthy, and temperamentally adapted to patients. Promiscuous mingling of magnetisms is deleterious, inducing nervous unbalance, and .opening the way for obsessions. Those
so inclined pursue the study of medicines in spirit-life, that
they may benefit the inhabitants of earth."

SÉANCE II.

Mr. Knight, entrancing, said, —

. . . " I see, looking at the mental workings of your brain,
that the extreme contradictions in the teachings of spirits
disturb you. . . . In previous conversations, we have told
you that the spirit-spheres — hundreds in number — are
inhabited by those just adapted to them intellectually and
morally ; and, as the spheres, such the aims and acts of
the spirits peopling them. Death is not a Saviour ; nor does
it produce any immediate, miraculous change. . . . Those
basking in the higher conditions of purity, truth, and love,
shed or impart the divine influence of the sphere from which
they come. And the same law applies to the lower spheres.
As there are evil-minded men, so are there evil spirits, self
ish, scheming, wicked spirits ! And to offer suggestions
relative to the means of avoiding the influences of these, is
the object of my present visit.

" I. In order to know men, you must try them : so to
fathom the real purposes of spirits, try *them*, *test* them by
rigid observation and patient experience ; and, further,
study the effects they produce upon their mediums.

" II. All mediums, not controlled by a fixed and reliable

circle of three or more spirits, are subject to such deleterious influences as low spirits may choose to throw around
them. And the control of this class of spirits is often
beyond the power of the guardian spirit, who may not have
the advantage of an established circle. The immediate
power of control lies not in superior intelligence or spirituality, but in magnetic force, or the great will-power of the
spirit. Entrancement is the result of the mesmeric influence of spirits; and it excels that of mortals only in this,
that it proceeds from spiritual beings, relieved from the
grossness of the flesh. The inference is, that persons hold
ing indiscriminate intercourse with spirits through mediums
unprotected by circles of pure, exalted spirits, are liable to
be flattered, and to receive false communications from spirits
under assumed names.

"III. Guardian spirits with fixed circles, and deep desires
to promulgate truth, seldom allow their mediums to be controlled by others than members of their own circle. Each
mortal has a guardian spirit; and the assistants of this guardian are properly denominated guides. A guardian spirit,
giving communications from spirits outside the circle to
mortals, — his own circle acting as means of conveyance, —
always states his non-responsibility relative to the message.

" The laws of mental science should be diligently studied,
and applied to mediumship. And all persons developing as
mediums should seek from their *guardian* the immediate
formation of a sympathizing circle in which they have faith,
and upon whom they can rely. When this is *not* done,
mediums, if not seriously injured, are often led into vice and
crime, — crimes instigated by low, undeveloped spirits. And,
further, they produce perversions, nervous diseases, obsessions, and insanity. Entering upon the career of mediumship,
therefore, is treading a pathway of danger and responsi-
bility. Incipient development should be carefully guarded.
Much depends upon mediums themselves. They should not
only · carefully remain away from improper society, but

should keep their minds upon subjects high and spiritual, in prayer seeking such controlling intelligences as must necessarily benefit humanity.   On the other hand, if they take the opposite course, — seeking such spirits as promise wealth by finding treasures, such as promise fame and worldly glory, or such as will pry into the secrets of others from selfish motives, — they will certainly be led to ruin.   As self-denial, as abnegation of good to one's self, and earnest labors for others' benefit, gives that for which one has *not* sought, — *happiness;* so the converse is true, that seeking for comfort and for self-aggrandizement at the expense of others, leads to one's utter defeat and destruction.

"The reality, the philosophy, of spirit-control, then, are matters of almost infinite importance.   And the subject should be approached with care and caution, and be used only by the wise, by the pure in purpose, for mental growth and higher spiritual attainments.   These ends sought, and humanity will reap the rich reward for which the faithful few have toiled, — the universal ministration of angels, the enlightenment of the races, and the redemption of the world!"

· SÉANCE III.

A French Normandy spirit, claiming to have been in the higher existence some three hundred years, coming by permission of the circle, advocated these theoretical dogmas : —

1. "There is no God ; *nothing* in the universe of being but matter, and the negative forces in matter."

2. "Annihilation is true ; or, a conscious future existence, in the sense of endlessness, is a farce.   Spiritual beings, by becoming more pure and etherealized, are finally absorbed in the great ocean of refined matter, — snuffed out, losing their consciousness and their identity."

3. "Fatalism is a truth.   Man is not responsible for an act of his life. All things, including men and their actions, are fated, or necessitated to be precisely as they are.   Man is a thing."

These exploded theories, once popular among atheists in France, are still taught by this shrewd, intelligent spirit.

They were grounds of sharp debate between us during several sittings. It was a drawn battle. Grant him his premises, and he will succeed admirably in the argument. Dispute them, demanding the proof of his proofs, and the foundation of his premises, and he fails to establish his untenable positions. He is evidently sincere and conscientious, delighting to propagate his metaphysical theories in spirit-life. Can any one conceive of notions that spirits have not taught? The lesson of these controversies was this : Spirits are fallible, and many of them long continue, though disrobed of mortality, to hug their earthly ideas and idiosyncrasies. Therefore, in listening to the teachings of immortals, we must be governed entirely by our intuitions and maturest judgment. Reason is the final judge.

SÉANCE IV.

The spirit Aaron Knight present, the following conversation ensued : —

Now that you have come, I desire your opinion upon the subject of my thoughts for the past few days.

" I should be happy to hear the substance of them."

Spending the winter in London, a few years since, I was deeply interested, listening to Mr. Tyndall's famous lecture upon " Dust," delivered in the Royal Institution. The professor clearly proved that the air is filled with fine atoms and living germs, which, inbreathed, enter the human body. He also explained how dust, and other unseen particled substances, might be filtered away by means of cotton-wool tightly impacted, and worn over the mouth. And M. Pasteur, a French scientist, carrying the investigation a step further, made filters of gun-cotton, using that variety which is soluble in ether. The filters, having done their work, were dissolved in ether ; and the solution, when microscopically examined, was found to contain millions of organized germs, — living entities. These could not only be seen, but the genera and species could be detected. Therefore the very atmosphere we breathe is full of air-borne germs and living life-cells. And these, for some wise purpose, must be continually entering into the human organization, must they not?

" Certainly: and you have suggested a subject of vast importance; one relating to, if not involving, the very origin of living beings. Logically speaking, there is *no* creation, — that is, the creation of something from nothing. Surveying earth and spirit-life, I see only evolution or unfoldment; and so pre-existence is true. The minutest monad in space is intelligent on its plane. Intelligence, or mind, is a result, or an effect of essential spirit and matter. But as these were never separated, and as the cause was eternal, so was, and so *must* be the effect also; which effect *was* and *is* intelligence. There are no vacuums. Interstellar spaces are filled with the life-principle, with infusoria, cells, and unseen atoms. Nothing but life can sustain life. Infusorial animalcula, and monadic germ-cells of life, pass into the cranial sensorium by organic attraction and imbibation. In the human organism they become more thoroughly vitalized; and in the brain itself they receive necessary magnetic influences prior to the projected descent by will-power, through the spinal column and seminal glands, to their conceptive destinies. The brain, remember, cradles, rather than generates spermatozoic germs aflame with conscious life. These, pre-existent, were afar back in the measureless past aggregating, throwing off, accreting, pulsing, and passing through various occult processes preparatory to incarnation. As in the acorn, germinally hidden, lies the oak, so in the spermatozoic life-germ, the future man."

SÉANCE V. — QUESTIONS ANSWERED BY THE SPIRITS.

" The cross is the most angular of geometrical figures; and, though connected with the martyred death of Jesus, it originated as an objective symbol in the phallic ages, and referred primarily to generation." . . .

" Emanations electic and magnetic, from the physical and

spiritual bodies, extend outward from the person quite a distance; and, although indicating, they do not unmistakably index the mental characteristics. And so the aural lights, and odylic sprays from the brain, give only the general bent and tendency of the mind." . . .

" Undoubtedly I could go to the planets; but I've no desire to so do. My work as yet is connected with the earth. Parisi's researches lead him in such directions. I think he has visited Jupiter and other planets." . . .

" The future is more important than the past; the destiny than the origin of humanity. Though generally outlined by your guardian angel, your future, morally considered, is not irrevocably fixed. Man is a mental and moral, as well as a physical being. To all moral beings endowed with reflection, there is a field of moral action. *You* are now paving the highway your feet must press in spirit-life, and laying, too, the foundation-stones of the temple you will inhabit. That chain of pearls was not a mythic farce, but a reality put around your neck when reaching the years of accountability by Parisi Lendanta, who for a time was John's medium. These pearls magnetically reflect, otherwise spiritually mirror, the deeds of your whole life, — deeds and events that you will be necessitated to read when entering the higher state of existence. Personal identity implies memory, and memory retribution. This is the judgment, — the opening of the books." . . .

" Living a celibate life for the purpose of boastingly saying, ' I am a celibate, I am pure : stand by, for I am holier than thou,' is selfish, and therefore morally deleterious; but if in laboring, on the other hand, to save others from passion, from fleshly gratifications, and *all* that opposes chastity and absolute purity, men become virgin celibates pure-minded and spiritual, then are they truly angelic. Such, having been raised from the dead, walk in the resurrection.'

Memory serving me, Mr. Knight, you once informed me that you had been privileged to attend councils of the glorified in supernal spheres, — that you there saw sages, seers, martyrs, and among them the Apostle John, with whom, as a pupil, you had held many interviews. This deeply interested me ; and, if consistent, will you answer certain inquiries relating to matters with which John, in his period of time, must have been conversant ?

" Certainly, to the best of my ability."

Where was John born ?

" In Syria. The Assyrians were once a great and truly enlightened nation, occupying a prominent position in Asia. But, by formidable combinations of foreign powers, their territory was conquered, and their national name abbreviated to Syria. He lived in that mountainous portion of Syria known as Judea ; which word was abridged from Jew-deity, so called because of Jewish reverence for Jehovah, the tutelary god of the Jews."

Did he travel in different countries ?

" Yes ; he traveled not only into the remotest provinces of Assyria, but even into Egypt and Persia. John was a linguist, highly educated for that period, and conversant with the teachings of Plato and Buddha. John and James were most intimately associated in their apostolic life. Occasionally John served as an interpreter for Jesus.

" Returning from a long season of travel in the East, he found his parents in great disrepute from connecting themselves with the Nazarenes, known at that time as Nazarretas, a poorer branch of the Jews, charged with sensualism, with holding intercourse with familiar spirits, and believing in the immediate coming of the Messiah. This sect originated long before Jesus' time."

Did the prophet Daniel impress these visions upon John's mind ?

" No : John was not only highly inspirational, but was a trance-medium ; often leaving his body, and traveling as a spirit in the highest spheres.   Those Apocalyptic images symbolized eras and principles.

" Written in the mystic language of correspondence, and little tampered with by scribes and Christian copyists, John's revelations are capable of an outer and *inner* interpretation. Inspirational men of those times understood them.   Jesus and the apostles constituted a sort of secret society among themselves.   The similarity of Daniel's and John's visions are traceable to oneness of nationality, and similarity of culture in the schools of the prophets."

What were the " deeds of the Nicolaitans " that Jesus " hated " ?

" John was Jesus' medium after he passed to the heavenly life from Calvary ; and he inspired John to write to the seven churches, i.e., the seven sympathizing assemblies of believers in Asia.   The " deeds of the Nicolaitans" were hypocrisies and the " unfruitful works of darkness."   The clan originated with one Nicolas, who sought to compromise the principles of Jews and Christians.   They were policy-men, full of flattery, and given to hypocrisies and licentious practices ; which ' deeds Jesus hated.' "

Who was Melchisedec, King of Salem ?

" There were two, and hence the confusion.   One was a spirit.   The other, a distinguished personage remote from the tenting Abraham, was called the ' King of Peace,' because baptized of the Christ-spirit.   To him Abraham paid tithes. The ancestors of Abraham were Aryans given to war and pillage."

Who were the Essenians ?

" A rigid and exclusive people, originally known as As-senians.   Strictly constructing the moral law, they were stern reformers, very industrious, and inclined to be self-righteous.   Those entering the inner court of the order were diviners and celibates.   Joseph, John the Baptist, Jesus, the apostles John and James, and nearly all of the disciples, were Essenes."

Who were the spirit-guides of Jesus?

" He had a large circle, over two hundred attending spirits, — ' a *legion*.' They were mostly from the earlier Jewish prophets; and among them were Moses, Elijah, Isaiah, Jeremiah, as well as sages from India, China, and Persia."

Do the prayers of sectarian Christians affect Jesus?

" Yes: the millions of Christians praying to and persistently calling upon Jesus, very slightly and indirectly affect him; and I must say not pleasurably, because of incorrect ideas concerning him and his mission, and because they ask him to do what they themselves should do. . . . The scriptural records of Jesus are very imperfect. He did not whip the money-changers out of the temple, but so sharply rebuked them that they voluntarily left. Neither did he call men ' swine,' ' dogs,' and ' whited sepulchres;' but said, ' If you persist in your unrighteousness, others will compare you to whited sepulchres.' . . . Jesus was overshadowed by spirit-presences from the sacred moment of conception, and therefore the prophetically expected of the Nazarettas. After the anointing, and descent of the baptismal Spirit, he was Jesus Christ, pre-eminent; the greatest medium ever born upon this earth. And in him, as apostolically expressed, ' dwelt the fullness of the Godhead bodily,' — that is, the full power of the Christ-spirit. And the races will ultimately acknowledge the sublimity of his precepts, as well as his moral superiority among the world's Saviours. The great moral battle in the future as we see it will not be between Spiritualism and true Christianity, but between Spiritualism and a cold, chilling, dreamless materialism. Christianity is becoming more broad, spiritual and tolerant, and Spiritualism is becoming more Christly and constructive. In the coming centuries, therefore, the twain shall become one."

CHAPTER XVI.

ENGLAND'S flag waves over India! The republic that is to come will be founded in justice, equality, and peace.

We have spent the day rolling and tossing upon the Bay of Bengal. I shall spell it hereafter Ben*gall*, emphasizing the last syllable. It deserves the bitter epithet. For three full days we endured a terrible monsoon-storm. It was a cyclone, save the rotary motion usually attending these hurricanes. The frightened Jews aboard rushed for Moses and the Prophets, and began to intone the psalms in Hebrew. The wind, increasing, came in maddened gusts; the waves surged and heaved; the lightnings flashed; the rain fell in sheets; the fore-stay-sail struggled in tatters; trunks, tables, upset; the dishes jingled in scattered fragments; the Fates and the Furies seemed, in fact, to have let loose the very artillery of the hells! Oh, it was fearful! The following day we passed a wreck. What became of the crew — what? Our ship, under the command of Capt. Valiant, behaved valiantly. It was a relief to sail into the Hoogly, one of the river-mouths through which the Ganges empties into the ocean.

INDIA.

Oh, marvelous country! Land of tree-worship, serpent-worship, the lotus-flower, and the mystic *ling*-land of the ancient Vedas, and those unparalleled epics the Ramayána and the Máhábharatá with its hundred thousand stanzas! land of the ascetic Rishis, the eighteen Puranas, and the *Tri-Pitaka* of the Buddhists! land of pearl-built palaces, templed caves, marble pillars, dust-buried ruins, walled cities, mud villages, and idolatrous worship! These, *all* these, are among the sights, the lingering memories, of India's mingled glory and shame.

When legendary Rome was a panting babe, and proud Greece a boasting lad, overshadowed by Egyptian grandeur, India was gray-bearded and venerable with years, worshiping one God, and using in conversation the musical Sanscrit, a language not only much older than the Hebrew, but conceded by all philologists to have been the richest and most thoroughly polished language of the ages. Well may India have been considered the birthplace of civilization, and the primitive cradle-bed of the Oriental religions.

APPROACHING THE LAND OF THE BRAHMAN.

Steaming through wind and wave out of the Bay of Bengal, Indiaward, we entered the broad mouth of the sluggish Hoogly, one of the outlets of the Ganges, and consequently to Hindoos a sacred stream. Calcutta is something like a hundred miles from the mouth of this river. Though the banks are low and nearly level, the stretching jungle thickly shaded, and the cultivation only ordinary, the stately palms, cocoanut-groves, and luxuriant vegetation, along this winding Mississippi of the East, rendered the scenery decidedly attractive.

Just previous to reaching the city, we passed the royal mansions of the ex-king of Oude. This prisoner of state, though despising the English, as do the rajahs generally, maintains much of his kingly magnificence, and gets, besides, a yearly stipend from the English government. A Mohammedan in religion, preferring polygamy to monogamy, his social instincts are said to be decidedly animal. Several European women grace — rather *disgrace* — his harem. Within the inclosure of his private, high-walled grounds, he keeps quite a menagerie of wild beasts, and continues in repair a large artificial mound, said to contain two thousand hissing serpents. It was feared, at one time, that he would let loose beasts and serpents upon the city.

CALCUTTA.

Quite early in July, by the steamer "Statesman," we reached the capital of British India, — the famous City of Palaces. The impertinence of custom-house officers, dilated upon by some of our fellow-passengers, proved a fraud. They were simply gentlemen doing their duty.

The hot, rainy season had just commenced. It was truly oppressive the first few days. In the city, and along the Delta of the Ganges, the mercury frequently rises to one hundred and twenty degrees, reminding one of the sun-scorched clime of Africa. In landing, half-naked coolies clamored loudly for our baggage; actually they excel the New-York hackmen! Dr. Dunn, fighting his way through the crowd bravely, soon saw the trunks safely aboard the *Gharrie* for "The Great Eastern." The rooms in these Asiatic hotels are high, commodious, and Oriental, even to the *punkas*.

TERRITORY AND ENGLISH RULE.

The empire of India, extending over a territory of a million and a half square miles, equals in size all Europe except the Russias. Swarming with two hundred millions of people, exhibiting almost an endless diversity of soils, productions, and climate, the deltas of India's great rivers are befitting granaries for the world. And England, claiming that the sun never sets upon her dominions, holds direct rule over three-fourths of this vast country.

Early in the seventeenth century, British cupidity, looking at the immense wealth of Indian kings and princes, coveted their possessions. Under the pretext of Christianizing, and other reasons, a cause for war was manufactured. Reck-

less of justice, fraternity, and the New-Testament principles
of peace, England, in brief, decided upon a war of conquest
for territory and trade, for gold, diamonds, and precious
stones.   No historian pretends to whitewash Britain's course
of crime and infamy in the East.   Learned Brahmans understand that history well, and, understanding, secretly hate
English rulership.   Still they prefer Englishmen to Mohammedans for masters.   Disguised in any way, however, slavery
is *slavery*, — a condition to be hated!

The "mild Hindoo" is a common term in the Orient; and
while the Hindoo is mild, forbearing, peace-loving, and con-
templative, the Englishman is ambitious, stern, and dictatorial.   The theistic reformer, Keshub Chunder Sen, sensibly
said, in a late Calcutta speech, "Muscular Christianity has
but little to do with the sweet religion of Jesus; and it is
owing to the reckless, warlike conduct of these pseudo-
Christians, that Christianity has *failed* to produce any whole-
some *moral influence* upon *my countrymen*."

There was a monstrous mutiny in 1756; there have been
minor mutinies since; and, mark it well, there is destined to
be another, eclipsing in blood and carnage all the others.
The Aryan-descended Indians love liberty and self-government.

WHENCE THE HINDOOS?

The Aryan tribes inhabiting Central Asia entered India
by the northern passes, and descended first the valley of the
Indus, and then that of the Ganges, attaining their full
strength and development along the rich alluvial valley-
lands of the latter river.   They brought with them agricultural implements, some of the fine arts, and the elegant
Sanscrit.   "Brought it from where? or in what country did
it originate?"   The inquiry, natural enough, shall be noticed
hereafter.

In this great and fertile country, the Aryans — primitive
Hindoos — located themselves in comparative security.   The

aborigines, supposed by some to be of " Turanian descent,"
fled, in many cases, to the mountain fastnesses before them,
as though conscious of their physical inferiority.

The Aryan type, including the pre-historic races of Central and Northern Africa, the Caucasians of Europe, the
Assyrians of Western Asia, and the fair-skinned, Sanscrit-
speaking people who entered India from the north, developed, wherever it settled, marvelous civilizations.   The
purest Aryan blood at present is found in Northern India ;
but wherever within the bounds of the Indian Empire to-
day you find light-complexioned, noble-featured Brahmans,
you find direct descendants of the ancient Aryans.

The non-Aryan natives, called, in the Rig-Veda, Dasyns,
Rakshasas, Asaras, and others with outlandish-sounding
names, were dark-complexioned, yet timid, spiritually-minded
tribes.   Remnants of them, ever the physical inferiors of
their northern invaders, are still found in the mountainous
districts of Interior and Southern India, known now under
the names *Todas*, *Gonds*, *Bheels*, *Kols*, *Korkus*, *Bygás*,
Chamars, down to the *Pariahs*.   Some of these tribes have
curly hair and protruding lips.   The infusion of the Aryan
element into the aboriginal stock took place rapidly ; and
yet the observant traveler among them will come upon
stratum after stratum, showing in a distinct manner the
intermediate stages between the two races.   Generally, the
physical type diverges from aboriginal features and manners
towards Brahmanical Hindooism.   Some of these aboriginal
races have so verged towards the status of Brahmanism that
they have assumed the " sacred thread," claiming member-
ship with the " twice-born caste."

GROWTH AND LITERATURE OF THE ARYAN HINDOOS.

None of the other Oriental countries have clung to so
many of their primitive customs, retained so much of
their early literature, experienced so few internal dissensions, or suffered so little from ancient Vandal invasions, as

the Hindoos. Strongly sea-guarded on three points of the compass, the dangerous defiles and mountainous ranges along the northern boundaries of India presented formidable barriers to conquering hordes from Northern Asia. Accordingly, while the nationalities of Central and Northern Africa, in pre-Pyramidal times, as well as the populous countries of Central and Eastern Asia, were engaged in wars both civil and aggressive, destroying, so far as possible, all the historic monuments of antiquity, and exterminating every vestige of literature within the enemy's reach, the Aryans of India seem to have been left in comparative peace and isolation, — left to work out the problem of civilization and mental culture, unaffected by foreign influences or ravaging internal revolutions.

The advancement for a time was all that could be desired. The Aryan Hindoos stood upon the world's pinnacle of progress. This was the era of the Máhabháratá, 1300 B.C., of Manu the lawgiver, and Panini the great grammarian, of the Sanhitas and Brahmanas, of the Vedas and of the Sastras, *all* something like 1000 B.C. Brahmans educated in English colleges, and learned in the Sanscrit, insist that Homer modeled his verses after their ancient poets. Putting it plainer, they boldly *affirm* that Homer's Iliad was " prigged," — largely borrowed from the Máhabháratá.

Though this was the golden age of Aryan learning, mental friction was wanting. The national intellect, at this point, became either stationary, or shaded off into the metaphysical and the speculative. The inductive method of research was abandoned. Mystical theorizing ran rampant. Though the Vedas distinctly taught the existence of one Supreme Being, a dreamy mythology slowly sprung into existence, and fastened its fangs upon the national mind. Chieftains and heroes were made gods. Imagination painted, and tradition ascribed to them valorous deeds and marvelous attributes as unnatural as monstrous. The ignorant masses, carving their images in stone as keepsakes, finally fell to worshiping

them ; while the higher classes either cultivated philosophy
and deductive abstractions, or mentally merged away into a
passive self-meditation, looking for final rest in *Nirvana*.

MEN IN THE CITY.

The first movement, after landing in Calcutta, was to report in person to the lately appointed American consul,
whom we found a most genial and sunny-souled gentleman.
His family residence is Grand Rapids, Mich. Gen. Grant
was singularly fortunate in his consular appointments at
Calcutta, Singapore, Hong Kong, and Melbourne.

Having made the acquaintance of Keshub Chunder Sen
in London, several years since, to inquire about Spiritualism
and the progress of the Brahmo-Somaj in India, I sent him
my card, receiving in reply a most cordial welcome to his
country. Our future interviews, I trust, were mutually
pleasing and profitable. Though singularly non-committal
upon the causes of Spiritual phenomena, he extends the
hand of fellowship to Spiritualism, because a phase of
liberalism.

Knowing something of the Unitarian missionary, Rev. C.
H. A. Dall, through " The Liberal Christian," and being the
bearer of a letter from Rev. Herman Snow of San Francisco.
Cal., I called upon him at No. 24 Mott's Lane, Calcutta,
where he has a flourishing school for boys, with several
native teachers. He has joined, so I was credibly informed,
the Brahmo-Somaj, preaching at present little if any. Unitarianism, American-born, had nothing new in the way of
religion to send to the Brahmans of India.

Busily counting money, Mr. Dall was at first not very
communicative, although he warmed up a bit when the
conversation turned upon progress, and the natural relations existing between radical Unitarianism and true Spiritualism. Having read of " free love," " fanaticism," and
other rubbish floating upon the spiritual river of life, if not
prejudiced, he certainly lacked a knowledge of the Spiritual

philosophy. Our chat became quite spicy. In no residence
priestly presence, or princely palace, during these round-the-
world wanderings, have I evaded or hidden my belief
in Spiritualism. No one principled in truth, or fired with
a spark of genuine manhood, would so do, even though
shunned by the sham god of the age, — "*society.*" Policy,
cunning, and craft, are kin of the hells. Worldly gain is
spiritual loss.

Calcutta, founded by the "Old East India Company,"
near the close of the seventeenth century, on the site of an
ancient city called *Kali-Kutta*, sacred to the goddess Kali,
has a population of about eight hundred thousand, some
seventeen thousand of which are Europeans.

CITY SUBURBS AND SIGHT-SEEING.

The gardens, the bright foliage, the luscious fruitage, and
the palm-crowned suburban scenery generally, win at once
the traveler's admiration. The Government House, the
High Court, the massive Museum, yet unfinished, and other
city buildings, are magnificent structures. The Post Office,
imposing in appearance, is built upon the site of the notorious "Black Hole" of mutiny memory, where one hundred
and forty-six prisoners, thrust into a room eighteen feet
square, were left in a sultry night to smother and perish.
Only a few survived. The act was infamous. The Maidán
below the gardens, crowned with a Burmese pagoda, is the
fashionable resort in evening-time. The drive skirts the
river; and, for gayety and costly equipage, Paris can hardly
parallel it. Through the kindness of our consul-general, I
was privileged with a carriage-ride in the gray of twilight,
down the river, and around the square, to the music-stand,
where the Queen's Band nightly discourses delicious music.
The scenic surroundings, the blending of Occidental style
with Oriental grandeur, can not well be described. Many of
the costumes were singularly unique, and the social intercourse remarkably free from any stiff provincialisms. All had

fashions and styles of their own. The rich *baboos* — Hindoo gentlemen — occupied prominent positions in the gay procession and motley gathering.

Lower-caste Hindoo life is seen in the bazaars ; and though there are disgusting sights and rank odors, along the narrow native streets, we neither heard nor saw the Calcutta jackals so often described by romancing writers. Crows, however, may be numbered by myriads. Nestling at night in the ornamental shade-trees of the city, they engage early in the morning at the scavenger business, and often mistake the kitchen for their legitimate field of operations. Tall, stork-like birds, called " adjutants," also do scavenger-work. At night they perch upon the tops of the public buildings, standing like sentinels on guard.

The city is watered from immense reservoirs. The natives bathe in them, wash their garments in them, and then, filling their goat-skins for domestic purposes, and slinging them under the arm, supported by a strap, they trudge moodily away to their employer's residence. Drinking-water is drawn from wells in a very primitive way. Women have but few privileges. They seldom appear in the streets ; and then, if married, they veil their faces. One is continually reminded, while studying the Hindoo socially, of Old Testament manners and customs.

RIVER SCENES. — JUGGERNAUT. — THE BANYAN-TREE.

Occupying a place in Gen. Litchfield's barouche, we drove along, early one morning, by the river's side some four miles, witnessing the bathing and worshiping of the Hindoos in the flowing Hooghly. Gesticulating, bowing, sprinkling themselves, and intoning prayers, these worshipers counted their beads much as do the Catholics. Paying no regard to the Christian's Sunday or the Mohammedan's Friday, these sincere Hindoos hold in great reverence festival days of their gods. The English government grants the different religionists of the country some sixty holidays during the year.

Unfortunately, we reached India just too late to see the yearly Juggernaut festival, during which the great idol-car in Eastern India is drawn with such gushing enthusiasm. Believing devotees do not, however, throw themselves voluntarily under this idolatrous engine to be crushed, as falsifying churchmen have widely reported. While the excitement is at a high pitch, careless devotees may accidentally fall under the rotating wheels, and perish. This actually happened the present year. And so similar accidents often occur on Fourth of July occasions in America. That a few impulsive fanatics in the past may have purposely rushed under the ponderous wheels, — much as Christian pilgrims in the Crusade period walked through Palestine with bared feet, to die by the Holy Sepulchre, — is quite probable. Fanaticism has been common to all reli·· gions.

But crossing the river on this delightful morning, by the banks of which nestled neatness and filth, — Christly and demoniac men in close proximity, — we were soon strolling through the Botanical Gardens, admiring tropical flowers, with the lilies white, golden, and purple, on our way to the crowning glory of the gardens, the great banyan-tree, *alias* the bread-fruit tree of the East. This grand old tree fully met our expectations, only that it bore berries about the size of acorns, instead of bread. The natives are very fond of them. While this gigantic tree is not tall, it is wide-spreading and symmetrically shaped; and, though not an evergreen, it is clothed in a dark-green, glossy foliage, reflecting at sunrise a thousand vivid tints, varied as beautiful. This Calcutta banyan-tree, throwing down to the soil one hundred and thirty creeper-like limbs, *all* forming trunks, — symbol of the American Union, many in one, — would afford shade or shelter in a light rain-storm for two thousand persons. No traveler in the East should miss of seeing it. Tradition says that Alexander's army of ten

Toddy Palms of India.

thousand, in the fourth century B.C., sheltered itself, while in Northern India, under the far-reaching branches of a princely banyan. Just after leaving this kingly tree, there fluttered up before us, from a clump of date-palms a fine flock of green-plumaged parrots.

Descriptions of one part of India will not serve for all portions of it. The country is immense. It is reported that 8,000,000 perished during the late famine in India — but what is this in a country of nearly 300,000,000? The government allowed as little as possible to get out about the famine, as it might incite to mutiny. The Hindoos depend more upon the monsoons than upon cisterns or wells for water. A rain failure means famine. Rice culture requires great flooding, and the Madras presidency has vast irrigation works. As these works increase throughout the country, carefully conserving the water, famines will cease.

Calcutta has a population of nearly 900,000 ; some 20,000 or more are nominally Christians. It has been, not inaptly, called the City of Colleges. It is reported that 10,000 Bengalese students take their entrance examinations here every year. The religions of India are frequently in conflict. The Mohammedans are naturally aggressive. There are nearly 60,000,000 of Mohammedans in India. They quite generally do not favor the National Indian Congress, thinking it too favorable to Brahminism. Buddhism is making an effort to re-instate itself in India. Mr. Dharmapa, a Buddhist monk, has already established the temple of the Buddha-Gya as a Buddhist shrine in Calcutta. Buddhism will certainly return to India and become a great spiritual power.

CHAPTER XVII.

INDIA'S RELIGIONS, MORALS, AND SOCIAL CHARACTERISTICS.

THE higher classes of these Asiatics have fine-looking faces. Tall and rather commanding in person, easy and graceful in movement, they have pleasant, open countenances, dark eyes with long eyebrows, glossy black hair, — of which they seem proud, — thoughtful casts of expression, and full, high foreheads. The complexion is olive, shaded, according to caste and indoor or outdoor exercise, towards the dark of the Nubian, or white of the Northman. In Northern India they are nearly as fair as Caucasians; and, what is more, English scholars have been forced to admit that the Hindoo mind, in capacity, is not a whit behind the European. In hospitality they have no superiors. The lower, oppressed classes, as in other countries, are rude, rustic, and *vulgar!*

As a people I have found the Hindoos exceedingly polite. When two Brahmans meet, lifting each the hand, or both hands, to the forehead, they say, "*Namaskar*" (I respectfully salute you). Sometimes the inferior bows, and touches the feet of the higher personage, the latter exclaiming, "*I bless you: may you be happy!*" The Hindoo, naturally mild, meek, and fond of peace, will sooner put up with oppression than engage in a battle of recrimination and violence. An English ethnologist considers him sufficiently "womanly to be considered effeminate." Certainly, his patience and cool self-possession, inclining him to sail tranquilly along the placid waters of life, present a striking contrast to the impatience, ambition, and dictatorial spirit of Anglo-Saxons. Each and all, however, fill their places in the pantheon of history.

THE KALI GHAUT AND SLAIN GOATS.

Religion, when unenlightened by education and unguided by reason, degenerates into superstition. The Kali temple, situated in the suburbs of Calcutta, sacred to the ugly-looking, bloodthirsty goddess *Kali*, was to me a deeply interesting sight, because showing unadulterated Hindooism in its present low, degraded state. The shrines and the altars, the flower-covered *ling*, and the crimson yard all wet and dripping with the blood of goats sacrificed at the rising of the sun, forcibly reminded me of the Old Testament sacrifices offered as sweet-smelling savors to Jehovah, the tutelary god of the Jews. The bowing of the face to the earth, the kissing of cold stones, the smearing of the face with mud, the liturgical mutterings, and the howling beggary by the wayside, were all repulsive in the extreme. The temple was only a coarse, ordinary structure. Being Christians, we were not permitted to pass the threshold. These temples are not constructed, as are churches, to hold the people ; but rather as imposing shelters for the gods, priests, and sacrificial offerings. The worshipers around them are generally of the lower castes. Conversing on the spot with one of these officiating Brahman priests, he assured me that the throng present did *not* worship the Kali image. "It is a symbol," said he, "leading the mind to the higher and the invisible." Doubting his statement, and pondering, I silently said, *Here is retrogression*, for the most ancient of the Vedas taught the existence of one infinite God. The Orientalist, Prof. Wilson, says, "The Aryans believed in one God, who created the world by his fiat, and organized it by his wisdom." After the composition of the first Vedas, with the post-Vedic priesthood, came mythology, and the different castes.

THE BURNING GHAUTS. — CREMATION.

How are the dead best disposed of? Certain American
Indians, lifting their dead warriors into forest-trees, leave
them to assimilate with the elements; Christians inter the
mortal remains of their loved ones beneath the turf; Persians expose the bodies of the dead to the sun on their
" towers of silence," while the Hindoos burn theirs in *ghauts*
consecrated to this purpose. Many scientists and hygienic
reformers consider the last the preferable method. With
Gen. Litchfield for guide, we repaired one afternoon to the
ashy *ghaut* of flame to witness the burning of the dead.
Entering the brick-wall-inclosed arena, the eye fell upon
several piles of smoldering ashes; while near by was the
corpse of a pleasant-faced young girl of some eleven years,
awaiting the priestly preparations for burning. The red-
paint spot on the maiden's forehead indicated that she was
married. A tearless mother sat by the rude bier, with a
naked· babe at the breast. A sad stillness pervaded the
scene. When the dry hard-wood, intermixed with light
sticks of bamboo and sandal, was laid across the shallow
trench, and the pile ready for the cremation, the priests
anointing the head with oil, and sprinkling the body with
sacred water, placed the poorly-clad and ghastly corpse upon
the rough pyre. Then, bending the limbs to occupy as little
space as possible, and putting seeds, boiled rice, and bananas
to the mouth, the lighted torch was applied to the husky
bamboo. Soon the fire, flame, and smoke, curling and
hissing around the sandal-scented pile, transformed the
organized dust to its original dust and ashes. During the
burning, the priests paced around the fiery pyre, chanting
their prayers of consolation. Thousands flock to the Ganges
to die and be burned. Nothing can be sweeter than for a
Hindoo to die with his eyes resting upon the sacred river.
The funeral pyres of the wealthy are made of the sandal-
tree, spice-wood, fragrant flowers, incense, and ointments:

and, while the body is being consumed, priests and distant friends chant the Rig and the Sama Vedas. The immediate mourners stand around, dressed in white. Often the ashes are gathered up, and preserved in urns.

HOW SHALL WE DISPOSE OF OUR DEAD?

Touching the removal of the dead, these have been the common methods: interment, exposing upon towers of silence, mummification, and incinerating or burning upon the prepared pyre. Considering the loathsome changes of decomposition, with the liberation and discharging of poisonous gases into the atmosphere, the burying of deceased bodies is open to serious objections. It is well known that sulphuretted and phosphuretted gases are active poisons; and their influence, when breathed even in infinitesimal quantities, must be deleterious to health. Dr. Walker, a London surgeon, shows in his " Gatherings from Graveyards," that from the surface of the ground, above dead bodies, there are continually rising poisonous miasmas. These impregnate and infect the germ-cells and dust of the air breathed; and thus disease is borne upon the winds. There are few unhealthier places than the cemeteries of crowded cities. In them epidemics and pestilences often originate. People should avoid rather than visit them. In the early history of Judaism, to merely touch a dead body rendered the person "unclean for seven days."

Extravagant coffins, pompous ceremonies, costly monuments, gloved priests, expensive mourning apparel, and bearing corpses long distances for burial, *all* violate the genius of that Spiritual philosophy which sees that the spirit

> " Sings now an everlasting song
> Amidst the trees of life."

The opposition of churchmen to cremation arises from their theological belief that graveyards are temporary resting-places for bodies awaiting the trump of the resurrection. It is evangelical teaching, that the departed are " locked in the embrace of death ; " that they have " fallen asleep in Jesus ; " or have died "in the hope of a glorious resurrection " of their decomposing, putrefying bodies.   As the shirt of Nessus, so clings superstition to the sectarist.   The tendency of solid thinkers, however, is turned towards cremation, because a quicker method of turning dust to dust, as by the "refiner's fire " of Malachi; because less expensive than burial; because conducive to the general health ; because preserving portions of the ashes in urns is less costly than gravestones ; and because it obviates all fear of being buried alive.   Science will readily devise means to deodorize the gases given off during the process of burning; while the ashy *débris* will the more readily revert back to usefulness as fertilizers of the soil.

CASTE, AND BRAHMAN PRIESTS.

Under any sky, caste is an unmitigated curse.   Buddhism in the sixth century B.C. was a brave inspirational protest against Brahmanical assumption and caste.   Though Buddhistic preaching and practice quite checked this caste system for a time, it revived again with the revival of Brahmanism, 200 B.C. ; and, intensified by an unrelenting social despotism, it is to-day the scourge of India.   Women feel the chains more keenly than men.   This great nation is slow to feel the pulsations of progress.   English rule has done little, *nothing*, to tone down or overthrow the caste-venom of the ages ; and how could it, when caste in English society is nearly as marked as in Hindostan ?

This social pest pervades all gradations of life in India. Each servant has his own sphere, and out of it he will not budge.   This necessitates in wealthy English families a large retinue of servants.   Brahmans, though sometimes poor, never " sink " to be tradesmen !   They are generally clerks and draughtsmen.   And then there is the messenger, the

Taj Mahal, Agra.

butler, the cook, tailor, coachman, market-man, washerman, palanquin-bearers, sweepers, and others, down to pariahs.

As is well known, there are four general castes, — *Brahmans*, priests and writers ; *Chattries*, soldiers ; *Vyshes*, merchants ; and *Sooders*, tradespeople and toilers, — with scores of subdivisions. Castes never intermarry, though there is occasionally an elopement. All Brahmans are not priests; but all priests *must* be Brahmans. When a Brahmanian lad reaches the age of nine, a thin, light cord, called *Janeo*, is given him after religious ceremonies and a family festal feast. This, going over the right shoulder, is continually worn around the body. It is symbolical. From the time of its adjustment by the priest, he must abstain from defilement, and engage in stated bathing and worship. Brahmans, living abstemiously, eating no meat, ignoring war, avoiding the sight of human blood, drinking no liquors, and punctually attending to worship, are considered, by the Hindoos, holy men. These Brahman priests, called *Shastris*, read the Vedas and the laws of Manu to the people. They also preside at festivals, celebrate marriages, and affix the sacred cord upon the young.

If a Brahman becomes defiled, losing caste, it can only be regained by the most mortifying penances, and submission to a tedious system of purification. We saw one of these unfortunates doing penance by crawling serpent-like on the ground, and then rising and falling again ; he actually measured his length in the streets on his way to the temple. The poor dupe was pitiably filthy. After his penances comes the bathing for purification.

India originally rooted her caste-system in the priesthood ; England based her caste upon ancestral "blue-blood; " while America is grounding hers upon wealth. The principle is abominable, and means just *this:* three men are ascending a ladder ; the middle one licks the dust from the boots of the one above him, and *kicks* the one below him !

VILLAGE LIFE. — BATHING IN THE GANGES.

The longer that missionaries and merchantmen remain in the "land of Ind," the more do they become attracted to the people, and attached to the country. Old men residing in India can hardly be induced to return to England. Book-making travelers, of the Rev. Prime school, are shamefully partial in their descriptions of the effeminate Orientals. It is chronic with these clergymen to write contemptuously of the "heathen." Idolatry in any form is deplorable ; but it is just as absurd to idolize a *book* labeled " holy," as a bit of carved stone.

The native Indians are not only exceedingly social, but trusting and reverential. They are not as moral, however, as they were in the days of Warren Hastings and Sir William Jones. Their habitations, afar back from the great cities, are all clustered in villages. None reside by themselves on farms. Ditches, rather than fences, indicate boundaries. Many of their houses are mere mud hovels, the flooring matting, the furniture scarce and oddly-shapen. The wealthy clothe themselves in costly apparel ; while the dresses of the poor are mere breech-cloths, the children sporting in utter nakedness. Wages are exceedingly low. Women do outdoor work the same as men, even to the carrying of dirt in baskets upon their heads, where railroads are in process of construction.

Saying nothing of the filth of the poverty-stricken classes, the Hindoos, as a nation, are noted for physical neatness. Watching them, the other morning, by the river, I silently said, " Your bathing is as natural as your breathing." Brahmans frequently bathe three times per day. The Ganges' banks, along the Ghauts, are often lined by the faithful before sunrise, performing their ablutions. The women are clad in loose, robe-like garments ; the men are nude, save close-fitting *lingatees*. These Brahmans, by the way, wearing shoes open upon the top, bathing frequently, being thorough vegetarians, and considering themselves, in consequence, physically sweet and pure, complain that Europeans emit an unsavory smell — a filthy, beef-eating *odor* — from their persons, exceedingly offensive and loathsome to *all* true Brahmans. The Shakers of Mount Lebanon are no stricter peace-men or vegetarians than are these high-caste Brahmans. Often, at the family table, Hindoos stop eating for a few moments, to chant Sanscrit *sloka* — a sort of jolly thanksgiving song.

Genuine Hindoos wear neither pantaloons nor coats, but *dhotars*. Parsees wear trousers, robes, and tall, pyramidal shaped hats; and Mahommedans, long beards and turbans. Noting these costumes, the prominent races of India are easily distinguishable.

The earnest desire of even the lower castes to secure an English education is manifest by their studying along the public streets in Calcutta by gas-light. This is a nightly practice. Such Brahmans as have acquired an education teach others gratuitously. Temperate themselves, wondering at the liquor-drinking customs of Christians, and the downright drunkenness of Western nations, they even blame Jesus for " turning water into wine."

Out of the cities, profanity is unknown among the Hindoos. They have too much reverence for the Christian's " Our Father," and for their own gods, to curse and profane their names. Wealthy Hindoos have their favorite symbol-gods in their houses. A certain room is set apart, flower-perfumed, and consecrated to the household deity, once a hero or saint. On festival days of remembrance, they invite in their European acquaintances. Departing, they put garlands upon their necks, and throw flowers at their feet. In courts of justice, Hindoos brought upon the stand make a *solemn affirmation*. If there are doubts of their speaking the truth, " they swear them by the Ganges, or the sacred *Toolsi-*flower." For some of these singular customs, I am indebted to a personal acquaintance, seven years in India, inspector of schools in Ommeraottix, — famous in England only as a cotton-market.

THE ASIATIC SOCIETY.

No place in Calcutta so completely chained me as the Royal Asiatic Society, with its Museum of Ancient Art and Sculpture. If the command had read, "Thou shalt not covet thy neighbor's library," I should long ago have committed the "unpardonable sin." That eminent scholar, Sir William Jones, who went to India in 1783, established the institution, and Warren Hastings was the first president. In this immense collection of volumes, manuscripts, scrolls, and unread Oriental rolls, are treasured the priceless memorials of the past. The original building, long ago overflowing with its shelved lore, necessitated the storing of manuscripts elsewhere, with many of the precious relics. We found the assistant secretary, a native Hindoo, a most scholarly and gentlemanly man. Gladly we exchanged several books, his treating of Brahmanism, and ours of Spiritualism. All library-books were free to us during our stay in the city. But time was flying. Longingly, regretfully, we left this library, — a very monument of research and reflection, — to penetrate the heart of the country. It was nearly nightfall when we left the City of Palaces, crossing the Hoogly to Howrah, taking the East-India Railway train for the north and west. The depot was dimly lighted, the confusion disgusting, but the cars cool and comfortable. Travelers by English railways painfully miss their accustomed sleeping-cars.

UP THROUGH THE COUNTRY.

The railroad extends along the Ganges Valley up the country in a north-westerly direction, and ultimately reaching Allahabad, between the Ganges and the Jumna, where these rivers form a junction. They both rise in the Himalayas. The scenery, with its vast unfenced rice-fields, clumps of deeply-wooded jungles, hedges of cactus, grazing herds, and nestling native villages, was decidedly attractive, though dulled by sameness. Occasionally broad, rolling ridges reminded us of our fertile prairie-lands in the West. Though camels and elephants are pressed into farming-work, hump-shouldered Asian bullocks do most of the plowing, rather a light *scratching* of the soil. The flocks of sheep along the way were, with hardly an exception, black. Shepherds with bamboo rods, instead of " crooks," tended them. Northern India produces large quantities of wheat and corn.

The cultivation of the Ganges Valley is of an inferior kind. This must necessarily continue till the Hindoos become landholders, owning the proceeds of the fields they cultivate. Though the vast plains of India have scattered groves of acacia, guava, mango, palms, and other Oriental trees, there is a destitution of deep, dense forests, from the fact that, in past centuries, they were ruthlessly cut, and the fields tilled to support the over-population of the country. The telegraph-poles along the way are either of iron or stone, to prevent destruction by white ants. The prying, greedy nuisances soon found their way into our trunks.

BENARES THE BLESSED.

Reaching Mogul Serai Junction, we were soon transferred to the branch-road leading to the river whose waters were anciently thought to insure eternal life. Tread lightly, speak softly; this is the winding Ganges, and that magnificent and moss-crowned city on the western bank, with its temples, mosques, palaces, tapering domes, sacred shrines, and the Golden Temple of Siva, — guardian divinity, — is Benares, *holiest city of the Hindoos!*

All sincere religionists are to be respected. What Mecca is to the Mohammedan, Jerusalem to the Christian, and Rome to the Catholic, Benares is to the Hindoo; and the Ganges, that washes its feet, is the Eden river of immortal life. The grayed pen of antiquity failed to record the names of its founders.   But, full two hundred years before the Grecian Plato discoursed in the groves skirting classic Athens, Benares was summering under the sunshine of her palmiest days, boasting of seven hundred flourishing seminaries of learning, with ambitious students from all portions of the Orient.   Here metaphysicians, both Brahmans and Buddhists, held their discussions upon philosophy, the duty and destiny of humanity ; and, in all probability, no keener logicians ever met upon the field of controversy.

The city of Benares, — anciently called *Kasika*, — having five thousand sacred shrines, is supposed to number some five hundred thousand inhabitants; but during festivals, or in the season when pilgrims flock thither, the population is greatly increased.   *Sekrole*, the European part, about three miles from the old city, is handsomely laid out with government buildings, two English colleges, finely shaded streets, and a broad esplanade for military practice and display.

The mention of Sekrole must ever remind us of the hospitality and favors of Dr. Lazarus and his estimable family. His son, a collegiate youth, aflame with genius, informed us that his college class had quite a number of natives, ranging in years from sixteen to nineteen, nearly all of whom were married, some being the fathers of two, three, and four children.   " Do these Hindoos keep up with their classes ? " we inquired.   " Certainly," said this student : " they even excel in mathematics, metaphysics, and moral philosophy, and would be wranglers in English colleges."

EUROPEAN METAPHYSICS OLD IN INDIA.

An English professor in Queen's College, Benares, asssured us that, reading of new methods in metaphysics, or recent mental phenomena in Germany considered *new*, and referring them to the pundits (learned Hindoos in Benares), they would turn to their Sanscrit scrolls, and, finding the same formula in metaphysics, or similar phenomena, they pro-

Hindoo Fakir.

nounce them *old;* and then, smiling among themselves, would add, " Western scholars are tardily following in the footsteps of our sages who lived full three thousand years ago."

The streets of Benares, as in all old Asian cities, are exceedingly narrow ; but the palaces of the wealthy, the mossy ruins, the massive masonry fringing the river, and the magnificent architecture, gorgeous even in decay, beggar description. Taking an open *dinghy,* and drifting down the Ganges one morning by the city, we not only saw floating corpses, but saw them bring their dead to the burning Ghaut ; saw them take the muddy waters in their mouths ; saw them perform their religious ablutions and immersions, expecting, like sectarian Baptists, to wash away their sins ; and saw them bring their offerings, and lay them upon the altars of their gods ; and then, climbing a long stone stairway, we went up the Mohammedan Man-Mandil, on the roof of which are astronomical charts, drawn by old Indian sages ; then to the Golden Temple, the domes of which are literally washed with gold ; and then to the Monkey Temple, sacred to Durgha, where hundreds of monkeys are kept and petted, if not worshiped, by the lower-caste Hindoos.

EASTERN FAKIRS.

Like the dervishes of Islam, these fakirs go by various names, and belong to different orders. Some continually chant praises to Vishnu. Others, inflicting tortures upon themselves, engage in constant prayers ; and others still seek to suspend the breath, restrain natural desires, and abstract the mind, preparatory to deeper communion with Brahm. While smiling at their superstitions, let us not forget their sincerity. Their subdued hearts seem to continually sing this sad refrain, —

" Oh ! where shall rest be found, —
Rest for the weary soul ? "

One of these fakirs, stopping for a night in a quiet Hindoo village, is received with profound respect. They consider him a holy man ; and, after washing his feet, they supply his wants. Some of these ascetics, renouncing homes, giving away their property, fast, pray, sleep on beds of stone, and practice other severe austerities.

During our second day's wanderings in Benares, we saw in the street, under a burning sun, one of the Hindoo fakirs, — a *Gosain*, holy beggar! This branch of fanatics do penance and work merit for others, by standing on one foot, or holding up one hand, for a term of years ; repeating the while pleading prayers. The one we saw, sitting cross-legged, with a three-forked tripod by his side, was exceedingly filthy. His coarse, uncombed hair was sprinkled with ashes, rice, leaves, and lotus-flowers. He kept the index finger open and fixed ; his body, nearly naked, was smeared with clay ; his ghastly eyes, almost closed, were turned upward ; and he seemed striving to cease breathing. He speaks to no one, but "aims," said Hindoo bystanders, "to do works of merit, separate the soul from the body, and commune with God." The next morning, with one of the Benares missionaries, we strolled away some four miles, to the ruins of *Sarnath*, once a very extensive Buddhist establishment, supposed by some to have been the birthplace of Buddha ; a grand old monument, with its architectural designs and elegantly carved images, still standing, and commemorating the event. We confess to admiration and veneration for such time-defying ruins. But why so dumb, O tongue of tradition? Speak, and tell us by whom, and for what purpose, were these acres of templed stone and mighty ruins once built!

ALONG THE WAY TO BOMBAY.

It is fifteen hundred miles, by rail, from Calcutta to Bombay, the two rival cities of India. Previous to reaching Bombay from Jubbulpore, famous for marble rocks, there is mountain scenery sufficiently bold and diversified to show a striking contrast to the valley of the Ganges, and others of India's lowlands through which we had passed. The country now rougher and higher, the cultivation of the lands changed, becoming better as we approached the western coast, rice-fields giving place to wheat, millet, and other grains. In Northern India, corn (*Indian maize*) does finely.

There is an extensive network of railroads in this country; and, what may seem singular, they are liberally patronized by the natives. Brahmans, Mohammedans, Sikhs, and poor Christians, rush into the "second-class" cars, riding as cozily as the caged "happy family" of Barnum memory. The steep grades, dark tunnels, dancing cascades, and heavily-wooded hillsides, reminded us of home scenery in New England.

Reaching Bombay in the waning part of the day, a glance convinced us that it was a seaport mart, aflame with business. Numbering over six hundred thousand inhabitants, this city is considered by the unprejudiced the most stirring and progressive of any in India; while the Parsees, whose forefathers brought their holy fire with them from Persia in the seventh century, now constitute one hundred thousand of the city's population. Acquisitive and enterprising, much of the mercantile traffic of the East is under their management. As there are no beggars among Shakers, Quakers, and Jews, so there are none among the Parsees.

Going out leisurely upon the esplanade in early evening, the streets are thronged with multitudes of Hindoos, Mussulmans, Parsees, Indo-Europeans, English half-castes, with occasionally a straggling American; and all either on foot, on horseback, or in *gharries*, or queer, gaudily-decorated and covered-in carriages drawn by bullocks. Costumes are gay and varied. Jewelry, even to rings in the nose, is worn in costly profusion. Wealthy Hindoos are lavish in dress, precious stones, pearls, and diamonds. The bazaars here, with their narrow streets, and filth, their trade and traffic in trinkets, silks, brocades, &c., are but a repetition of those in all Asian cities.

Bombay, built upon a cluster of islands connected one with the other and with the mainland by causeways, forming a sort of peninsula, and fanned by invigorating sea-breezes, is considered the most desirable residence for Europeans in India. The city is supplied with excellent water from Vehar Lake, some two miles out, at the foot of the Salsette Hills. Rich Europeans, and some of the missionaries, reside at the fashionable suburb, Malabar Hill, from December to February; but during the rains and hot weather, from June to September, they migrate to the highland plateaus and cool mountains.

Jesus, worn and weary under Syria's scorching skies, went up on to the mountains, not to escape the heat, and do a bit of cozy lolling around champagne-tables with Peter, James, and John, but to pray, and to heal the sick. It is deliciously comfortable to be a " Christian " in the nineteenth century. But what about that old apostolic word, the " cross " ? — " bearing the cross," and suffering for the " truth's sake " ?

ORIGIN OF BRAHMANISM.

The Aryans, more properly *Aryas*, meaning, in the Zend language, honorable men, — occupying the high table-lands of Central Asia, known in later times as the Plateau of Iran, —left in the pre-historic past their ancient agricultural seats, traveling westward and southward in the character of emigrants, explorers, and conquerors.

The Aryan conquest of Hindostan, effected before and during the period treated of in the Máhábhárátá, and the Rámayana, was mainly accomplished in the palmy days of those kingly chieftains known as the Máhárájás. These in the pre-Vedic period were their own priests, kindling their own altar-fires. As Thales, Solon, and Socrates were called *Sophoi*, — knowers, — the wise among the Aryans were denominated Rishis, and, in a much later period, Gymnosophists.

It is conceded by Oriental scholars that 1200 B.C. the Aryans were not only a powerful people along the banks of the Indus, but around the mouths of the Ganges, on the extreme east of India. This was the latest period that can possibly be assigned to the Rig-Veda, oldest of the four Hindoo sacred books. And yet these Aryan seers who composed the Veda speak, in their sacred works, of "older *hymns* which the fathers sang," of "ancient sages and elder gods." "They were old," says Samuel Johnson, "at the earliest epoch to which we can trace them. Their religion, like their language, was already mature when the Rishis of the Veda were born." Marriages in this period were performed by the Máhárájás, or by the father of the bride; while the Rishis — seers or wise teachers — instructed the children, offered sacrifices, and spoke comforting words over the dead.

Sacrifices have in them an underlying truth. On the higher planes of thought, they imply the consecration of the dearest possessions to the highest ideal. On the lower, superstitious stratum of life, the term "sacrifice" is made to mean the shedding of blood, and the remission of sins. The primitive Aryans offered three gifts as sacrifices, — fire, clarified butter, and the plant whose juices stimulate to a new life. The Jews offered goats and kids, heifers and rams. Certain superstitious Hindoos, in their degenerate present, engage in similar sacrifices. Enlightened men and women sacrifice strength, ease, comfort, to educate and bless humanity.

Owing to wealth, luxury, and multiplying responsibilities of the earliest Máhárájás, they employed the Rishis as substitutes in religion, — employed them to attend to the sacrificial gifts, and serve as mediums of communication between them and their gods. How natural for Rishis, seers, prophets, to slide into the attitude of priests! Thus employed, these seers, *alias* priests, soon assumed authority, and professed supernatural powers; and knowing something of philosophy, magic, astrology, and seership, they perfected an organization which resulted in the priestly or *Brahman caste*, the features of which were defined in the laws of Manu. As the Brahman priests believed in Brahm, molded the rising thought, and officiated at religious ceremonies, the religion of Hindostan was naturally denominated Brahmanism.

Aryanic in origin, 13.4 per cent of the world's religionists are Brahmans, and 31.2 per cent are Buddhists. These together make a decided majority over any religious sect on the globe. Buddhism bears something the same relation to Brahmanism that Christianity bears to Judaism. I class them together because Aryan in their origin and growth.

BELIEF OF THE ANCIENT BRAHMANS.

" There is," says Max Müller, "a remembrance of one God, breaking through the mists of idolatrous phraseology, — a monotheism which precedes the polytheism of the Veda." * Mr. Müller, who as authority is unrivaled, further says, " A Hindoo of Benares, in a lecture delivered before an English and native audience, defends his faith, and the faith of his forefathers, against such sweeping accusations " as polytheism and idolatry.

" 'If by idolatry,' says this Hindoo scholar, ' is meant a system of worship which confines our ideas of the Deity to a mere image of clay or stone; which prevents our hearts from being expanded and elevated with lofty notions of the attributes of God, — if this is what is meant by idolatry, we disclaim idolatry, we abhor idolatry, and deplore the ignorance or uncharitableness of those that charge us with this groveling system of worship. . . . We really lament the ignorance or uncharitableness of those who confound our representative worship with the Phœnician, Grecian, or Roman idolatry as represented by European writers, and then charge us with polytheism in the teeth of thousands of texts in the Purânas, declaring in clear and unmistakable terms that there is but one God, who manifests himself as Brahma, Vishnu, and Rudra (Siva), in his functions of creation, preservation, and destruction.' " †

* Müller's Sanscrit Literature, p. 559.
† Müller's German Workshop, p 17.

It is the common reply of the modern Hindoo to the missionary, when accused of worshiping many gods, "Oh! these are various manifestations of the *one* God; the same as, though the sun be one in the heavens, yet he appears in multiform reflections upon the lake." That there are ignorant Hindoos who worship images, is doubtless true; and equally true that there are Roman-Catholic Christians who worship pictures and the Virgin Mary, and Protestants who worship the Bible, instead of accepting its inspired truths.

Defined in general terms, Brahmans believe in Brahm, the One self-existent, manifesting himself in the relation of creator, destroyer, preserver. Up to the present time, there have been, say these Hindoos, nine incarnations; the ninth is that of Christna, son of the virgin Devanaguy. He was begotten by the thought of Vishnu; and, at the moment of his birth, celestial music filled earth and heaven. Christna signifies, in Sanscrit, *sacred.*

"The initiated Brahman," says Manu, "should take the vow of chastity, that he may present himself at the holy sacrifice with heart and body pure." The Catholic missionary Dubois says in his work entitled "*Mœurs des Indes,*" —

"Justice, humanity, good faith, compassion, disinterestedness, all the virtues, in fact, were familiar to them, and taught to others both by precept and example. Hence it comes that the Hindoos profess, at least speculatively, nearly the same moral principles as ourselves; and, if they do not practice all the reciprocal duties of men towards each other in a civilized society, it is not because they do not know them."

The sacred books of the Brahmans are rich in moral teachings; to wit: —

"Love of his fellow-creature should be the ruling principle of the just man in all his works; for such weigh most in the celestial balance."

"As the body is strengthened by muscles, the soul is fortified by virtue."

"As the earth supports those who trample it under foot, and rend its bosom with the plow, so should we *return good for evil*."

"The virtuous man is like the gigantic banyan-tree, whose beneficent shade affords freshness and life to the plants that surround it."

Brahmans further believe the soul emanating from Brahm to be divine and immortal; and, as it was given pure from all stain, it can not re-ascend to the celestial abode till it shall have been purified from all faults committed through its union with matter. They teach universal charity, —teach that self should be secondary, and that selfishness leads to hells and re-births; while happiness and ultimate redemption come through purity and entire self-renunciation. Benevolence and good deeds lead to homes among the gods. Some of the Vedic "hymns are addressed to deified men who had attained their divinity through beneficent work." Other of these ancient hymns treat of charity and good works as means of salvation. Listen : —

"He who keeps his food to himself has his sin to himself also."

"He who gives alms goes to the highest heavens, —goes to the gods."

"To be kind to the poor is to be greater than the greatest there."

"Mortal life ended, go thou home to the fathers, and, if thou hast deserved it, dwell in a shining body with the gods."

The religious hymns of the Rig-Veda date back to 1500 B. C. — but were not put in writing until about 500 B. C. They were retained in memory and transmitted to others before book-making. The Vedas abound in Spiritualism. The Devas were the "bright ones gone beyond." Departed ancestors were called *Pitris*. Converse with these *Pitris* led at a later period to ancestral worship.

CHAPTER XVIII.

THE RISE OF BUDDHISM IN INDIA.

BUDDHA, of the family of the Sakyas and clan of the Guatamas, was not properly a Brahman by birth, but belonged to the line of royalty. History pronounces him the son of a rajah of Kapilavastu, a kingdom probably in Nepál, near the foot of the Himalaya Mountains, north of Oudh. As a boy he was beautiful and brilliant, as a youth remarkable for his candor and contemplation. His wife was the accomplished Gopá.

Riding as a prince in his father's city, in a chariot, observing the poverty, misery, and death around him, and contemplating upon the vanity of earthly things, he contrasted all this anxiety, this misery, with the calmness and true freedom of a religious devotee, a sort of an ascetic beggar, sitting at the city gate. The sight opened in his soul a new fountain; and, though a proud prince, he threw aside his royal attire, crushed caste under his feet, and retired to a hermitage for six years.

Brahmanical theology, with its sacrifices, ceremonial practices, and Pharisaic conceits growing out of caste, early disgusted this religious enthusiast. The world was selfish and hollow. He renounced it, — renounced all pleasure, and, through humiliation and meditation, sought to conquer himself. Subjecting the lower nature to the higher, engaging in fasting, prayer, and penances, he was blessed with ecstatic visions which pointed to true knowledge — the way of salvation.   Soon he became divinely illumined, and claimed the title of *Buddha.*

His first public ministry, attended with spiritual marvels, was at Benares, where he made many converts.   This accounts, in all probability, for the Buddhistic ruins at Sarnath, near this sacred city of the Hindoos.

Scholars generally agree in placing his death 543 B.C.

BUDDHISTIC ETHICS.

The gist of Buddha's teaching was this: all earthly objects, cognized by the senses, are unreal.   All is change, all is vanity.   There's nothing but sorrow in life.   This sorrow is caused by ignorance, and the flow of the passions. Accordingly, the passions must be subdued, the affections toned down, the mind enlightened, and the life consecrated to good works : *these* moral and meritorious altitudes gained, and the soul is at the threshold of salvation, the gate of divine repose, conscious rest and peace in *Nirvana.*

In addition to its prohibitory commandments, not to kill, nor steal, nor commit adultery, nor lie, nor be drunken ; it enjoined such positive virtues as purity, charity, integrity, contemplation, forgiveness of injuries, equanimity of temper, and self-abnegation.   In brief, holiness of life released from further transmigrations, and secured eternal salvation. *Nirvana !*   Buddhism was never nihilism or atheism. Nirvana — derived from the negative *nir*, and *va*, to blow as the wind — implies calm unruffled, the peace and rest of a spent breeze, perfect felicity.   Until this high position is attained, transmigrations are moral necessities.

" Buddhism," says Dr. Wuttke, " stands in history as a religion not of one people, but of humanity.   It conceived in the commencement the grand idea of peacefully converting the world."   While maintaining the right of religious freedom, its rejection of war and bloodshed has been absolute.

Priests and others, both men and women, ministering in spiritual things, must live celibate lives.   Buddha's doctrines spread rapidly. After his death, some 543 B.C., occurring while sitting under a sàl-tree, the first general council of his followers was held to settle theological dogmas. At a third council, held in the reign of King Asoka, commencing 263 B.C., when Buddhism had become the state religion of India, the canon, or holy Scriptures, — *Tri-Pitaka*, — of the Buddhists, were drawn up, and pronounced canonical.

THE REV. MURRAY'S "CIVILIZED HEATHEN."

This distinguished Congregational clergyman, in a lyceum lecture delivered through New England upon the " Civilized Heathen," said in substance : —

" Christian civilization might profit from Buddhism, and New England and Boston might go to school to China and Canton. The underlying idea of Buddhism is a belief in the infinite capacity of the human intellect ; belief in the availing of true merit, and in the development of all the human faculties. It is not a heavy, sensual religion, but one purely rational, appealing to consciousness and intellect for support. While Old England and New England have used the rack, the cell, the dungeon, the inquisition, and thousand implements of torture, there were twenty-three hundred years of Buddhism with not a drop of blood in its onward march, nor a groan along its pathway. It has never persecuted. It has never deceived the people, never practiced pious fraud, never discouraged literature, never appealed to prejudice, never used the sword. If the Buddhists are heathen, are they not *civilized heathen?* . . . Their priests depend upon voluntary subscriptions. We have homes for the sick, the poor, and the aged. But the heathen Buddhists go one step farther, and provide hospitals for sick and worn-out animals. They plant shade-trees along the way to shelter men and animals from the scorching sun. Grazing herds and all insect-life represent the divine thought. All life in their eyes is sacred. Christians entertain travelers at hotels if they pay their bills. You are respectfully received by the wealthy if you bring

with you letters of introduction from aristocratic circles; but
the door of the Buddhist is ever open to the stranger, with
the mat and waiting pot of rice.   The Burmese missionary
Smith, said he ' could traverse the whole kingdom without
money ; ' and during his missionary stay he saw no drunkenness, not an indecent act, nor an immodest gesture.   Compare this with the gross, filthy, night-walking prostitution of
New York or London.   Unselfishness, or forgetfulness of
self, is a cardinal virtue.   Struggles, sufferings, and sacrifices
for others' good, purify and prepare the soul for heavenly
rest."   And these, *these*, are the heathen Buddhists, whom
Orthodox theologians have for centuries preached to perdi-
tion for not believing in Christianity, — this American Christianity that speculates, loans money, persecutes heretics, rents
pews, cheats, fights, and gambles at fairs and festivals, for
religion's sake.   I am not writing of the Christianity of
Jesus, but the civilized Christianity of America, that sends
missionaries to Asia's coral strand " to convert the Buddhists."

BUDDHA AND JESUS.

The Buddhists consider Sakya Muni Guatama Buddha a
much greater Saviour than Jesus Christ ; because the latter,
born in poverty, a carpenter's son, sought, upon Jewish
authority, to enthrone himself as king ; while Guatama
Buddha, a king's son, laying aside royalty and a prospective
crown, humbled himself, walking the companion of beggars,
that he might the more effectually break down caste, reaching and enlightening the lowest classes of humanity.   In
preaching, Buddha continually magnified the " wheel of the
law," the four great principles : —

I. There is sorrow, want, pain.

II. Examining the source of pain, be found it to be selfish desire.

III. Pain was destroyed by regulating the natural demands of life, and
destroying selfish desire by self-control.

IV. The means of destroying it, in the sense of extirpation, were
meditation, self-abnegation, and the practice of every virtue.

Guatama Buddha.

A Brahman accusing Guatama Buddha of idling away his time, neither sowing nor reaping, was met with this reply: "I do plow and sow, reaping thence fruit that is immortal."

" Where are your implements, O Guatama? "

" My field is the law; the weeds I clear away are the cleaving to life; my plow is wisdom; the seed I sow is purity; my work, attention to the precepts; my harvest, *Nirvana!* "

TEACHINGS OF BUDDHA AND HIS DISCIPLES.

" The taint worse than all others is ignorance."

" In a corrupt world each ought to be a lotus without spot."

" So long as the desire of man towards woman is not subdued, so long is his mind in bondage."

" Sin will come back upon the sinful, like fine dust thrown against the wind."

" The way of release is through the practice of the virtues."

" When the just man goes from this world to another, his good deeds receive him as friend greets friend."

" Thyself is its own defense, its own refuge; it atones for its own sins; none can purify another."

"Master thyself; so mayest thou teach others, and easily tame them, after having tamed thyself; for self is hardest to tame."

" Let us live happily, free from greed among the greedy, — *happily,* though we call nothing our own."

"Proclaim it freely to all men, — my law is a law of mercy for all. . . . Whoever loves will feel the longing to save not himself alone, but all others."

" The talk of the ' high and low castes,' of the ' pure Brahmans, the only sons of Brahma,' is nothing but sound: the four castes are equal."

" Are the Buddhas born only for the benefit of men? Have not Wisakha, and many others, entered the paths? The entrance is open for women as well as for men."

" Of all the lamps lighted in Buddha's honor, one only, brought by a poor woman, lasted through the night."

" Forsake all evil, bring forth good, master thy own thought; such is Buddha's path to end all pain."

" And you yourself must make effort. The Buddhas are but preachers."

" The good delights in this world and the next; he delights in his own work, and is happy when going on the good path."

" All we are is the result of what we have thought. If a man speaks
or acts with evil thoughts, pain follows, as the wheel the foot of him
who draws the carriage."
"' Better than ruling the world is the reward of the first step in
virtue."
" Not even a god, not Mára nor Brahma, could change into defeat the
victory of a man over himself."

The Dhammapada, otherwise " Path of Virtue," is put
down as among the oldest records of the Buddhistic doctrines. Most of the above precepts are taken from it, as
stars from shimmering skies. The erudite, especially of the
East, believe that they either refer directly to, or fell from
the inspired lips of, Guatama Buddha himself. These and
other sacred writings were carefully transmitted, as canonical, by the son of King Asoka, the Constantine of
Buddhism.

DECLINE OF BUDDHISM IN INDIA.

Though Buddhism arose in India, it soon spread into
Ceylon, Thibet, Burmah, Siam, China, Mongolia, and the
extreme north of Asia. There are few or no Buddhists at
present in India. The decline commenced in certain portions of India, about 200 B.C. The subsequent *Jaina*
religion, denying the authority of the Vedas, was a modified
Buddhism. While the Brahmins use no language in their
sacred writings but the Sanscrit, the Ceylon Buddhistic
Scriptures are in *Pali*, a rich, poetical language, attaining
its highest refinement near the advent of Buddha, something
like 588 B.C. This *Pali*, of which Max Müller so frequently
speaks, is little more than the Brahminical Sanscrit melted
down to the softness of the Italian.

It was in the palmy days of the Buddhistic period that
the Greeks under Alexander invaded India, 327 B.C.; shortly
after which, Grecian orators visited, and Greek ambassadors
resided at, the court of a distinguished Indian king. Subsequent to these invasions, Greek historians, while giving

very interesting descriptions of the Brahmanical caste system, the wealth of the country, the republican tendencies of government, and the great learning of the Indian scholars, expressed the most surprise at the self-abnegation and asceticism practiced by the hermits of India. They further speak of schools of prophets, or communities where men lived abstemiously and peaceably, holding " all things in common."

The Greek and Persian invasions into India, several hundred years before Jesus' advent, opening up an interchange of learning and letters, put into our hands keys to be used in the elucidation of religious questions, growing out of the *Alexandrian School* in Egypt, where the Indian philosophy, Hellenism, and Judaism grasped in deadly conflict, affecting and coloring the future Christianity of the ages.

THE WORLD'S RELIGIONS.

Religion as a soul emotion is universal ; but the expression as a sentiment, owing to organization and racial tendency, manifests itself in several great sects. The most primitive worship of all is Fetichism, or Sabaism, so-called.

This is professed by	100,000,000.
The religion of Zoroaster and Confucius	40,000,000.
Brahmanism, the original faith of India	60,000,000.
Buddhism, the reformed faith	270,000,000.
Mohammedanism	96,000,000.
Judaism	4,500,000.
The Greek Church	62,000,000.
The Roman Church	139,000,000.
The sects of Protestantism	115,000,000.

These numbers profess to be approximations only. The Tauists of China, numbering millions, are not mentioned. The Buddhists, here estimated at one hundred and seventy millions, far outnumber any other sect of religionists upon the globe. This admits of no doubt.

THE ELEPHANTA CAVES.

Shri Gunesha-aya-Namaha! — To glorious Gunesha, salutation! Gunesha, the elephant-god of India, is connected
with literature as well as worship. When first reading that
misleading work, Godfrey Higgins's Anacalypsis, I was
peculiarly struck with his reference to the " Elephanta
Caves of India." They are situated upon the island of
Garipurix, only a few hours' sail from Bombay.

Landing, a long, winding stone stairway leads to this
mountain of sculptured marvels. A stroll through these
churchal-looking caverns, old Buddhistic temples, cut into a
yielding, yet solid mountain rock, was a sight truly impressive, a day long to be remembered. The ceiling to the first
we entered was about twenty feet high, the depth back to
the rock-carved gods, Brahma, Siva, and Vishnu at the
rear, something like one hundred and fifty feet by perhaps
one hundred and twenty in width. The divisions, compart-
ments, pillars, aisles, alcoves, and niches, filled with exquis-
itely-cut gods, and panoramic festival scenes, grim as grand,
kindling the wonder of travelers, *all* literally charmed me :
it was tradition in earnest, a feast to my love of antiquity.
In one compartment is symbolized the Trinity, — Brahma,
Siva, Vishnu, — the Christian " Three in One." In another
division is Christna, with emblems referring to his incarnation. Behind the left thigh of this *god* is carved — what?
the *cross*, or a heavy-hilted *sword*, which? No matter
whether cross or sword, it can not fail to remind one of
Abraham's position when taking an oath.

Every thing connected with these caverns inspires one with
the grand and the reverential. Scores of lifelike figures,
from twelve inches to fifteen feet in height, elegantly carved
in and forming a part *of* the original rock, with corridors and
tapering columns, *all* exhibit a high order of architectural
talent, considering that it antedated the Christian era by
several hundred years. These Buddhistic monasteries, though

conceived and constructed long before the birth of Jesus, and still the resort of Hindoo pilgrims, are admirably adapted to religious meditation and anchoretic life. Many years since, the Portuguese anchoring on an adjoining island, shelled these caves for sport. "May God have mercy on their souls, and all other such Christian vandals!" Dr. Bhâu Daji, a Hindoo scholar, and vice-president of the Asiatic Society of Bombay, takes a deep interest in exploring and explaining the histories of cave-cathedrals in India, to all lovers of antiquarian studies.

There's not a vestige of proof in these caves, — rock temples of worship, that Christianity and Christian symbols were borrowed from Buddhism. There's not a carving in these weird caves that can be tortured into a resemblance to "the Holy Family" or the "Crucifixion of Krishna." I examined them with an erudite Bombay gentlemen carefully; and the testimonies of men, who will sit in their comfortable homes, as did Higgins, Taylor and others, and write "hearsay" about cave symbols and the pillar-inscriptions of India, to make out a case against the Palestinian origin of Christianity — are worse than worthless. Study and genuine Oriental research doom all such men and their books to eternal forgetfulness. No scholar presumes to quote them as authority.

CHAPTER XIX.

" THE FRIEND OF INDIA," published at Serampore, had among its selections, just before our arrival, this telling paragraph : —

"The Bombay papers contain accounts of a mania for spirit-rapping, which they say has set in among the natives there. If the statements are correct, it would not be surprising if the mania ran through India. Every thing connected with the spirit-world is a profound mystery to the native of India. He has no definite ideas as to the future. He confesses at once that it may be this or that, — he knows not what. A city with golden pavement astonishes him, but really the definiteness is what puzzles him. If spirit-rapping finds its way among such a people, we shall have queer revelations by and by. They will intensify a hundred-fold all the mysteries, and. will make a thousand more. Religion will not stand in the way in the slightest degree. A Hindoo is free to examine any thing on the face of the earth, and speculate to his heart's content."

A rare tissue this of the true and the false! Hindoos, thank Heaven! are "free to examine any thing on the face of the earth." And this confession, all unwittingly made, should put to shame the churchman's bigotry. "Every thing connected with the spirit-world," however, is not a "profound mystery to the native of India." Converse with spirits is as old as the Vedas, while Indian Oriental writings generally are freighted with the teachings of inspired seers and sainted Rishis.

Opening Capt. Forsyth's volume on "Central India," I find important passages on p. 362 and others. Here is the substance : —

"Theirs — the *Bygás* — it is to hold converse with the world of spirits, who are everywhere present to the aborigines; and theirs it is also to cast omens, call for rain, and charm away disease. The Bygá — medicine-man — fully looks his character. He is tall, thin, and cadaverous, abstraction and mystery residing in his hollow eyes. A great necklace, carved from forest-kernels, marks his holy calling. Ghosts are supposed to be ever present, inciting to either good or evil. Many profess to see them. . . . These Bygá medicine-men further possess the gift of throwing themselves into a trance, during which the afflatus of the Deity is supposed to be vouchsafed to them, communicating the secrets of the future. I am thoroughly convinced [says the captain], by evidence from other quarters, that this *trance is not mere acting.*"

Mr. Tscherepanoff, a Russian scientific man, published in 1854 at St. Petersburg the result of his investigations with the lamas — Buddhist priests — in Thibet. He says, "The lamas, when applied to for the discovery of stolen or hidden things, take a little table, put one hand on it, and after nearly half an hour the table is lifted up by an invisible power, and is carried to the place where the thing in question is to be found, whether in or out of doors, where it drops, generally indicating exactly the spot where the missing article is to be found."

The missionary M. Huc says, —

"When a living Buddha is 'gone,' i. e., deceased, it is not a subject of mourning in the lamasery, for all know he will soon come back."

THE ORIENTAL SPIRITUALISTS.

Readers of the "Banner of Light" remember to have heard me speak of receiving India letters from Peary Chand Mittra, a commission-merchant, writer, and Spiritualist. It can well be imagined that it gave me much pleasure to clasp the hand of this Hindoo thinker, author, and Spiritualist; and the more so when I found his soul deeply absorbed in spirituality as against the vices of this sensuous life. The Brahmanical tinge permeating his Spiritualism had for me a thousand charms. He was for a time a writing medium ; but at present his gifts pertain more to spiritual insight. He assured me that his ascended wife was as consciously present, at times, as though in her body. Parting with this excellent man, he gave us, besides other presents, a small volume from his pen entitled "The Development of the Female Mind in India." Perusing, I find it rich in historic references to woman's independence in the Vedic period, — the golden age of the Aryans.

Mohindro Saul Paul and Romanath Senx — two interesting young gentlemen connected with the higher castes — called upon us several times to converse of Spiritual phenomena in America, and the best methods of holding private séances. Conversant with the Spiritualistic literature of England through the mails, these young men are Spiritualists; and yet they have never witnessed a shred of the phenomenal. A correspondence was agreed upon with these gentlemanly Hindoos. Are we not brothers *all?*

Shibchunder Deb — another devoted Spiritualist, introduced by P. C. Mittra — presented us a neat volume that he had recently published upon Spiritualism. It contains liberal extracts from American authors; in fact, the works of Davis, Tuttle, Sargent, Denton, Edmonds, and others are well known in India. This gentleman had also translated a large portion of my book "Seers of the Ages" into the Bengalese language; and they are now being circulated as tracts in India. We saw several Hindoo *healers* relieving the sick in the streets.

Expressing regrets that I had not a copy of the "Seers" to tender him in turn for his valuable volume, smiling, he said, "I have read 'The Seers of the Ages,' and others of your later works, quite a number of which have reached our country from Mr. Burns's publishing house in London." So courage, brave fellow-workers all, courage! Your pens preach where your eloquent tongues are never heard.

India's better class of minds — metaphysical and contem-
plative — are singularly adapted to accept the harmonial
philosophy. It is a common saying that " Hindoos, educated in English colleges, return to India theists and pantheists." Though willing enough to believe in Jesus as one
of the Asiatic saviors and prophets, they can not believe in
the immaculate conception and vicarious atonement. Oh
that there were self-sacrifice, sufficient liberality, generous
enthusiasm, and missionary spirit, among Americans, to send
Spiritualist papers, pamphlets, books, and lecturers even, to
India, to disseminate the beautiful principles of brotherhood,
free thought, and a present spirit ministry! The seed has
already been sown by the angels; there are many Spiritualists in different parts of this great country: can they, *will*
they not perfect organizations, and thus come into working
order?

THE ABORIGINES OF INDIA. — A SAGE-LIKE SPIRIT'S COM-
MUNICATION.

As the present is born of the *past*, I am ever anxious, so
far as possible, to get at the foundations of the old civilizations and religions; and for the reason that many of them
were so far in advance of ours in this boastful nineteenth
century. Comparative philology, coins, and inscriptions
upon monuments, with the testimony of ancient spirits, —
these must decide upon the *status* of the pre-historic periods.
Sitting one evening by the side of Dr. Dunn aboard the
steamer " Aretusa " in the Arabian Sea, reflecting how the
rude, stalwart Northmen descended upon cultured Rome in
the long ago, and pondering upon the thought that physical
"might makes right," the doctor all unexpectedly became
entranced. The controlling spirit, bowing low after the
Oriental manner, said, —

" Good evening, stranger. I see you are wrapped in meditation; perhaps my coming is an intrusion."

Not in the least, sir; am glad to welcome you.

"The origin and destiny of races is a subject of vast import. I lived in *Hindusta*, the land of plenty, — now called India, — about four thousand years ago. We spoke the *Sansar*, the language of the sun, — vulgarized into Sanscrit. It was the language of sounds, and compassed the uttered emotions of man, beast, insect. The most learned *savants* of my time professed to understand the out-breathed and meaning sounds — pleasure, pain, desires — of all animated life. Generally poets understood one part, Rishis another, metaphysicians still another; but none knew it *all*, for it was the study of more than a single life. Our government, embracing a portion of Africa, Egypt, Assyria, Persia, and India, was patriarchal; the emperor being considered a father, under whom were kings over smaller divisions, lords of cities, and head men of villages. This extensive government, having no coin currency, and transacting business, even of a commercial character, upon the principle of *equivalents*, was largely sustained by voluntary contributions. A moderate competency was regarded a sufficiency with my countrymen.

"Indeed, it was a maxim among us that man wants only what he lives upon; and accordingly at the end of the year each city, village, and family paid over to the government all its surplus produce and treasures of every kind. And then, in times of scarcity or famine, the government, upon the principle of compensation, supported the people from its public granaries and accumulated stores. Disputes were settled by arbitration. Capital punishment was unknown among us.

"The Aryans, or rather the *Aryas*, who came down from the north, were among the first of the blood-spilling nations. They were the lower, athletic classes, the rovingly disposed, in Central and Northern Asia, speaking a mongrel Sanscrit. Their descent into India was long after my time. Our system of marriage was monogamic; after this came polyandry, the marriage of one woman to many men, of which your histories speak; still later came polygamy, which, as you are aware, continues in many countries. We worshiped one God, incarnate in all things. The pyramids, of which in due time you shall know more, were built before my time on earth."

Pardon me, but had you commerce in that age?

"Yea: we not only carried on shipping with Africa and other foreign countries, but had extensive canals through India, Egypt, and other portions of Africa. Some of these countries have been greatly changed by convulsions since I left the body. We counted time by sun-changes, and long periods by the reigns of emperors. Literature was patronized among us, and beggary unknown. I lived through about eighty *sun-changes*, or years according to your reckoning. We understood spirit-communion, and many of us held mediumistic converse with spirits. I was cognizant, long after my ascension to the heavenly life, of the spirit-world's raising up, some two thousand years since, through inspirational and magnetic processes, an Israelitish Nazarene, a *prophet*, to spiritually enlighten his people, and afterwards the nations of the earth. He was guarded by angels, and guided by the spirit of truth. There have been many ages of iron and ages of gold. Nations are ever rising and descending as do waves upon fathomless oceans."

There, reader, is the communication — the sentiments, at least — with much of the language *verbatim*. Take it as I did, with all other spirit communications, for what it is worth, weighed by reason, and sound, practical judgment.

"Is there any historic evidence," says one, "of non-Aryan races with culture and literature, inhabiting India long before the Aryans came down from the north?" Certainly there is. We have room for only this from Prof. E. Lethbridge, M.A., Oxford, and now professor in a Calcutta College. He says ("History of India," pp. 17, 18) : —

"Remnants of a large population, non-Aryan in origin, yet hardly, if at all, less civilized and polished than the Aryans, are found among the hills and river-basins south of the mountain-ranges. Their personal appearance testifies that they are not connected, by descent, with the Aryans; while their language proves decisively that they belong to an entire different race. It has been called Dravidian, — the language *Telugu;* others term it *Támil.* . . . The architectural and other remains that are scattered over the country, and the state of the language, confirm the traditions that the Tamilian race attained a high state of civilization in *very remote ages, probably long before the Aryan invasion of India.*"

ALLAHABAD.

"India of the East, o'er whose valleys sweet
Too quickly pass my ever-wandering feet,
Ere yet your shores in lengthening distance fade,
Let faithful Memory lend my pen her aid."

Unfortunately, it was long after nightfall when we crossed the magnificent bridge spanning the Jumna, to enter *Allahabad*, "the City of God," anciently called by the Hindoos *Prayaga.* Here, at the junction of the Ganges and Jumna, is the great fortress, built on the ruins of an old Hindoo fort by Akbar, a Mogul emperor, reigning about three hundred years ago. Travelers consider this — because of wide, well-shaded streets, beautiful avenues, mausoleums, and marble domes, commemorating Mohammedan glory — the handsomest city in India.

Historically speaking, it should be remembered that there were five Mohammedan invasions into India, the first being one of disgraceful plunder and downright murder. Mussulman power was not established to any great extent till nearly the twelfth century. Sultan Mahmoud, of Ghazin, fought seventeen distinct campaigns in India, carrying away immense treasures to enrich his country. His zeal in destroying idols gave him the name of "Iconoclast," — *the image-breaker.* There is a deep, silent hatred existing between the Hindoos and Mohammedans, and yet they peaceably worship side by side.

Allahabad is a wonderful resort for pilgrims. It is said that a million are sometimes encamped about the city. Some of the Brahmanical priests are evidently very saintly men ; others, doubtless, encourage these pilgrimages and festivals from avaricious motives. Priestcraft is the same in all countries. It is two hundred and fifty miles from Allahabad to Agra, world-famed for the Taj, — a tomb of exquisite and unparalleled magnificence. The structure, peerless and unrivaled, was built at a cost of fifteen million dollars, to immortalize the memory of a woman, — Noor Mahal, — the favorite wife of Emperor Shah Jehan. This Mogul ruler was the grandson of Akbar, who was sufficiently enlightened to patronize literature, and tolerate all religions. Nowhere on earth has human dust been buried in style and grandeur so sublime. Here at the Taj lie the forms of emperor and empress beneath a splendid dome, "each in a couch of almost transparent marble," set with precious stones, topaz, ruby, jasper, carnelian, chalcedony, all beautifully inwrought in running vines and blossoming flowers. It is said that the whole of the Koran in Arabic is most skillfully wrought in gemmed mosaics into this templed tomb; and *all* for what? To perpetuate in memory the pitiable pride and vanity of mortals even in death! Were there no ignorant to be educated, no hungry to be fed, and no thirsty to give a cup of water, in Shah Jehan's time? Looked down upon from the spirit-land, this tomb can only be a sting!

THE BRAHMO-SOMAJ WORSHIPERS.

As progress in all countries necessarily interests Americans, they must like to know more of the Brahmo-Somaj, — "Society of God," and real theistic church of India, — originally founded by Rajah Rahmohun Roy, a distinguished Hindoo reformer of the Brahman caste. Being a fine scholar, versed in the *Sanscrit*, he became convinced that the earliest Vedas taught a system of pure theism. Thus believing, he wrote against the "idolatry of all religions," encouraged education, advocated free thought, and opposed *suttée*, — voluntary widow-burning, then a common practice in India. Universally esteemed, Rahmohun Roy died while on a visit to England in 1833.

These first Hindoo reformers, though exceedingly liberal in most matters, firmly believed the Vedas to be the infallible word of God. Ere long, however, some doubting the infallibility of the Vedic scriptures, four young yet scholarly pundits were sent to Benares to study and copy from the four Vedas. This research dispelled the gathering fog of infallibility; and the Brahmo-Somaj, numbering many of the choicest intellects in India, ceased to be a Vedantic church. From this time the sacred books of all nations were taken for what they were worth, and no more.

No band of reformers, whether in India or America, can expect to ever sail on sunny seas. Storms, petty dissensions, will arise; some within, others without. Social persecution from orthodox Hindoos lifted its hydra head; and a partial eclipse came on, followed by indifference to the interests of theism.   17

At this critical hour there came upon the stage a caste Hindoo, and graduate from the Presidency College, *Babuo Keshub Chunder Sen.* This religiously inclined scholar, reading and admiring English literature, and the works of Theodore Parker, soon shook off every vestige of idolatrous superstition, becoming a stanch theist. Connecting himself with the Brahmo-Somaj, he quite unconsciously found himself in a short time a leader in their ranks. Expressed in a sentence, these Brahmo-Somaj worshipers are simply radical Unitarians, practicing the same order of Sunday worship, only engaging in more singing. Among their innovations are the equality of women, the ignoring of caste, the rejection of the " sacred thread," and the performance of the marriage ceremony without absurd Hindoo rites.

When proud Brahmanical Hindoos found that these iconoclastic Brahmos not only denied the infallibility of the Vedas, but did not respect the custom of child-marriage, nor cherish faith in Hindoo theology generally, they reproached them as heretics. On the other hand, "when Christians find," says Keshub Chunder Sen, "that Brahmos call in question the authority of the Bible, dispute the divinity of Jesus, and freely criticise Christian doctrines held in reverence by the best and wisest of Europe, an utter *contempt* is felt for the poor, misguided, presumptuous theists of India, whom the Rev. Dr. Duff styled as ' striplings on the banks of the River Ganges.' "

Here are sketches from their articles of belief : —

" God is spirit, not matter. He is perfect, infinite, and eternal. He is omnipresent, omnipotent, omniscient, all-merciful, all-blissful, and holy. He is our Father.

" The soul is immortal. Death is only the dissolution of the body : the soul lives everlastingly in God. There is no new birth after death : the life hereafter is only the continuation and development of the present life. Each soul departs from this world with its virtues and sins, and gradually advances in the path of eternal progress while realizing their effects.

" Brahmoism is distinct from all other systems of religion ; yet it is the essence of all. It is based on the constitution of man, and is therefore ancient, eternal, and universal. It is not sectarian, not confined to age or country.

"All mankind are of one caste, and all are equally entitled to embrace the Brahmo religion. Every sinner must suffer the consequences of his own sins sooner or later, in this world or in the next; for the moral law is unchangeable, and God's justice irreversible.

"It is the aim of the Brahmo religion to extinguish caste hatred and animosity, and bind all mankind into one fraternity, — one brotherhood of *souls*."

The Brahmos, having quite a number of organizations in India, publish a theistic annual, print six or seven journals, and send out missionaries into different parts of the country. They also have branch associations in England, Belgium, Holland, Italy, Spain, and the United States; the president of the latter being Rev. O. B. Frothingham, and the secretary, Rev. W. B. Potter. The attitude of these Indian Liberalists is exceedingly friendly and cordial toward Spiritualism. Frothingham and Potter are both now dead.

This religious movement, originating as it did among the Brahmans of India, is one fraught with vital importance. And while tendering to the Brahmos of the East and all parts of the world the hand of hearty fellowship; hoping for their growth in peace, purity, and that charity which crowns the Christian graces, — I sincerely pray that they may "add to their faith" *knowledge*, knowledge of a conscious immortality through the present ministry of spirits; thus preparing them to "go on unto perfection," holding "all things in common," and living daily the "resurrection life."

Already more than a year has passed since leaving my native home. Time flies. August days are upon me; and I must take my departure from this ancient mother-country of civilizations and religions. Egypt and Palestine are before me. But, dear old India! land of my early dreams, receptacle of Oriental learning, and the most interesting of all the countries my eyes have yet seen, I leave you reluctantly, sorrowingly. Peace, *peace*, be unto you, — *peace* from God and his good angels!

THE PARSEES.

Youth is the dreamland of life. Reading, when an academic student, of the famous Persian King Darius, contemporary of Buddha, leading an invading army into India, and also of Zoroaster the great Persian religionist, implanted in my soul a deep desire to know something practically of Persian character and religion. Next to Central Persia itself, India, containing over a hundred thousand "fire-worshipers," was just the place, inasmuch as they tenaciously retain most of the customs of their ancestors. Exceedingly clannish, dressing in Oriental, robe-shaped apparel, generally white, the Parsees do not intermarry with other nations, nor do they like to eat food prepared by other people. They consider themselves the chosen of God, and the subjects of special angel ministry. Fair-complexioned, their general appearance is graceful and commanding. They are the Jews of Bombay, the bankers, the money-lenders, the traders. On Malabar Hill they have great wealth and elegant villas. Pious Parsees pray sixteen times each day, maintain their own schools, and take care of their own poor.

ZOROASTER, FOUNDER OF THE PARSEE FAITH.

It is difficult to determine with exactness the precise period of the world's saviors. That eminent Oriental scholar, M. Haug, puts Zoroaster — Zarathustra Spitama — 2300 B.C., thus antedating Moses. But far better authorities than Haug or Rénan are the earliest Greek writers. It is a momentous consideration, that all the Greek authors who wrote upon the Magi and the Parsee religion, previous to the Christian era, put Zoroaster back to a period of full six thousand years B.C.

Xanthos of Lydia, one of the first writers upon the subject, living about 450 B.C., was a younger contemporary of Darius and Xerxes. His reckoning makes Zoroaster to have been living at a period nearly 6500 B.C.

Aristotle, the philosopher and teacher of Alexander the Great, states that Zoroaster lived about six thousand years before the death of Plato (348 B.C.), which would carry us to about 6350 B.C. Eudoxus, Harmodorus, and other Grecian writers, made similar calculations.

Hermippus of Smyrna, one of the most ancient authorities among the Greeks upon the religion of the Magi, lived about 250 B.C., making the Zoroastrian books the study of his life. This Hermippus, according to Pliny, was informed by his teacher, Agonakes, a Magian priest, that Zoroaster lived about five thousand years before the Trojan war, occurring 1180 B.C. This would take Zoroaster back to 6180 B.C.

That there was a Zoroaster in the time of Hystaspes, Darius' father, is not disputed. Zoroaster was a common name in Persia, as was Jesus in Syrian countries. But Zoroaster of the Avesta, the prophet and founder of the Parsee religion, flourished more than eight thousand years since.

RELIGIOUS DOCTRINES OF THE PARSEES.

Conversing with Ichangir Burjorji Vacha, a Parsee Oriental scholar of Bombay, and perusing the books he so kindly presented, the following is submitted as a general statement of their religious opinions : —

They believe in one God, eternal, invisible, — Ahura-Mazda, unity in duality. Ormuzd, the "highest of spirits," was a tutelary divinity, as was the Jehovah of the Old Testament. This God, Ahura-Mazda, infinitely wise and good, punishes the sinful, and rewards the virtuous for their good deeds. Their theology knows nothing of any sin-atoning Saviour. Their fire-temples have no pulpits. Their priests are teachers, abounding in prayers.

Zoroaster was the exalted prophet, the chief of the wise, who wrought miracles, who taught men to pray with their faces towards the light, who enjoined upon men to practice good deeds, and look for a reckoning on the fourth morning after death.

There are both good and evil spirits. The wise ask the protection of their guardian angels. The truly pious guard the sacred fire, bathe often, avoid pollution, encourage knowledge, and perform acts of beneficence. The Kusti and the Sudra form the badge of the Parsee worshipers. The Sudra is a plain, robe-like vest reaching to the knees ; the Kusti a hollow woolen cord, woven by women of the priest-caste only, and consisting of seventy-two threads in the warp. The Kusti, blessed of the priests, is tied over the Sudra, and wound three times around the waist. The *Nirang*, or the use of Nirang during the first morning prayer, is not enjoined in the Avesta ; nor is it practiced by the progressive Parsees of Bombay or Persia. Previous to prayers, they wash the face and hands. Each month of the year is named after an angel. All prayers are recited in the Zend language. The Parsees are not polygamists, but strictly monogamists.

PARSEE CEMETERIES, AND THE VULTURES THAT DEVOUR THEIR DEAD.

The Persian method of disposing of their dead must, to an American believing in the evangelical doctrine of the resurrection of the body, be absolutely revolting. The Parsee cemetery in Bombay, *Dokma*, situated several miles from the center of the city, is designated by some writers " the Tower of Silence." The area devoted to this purpose is located on the north-east crest of Malabar Hill, and surrounded by thick walls some thirty feet high, within which are walks, flowers, seats for meditation, and tall, round stone towers, capped with descending, concave-shapen gratings. Upon these the bodies of their dead are placed, and left to return to the elements, or be devoured by the scavenger-birds of the East. Flocks of these filthy, flesh-eating birds are said to be ever in waiting for a corpse. All avenues to these " *Towers of Silence* " are carefully guarded. Parsees themselves, even the mourners, are not permitted to enter the gateways leading to these cemeteries : only priests and a certain caste, "bearers of the dead," officiate within the walls. When suns and rains have changed, and ugly vultures torn and devoured, the flesh of these exposed bodies. the bones slide down into deep sepulchral vaults.

Owing to diet and bathing, the Parsees are long-lived. They eat neither pork, beef, nor meat of any kind. Holidays are employed in prayers and feasts. When a Parsee dies, prayers are offered at the house. The soul goes to heaven, and the body must not be tainted with corruption. Therefore it is at once washed, purified, dressed in white, and borne by the dead-bearers to the Towers of Silence. There are six of these within the walled inclosure, which overlook bungalows, public buildings, forests of palm-trees, Elephanta, and other mountain-islands studding the deep waters.

THEIR TEMPLES, ALTAR, AND FIRE.

There is little in style or architecture to outwardly distinguish a Parsee temple from a Jewish synagogue. Their edifices in all countries are considered consecrated to worship, to prayer, and the "sacred fire" originally from heaven through their prophet Zoroaster. They do not worship this *fire*, but consider it, as they do the sun, a symbol of the infinite Light, that "*eternal fire*" which must ultimately burn up the dross of the universe. Though the mosaic floors of Parsee temples are never paced by unholy feet, nor their perpetual fires seen by infidel eyes, the following description, paradoxical as it may seem, is dictated by one who has explored their temples, and gazed upon their sacred fire, ever burning in the innermost sanctuary : —

Within their temples are three courts, Parsees themselves entering only the outer. The high priest with veiled face, that his breath even may not pollute, approaches alone to see and feed the fire with sandal, precious woods, and fragrant spices. Those in the second, or intermediate court behold a dimmed reflection ; while those in the inner court only catch a glimpse of the light from the altar, and freely

breathe the incense-fumes of the spice-woods. Their altars
are of stone, and parallelogram-shaped; some rough-hewn,
and others choicely polished, shining like alabaster. On the
top of the altar is an excavation, or hollowing-out for the
fire. On one side of the altar is an exquisitely carved
figure of the sun ; on the opposite side, creation, or chaos
unfolding into *Kosmos ;* on one end is a high tower, with a
human form chiseled thereon, catching the first rays of the
rising sun, signifying the entrance of the spirit into the light
of immortality ; and on the other side is a shadowy reflection
of the sun fading away into total darkness, prefiguring
Hades, the under-world of darkness and destruction. As no
good Mohammedan drinks wine, nor Jew eats swine's flesh,
so no Parsee smokes tobacco. Such a use of *fire*, applied to
a weed, would be both a disgrace and a desecration.

Fortunately I met at Madjura, India, Dr. K. R. Divecha,
a very learned Parsee physician. From both him and his
good wife I received many kindnesses. All Zoroastrians are
Monotheists. They wear a sacred girdle, the *Kusti*, on the
shirt next to the skin. They pray while tying and untying
this girdle. They regard the cow and cow's urine as powerful means in removing disease. Intercourse with a pregnant
woman is considered a crime. Every one touching a corpse
becomes defiled. Women during menstruation must isolate
themselves from the family. They consider a corpse too
filthy to be touched and too poisonous to be buried in the
soil. The dog is a sort of sacred animal and precedes the
corpse on the march to the Tower of Silence. After a
funeral all are expected to use cow's urine to purify themselves. They pray for the dead. They look upon the
"Fravashis of the Holy" as guardian spirits. Every
family has its consecrated room. The Indian Parsees are
a very neat, thrifty and religious people. They are most
numerous in Bombay.

CHAPTER XX.

THE usual sailing distance from Bombay across the Indian Ocean to Aden, a seacoast city of Arabia, is some seventeen hundred miles; but our Austrian captain commanding the steamer "Aretusa," considering the fierceness of the monsoons at this season, decided upon the southern course, making the route full twenty-five hundred miles, and subjecting us to an eighteen-days' drag upon the deep!

This Aden in "Araby the Blest" is called the "Gibraltar of the East," because so thoroughly fortified, and consequently prepared to manage any military movements on the Red Sea. Though once held by the Portuguese, afterwards by the Turks, and now by the English, it has ever been a city of sand, nestling at the feet of volcanic peaks, and destitute of vegetation, even to a blade of grass.

Dreary and desert-looking, Aden claims a population of twenty thousand; the cantonment portion of which, being five miles from the landing, is cozily located in the crescent-shaped crater of an old, extinct volcano. It is a great mart for ostrich-feathers. Rumor declares that it rains here but once in three years.

Owing to the protracted droughts, those holding this barren place in the sixth century excavated immense reservoirs in the rocks at the foot of the mountains, for the tardy yet heavy rains to fill. Still in preservation, and called the "ten tanks," they are largely utilized to supply the present demands of the city. Standing upon heated sands, by the lowest of these tanks, surrounded by donkeys, camels, and Arabs, never did water taste sweeter to parched lips.

Back into Arabia, about seven miles from Aden, there begins to be quite a show of vegetable life. Oases multiply and widen, till farther on are green fields, small trees, and living streams, along which Arabs pitch their nightly tents. Thirty miles from the city is a fine river, which English enterprise thinks of turning into Aden.

Arabia is not the vast, barren desert once supposed. In the interior, and among the mountainous portions, are beautiful rivers, dense forests, vast pasture-lands, with choice fruits and grains.

ARABIC LITERATURE.

No traveler can say much in favor of the Arab character. The Bedouins, athletic, stout, treacherous, and roving, — wild men of the desert portions, — are the degenerate sons of Araby's better days. Like all Eastern countries, this, too, had its golden age, its period of literature and fine arts.

While the sacred canon of the Mohammedans was in Arabic, the great bulk of their general literature has been in the flowing and more musical Persian. During the latter part of the dark ages in Europe, the Arabs were the chief cultivators of science ; their literature having previously attained a high stage of development. They excelled in chemistry, mathematics, history, and poetry. One of their poets, Ferdansi, has been compared to Homer.

Whewell, in his "Ethics of Sir James MacIntosh," says : —

"In the first moiety of the middle ages, distinguished Mohammedan Arabians, among whom two are known to us by the names of Aviesura and Averroes, translated the ancient Peripatetic writings into their own language, expounded their doctrines, in no servile spirit, to their followers, and enabled the *European Christians* to make those translations of them from Arabic into Latin, which in the eleventh and twelfth centuries gave birth to the scholastic philosophy.''

This is Aug. 8, and we ship this afternoon for the Red Sea and Egypt.

> " We'll away to Egypt, and rest awhile
> In palm-girt palace beside the Nile,
> And watch from our roof Canopus rise
> In silver splendor 'mid opal skies.''

PARTING : STEAMING ALONG THE RED SEA.

We sailed into the Red Sea through the Straits of Bab-el-Mandeb, — " the gate of tears," — so named, doubtless, from the dangers of the sea ; which, while lacking a sufficient number of light-houses, abounds in African coast-winds, rough coral-reefs, and half-hidden rocks, ever the terror of navigators.

Steaming northward, the third day out, and rising with the gray gleams of morning, I had another magnificent view of the Southern Cross, hanging low in the hazy south-west distance.   A few nights and mornings thereafter, and it faded from our sight forever ; or, at least, till seen by us with unsealed eyes from the evergreen shores of the Morning Land.

The withering heat upon the Red Sea was almost beyond human endurance.   The winds, sweeping from African sands west of us, fell upon our panting persons at noonday like breaths of fire.   Thermometer measurements showed that the mercury stood in the sea-water at 90°, and in the air, from 95° to 115° in the shade.

Approaching the terminus of this sea, and standing upon the ship's deck in the Gulf of Suez, one sees, lying to the east and west, bald, arid deserts, and shrubless mountain ridges, warm in each morning's glow, and at noon a tremulous *mirage* of burning, glistening mirrors.   Farewell, O sea of fire !

For several miles out from the Suez landing, the sea is only from a mile to two and three miles in width.   A roughly-cut and rugged mountain shuts in the desert upon the left; while from a projecting tongue upon the Egyptian side, to a corresponding point upon the Arabian, the Israelites, led by Moses, are supposed to have crossed. Soundings at the present time show six fathoms of water. Sands are ever shifting in these Eastern seas: accordingly, a few thousand years ago, there might *not* have been six *feet* of water at this point. And then, again, the heavy north winds pushing, piling the waters southward with a six-feet ebb tide, the Israelites might easily have crossed upon dry land. On the other hand, a sudden change of wind, the inflowing tide, with a *not* uncommon "water-whirlwind," would naturally overwhelm and submerge the advancing Egyptians. Admitting the literal truth, therefore, of the scriptural record, no miracle was necessary for the preservation of one, or the destruction of the other party. Miracles, defined as abrogations of natural laws, are simply impossibilities.

SINAI.

Naturally skeptical, unbelief arose when our kind-hearted captain of "The Aretusa" — who, by the way, is an Austrian Spiritualist, well read in the works of Allan Kardec — pointed out to us the mountain that, 'mid reported convulsions of nature, saw the "law inscribed on tables of stone." Doubts in abeyance for the time being! Previous to reaching Suez, there loomed up in the haze upon the Arabian side grim and bald mountainous peaks, the highest and most forbidding of which is pronounced to be the Mount Sinai of the Pentateuch. Hushed forever are those thunders; lost are the voices of the Syrian prophets; and the land once flowing with milk and honey is but a desert waste. Near the foot of this ragged Sinai range is the site of Moses' wells; and bright, green spots they are, — the only verdure visible. Here it was — so say Jews and Mohammedans — that the Israelites quenched their thirst, while Jehovah displayed his power in drowning the wicked Egyptians. This Jehovah of the Old Testament, the war-god of Christians,

must have been an incorrigible sinner, if the peace principles of Jesus are divine.

SUEZ AND ITS SANDS.

Mostly a straggling mass of low mud houses, this city of
ten thousand inhabitants, including some three hundred
Europeans, is surrounded by a desert region, and naturally
repulsive to an American. One good hotel, the " Suez," with
any number of disreputable ones, a tall mosque tower. a
square with no shrubbery, and bazaars full of Oriental goods,
with Copts and Arabs for salesmen, tell the story of the
place. Not to mention fleas and lizards, one becomes disgusted while looking at the sand-clad children who brush
the flies from their sore, gummy eyes, to look upon the traveler, and cry " Backsheesh! " Evidently the glare of the
noonday sun, and the flying sand, have as much to do with
the eye-diseases of Egypt, as syphilis and other scrofulous
taints. Begging is a profession in Suez. Healthy Arab lads
will follow you, shouting, " Backsheesh! " while old men,
hoary, ragged, and toothless, hobble along after one, muttering, " Backsheesh! " It is not strange that the Israelites
wanted to leave this part of the country.

THE SUEZ CANAL.

Just previous to dropping anchor at Suez, our eye caught
a glimpse of a faint blue thread stretching away into the
desert toward the north. It was that modern triumph of
genius, the Suez Canal. Observing ships dragging slowly
around the coast of Africa and the Cape of Good Hope, and
through the Indian Ocean, for the East, that enterprising
French engineer, M. F. de Lesseps, proposed to Mohammed
Said to re-open the ancient canal of Sesostris. Be it remembered that two, three, and five thousand years ago, when
Europe had no history, Egypt not only had her *canal* through
the lakes across the isthmus, — remnants of the ruins still
remaining, — but proud old Egypt had other canals, with an
extensive commerce.

This canal, uniting the Mediterranean with the Red Sea and the vast waters of the Indian Ocean, one hundred miles in length, three hundred and twenty feet in width at the top, two hundred and forty-six feet at the bottom, and twenty-six feet deep, was formally opened on the 13th of October, 1867. At this time, as fortune would have it, we were in Constantinople, privileged to see the Austrian Francis Joseph, the Prussian Frederick William, the Italian Amadeus, now ex-King of Spain, with others in authority, on their way to the *fêtes* and festivities consequent upon the interesting occasion. Prophetic politicians, Lord Palmerston, and English aristocrats, to the contrary, the Suez Canal is a grand success.

Formerly five thousand vessels sailed to India every year around the Cape of Good Hope. Now over a thousand of these pass through the Suez Canal; and the number will increase, especially since the tolls are so fairly assessed. By this canal the distance between London and Bombay has been reduced to 3,050 miles, from 5,950 by the Cape. This canal, a colossal work, was built at an expense of sixty millions of dollars, one-half of which was contributed by the Khedive himself. Such ambition is laudable.

Considering the shifting nature of the sand, the heated barrenness of the desert, the difficulty in procuring fresh water, no one can gaze upon the numerous steamers — English screws of two thousand tons and more — driving along this desert-cut furrow filled with water, and not admire the skill of the French engineer, and the enterprise of the Khedive. Egypt that was, and then was *not*, is now waking from the dreamy slumbers of weary centuries.

FROM SUEZ TO CAIRO.

The Dead, Red, and Mediterranean Seas evidently constituted, in the almost measureless past, one body of water. At a later period the Red and Mediterranean Seas were united, as the sandy contour of the country each side of the isthmus plainly indicates.

It is about one hundred and fifty miles, if memory serves me, by railway from Suez to Cairo, much of the way lying across vast sand-plains, with only an occasional oasis. Let us hasten. Here is a patch of palms: how drooping they look! There is a slowly-pacing caravan: how patient the poor camels! There are tenting Arabs; there a lonely pelican; there camels and donkeys browsing on a sort of sage-brush; there a squad of Egyptian soldiers; there a storm of sand whirling across our track; and here a mud-built village, a very hive of squalid humanity. Around it cluster dates, figs, plums, and flourishing vegetation, the results of energy and irrigation. Many of the desert tracts of the East may, by this and other methods, be reclaimed, and made to blossom as the rose.

But see! there are piles of old, moldering ruins; there crumbling walls, and prostrate pillars! What a field for exploration! How often ancient spirits have told us of sand-buried cities! Surely, this was not once the picture of desolation that it now is. Oh the sand, the scorching sand! On this August day the thermometer stands at 136 ° Fahrenheit. It is living at a poor " dying rate ! "

But we are on the way to the Nile. Wonder if this is the route the patriarch Abraham took when going down to Egypt to escape the famine? And was it anywhere in this locality that, returning from the " slaughter of the kings," he met Melchisedec, the king of peace, the baptized of Christ?

Worn and weary, this day's railway travel across sands reminded me of the Arabian sheik's prayer. " An Arab," says Saadi, " journeying across a vast desert, wearily exclaimed, ' I pray that, before I die, this my desire may be fulfilled: that, a river dashing its waves against my knees, I may fill my leathern sack with water ! ' "

DELICIOUSLY gratifying was it to gradually leave the sands, and approach, with the lengthening shadows of the day, the wide and fertile Valley of the Nile. It was nearly twilight when the train reached the city; and yet, on our way in the carriage to the Oriental Hotel, we caught a distinct view of Cheops and Belzoni, — two of the great pyramids. The sight shot a thrill of satisfaction into my being's core.

August 18. — This, in one sense at least, was an auspicious time to reach Cairo, because the third night of the yearly illumination in honor of the Viceroy of Egypt. The estimated expenditure for the display was half a million.

They dine in the East at eight o'clock. Strolling out in evening-time, after dinner, accompanied by an Egyptian guide and Dr. Dunn, I mentally asked, "Is not this dreamland? the lotus-clime of the poet? the palace realm of the 'Arabian Nights'?" Bright globed and various colored lights were distributed through the gardens, and along the streets, arching the avenues, whitening the pavements, flickering in the branches, and sending silvered shafts down into playing fountains; while rockets, serpents, revolving wheels, and other kinds of fireworks, blazed out upon the night, half paling, for a time, torch and lamps. Not only were triangular and pyramidal-shaped figures hung with glass lanterns, trimmed and illumined, but theaters, palaces, mosques, up to the very summits of their minarets seemed all ablaze with a weird, gaseous brightness. The streets and lanes, fringed for miles with flags, banners, and costly tapestry and transparencies, were literally thronged with carriages and giddily-gaping multitudes, some in rags, some in silks and satins, and others in the gilded trappings of state. Seen externally, it was a most magnificent pageant. Considered spiritually, it was the quintessence of babyish folly, — the glittering pampering so pleasing to vain royalty. This half million, worse than squandered, should have been spent in educating ignorant subjects, freeing the country from slavery, and feeding the wretched street-beggars.

Disgusted with the confusion, the wild excitement, and the sham of the show, I returned to my apartment to meditate.

Is it a dream? or am I really in Egypt, the country of Hermes, Trismegistus, and Menes the founder of Memphis? Am I in the land of ancient symbolical art, of hieroglyphs, obelisks, pyramids, and paintings, of monoliths, sarcophagi, and templed tombs? Changed, oh, how changed during the devastating decades of two, three, and five thousand years! The sacred Nile still moves on in silent majesty; but no wandering Isis weeps, searching for the dead Osiris. The shadow of Typhon's frown falls no more upon the tremulous waves of this great rolling river. The lips of Memnon, touched, smitten even by rising sunbeams, remain voiceless as the sphinx that gazes coldly out upon the vast granary-valley of Egypt. Cleopatra and the kingly Ptolemies are only dimly, dreamily remembered; but those marvels of towering masonry, those *pillared Pyramids*, though stripped of their marble casings, continue to stand in peerless grandeur, the wonder of the races, the riddle of the ages!

THE KHEDIVE AND HIS PURPOSES.

Işmael Pasha, Kheılive of Egypt, formerly resided in a magnificent palace on the Bosphorus, surrounded by lawns and gardens, *all* arranged in the highest style of Oriental elegance. He was educated in Paris. The clear complexion and light blonde hair, that he inherited from his Circassian mother, give him more the appearance of an Anglo-Saxon than an Oriental. He is of medium height, stately in gait, with a full forehead, gray eyes, and shrewd expression of countenance.

He is immensely rich, virtually holding the land of Egypt in fee simple ; his subjects working it on *his* terms. The proceeds fill his purse too, rather than the pockets of the fellahs. Irrigation-canals are bringing a vast amount of barren land under cultivation ; four thousand miles of telegraph stretch from the Delta over the Nile Valley in every direction ; and surveys have been made for the purpose of rendering the Nile navigable its whole course. There will be, within a few years, a continuous line of railway from Alexandria to Khartoum, near the site of the ancient Meroe at the junction of the Blue and White Nile, a distance of fifteen hundred miles. Ere long the confines of Egypt will be extended over Darfour, Abyssinia, and the Soudan, to the Mountains of the Moon, — countries burdened with heavy forests, and abounding in medicinal plants, in gold, silver, iron, and copper, in cotton, rice, and other productions of great commercial value. It is said by the Khedive's ardent admirers that wherever he pushes his conquests he abolishes the slave-trade. This is seriously doubted. Domestic slavery, and polygamy, are common in most Mohammedan countries.

THE CENTRAL AFRICANS AS THEY ARE.

English scientists sitting in their cozy homes, consulting the reports of sea-captains, slave-buyers, and the tales of ivory-dealers, write glibly of Africa, and the degraded African tribes. Opinions derived from such sources are utterly worthless, as compared with the testimonies of Sir Samuel Baker, Prof. Blyden of Liberia, Dr. Livingstone, and other distinguished men, long residents in Africa. Dr. Livingstone says, —

" If I had believed a tenth of what I heard from traders, I might never have entered the country. . . . But fortunately I was never frightened in infancy with ' bogie,' and am not liable to ' bogiephobia;' for such persons in paroxysms believe every thing horrible, if only it be ascribed to the possessor of a black skin." *

After speaking of the insight and practical good sense of the Bushmen, Livingstone remarks, —

" We all liked our guide Shobo, a fine specimen of that wonderful people, the Bushmen." †

Referring to the race of Makololos, he observes, —

" Their chief Sebituane came a hundred miles to meet me, and welcome me to his country."

This is an intelligent, kind-hearted race, having no fear of death, because believing in immortality. " When I asked the Bechuanas to part with some of their relics, they replied, ' Oh, no ! ' thus showing their belief in a future state of existence. The chief boatman often referred to departed spirits who called a Placho." ‡ Treating of the Bakwains, a large inland tribe of Africans, Livingstone says, —

" Though rather stupid in matters that had not come under their observations, yet in other things they showed more intelligence than is to be met with in our own uneducated peasantry. . . . They are well up in the maxims which embody their ideas of political wisdom." §

Mentioning the keenness of perception manifest among the tribes north of the Zambesi, he says, —

" They all believe that the souls of the departed still mingle among the living, and partake in some way of the food they consume. . . . They fancy themselves completely in the power of disembodied spirits." ||

.* Livingstone's Africa, p. 542.   † Ibid., p. 47.   ‡ Ibid., p. 121.
§ Ibid., p. 21. || Ibid , 283–287.

Describing the far inland Manyema men, he pronounces
them, —

" Tall, strapping fellows, with but little of what we think distinctive
of the negro about them. If one relied upon the teachings of phrenology,
the Manyemas would take a high place in the human family. . . . Many
of the Manyema women, especially far down the Lualaba, are very pretty,
light complexioned, and lively."

Speaking of another race in the interior of Africa, Dr.
Livingstone says, —

" They are slender in form, having a light olive complexion. . . . The
great masses of hair lying upon their shoulders, together with their general features, reminded me of the ancient Egyptians. Some even have
the upward inclination of the outer angles of the eyes." *

" The London News," commenting upon Livingstone and
Stanley, expresses the conviction that " enterprising travelers
will soon find a full confirmation of those old Egyptian traditions handed down to us by Herodotus, which until recently were supposed to be romance rather than actual fact. The
account of the races that Livingstone met indicates that the
inhabitants of Central Africa have a civilization little dreamed
of by European anthropologists. And then, the whole
country is exceedingly fertile, especially in those resources
which repay commercial enterprise."

Sir Samuel Baker in his Cambridge lecture made this
observation: " Central Africa will awake when the first
steam-launch is seen upon the Albert Nyanza; " and he added,
" Nowhere in the world does scenery exist more beautiful, or
soil more fertile, or climate more healthy to the temperate
and strong, than those vast and diversified highlands of Central Africa, which inclose these glorious, sparkling seas of
sweet water, and feed the mighty rivers whose course is so
far-winding that to this day no man has yet traversed them
from mouth to fountain."

The mayor of Monrovia, Liberia, confirming the above

* Livingstone's Africa, p. 296.

statements of Dr. Livingstone and Sir Samuel Baker, assured me that the lowest of the Africans were found along the sea-coasts : while, the farther one ventured into the interior, the finer and more intelligent races he found. "Some of the tribes," said he, " in Central Africa, bear little or no resemblance to negroes ; being tall, light-complexioned, ingenious, and thoughtful men." Of what racial division of humanity are these tribes the lingering remnants ? What of their origin ? And when was their palmy period ?

AFRICA THE BIRTHPLACE OF THE SANSCRIT.

None interested in the " lost arts," or conversant with the matchless grandeur of the past, need be informed that the ancient Greek and Babylonian historians ever reverted to Africa as the once garden of the world. And, marvelous as it may seem, many of the root-words applied to the rivers and mountains in Africa are directly traceable to the Sanscrit language. Wise spirits, of remotest antiquity on earth, have assured us that the Sanscrit in distant, prehistoric periods, was, if not the universal language, the language of the cultured Africans. It was in Africa that this, the most perfect of written languages, according to Sir William Jones and other Orientalists, originated. Those primitive peoples, acquainted with agriculture, mechanics, art, literature, and withal becoming as ambitious as populous, moved slowly off in time, through those regions denominated in later periods Mizraim (Egypt), Assyria, Iran, Media, into Central Asia, where, multiplying, they were called Aryas. In a long-subsequent era, they swarmed out from those high table-land localities in all directions. A branch of them met and mingled with the progenitors of the Cathayans. The Malays sprang from this intermixture. The more warlike division of these Aryas that moved southward, invading India, came to be known as the *Aryans*.

This country, protected by mountains on the north, and oceans on the south, largely escaped the vandal influences of war. Prospering, they modified and reconstructed their literature, preserving it from entire destruction. What remains is known as the ancient Sanscrit of India, a reflex wave of which ultimately returned to Egypt. Fading remnants of this fairer race, degenerate descendants of the original African Aryas, still exist in Central Africa. Dr. Livingstone describes them as " tall and slender, olive complexioned, and as intelligent to-day as the peasantry of Britain."

SWEDENBORG'S MOST ANCIENT OF ALL BIBLES.

Those African Aryas not only possessed a literature, but a Bible rich in nature's teachings. Was not this the veritable Bible referred to by the Swedish seer ?

Swedenborg, giving an account in his " Memorable Relations " of what he saw and heard in the world of spirits, says, " There was a Bible far more ancient than the Jewish Scriptures, harmonizing perfectly with the revelations of nature, most of which was lost. But some scraps were gathered by Moses, and preserved, appearing in what is now termed the Old Testament. In this remote period of time people talked in the language of correspondence ; afterwards the symbolic, or pictorial ; this degenerated into the hieroglyphical ; and this again into the various dialects spoken by the Semitic races." He further says (A. C. 1002). " The people of these most ancient times never on any account ate the flesh of any beast or fowl, but fed solely on grains, fruits, herbs, and various kinds of milk." Referring to the degeneracy of men, he says, " In the course of time, when mankind became cruel and warlike as wild beasts, they began to slay animals, and eat their flesh."

CAIRO AS A CITY.

The Cairo of to-day, including the old city and the new, has an estimated population of five hundred thousand. The mixture of races puts to defiance the classifications of ethnologists. Under the administration of the Turkish Khedive, or reigning viceroy, the city is rapidly improving. The palaces, the public buildings, and the substantial bridge across the Nile, are fine specimens of architectural masonry. Old Cairo is three miles from the new, and yet there is no real break of buildings between them. Modern Cairo seeks its model in Paris, not only in extravagance, fashions, and luxuries, but in its amusements, gardens, sparkling fountains, marble walks, mosaic pavements, and reception-rooms inlaid with porphyry and alabaster. The viceroy is still building for himself new palaces. Those who wish to see the Cairo of the past should not delay. The weird old houses, with their polished and fantastic lattice-work, are fast disappearing. All day long the remorseless chipping and hammering of the mason is heard. The constructor is upon his heels; and soon boulevards and flowering gardens will cover alike the ruins of the Christian Coptic and the more ancient Egyptian.

THE CITADEL AND THE MUSEUM.

Rising above the rest of the city, is the grand mosque, called the citadel. Standing by this Mohammedan structure, one may catch a panoramic view of the whole plateau; the Nile, fringed in living green, rolling at your feet; at the right the tombs of the old caliphs and Mamelukes; on the left the ruins of ancient Cairo; in the distance emerald islands, dotting the now swollen Nile; and, farther off, scores of monuments and pyramids pushing their gray shafts up toward the heavens. The prospect is magnificent.

During the day we visited one of the old Coptic churches, said by our guide to have been built in the seventh century. The paintings of Bible scenes were unique and fantastic, the crypts cold and gloomy.

Among objects of deep interest to travelers is the Egyptian Museum, situated upon the banks of the Nile, and enriched with rarest specimens from ancient Memphis, Heliopolis, and hundred-gated Thebes. Many of the museums of Europe abound in the rare curiosities of old Egypt, and yet her ruins are not exhausted. New discoveries are constantly being made, both in Upper and Lower Egypt. Walking through the cabinets of this museum in Cairo, free to the public, one may read the history of Egypt for five thousand years, — its religion, its art, and domestic life

WHAT A SPIRIT SAID TO THE CLAIRAUDIENT EAR.

While studying the relics of antiquity in this museum, and wondering what this and that hieroglyphical figure meant, an ancient Egyptian spirit came, and explained them clairaudiently to Dr. Dunn. Referring to the manners and customs characterizing his period, he said, among other things, that the "Great Pyramid, constructed upon mathematical and astronomical principles, with its seven well-aired chambers, was built for a *granary*, and the *coffer* for a measurer. Others in after periods were constructed for different purposes." Speaking of the hieroglyphs, he said, "The hawk symbolized war; the deer fleetness; the triangle, trinities; the *yoni*, purity, also generative life; and the circle, immortal existence."

Though the opinion may be considered a wild one, I venture the belief that the original Sanscrit was simply phonetically abbreviated hieroglyphs. The ancients, instead of carefully chiseling the whole hawk, would naturally, after a time, convey the thought by drawing the head of the bird, then the bill, then the bill-shaped curve, which *curve* would signify war, and emphasized a *warrior*.

THE NILOMETER AND NILE.

Opposite Old Cairo, nestling in the Nile, lies the little isle of Roda, the north part of which is occupied by beautiful gardens. Arabic tradition assures us that it was here that Pharaoh's daughter found "Moses in the bulrushes." If these guides are sincere, they deserve only pity.

The famous Nilometer — *Nile-measurer* — is located upon this island. It did not strike me as any thing very wonderful. It consists of a square well, in the center of which is a graduated pillar, divided into cubits, and surrounded by circular stones with inscriptions upon them. Along the arches are passages from the Koran in sculpture. The whole is surmounted by a dome. The Nile begins to rise the latter part of June, reaching its maximum about the 25th of September. It is watched during this period with intense interest; because, if rising too high, it produces inundations, destroying crops ; and if not high enough, filling the canals and reservoirs, the means of irrigation fail, causing infertility and famines. The yearly rise is from twenty to forty feet, depositing over the fertile valley a rich sediment of nearly two inches in thickness. It is to be hoped that before our Stanley leaves Africa, the sources of the Nile will no longer be geographical problems. Strabo, the ancient geographer, mentions the Nilometer. Diodorus informs us that it was in use during the period of the Pharaonic kings; and Herodotus speaks of its measuring the Nile waters when he visited Egypt twenty-three hundred years ago. Though not a vestige of rain has fallen now for nearly six months, the river at the present time is very high and muddy. During inundations the rise is proclaimed daily in the streets of Cairo. The rainy season lasts about three months.

CAIRO STREETS.

These are crowded in evening time with unique vehicles, veiled women, loose-jointed camels and little donkeys with their dark-skinned drivers. The back streets are narrow and ill-smelling. The electric cars are poorly manned. The pyramids, forty centuries old, here look down upon electricity and steam. Pharaoh and Edison shake hands. The most ancient and the most modern civilization jostle each other along the streets. Let us meditate !

CHAPTER XXII.

EGYPT'S CATACOMBS AND PYRAMIDS. — APPEARANCE OF
THE EGYPTIANS.

IN physique the Egyptians of to-day are larger and much
stouter in organic structure than the Hindoos, yet evidently
lack their intellectual activity. Physically they are a well-
formed race, with an expressive face, retreating forehead, jet
black eyes, full lips, prominent nose, broad shoulders, and
beautiful teeth. Their complexions — strangely blended —
vary; the darkest are doubtless the descendants of the
pyramid-builders. Those having an infusion of Arabian
blood in their veins are exceedingly hardy and stalwart.
The women veil their faces, *all* except their eyes. A certain class, however, as do some Syrians, veil their faces completely. The reasons assigned refer to the harem, and the
" look " of temptation.

Dress, with Egyptian men, consists of trousers, — literally
a red bag through which the feet are thrust, — a tight under-
shirt, probably white when clean; a short, flying over-
jacket; a heavy, sash-like fold of cloth about the waist; and
a red-tasseled " tartouche " upon the head, around which is
twisted a fanciful coiffure. All classes wear the tartouche,
even those who otherwise doff the European dress. Travelers frequently put it on, thinking to pass for old citizens.
Have they forgotten the " brayer " in the " lion's skin " ?
Could I speak but one word to the Khedive of Egypt, that
word should be *education*, — educate the people !

THE PYRAMIDS, THE PYRAMIDS!

A picnic from Cairo to the pyramids is one of the easiest things, nowadays, in the world. The Great Pyramid, Cheops, is only some ten or twelve miles from the city, and a fine carriage-road; but this is not the route for tourists desirous of seeing other pyramids, the ruins of Memphis, Heliopolis, and the tombs at Sakkarah.

Accompany us. It is seven o'clock in the morning, carriage at the door, the lunch-basket filled, the guide ready. The streets are yet comparatively quiet. Starting westward, we cross the bridged Nile, and pass along its banks, under overarching acacias, by a palatial structure of the viceroy's, in process of completion, by quaint buildings of less prominence, by mud-built huts, toward Geezah. Here we alight, and take to the cars as far as the Bardshain station, where, finding mules and muleteers, we are off through crooked paths to the ruins of Memphis. Donkey-riding is doleful business for a tall man, inasmuch as feet dangling in the sand become neither grace nor comeliness. But see those heavily-laden camels on their way to the market, those toilers winnowing grain by fickle wind-gusts, and, beyond, those beautiful groves of date-palms, reddening and ripening to load the tables of the rich!

Now we are upon the threshold of the Memphian ruins. Though level with the ground, or buried in the sand, they cover a vast plain. Egyptian priests informed Herodotus that Memphis was founded by Menes, a very ancient king of Egypt, and noted for having turned the Nile from its course, making a large tract of dry land upon which to build a city. In hieroglyphs, Memphis was styled Manofre, the "land of the pyramids," the "city of the white wall." According to Diodorus, this wall was seventeen miles in length, girdling and guarding the city against armies, and the annual overflow of the "Eternal River." The city, once or twice rebuilt, had suffered terribly from the Persians when Herodotus saw it. Among its most magnificent temples was that of *Phtah*. Near this temple, at the gate, were statues, one fifty feet high, made of light-colored silicious limestone. At the entrance of the east gate, there lies, at present, the statue of a Memphian god, two-thirds buried in the sand. It is red granite, about twenty feet in length, beautifully chiseled, highly polished, and lies nearly upon the face. Other statues and unique relics have been found in this vicinity. If you look at them, however, a swarm of beggars, with their attending flies and fleas, fasten to you. The pest of travelers are these begging Bedouin Arabs. Their bullying, gesticulating, importuning impertinences are supremely contemptible. Giving them less or more, they are still unsatisfied.

Let us on, over brick-dust, broken pottery, carved images, and shifting sands, some two miles to Sakkarah, the vast subterranean tomb-lands of the old empire, called the "Sakkarah plateau of the dead." With the exception of a single modern stone building, Sakkarah is a grassless, shrubless, houseless cemetery of robbed tombs. Acres are honeycombed and mummiless; and still nearly a thousand men, under the auspices of government, are employed excavating and digging for relics and antiques. The treasures found daily are kept secret.

Ascending a little hill, the eye could take in, at a single sweep, eleven pyramids. They are neither of the same size nor shape, nor have they the same angles. One very large one before us is square, yet pyramidal-domed. Others, square at the base, are nearly round up a little distance, and pagoda-storied near the summit, *all* clearly indicating that they were built at different periods, and for diverse purposes. Travelers mention about one hundred and forty pyramids, and all within nearly one degree of latitude, clustering in and along through Middle Egypt. Thebes, on the same side of the Nile as Cairo, is about ten days up the river. They measure distances here in the East not by miles, but by hours and days.

Let us go into the Memphian catacombs. The ponderous gate of death swings on its rusty hinges. The guides light their tapers. The main passage, several hundred yards in length, is cut in a solid limestone rock. To the right and left of this arched avenue are niches filled with large sarcophagi. These, chipped and hewn from the hard granite, are beautifully polished and hieroglyphed, but empty. Vandals of the past robbed them of their embalmed remnants of mortality. There were twenty-seven of these sarcophagi, one of which, resembling pure porphyry, was constructed by King Bis for his last resting-place. History puts him down as a vain, ambitious ruler. Might he not, in his dying hour, have uttered the following ? —

> "Farewell, a long farewell, to all my greatness !
> This is the state of man : to-day he puts forth
> The tender leaves of hope ; to-morrow blossoms,
> And bears his blushing honors thick upon him ;
> The third day comes a frost, a killing frost,
>
> .   .   .   .
>
> And then he falls, as I do. I have ventured,
> Like little wanton boys that swim on bladders,
> This many summers in a sea of glory.
>
> .   .   .   .
>
> Vain pomp and glory of this world, I hate ye ! "

A little distance from this range of catacombs, we visited the excavated cave-tombs of *Seri-biana*. The mummied forms, with the gaudy casing and linen wrapping, had been removed. Approaching the grim cavity, a fox leaped out, and fled into the distance. It reminded me of Hosea Ballou's famous " Fox Sermon," from the passage, " O Israel, thy prophets are like the foxes in the desert ! " This was a magnificent tomb, with the two pillars at the entrance arranged in Masonic order, and twelve others surrounding the sarcophagus, each full four feet, made of a magnesian limestone composition, hard as rock, and decorated with hieroglyphics. Egypt wrote her public history on walls.

towers, and obelisks. But in these tombs are inscriptions setting forth the names and titles of the deceased, followed by an address to Anubis, guardian of tombs, and also to the gods beyond the river of death, asking them to be favorably disposed toward the individual in his journeyings to the Elysian lands of the blessed.

Wandering among the subterranean temples and tombs of Sakkarah, site of the ancient Memphis, and reflecting upon the gigantic size of these rock-cut granitic graves, long since ruthlessly deprived of their mummied wealth, the wonder increased how such huge masses of stone were ever brought here so finely cut, and each fitted to its place. Those ancient Egyptians certainly had mechanical knowledge, and powers of moving immense blocks, of which we are comparatively ignorant. And, by the way, these Ramsean temples and tombs were as much a marvel to the Grecian Herodotus as they are to us.

"SIX MILES TO CHEOPS!"

So sings out our jolly guide. It seems very much nearer. The sun is slowly declining; let us hasten. Any thing but a contrary donkey for locomotion! Effort is useless: the stupid brute will hunt his own sand-path. Now we pass a herd of breeding camels, with their young; there a miserable mud-built Bedouin camp; there a little patch of crisped vegetation; and, just beyond, a turbid-looking back-water cove from the swollen Nile. This we must drink, or thirst. Surely, —

"Every pleasure hath its *pain*, and every sweet a *snare*."

But here we are, under the shadow of the Sphinx, hewn, cut, and polished, from a reddish solid limestone rock, and resting in its original position. With the body of a lion, and the head of a man, emblematic of strength and wisdom, it has gazed coldly, with prophetic eye, for thousands of years, upon the fertilizing Nile. The rough-featured face, shame-

Egyptian Magician.

fully defaced, conveys the impression of thoughtfulness and a fixed resolution. The architect evidently fashioned it to represent *Che-ops-see*, the builder of the Great Pyramid. Cheops, *alias Che-ops-see*, was deified after his death as " Ramses the Great ! " Ram, Rama, Ramses, are famous names in India to-day, as well as historic landmarks in the palmier days of the Asia and Africa of the dreamy past. On the Sphinx was hieroglyphed the name of this *great king of the world*, " RAMSES THE GREAT ! "

The figure, according to the measurement of Prof. C. P. Smyth, Sir Gardner Wilkinson, and other distinguished explorers, is thirty-seven feet above the sand-surface, and something like thirty-seven feet below. It is twenty-nine feet across the wig, for the image, remember, has a colossal beard. The lips and protruding lower jaw typify a deficient moral organization. Owing to the perusal of imaginative and overdrawn descriptions of the Sphinx, it quite disappointed me, both in size and the architectural elegance of the workmanship. Still it is a wonder, — a deathless monument guarding a desert waste !

One quarter of a mile more to the foot of Cheops. Who would tarry long at the Sphinx ? Off and away, donkeys ! They become spirited. See, they actually gallop ! But, " ha ! *ha !* " here we are at the base of the Great Pyramid ! Casting an eye toward its dizzy summit, language proves inadequate ! Every fiber of my being flames with the grand, the majestic, the inexpressible ! Come, Beverly, — mad philosopher of New Zealand, — *come*, bringing your diagrams and figured calculations, and let us explore them together. Do you not remember, friend Beverly, how we nightly talked of the pyramids, last winter, till the clock struck ten ; ate fruit, and talked on about the Pyramids ; turned the slate, stirred the fire, and still talked about the old Pyramids ? *Hark !* the bell rings out upon the clear midnight air, — *Twelve !* and still the pyramid-mania rages. You, Mr. Beverly, in the estimation of the ignorant Dunedin rabble, was a crack-brained enthusiast; and self, a crazy Spiritualist just loose from some American madhouse. Laughing at all such pious rage, we remembered, that, when Bunyan's lions became too old and toothless to bite, they gratified their vicious dispositions by growling. Sectarians, harmless nowadays, can only growl.

But the pyramids! Cheops, built strictly upon geometrical and astronomical principles, faces due north, south, east, and west. And, according to the measurement of Col. Howard Vyse, the base of this pyramid is 764 feet, and the vertical height 480 feet, with a basical area of thirteen acres, one rood, and twenty-two poles. The quantity of masonry is 89,028,000 cubic feet, with a weight of 6,848,000 tons; the space occupied by chambers and interior passages being something over 56,000 cubic feet of the immense mass. Greek authors state that 500,000 laborers, comprising government captives and bondsmen, were employed during a period of twenty-five years in putting up and completing the structure. To fully realize the magnitude of this desert Titan, one should walk around it, and then, looking up to its dizzy height of five hundred feet, reflect that the granite blocks which furnish the outside of the third, and a portion of the inside of the first pyramid, came, if not manufactured on the spot, all the way from the first cataract; and that outwardly these monumental giants were originally covered with silicious limestone, or marble, highly polished. These facts considered, and the magnificence, the pristine splendor, begin to become manifest.

UP, UP TO THE APEX.

Our dragoman engaging three Bedouin Arab assistants for each, we were ready for the ascent. Full of pluck, we start up the stony steep, scaling block after block. A stout Arab clasps each of our hands firmly. Getting weary, the third "*boosts*," — if there's a more classic word to convey the idea, use it. Though fun at first, fatigue and exhaustion soon follow. "Bravo! a third of the way up: take a rest," shout the guides. Another start, but not so gay and gritty as the first. Up, and still upward; the air seems too light for breathing. Pity be to the short-winded! blessings to the long-legged! all deformities have their uses. 'Tis done! Our feet press the summit! Hallelujah! The apex, seen at a distance as a point, proves to be an area full twelve feet square, from which the view is absolutely magnificent. Northward, you look down the river upon the Delta, with its patches of green, groups of palms, and long files of patient camels. Southward, you gaze up the river, fringed with waving date-palms, penciled in gold against the delicate sky; fields of vegetation, green and yellow; flocks of black and brown sheep, with attending shepherds; peasant-women bearing water-jars upon their heads; and, farther on, the ashes of the ancient Memphis. Eastward, upon Cairo, with its glittering domes, minarets, labyrinthine streets, dazzling bazaars, public squares, coffee-houses, three hundred mosques for Mahometan prayers, and the gracefully-towering citadel, grand and gorgeous, crowning the whole. Westward stretches in the clear distance the African Sahara, undefinable and immeasurable; while at your feet, seemingly, rolls the majestic Nile, great river-god of the old Egyptians, whose sculptured figures they wreathed with lotus-flowers, and filled his extended arms with their ripened fruits and grains. Let us linger upon this desert Mount of Transfiguration, and meditate. But where — where's the doctor?

A SÉANCE ON THE PYRAMIDS.

Sunny and joyous, Dr. Dunn and his Arab aids started first to make the ascent; but for some unaccountable reason they had not yet reached the pinnacle. Looking over the precipitous stone terraces, there he was, full a third of the way down. "What's the matter?" we inquired. "Why those gesticulations, and why the delay?" — "Dun no," was the Arab response in broken English. "Well, go down and

help them." A shrug of the shoulders said *No!* Becoming
alarmed, I exclaimed with strong emphasis, " *Go down after
them!*" They stood mute and stolid as statues. Impul-
sively taking all the silver from my pocket, — a precious
little, — and giving it to the leader, I repeated, "Go to the
rescue!" Down they went. Alone now upon the Pyramid!
what a moment! But here the whole party comes; Dr.
Dunn unconsciously entranced, and the Arabs, all excited,
frightened at his "fits." The mystery was solved.

The trance is closely allied to hypnotism, originally called
mesmerism, and later termed psychology, biology and electro-
biology.

Hypnotism is from *hypnos*, a Greek word signifying sleep;
and this sleep produced by the will may be accomplished
either by the transference of a refined, etherealized fluid, or
by suggestion.

The brain is a magnet; and around every object in nature,
the atom, the crystal, the ivy, there is an invisible atmosphere, an emanating aura. Independent clairvoyants see
it.

This aural effluence, encircling all objects, extends off from
one to five and fifteen feet from the individual according to the will and soul-potency. Spirits make use of this
aura in entrancing their sensitive subjects.

A change; owing to inharmonious conditions, the entrancement is spasmodic. How the Arabs stare! It is difficult to
keep them at a distance.

But listen: another spirit has taken possession. What
dignity in the attitude! and what a deep-toned voice! —

"Traveler, you stand now upon the summit of one of the world's
wonders, — a mountain of stone rising from trackless sands. I once
lived under these skies, vestured in a mortal body. The same majestic
river rolled through the valley; but winds, storms, shifting sands, and
maddened convulsions, have changed all else. This pyramid, upon
which I often gazed, was even *then* more a matter of tradition than history. It must have received its final cap-stone over ten thousand years
since. Our time was measured by ruling dynasties. My years on earth

seem now like a half-forgotten dream. Starry worlds have faded, islands have risen from the ocean; continents have disappeared; thronged cities have perished; conquering kings have been born, ruled, died, and been forgotten; but this Titanic monument of the desert still stands in stately solitude. And yet nothing earthly is immortal; this pillared pile of composite, of granite, and of porphyry is slowly, surely crumbling. Only the undying soul, the templed pyramid of *divinity* within, is eternal. See, then, O stranger and pilgrim! that every thought, deed, act, — *each* a 'living stone' placed in the spiritual temple you are constructing, — is polished, and fitted to its place with the master's 'mark.'

"But you wish to know the purpose of *this*, the oldest of the pyramidal structures. The aim was multiform. Carefully considering the constellations, the position of the North Star, and the shadow cast by the sun at the time of the equinoxes, it was built upon mathematical principles, to the honor of the *Sun-God* that illumines and fructifies the earth; built for the preservation of public documents and treasures during wars of invasion, and built as a storehouse for *grains* during famines and devastating floods, with that mystic *coffer* in the center, as an exact measurer for the world. A universal system of weights and measures, a universal currency, and a universal government, were Utopian theories of the ancients before my period of time. This pyramid was not built by forced toil, and at a great sacrifice of life, but by gratuitous contributions, the servants of the wealthy doing the manual labor. There are seven granary apartments in the structure, with shafts leading from each to the common granary of the coffer, now called the King's Chamber. These shafts have not yet, to my knowledge, been discovered.

"During long rains and terrible floods, ancient Memphis was twice swept away, — once even to its walls, with all its inhabitants, in a single night. Convulsions of nature, and terrible floods, were then common. Immediately after one of these, this pyramid was commenced, requiring more than a generation in the construction. It was completed before the great flood, and the wars of the shepherd kings.

"Once in my time the water rose, and rolled over the very apex of these stones. It rained *forty-five consecutive days;* and, while torrents swept down the Nile Valley from the south, stout, heavy winds from the Mediterranean drove the water up the country, piling wave upon wave, till this structure was completely submerged. But, though thus buried in the flooding waters, the treasures and well-filled granaries remained to feed, when the waters subsided, the famishing people who had fled southward to the hilly country. There seems to be less water upon the face of the earth now than then. Liquids are becoming solids, and change in every department of being is doing its destined work. Only pyramids of truth, constructed of immutable principles, are eternal.

"*Che-ops-see*, the great king of the world, died in Thebes. Embalmed by the priests, he was placed, after a time, in this pyramid, as a
mark of *honor* for having conceived and planned a monument serving as
the savior of his subjects. Finally, the sarcophagus removed, he was
godded, or deified, *Ramses the First;* and the Sphinx, that calm, weird,
unreadable face, now mutilated by a degenerate people, was designed to
hand the outlines of his physiognomy down to posterity. I must leave.
Stranger from a foreign country, do well the work appointed you, that,
when ashes and sands claim their own, you may be prepared for the
fellowship of those ancient spirits of whom you seek counsel."

We have reported this Egyptian spirit's ideas and words
as best we could. Take them for what they are worth, making history, hieroglyph, and reason the umpire of decision.
Powhatan, the good Indian spirit, came, and, noting the
waning of the western sun as a symbol of the fading-away
of the aboriginal tribes before a merciless civilization, said
they went down like setting stars, to rise into the better conditions of the Morning Land.

CHAPTER XXIII.

THOUGH in no wise smitten with the pyramid mania, still I must say that the image of the Great Pyramid, sitting so kingly upon the African side of the Nilotic Valley, can never be effaced from the picture-gallery of my soul's memory chambers.

WHEN? — WHAT OF IT?

"I asked of Time : ' To whom arose this high,
　Majestic pile, here moldering in decay ? '
He answered not, but swifter sped his way,
　With ceaseless pinions winnowing the sky.

. . . .

I saw *Oblivion* stalk from stone to stone :
　' Dread power ! ' I cried, ' tell me whose vast design ' —
He checked my further speech in sullen tone :
　· Whose once it was, I *care not :* now 'tis *mine !* ' "

Strangely, and with widely different eyes, do men of culture look at the tablets, carvings, memorials, and teaching monuments of antiquity. Many surface-thinking Americans have sneered at them; while others have scoffingly mocked the fading memories of their inspired constructors. A New York journalist, while traveling in the East a few years since, spotted a bit of clean manuscript paper with this paragraph : " These old pyramids, useless and crumbling, are only ugly piles of stones, covering a few acres of howling desert." This style has been too common with the flippant, the facile, and the ambitious, from the time of Pliny, down to the novelist Sir Walter Scott.

It is needless to remind the historian that the old Greeks were exceedingly indignant with their distinguished traveler, Halicarnassus, who, after having explored, extravagantly praised the pyramids

"What!" said these vain Greeks; "does not our own divine Greece possess monuments more worthy of intelligent admiration? Had not Greece the *omphalos*, or navel-stone of the whole earth, to show in the temple of Delphi, in order to prove that Greece was the center of the vast world's plain? Were not Greek rocks and hills, Greek fountains and groves, all hallowed by the presence of Grecian gods and goddesses of every degree? And were not the then inhabitants of Greece descended by direct line from those superhuman beings? What need had a Greek to go to distant Egypt, and admire any thing not erected by genius of Grecian artists?"

Still, in the face of the most virulent opposition, in spite of the boastful Greeks 500 B.C., in spite of Rome's proud Cæsars, in spite of twenty-five hundred years of persistent attempts to sneer down and write down these monarchs of the ages, there they stand, *irrepressible*, — absolutely refusing to be driven or scribbled into oblivion!

OPINIONS OF THINKERS AND SAVANTS.

Saying nothing of German and French scholars who have visited, measured, and written of the pyramids, — nothing of Prof. John Greaves, Col. Howard Vyse, Sir Gardner Wilkinson, and other men of letters, — we turn with pride to Prof. C. Piazza Smythe, Astronomer Royal of Scotland. When this erudite and eminent gentleman proposed to make accurate measurements and scientific observations touching Egypt's pyramidal glories, his fellow professors in the university exclaimed, "What! you, too, a believer in the pyramids? Can you imagine for a moment that the ancients had a knowledge of mechanics, of science, lost to moderns? You will lose your reputation as an astronomer if you begin to meddle with the pyramids!" Prof. Smythe replied thus in substance: —

" As a university professor, I deem it strictly in accordance with the methods of modern science to test any and every material thing whatever by observation, by measure, and by the most rigid examination. These ever-recurring questions demand rational answers: Why hangs there so much historic lore about the Great Pyramid? Why is it referred to in the legends of nearly all the Eastern nations? Why has it so often been claimed as a treasure-house of scientific information? What need, upon the Egyptian-tomb theory, had the corpse of a king for a thorough and complete system of ventilation to his sarcophagus-chamber? Why was the interior of the king's tomb so perfectly plain, and void of all ornament of carving, painting, or hieroglyphics, when his subjects reveled in such things up to the utmost extent of their wealth? Why were the passages leading to the supposed secret sepulchral chamber lined with white stone, as if to lead a would-be depredator, and without a chance of missing his way, right up to the very place where, on the sepulchral theory, he ought not to go? Why was so different a shape employed for a king's tomb to all his subjects' tombs, prince and peasant alike? Why did pyramid-building cease so early in Egyptian history, that it had become a forgotten art in the times of Egypt's chief greatness under the so-called new empire at Thebes, Luxor, and Karnak, yet an empire earlier than the siege of Troy; when the Egyptian kings, too, were richer, more despotic, and more fond of grand sepulture, than at any former period of their history? "

To investigate, and, if possible, rationally answer these pressing inquiries, Prof. Smythe, collecting and packing his measuring instruments, sailed — accompanied by his brave wife — on a stormy November's morning, for Egypt, to spend the winter in the study of the pyramids. Consulting the viceroy, "his royal highness" granted him twenty men to remove *débris*, clear the passages, and otherwise assist in the measurements.

Fixing his abode in the eastern cliff of Pyramid Hill, the professor, in due time, with lamps, measuring-rods, notebooks, and Arab assistants, went into the entrance-passage on the north side, forty-seven inches high by forty-one wide, to commence the all-important work of exact measurements. These were necessary steps in order to draw the legitimate deductions.   And the whole enterprise was worthy the Scotch astronomer, and the occasion.

THE GLORY OF GHEEZEH.

Reaching the great pyramid of Gheezeh, across the desert from Sakkarah, quite late in the afternoon, we lost no time in commencing the work of sight-seeing.   The general mass of this giant edifice, covering, as it does, over *thirteen acres* with solid masonry, is rather roughly, yet substantially built. The blocks of stone upon the outside — the largest, I should judge, being four feet in width, by six or eight in length — are handsomely squared, keyed to each other, and cemented on their surfaces.   The material is mostly limestone ; and the blocks have the appearance of "made material," — a composition of magnesian limestone, sand, and cement.   These constituents constitute a species of rock much like that now being made in the city of Alexandria to outline and bulwark the harbor.   It is the opinion of many that all the blocks were chemically manufactured by the ancient Egyptians.   This class of writers put the construction of the pyramids back in the past some twenty thousand years.   Such of the polished stone   blocks   as   are   worked   into   the   astronomically-constructed entrance-passages are hard, and almost as white as alabaster. These evidently came from the *Mok-at-tam* Hills on the Arabian side of the Nile ; while those enormous granite slabs in the interior must have been brought — if not manufactured on the spot — from the Syene quarries, five hundred and fifty miles up the Nile.

> " Recount to me the beauties of the Nile :
>   No more of Tigris and Euphrates sing ;
>   Those days of joy in Gheezeh and the Isle,
>   Their memories ever round my heart will cling."

Mahommedan Hermit.

THE INTERIOR STRUCTURE.

Though the climate of Egypt is tropical, and generally dry, time with its disintegrating forces has rapidly changed the pyramidal monument of Gheezeh since the outside casings of polished limestone and marble were torn off by the Arab sultans of Cairo. Entering the pyramid at a descending angle of twenty-seven degrees, and wending our way downward at first half-bent, led by Arab guides, and then up the ascending passage for a long distance, we entered the King's Chamber, the floor of which rests upon the fiftieth course of stone forming the whole pyramidal mass. This chamber is a magnificent oblong apartment thirty-four feet in length, seventeen feet broad, and nineteen feet high, formed of monstrous yet elegantly polished blocks of granite, but utterly destitute of ornament, painting, or every thing save that plain, puzzling, yet time-defying coffer. The glaring lights gave the room a dismal appearance; and our voices sounded fearfully strange and sepulchral. The granite walls of the chamber surrounding the *coffer* are divided into five horizontally equal courses; and there is also a sign of the " division into five " over the doorway outside. Five, it is well known, is the ruling and most important number in mathematics.

THE PORPHYRITIC COFFER.

But this hollow, lidless, rectangular box, chest, or coffer of imperishable stone in the center of the King's Chamber, — what of *this?* Why so very plain? Why lidless, and minus any inscriptions? And, further, why much of the pyramid made as though in subservience to it?

When this pyramid was first broken into, remember, by Caliph *Al Mamoon*, more than a thousand years since, he expected to find immense treasures, with the key to all the sciences. Tradition has it that this pyramid had been previously discovered, explored, and robbed by the ancient Romans. Be this as it may, the Moslem caliph, to his great disappointment, found nothing but the empty porphyry coffer, — the riddle of riddles!

CONTINUED INVESTIGATIONS.

Dropping all preconceived theories, this Edinburgh professor, after noting the sloping key-line stones in the passage, the mystic number five, and the seven overlappings of the grim walls, began his series of measurements by measuring the size, shape, and position of every stone in the passages; also the walls, the floor, the roof, and the ceiling of the King's Chamber; and, to guard against any possible error, he repeated these measurements at three different times. "It was not until after two months of apprenticeship at pyramid mensuration," says this *savant*, "that I undertook that most important question of the precise angle of the grand gallery." The mathematical mensuration finished, he ordered his assistants to carry the boxes containing the instruments — the large altitude azimuth circle and telescope — to the top of the structure, that, in connection with his geometrical calculations, he might make the necessary astronomical observations. This must have been a sublime spectacle! — a profound scholar studying the rising and culminating positions of different stars, those stellar milestones along the ethereal spaces, in the silent night-time, under those clear and cloudless skies of Egypt.

RESULTS OF RESEARCH.

Besides solving puzzling problems, these investigations of John Taylor, Profs. Greaves, Smythe, and others, with the mathematical calculations of A. Beverly, Esq., Dunedin, N. Z., demonstrate, clearly demonstrate, the marvelous foresight and wisdom of the most ancient Egyptians, especially in the application of symbolism, by a speaking arrangement of parts to science, and to pictorial expressions of the recondite principles of nature.

I. — The heaviest winds of the Orient, especially in the

monsoon seasons, are from the south-west and north-east. These strike the corner angles, rather than the facial fronts of the pyramids, thus tempering the storms to the preservation of the structures. And then they are located in that latitude best designed to prevent the African sands from swooping down upon certain fertile localities of the Nile. Further, the form of their structures is founded upon the *extreme* and *mean* ratio, so well known to geometricians.

II. — The size of the Great Pyramid, Cheops, is so nicely proportioned upon mathematical and architectural principles, as to indicate the number of revolutions made by the earth on its yearly axis in terms of a certain unit of linear measure; while *other numbers* measure the length of the semi-axis of the earth's rotation.

III. — The angle of inclination towards its central axis is such that its vertical hight is to the continued length of the four sides of its base as the radius to the circumference of a circle; and this is a fractional quantity lying at the very base of mathematics.

IV. — This unit of linear measure, *alias* unit of length, was the same as the cubit of the Hebrews, and identical with the inches of our ancestral Anglo-Saxons, and the present British inch, into less than a thousandth part. Practically, then, the unit of linear measure in the pyramid is the same in length as the American inch. Thus may our mensuration be traced through Britain, Rome, Greece, to Egypt of the pyramidal era.

V. — The geometrical knowledge of the pyramid-builders began where Euclid's ended; for Euclid's forty-seventh problem, said to have been discovered by Pythagoras, and to have caused the sacrifice of a whole hecatomb of oxen, is common all through the pyramids.

> " When the great Samian sage his noble problem found,
> A hundred oxen dyed with their life-blood the ground."

VI. — The subterranean chamber shows the extraordinary way in which it points out the pyramid's axis, thus indicating a solution of the problem which has occupied the attention of geometers in all ages, viz., the trisection of angles; while the *metrical square* shows how the unit measures of the pyramid are related to one another, to the earth's radius of curvature in lat. 30°, and the pyramid as a unitary structure.

VII. — The polished coffer in the heart of the pyramid, representing the cube of a marked linear standard, is based upon principles referring to the specific gravity of all the earth's interior substance; and, to use the language of. the celebrated John Taylor, " It precisely measures the four *cheoners* of the Hebrews, and also the one chalder, or four quarters, of the Anglo-Saxon system, to such a nicety, that the present quarters " in which British and American farmers measure their wheat are the veritable quarters of the stone coffer in the King's Chamber.

In brief, while the Great Pyramid indicates astronomically that the " North Pole is moving toward Eastern Asia," the coffer not only shows the method of dividing the circle into degrees, and bisecting angles generally, but this porphyry coffer is the standard measure to-day of capacity and weight with the two most enlightened nations of earth, — England and America, — " ruling," as Prof. Smythe says, " the approximate size of our British quarters, tons, and pounds. These admissions furnish the key-proofs, that, while the coffer was designed by the king for a standard measure, the hollow chambers were built for *granaries*, and the receptacle of *treasures* and *records* during wars and floods. Further explorations will discover other chambers, making seven, and all ingeniously connected with the King's Chamber."

This Edinburgh professor, treating of his astronomical observations, says, " I have ascertained by recent measures, much more actually than was known before, that the Great Pyramid had been erected under the guidance of *astronom-*

ical science, . . . and that the entrance-passage had been pointed at the star *á Draconis* when crossing the meridian below the pole, at a distance of 3° 42'; . . . accordingly this star's closest approach to the pole, and within only ten minutes thereof, occurred about the year 2800 B.C." Upon the hypothesis of the *á Draconis* observation and epoch, taken in connection with the precessional displacement, the Great Pyramid was built 3400 B.C.; but Lepsius puts it 3500 B.C.; the French Rénan 4500 B.C. That learned man, Baron Bunsen, in his world-famous volumes of "Egypt's Place in Universal History," claims a duration of six thousand seven hundred years of a civilized, well-governed, and prosperous Egypt, previous to their kings of the so-called Manetho's fourth dynasty.

Dr. Rebold, a French archæologist, treating of the Greek historians visiting Egypt in the fifth century B.C., makes the following observation : —

"From the date 13300 B.C. until the year 4600 B.C., when the zodiac was constructed and set up in the temple of Esneh, there occurred four periods; to the first is ascribed the reign of the gods, and to the last the consolidation of the lesser kingdoms into three large kingdoms, acting in concord with some thirty or forty colleges of the priests. . . . Hermes observing the star Aldebaran 3360 B.C., and writing upon astrology, and the certainty of immortality, said in dying, 'Until now I have been exiled from my true country, to which I am about to return. Shed no tears for me. I return to that celestial country whither all must repair in their turn. *There* is God. This life is but the death."

It can not be supposed that the Egyptians *suddenly* built their walled cities, carved and ornamented their monuments, established picture-writing, — the language of the stars, — and constructed their pyramids upon the principles of science, with a standard measure for their cities and all the adjoining countries. Did it not take a long period to invent those tools, to construct machinery for raising such immense weights, to establish laws to govern workmen for general concert of action? — and profound learning too. to build with such exactness upon principles geometrical and astronomical? And yet what grand results! Those pyramids are perpetual light-houses in the desert, speaking histories of once marvelous civilizations; mighty monuments, serenely, proudly overlooking the fading ruins of nearly-forgotten ages.

The learned Gliddon in his "Ancient Egypt" sensibly asks, —

"Can the theologian derive no light from the pure primeval faith that glimmers from Egyptian heroglyphics, to illustrate the immortality of the soul? Will not the historian deign to notice the prior origin of every art and science in Egypt, a thousand years before the Pelasgians studded the isles and capes of the Archipelago with their forts and temples? —long before Etruscan civilization had smiled under Italian skies? And shall not the ethnographer, versed in Egyptian lore, proclaim the fact that the physiological, craniological, capillary, and cuticular distinctions of the human race existed on the first distribution of mankind throughout the earth?

"Philologists, astronomers, chemists, painters, architects, physicians, must return to Egypt to learn the origin of language and writing; of the calendar, and solar motion; of the art of cutting granite with a *copper* chisel, and of giving elasticity to a *copper* sword; of making glass with the variegated hues of the rainbow; of moving single blocks of polished syenite, nine hundred tons in weight, for any distance, by land and water; of building *arches*, round and pointed, with masonic precision unsurpassed at the present day, and antecedent by two thousand years to the 'Cloaca Magna' of Rome; of sculpturing a *Doric column* one thousand years before the Dorians are known in history; of *fresco* painting in imperishable colors; of practical knowledge in anatomy; and of time-defying pyramid building.

"Every craftsman can behold, in Egyptian monuments, the progress of his art four thousand years ago; and whether it be a wheelwright building a chariot, a shoemaker drawing his twine, a leather-cutter using the selfsame form of knife of old as is considered the best form now, a weaver throwing the same hand-shuttle, a whitesmith using that identical form of blowpipe but lately recognized to be the most efficient, the seal-engraver cutting, in hieroglyphics, such names as SHOOPHO's, above four thousand three hundred years ago, — *all these*, and many more astounding evidences of Egyptian priority, now require but a glance at the plates of Rosellini."

When newspaper scribblers, when blatant talkers, pronounce Egypt of "little account," pronounce the pyramids "useless piles of stones, the largest covering four or five acres of sand," they will permit me to pleasantly express a pity for their egotism, and a scathing contempt for their ignorance.

Evidences difficult to gainsay incline many to the belief that the oldest pyramids are nearer twenty than five thousand years old. That eminent Egyptologist, Bunsen, concedes to Egypt an antiquity of twenty thousand, and to China a larger period.

HOW DID THE OLD EGYPTIANS MOVE SUCH MOUNTAINOUS MASSES OF STONE?

In Sakkarah Catacombs, near the site of the present Memphian ruins, are beautifully polished granite slabs, constituting the tombs of the kings, twelve feet in length, eight feet wide, and six feet high. Such sarcophagi are actually mammoths. In them I could and *did* stand erect. And yet these are but playthings compared to some of the obelisks, granite needles, and pyramidal stones, characterizing the Egypt of remotest antiquity. This one thing is certain: either the mechanism of ancient Egypt was vastly superior to ours, or these huge stones and pillars were manufactured where they now stand.

" Pliny describes some of the arrangements connected with an obelisk a hundred and twenty feet high, erected at Alexandria by Ptolemæus Philadelphus. A canal was dug from the Nile to the place where the obelisk lay. Two boats were placed side by side, filled with pieces of stone having the aggregate weight of the obelisk. These pieces were in masses of one cubic foot each, so that the ratio between the quantity of matter in the obelisk, and that held by the boats, could be determined by a little calculation. The boats were laden to twice the weight of the obelisk, in order that they might pass under it, the two ends of the mighty monolith resting on the two banks of the canal.   Then, as the pieces of stone were taken out one by one, the boats rose, until at last they supported the obelisk.   They were finally towed down the canal, bearing their burden with them.   So far, Pliny's account is clear; but he tells us little or nothing of the tremendous task, performed ages before, of originally transporting such masses from the Syene quarries to Thebes and Heliopolis.

" An account is given by Herodotus of the transport of a large block of granite to form a monolith temple.   The block measured thirty-two feet long, twenty-one feet wide, and twelve feet high ; its weight is estimated to have been not less than three hundred tons.   The transport of this huge mass down the Nile, from Syene to the Delta, occupied two thousand men for three years."

Several comparatively inferior Egyptian obelisks have been brought and reconstructed in Rome.   The Luxor obelisk, borne from Egypt by the skillful M. Lebas, at an immense outlay of money and men, and put up in the Place de la Concorde, Paris, 1833, weighed less than two hundred and fifty tons.   This is but a babe, compared to those remaining. There are single blocks, in that land of marvels, estimated by Glidden and others to weigh nine, and even twelve hundred tons.   Tell us, engineers, tell us, O moderns, how they were removed, and placed in their present positions !

CHAPTER XXIV

THE ancients swarming the Nile Valley seem to have
excelled in astronomy, as well as in mechanics. Smythe,
the astronomer royal of Scotland, sustains this position.
And in a lecture delivered in Philadelphia by Prof. O. M.
Mitchell, and reported for the press, he said, —

"Not long since I met, in St. Louis, a man of great scientific attainments, who for forty years had been engaged in Egypt in deciphering
the hieroglyphics of the ancients. This gentleman had stated to me that
he had lately unraveled the inscriptions upon the coffin of a mummy
now in the London Museum, and in which, by the aid of previous
observations, he had discovered the key to all the astronomical knowledge of the Egyptians. The zodiac, with the exact positions of the
planets, was delineated on this coffin; and the date to which they pointed
was the autumnal equinox in the year 1722 B.C., or nearly 3600 years
ago. Accordingly I employed his assistants to ascertain the exact
positions of the heavenly bodies belonging to our solar system on the
equinox of that year (1722 B.C.), and sent him a correct diagram of
them, without having communicated his object in so doing. In compliance with this, the calculations were made; and to my astonishment,
on comparing the result with the statements of his scientific friend
already referred to, it was found that on the 7th of October, 1722 B.C.,
the moon and planets had occupied the exact points in the heavens
marked upon the coffin in the London Museum."

HELIOPOLIS.

What Oxford is to England, and Yale to New England,
Heliopolis was to Egypt in the fifth century B.C. It is

only two hours and a half from Cairo by carriage. They tell me that in winter-time it is a very pleasant drive, over a splendid road bordered with orange, lemon, acacia, and olive trees. The gardens of ancient Heliopolis were famous, as the historian knows, for their balm-of-Gilead balsams. What think you, my countrymen, remains of this sacerdotal, this university city of antiquity, where Moses studied the "wisdom of the Egyptians," where Joseph's father-in-law officiated as a priest in the temple, where Plato the Grecian graduated, and where Herodotus, in his travels, sought counsel from the "wise men of Egypt"? Its colleges, its magnificent temples, are but isolated mounds now; and all that remains to determine the locality is a beautiful granite obelisk. This, fixing the site of the Temple of the Sun, is thought by some Egyptologists to have been erected by the Pharaoh of Joseph's time, bearing the name of Osirtasen I., founder of the twelfth dynasty. When the geographer Strabo visited this grand old country, Egyptian scholars pointed out the residences of Eudoxus and Plato during the thirteen years they remained in Egypt under the searching tuition of the priests of Heliopolis. Though relentless time long since transformed Plato's Egyptian palace to dust, it has not effaced the hieroglyphics from Heliopolis's stately obelisk.

The obelisk in the Hippodrome at Constantinople, which I visited several times while in Asiatic Turkey, is supposed to be the work of the fourth Thotmes. Those in Rome, brought from Egypt, bear inscriptions of various Pharaohs. But, of all the obelisks, the largest and most beautiful is that of Karnak, at Thebes, cut by Queen *A-men-see*, about 1760 B.C. It is a single towering shaft of the purest and most exquisitely polished syenite, in height about ninety feet, and in weight over four hundred tons.

In hieroglyphical symbol-writing, Heliopolis means "the abode of the sun;" and, as a celebrated seat of philosophy, its hierophants and seers professed to enlighten the world

After mentally and architecturally enriching other cities, the reputation of Heliopolis began to fade soon after the conquest of Egypt by Greece; the Grecianized city of Alexandria taking its place.

THE ROSETTA STONE, AND COPTS.

When visiting London the first time, nothing interested me more than the Rosetta Stone in the British Museum. Rosetta, in Arabic, Rasheed, is handsomely located on the west bank of the Nile, near its mouth. This modern town, founded by a caliph, 870 A.D., is built upon the site of some ancient city. Its present archæological celebrity was acquired by the finding of the trilingual stone, known as the "Rosetta Stone," discovered by the French in 1799, while digging foundations for a fort. This invaluable tablet contained a decree made by the priests of Egypt in honor of Ptolemy Epiphanes, 196 B.C. It was written in hieroglyphic, enchorial, and Greek. This gave the key to the Egyptian alphabet, the old Coptic, and to the reading of the hieroglyphical inscriptions. Copt is the language written on most of the monumental walls in Egypt.

The Arabic is the vernacular of the country to-day, though there are many dialects spoken in the various parts of Egypt.

The Coptic Church is the national church. Its archbishop of Alexandria, though residing in Cairo, is said to be the direct successor of Mark the Evangelist. So run these theological threads; the Catholics looking to Peter, the English Church to Paul, the Coptic Church to Mark, and the Greek Church to the embodied wisdom of the apostolic fathers. The liturgy of the Copts is in the ancient Coptic. Their forms of worship resemble the Catholic; but they utterly deny the authority of the Pope.

None doubt the Copts, so numerous in Middle and Upper Egypt, being the direct descendants of the ancient Egyptians. Their brown complexions, almond-shaped eyes, and heavy lips, resemble the face of the Sphinx, the ancient paintings,

and sculptured portraits ; and, further, they are slightly
under the medium size, as are the exhumed mummies.

ALEXANDRIA.

In the palmy days of the Ptolemies this city numbered
full half a million : it has to-day about one hundred and
fifty thousand.   Bating Pompey's Pillar and Cleopatra's
Needle ; broken columns, cisterns, aqueducts, traces of walls,
unexplored catacombs, porphyry, portions of Cæsar's palace,
fragments of statues, and library ashes, are all that remain of
this ancient magnificent city, founded by Alexander the
Great soon after the fall of Tyre, 333 B.C.   Strabo gives
a brilliant description of the streets, avenues, libraries,
museums, obelisks, groves inclosing retreats for learned
men, and temples of marble and porphyry that ultimately
enriched Rome and Constantinople.

The same architect, Dinocratus, who acquired such fame
from planning the Temple of Diana at Ephesus, was
employed by Alexander in the construction of Alexandria.
Upon the death of this Macedonian monarch, he became
governor of Egypt, and finally assumed the title of king 304
B.C.   Ptolemy Philadelphus, while adding much to the
grandeur of the city, and increasing its libraries, built a
marble tower, upon the summit of which a fire was kept
continually burning as a direction to sailors.   At this period,
and long after, it was the great cosmopolitan seat of theological controversy and moral philosophy.   One links with
it precious memories of Proclus, Plotinus, Ammonius,
Saccas, the Alexandrian school, and its modifying influences
upon Christianity.

THE ALEXANDRIAN LIBRARY, DESTROYED BY WHOM ?

This massive collection of literature was shelved in the
Temple of Serapeion.   Most of its rolls and scrolls were
originally brought from India.   Ptolemy Sotor has the
honor of being its founder.   Ptolemy Philadelphus enlarged

it. Others increased it to over seven hundred thousand volumes. To further add thereto, the following unique plan was devised: " Seize all books brought into Egypt by Assyrians, Greeks, and foreigners, and transcribe them, handing the transcriptions to the owners, and putting the originals into the library."

Book-burning is a business common to both ancients and moderns, Christians and Mohammedans. In an article on Alexandria, " The Encyclopædia Britannica " says, —

" This structure [alluding to the Serapeion] surpassed in beauty and magnificence all others in the world, except the Capitol at Rome. Within the verge of this temple was the famous Alexandrian library, . . . containing no fewer than seven hundred thousand volumes.

" In the war carried on by Julius Cæsar against the inhabitants of the city, the library in the Brucheion, *with all its contents*, was reduced to ashes. The library in the Serapeion, however, still remained, and here Cleopatra deposited two hundred thousand volumes of the Pergamenean library. These, and others added from time to time, rendered the new library of Alexandria more numerous and considerable than the former; *but, when the Temple of Serapis was demolished under the archiepiscopate of Theophilus, A. D. 389, the valuable library was pillaged or destroyed; and twenty years afterwards the empty shelves excited the regret and indignation of every intelligent spectator.*"

The blinded zealots of the agone ages strove to obliterate every vestige of that historic knowledge which distinguished the nations of antiquity. John Philaponus, a noted Peripatetic philosopher, being in Alexandria when the city was taken, and being permitted to converse with Amrou the Arabian general, solicited an inestimable gift at his hands, — *the royal library*. At first Amrou was inclined to grant the favor; but upon writing the caliph, he received, it is said, the following answer, dictated by a spirit of unpardonable fanaticism : " *If those ancient manuscripts and writings of the Eastern nations and the Greeks agree with the Koran, or Book of God, they are useless, and need not be preserved, but, if they disagree, they are pernicious, and ought to be destroyed.*" The torch was applied, and a wretched barbarism was for the time triumphant. Sensations of sadness thrilled my being's core, while walking over ashes and ruins that were once ablaze with the literature of the East Never for a moment have I felt that " it was all for the best," the burning of the Alexandrian Library.

Travelers visiting the present Alexandria naturally rush to see Cleopatra's Needle, a solid block of reddish granite, said to have been originally brought from Syene. This granite needle is sixty feet high, having to the top three columns of hieroglyphical inscriptions. Its twin column is buried in the sand near by. Not far distant is Pompey's Pillar, a single graceful column of pink granite, one hundred and fourteen feet high, and twenty-seven feet in circumference. During the reign of Tiberius, A. D. 14 to 37, these " obelisks were brought from Heliopolis to Alexandria." But how were they brought ? Ay, that's the question. It would be absolutely impossible for moderns to do it. The method is among the " lost arts." Was not this pyramidal stone estimated to weigh nine hundred tons ? were not these obelisks manufactured where they stand, historic opinion to the contrary ?

Just at the dawn of, and after the initiation of the Christian era, the history of Alexandria became singularly intermingled with that of Jerusalem, Greece, and Rome, in which the Ptolemies and Cæsars, Philo Judæus, Pompey, Cleopatra, and St. Anthanasius, all play conspicuous parts. Here I am reminded of Gen. Lytle's lines referring to Cæsar, Pompey, Antony, and Cleopatra : —

> "I am dying, Egypt, dying !
>   Ebbs the crimson life-tide fast,
> And the dark Plutonian shadows
>   Gather on the evening blast.
> Let thy arm, O queen ! support me,
>   Hush thy sobs, and bow thine ear,
> Hearken to the great heart secrets,
>   Thou, and thou alone, must hear.

Though my scarred and veteran legions
  Bear their eagles high no more,
And my wrecked and scattered galleys
  Strew dark Actium's fatal shore,
Though no shining guards surround me,
  Prompt to do their master's will,
I must perish like a Roman,
  Die the great triumvir still.

Let not Cæsar's servile minions
  Mock the lion thus laid low.
'T was no foeman's hand that slew him:
  'T was his own that struck the blow.
Here, then, pillowed on thy bosom,
  Ere his star fades quite.away,
He who, drunk with thy caresses,
  Madly flung a world away.

Should the base plebeian rabble
  Dare assail my fame at Rome,
Where the noble spouse, Octavia,
  Weeps within her widowed home,
Seek her: say the *gods have told me,* —
  Altars, augurs, circling wings, —
That her blood with mine commingled
  Yet shall mount the throne of kings.

And for thee, star-eyed Egyptian,
  Glorious sorceress of the Nile,
Light the path to Stygian horrors
  With the splendors of thy smile;
Give the Cæsar crowns and arches;
  Let his brow the laurel twine;
I can scorn the Senate's triumphs,
  Triumphing in love like thine.

I am dying, Egypt, dying!
  Hark! the insulting foeman's cry:
They are coming: quick, my falchion!
  Let me front them ere I die!
Ah! no more amid the battle
  Shall my heart exulting swell.
Isis and Osiris guard thee!
  Cleopatra — Rome — farewell!"

It is supposed that the two obelisks called Cleopatra's Needles once decorated the palaces of the Ptolemies. One of these has been presented to England by the Egyptian Government. It is questionable if decaying Britain has sufficient energy to transplant it upon her shores.

When Amrou conquered Alexandria, he was so astonished at the magnificence of the city, that he wrote to the caliph, "I have taken the City of the West. It is of immense extent: I can not describe to you how many houses it contains. There are four thousand palaces, four thousand baths, twelve thousand dealers in fresh oil, forty thousand Jews who pay tribute, and four hundred theaters, or places of amusement."

Bidding Egypt, the Mizraim of the Hebrews, farewell, I have to say, O Egypt! your reigning viceroy is an ambitious Mohammedan polygamist; your government in its taxation is oppressive; your slavery is a blotch upon the face of the nineteenth century; your religion is a gaudy show; your people are terribly ignorant; your guides are shameless liars; your donkeys are hopelessly impenitent; your "backsheesh" crying beggars are a disgrace to any country; and your hungry fleas and flies more numerous, if possible, than they were in the times of the biblical patriarchs. On the other hand, those pyramidal Titans standing in somber majesty; those hieroglyphical records, defying the wear and waste of time; that magnificent museum of antiquities upon the bank of the Nile; those far-stretching groves of palm; those broad fields of cotton, coffee, and rice, dotting the Nilotic valley; those gardens of fruits and flowers; those gorgeous sunsets of crimson and gold, translated into myriads of flashing jewels, to gradually melt away like Cleopatra's pearl into a sea of purple; and those skies so clear and golden by day, so blue and delicately studded with constellations by night, reminding one of that city immortal with the twelve gates of pearl, as seen by John in vision, — these, *all these*, are to be set down to the sunny side of the Egypt of to-day.

Mummy, Rameses II.

TALKERS. — EASTERN LIARS. — MARK TWAIN.

These everlasting talkers, who run all to tongue, continually put one in mind of a swinging sign on the hotel abandoned. They are the Cheap-Johns of civic life. Sap
drizzles and drops. Limber-lipped talkers talk what they
know, and what they do not know; talk what they imagine,
what they suspect, what they infer, what they dream, what
they have done, and what they intend to do, making themselves the heroes of all tales told. Men like Alcott and
Emerson, substantially great, are retiring and modest. Deep
rivers roll silently. The lightnings are voiceless. God
never speaks. Any thing, then, but a talkative, self-conceited
egotist, who, to put it alphabetically, shows off at A, spills
out at B, slops over at C, runs sediments at D, and then
repeats and re-repeats, commencing with the *ego*, and all —
all this — to seem "smart!"

If David in his "haste" said, "All men are liars," I
say it deliberately of all the "dragomen" and guides
employed by us in the East. Many would both falsify and
steal. Charity compels the opinion, however, that some of
their misstatements were grounded in ignorance, rather than
willfulness. Take this sample: Standing near the dome of
the Grand Mosque in Benares, and surveying the city circling the bend of the Ganges, we inquired of our guide the
number of the population. "Six millions!" was the prompt
reply. "What?" we doubtingly inquired. "Six — *six millions*, sir!" was the emphatic response. It was provokingly
annoying. London, the largest city in the world, has less
than three millions and a half. When looking up to the
summit of Pompey's Pillar in Alexandria, Dr. Dunn inquired
the hight. "Ten miles: he be ten miles high," was the
ready answer. This Arab guide neither knew the real
hight, nor the use of the English language. His professed
guidance, therefore, was an imposition.

Mark Twain does full justice to the "sheiks," to the

"dragomen," and to the beggars generally, of the Levant and the East. Generously admitting the genius of Twain in some directions, I nevertheless feel to say that, while *wit*, if original, is well; while fiction has its place, and romance its legitimate use, — still truth and falsehood, sacredness and sacrilege, history and tradition, indiscriminately mixed, and bound between two covers with no lines of demarcation, reveal not only a silly conceit, but show a lack of solid literary culture. Such "Innocents-Abroad" books of travel, read trustingly and believingly, lead the unwary strangely astray. True, their pages may excite interest : so do Gulliver's. They may produce laughter: so do clowns. And such volumes, too, may sell : so also does the Jack Sheppard style of novels. But is this the only object of bookmaking?

SPIRITUALISM IN THE EGYPT OF ANTIQUITY.

The *gods*, the guardian angels of the ancient Egyptians, were once mortal men. Sanchonianthon, whom accredited historians place before the time of Moses, wrote in the Phœnician. Philo of Byblus translated a portion of his works into Greek. Here follow a few lines : —

"Egyptians and Phœnicians accounted those the greatest gods who had found out things most necessary and useful in life, and who had been benefactors when among mankind."

Hermes Trismegistus acknowledged that the "gods of Egypt were the souls of dead men." And Plutarch informs us that the "Egyptian priests pointed out where the bodies of their gods lay buried." The eloquent Cicero wrote, —
"The whole heaven is almost entirely filled with the human race : even the superior order of gods were originally natives of this lower world." And with these gods, angels, *spirits*, the Egyptians of remotest antiquity held constant converse. They also thoroughly understood psychological

science. On their tombs, towers, and obelisks, are pictured mesmerists, in the act of pathetizing subjects.

The papyrus of Sne-frau, predecessor of Cheops, abounds in the marvels of a gifted priestess. On a papyrus-scroll from Thebes is a symbol of death; and just over the mummied form is hovering the resurrected spirit, with eyes turned towards the scales of justice and truth. In the distance are the expected mansions of rest. Several chapters in the ritual of the "Book of the Dead" treat of magic, trance, and magnetic healing. There are also pictorial illustrations of the different magnetic states, and operators with upraised hands mesmerizing their subjects. Aural rays are seen streaming upon the patient's brain; and consecrated priests stand by, holding in their right hands croziers, warding off the psychological influences of dark-hued, undeveloped spirits. The study and practice of Spiritism must have been common in the period of the pyramid-builders. The Hebrews obtained their knowledge of psychological science in Egypt.

SPIRITUALISTS IN CAIRO.

The Angel of Spiritualism has sounded the resurrection trumpet of a future existence in every land under heaven. Madame Blavatsky, assisted by other brave souls, formed a society of Spiritualists in Cairo about three years since. They have fine writing-mediums, and other forms of the manifestations. They hold weekly séances during the winter months. Madame Blavatsky went on later to Odessa, Russia. The lady whose husband keeps the Oriental Hotel is a firm Spiritualist. Fired with the missionary spirit, I left a package of pamphlets and tracts in her possession, for gratuitous distribution. "And, as ye go, *teach*," was the ancient command. Madame Blavatsky, the irrepressible, several years subsequent became a Theosophist, writing huge volumes of wisdom, of sense, nonsense and undemonstrated theories heavily seasoned and spiced with ancient Hindoo mythology.

CHAPTER XXV.

FROM ALEXANDRIA TO JOPPA AND JERUSALEM. — THE
CITY OF JOPPA.

EXCELLENT steamers leave Alexandria three times a week
for Jaffa, *alias* the Joppa of the New Testament. The passage requires two or three days, stopping only at Port Said,
the northern terminus of the Suez Canal. This city contains hardly seven thousand, — a motley gathering of all
nations, the Arab element largely predominating. It has an
artificial harbor, the huge blocks of which are manufactured
of limestone, sand, and cement, and then transported to their
position, forming a breakwater sufficiently substantial to
insure the safety of ships. Unless money were the object,
few would fix a residence in this sandy city.

This is Sunday morning, six o'clock, Joppa — the
Joppa of my Sunday-school dreams, with its domes, minarets, palms, and suburban orange-gardens — loomed up in
the distance like an amphitheatre from the ocean. To the
right and left of the city only a sandy beach was visible.
Joppa — a city of fifteen thousand, literally a " city set upon
a hill," and the natural landing-place of Jews, Christian and
Mohammedan pilgrims to Jerusalem — has a very insecure
harbor. Remnants of an old Phœnician harbor are yet
traceable ; but the precise spot where Jonah shipped for
Tarshish, — probably *Tarsus*, — to " flee from the presence of
the Lord," is not pointed out even by credulous monks.
The clergy of the East, knowing the nature of the finny

tribes that sport in the Mediterranean waters, consider it no heresy to doubt the whale-story of the Old Testament.

It was at Joppa that the Lebanon timber from Hiram, king of Tyre, was landed for the building of both the temples at Jerusalem. It was here that the Tabitha whose name "by interpretation was Dorcas" lived, whom Peter, by his mediumistic powers, "raised to life," and where this apostle also had the remarkable vision recorded in the tenth chapter of Acts. The "*Acts* of the Apostles" should have been denominated the practices and spiritual experiences of the apostles. Tradition points to the very house where lived "Simon the tanner, by the seaside." Certainly we visited this spot, as do all pilgrims. The "seaside" is still there: further, "deponent saith not." Houses perish, but the good, never. Peter still remembers his vision.

NEW-ENGLANDERS IN JOPPA.

Considerable interest attached to Joppa, a few years since, from the attempted settlement there of some Maine and New-Hampshire "Church of Messiah" religionists, under the leadership of the Rev. G. H. Adams, well known in some of the New-England States. This colonizing movement proved, however, a complete failure. Adams — originally an actor, a Mormon, a pretender — became dissipated; the colonists lost their property; an officious consul (since dismissed) took the fleece; and the flock became scattered, only a few of the original settlers remaining in the country. The tract of land secured and taken up by these New-England enthusiasts is now owned principally by Germans. Some of these American settlers became so poor that they actually begged bread of the Arabs. Contributions sent to them were appropriated by Adams and his wife. Only twelve of the original one hundred and fifty-six that went to Joppa remain. Adams is in England; and Mrs. Adams, the least respected of the two, is in California. The whole story is a sad one, the details of which will hereafter be given in full.

But how can we longer tarry in Joppa, when Jerusalem, once the "city of the great king," is only thirty-five miles distant, and that over an excellent road, considering the mountainous nature of these Syrian lands?

IN JOPPA, BOUND FOR JERUSALEM.

While yet in Cairo, Egypt, we unwisely engaged an Arab dragoman, at so much per day, to conduct us through Palestine; *unwisely*, because better guides can be employed in Jaffa at the same price. Mr. Rolla Floyd, a very candid, competent American gentleman, and an energetic young man named Clark, both thoroughly acquainted with the whole country, will prove excellent guides. They are remnants of the Jaffa colony, and quite conversant with the Arabic and the Palestinian dialects. I am particular to note these facts, because, in the Egypt of to-day, famous for flies, fleas, and falsifiers, they are sure to tell travelers that no guides can be procured in Jaffa. Our Cairo guide — Mahomet Selim — was a failure so far as intellectual guidance was concerned, yet a good and faithful "dragoman" in other matters. It is cheaper traveling in this than in the winter season. The dry and rainy seasons remind one of California.

Selim, having secured his sheik, well-armed, his muleteers, his horses, donkeys, and tents, we were off at ten o'clock on a sunny morning, horseback, for Jerusalem. Our horses were good ones. Passing through the bazaar, the narrow streets swarming with glittering raggedness, and the walls grayed with age, we emerged from this Oriental city buried in noble groves of orange-trees, out into the main thoroughfare, which was lined for some distance with irrigated gardens, lemon-orchards, and orange-groves. Suburban Jaffa is beautiful. The roadside, for a long way toward Ramleh, is fenced with cacti, and fringed with gardens. Residents tell us that these gardens in March and April are literally enchanting, the air being loaded with mingled fragrance of apricot and orange, lemon and quince, plum and china tree blossoms. During the dry season, lasting from May till November, these gardens are kept fresh and green by irrigation.

> " In Eastern land they talk in flowers,
>   And tell in a garland their loves and cares:
> Each blossom that blooms in their garden-bowers
>   On its leaves a mystic language bears."

But we are galloping away from garden and grove over vast plains, the biblical plains of Sharon. How flash upon the mind now the poetical phrases, " Carmel and Sharon," " the rose of Sharon, and the lily of the valley "! Who are these? " Pilgrims," says Selim, " coming back from Jerusalem and the Jordan." Some were Catholics, some Greek Christians, and others Mohammedans, *all* either riding camels, donkeys, or afoot, weary and dusty. Most of the traveling at this season is done in the night-time. Syrian, like Egyptian women, veil their faces. It is said that when the Sultan of Turkey was at Paris, in 1867, Louis Napoleon inquired of him, " Why don't you have roads in *your* country?" adding, " The empress wishes much to visit Jerusalem." " There shall be a road within a year," was the Sultan's reply; and so there was, a handsome carriage-road, twenty-five or thirty feet in width, the work of forced labor.

Sharon has not, as Isaiah prophesied, become a " howling wilderness." Its extensive plains, rounding up now and then into swells and long ridges, are very fertile, judging from the cultivated fields we passed, covered with corn and wheat stubble. Reapers and gleaners gather the harvests in June, or early in July. These plains, so eminently fertile, constantly reminded me of Sacramento and other rich valley-lands in California.

On this route from Jaffa to Ramleh, three hours distant, there are several little villages in orchards of olives, figs, pomegranates, and mulberries. These mulberry-trees, like those of Australia, are grown not for the silk-worm, but for their fruit, the berries of which, while resembling the largest blackberries, have a sharper acid taste. From the mountains of Judea and Samaria to the sea, and from the foot of Carmel to the more barren lands of Philistia, lie spread out the plains of Sharon, in spring-time like a flower-flecked island, beautiful as vast, and diversified as beautiful, fascinating the eye, and enchanting the imagination. It must have been paradisaic when Israel's king sang of Sharon's rose.

RAMLEH.

This old city, mostly in ruins, is said by Eusebius and St. Jerome to have been the Arimathea of Joseph, the Joseph into whose new tomb they put the body of Jesus. It was and *is* customary for Jews in distant localities to have tombs and burial-places in the immediate vicinity of Jerusalem, the holy city. This Ramlehan city of ancient buildings, cisterns, and subterranean vaults, has a grand old tower, believed by some to have been a minaret; others think it originally the campanile of a magnificent church. That it has an Arabic inscription, bearing date A.H. 710, A.D. 1310, proves nothing, as there are similar vaunting inscriptions on castles and temples in Syria much older than the Mohammedan religion. Among the old stone houses of this city rises a palatial Latin convent, the monks entertaining travelers. The kindness of these celibate monks is proverbial.

THROUGH THE JUDEAN COUNTRY.

" We have turned us away from the fragrant East,
      For the desert sand and the arid waste."

" Selim," our guide, announcing himself ready with horses watered, bridled, equipped, we are again snugly in the saddle under a scorching sun, on the way from Ramleh to Jerusalem. It is several miles yet across the plains of

Sharon to the foot-hills that fringe the more mountainous regions. The landscape is diversified and beautified with olive-orchards, the leaves resembling those of the willow, only more soft and delicate. This is a common tree in the south of France, in Greece, and Syria. The beautiful plain of Athens, as seen from Hymettus, appears almost covered with olive-trees. Olive-oil, quite an article of export in Syria and Asia Minor, is eaten with lettuce and other salads all through the East. The fruit is plucked by the hand, reduced to a pulp in the olive-mill, put into sacks of coarse linen, and subjected to a crushing pressure. This tree in portions of the Orient, like the oak in the West. is held in a sort of veneration. It was an olive-branch that the dove brought to the legendary ark ; while in Greece the wreaths that crowned the victors in the Olympic games were woven from the slender branches that tremble upon the leafy olive.

The road winding, the country now wild and desolate, we gallop along quite reckless of the thought that this portion of Palestine. storied in song and trodden by apostles, had given birth to Jeremiah, witnessed the duel of David and Goliath, and the recorded standing-still of the sun on the plains of Ajalon. Passing old stone villages and rude tombs, we meet more pilgrims. It is nearly noon, a burning August noon, and the way begins to seem long to the " city of the great king." Through ravines and cañons, how rugged the country, and barren too, save the orchards of figs and olives that dot the valleys, or terrace the hill-sides. What strange geological formations ! Giving our panting horses a little rest, we lunch to-day in an olive-grove, and have delicious prickly pears plucked fresh from a cactus hedge, and brought us by some sore-eyed Syrian girls, living a little distance from the wayside. " Selim," our dragoman, provides well, but the day seems long. Other hills and mountains are scaled. and Jerusalem is still before us. This is novel and odd-looking, surely. " What ? " Why, this summer threshing-floor in the open field. the grain being trampled out by the stamping of oxen. It is decidedly primitive. The Egyptians have a similar method.

Traversing these regions, one naturally asks, "How do the people live?" Only in dreams could it have been called a land " flowing with milk and honey; " and yet when irrigated there are tasty oases, and numerous vineyards too, burdened with white and purpling clusters. Cities and villages, built upon hillsides, frequently crown their summits Thus situated, these warlike inhabitants of Scripture records could better see the approaching enemy, and defend themselves in battle. Terraced up toward the steep hilltops, many streets are on a range with the stone houses below. And then these tile-roofed buildings are generally flat. Some are handsomely grassed over. In several places we saw goats and cattle feeding upon the housetops.

But see! here's a *restaurant!* Two men come out, American dressed. They speak English. One of them, originally connected with the American colonists to Jaffa, is now employed by the Palestine Exploration Society on the east side of the Jordan, in the land of Moab. These explorations are certainly confirming Jewish history. Our horses are weary and worn: so are their riders. The sun has now dipped his disk in the Mediterranean.

GLIMPSES OF JERUSALEM.

. There's not a cloud in sight. The skies are aflame with departing sun-rays, crimson and golden. Only " this hill to rise!" Ay, there — *there* it is! the very Jerusalem over which " Jesus wept." Some poet sings, —

> " Jerusalem! I would have seen
>   Thy precipices steep ;
> The trees of palm that overhang
>   Thy gorges dark and deep.
> Around thy hills the spirits throng
>   Of all thy murdered seers;
> And voices that went up from it
>   Are ringing in my ears.''

The fading light throws over the city a gray, somber, shadowy appearance; and yet you see around its entire circuit a lofty wall with beautiful parapets; and within, white roofs, balustrades, domes, minarets, majestic churches, and the Mosque of Omar crowning Mount Moriah. Though situated upon a mountain-top, Jerusalem is surrounded by still loftier mountains. It surprised us, however, that a city so historically famous should be so small. Pictures and Sunday-school teachings had impressed us with the belief that it must be marvelously great, because built and adorned by King Solomon. Nevertheless it is large and rich in Semitic associations. Here Abraham dwelt. Here patriarchs and prophets had their pastures, their wells, their tents, their tombs, and their altars. Here Jesus performed many of his spiritual marvels. Here apostles sat at the feet of their divine Teacher. Here disciples learned the commandment, "Love ye one another." And here the tender, sweet-hearted John lovingly leaned upon Jesus' bosom, giving to all these hills and mountains an associate sacredness. Well might Whittier write, —

> "And throned on her hills sits Jerusalem yet,
> With dust on her forehead, and chains on her feet;
> For the crown of her pride to the mocker hath gone,
> And the holy shekinah is dark where it shone."

OTHERS' IMPRESSIONS OF JERUSALEM.

Lieut. Lynch, of the navy, approaching Jerusalem, writes, —

"I rode to the summit of a hill on the left, and beheld the holy city. Men may say what they please; but there are moments when the soul, casting aside the artificial trammels of the world, will assert its claim to a celestial origin, and regardless of time and place, of sneers and sarcasms, pay its tribute at the shrine of faith, and weep for the sufferings of its Founder."

Prof. Osborne observes, —

"Though weary from the day's ride in the saddle, and exhausted as were the pilgrims by the way, it was near night when we obtained the first view of the city with its mosques and towers. How unspeakably charming was that moment's vision! Never did silence and loneliness appear so gratifying.''

Believing as firmly in Jesus' suffering, bleeding, and dying a martyr to a principle, as in Socrates' draining the hemlock draught, the sight of Jerusalem had for me a thousand charms.

> " Here circling vines their leafy banners spread,
> And held their green shields o'er the pilgrim's head;
> At once repelling Syria's burning ray,
> And breathing freshness on the sultry day."

To Strauss, Jesus was a wise rabbi; to Rénan, a moral teacher; to Fourier, a warm-hearted socialist; to Fénelon, the most rapt of mystics; to Paine, the most sincere of philanthropists; to Müller, the harmony of all history; to Emerson, a true prophet seeing the mystery of the soul; to Parker, a fellow-brother and self-sacrificing reformer; while to me he was the marvel-working medium of the East, the baptized of Christ, and the great Syrian *Spiritualist* sent of the gods to bear " witness to the truth." Previously I had looked upon the Isle of Samos that gave birth to Pythagoras; I had stood upon the spot where Socrates was imprisoned for corrupting the youth; I had wandered over the fields of Sarnath, where Buddha's feet had pressed the soil; I had traversed the land where Plato taught in the Athenian groves; and *now* I was at the gates of the city where Jesus had toiled and taught, healed and suffered, wept, and died with the prayer upon his purpling lips, " Father, forgive them!" The sainted John Pierpont sweetly wrote, —

> " A lonelier, lovelier path be mine;
> Greece and her charms I'd leave for Palestine;
> There purer streams through happier valleys flow,
> And sweeter flowers on holier mountains blow;
> I'd love to breathe where Gilead sheds her balm;
> I'd love to walk on Jordan's banks of palm;

I'd love to wet my foot in Hermon's dews;
I'd love the promptings of Isaiah's muse;
In Carmel's holy grots I'd court repose,
And deck my mossy couch with Sharon's blooming rose."

This is Aug. 24. We enter Jerusalem by the Jaffa Gate, and follow " Christian Street " to Mount Zion.

JERUSALEM AS IT NOW IS.

How often in life does sunshine fade away into cloudland, poetry into dullest prose! So Jerusalem, which was so beautiful an hour ago in the softening, fading light of the setting sun, shrunk away to a trafficking Turkish city the moment we entered within the gates. The city has at present a population of some twelve thousand, of whom three thousand four hundred are denominated Christians, three thousand Jews, and five thousand Mohammedans; each class largely occupying separate quarters. The streets are narrow, dirty, and poorly paved. The houses, built of stone, look like fortresses, presenting in front little more than blank walls. Morning and evening they are crowded with Turks and Arabs. The bazaars were sparsely supplied, with the exception of fruits. The principal trade of the city consists in beads and coins, crosses and relics. There are no gas-lights, as in Alexandria; and therefore it was impossible to see much of the city in evening-time. Stopping at the Mediterranean Hotel on Mount Zion, kept by Mr. Honstein, — a Free-Mason and a free-thinker, — we had a delightful night's rest. Waking rested and refreshed, we could say most heartily, " Pray for the peace of Jerusalem; they shall prosper that love thee. Peace be within thy walls, and prosperity within thy palaces."

OUR FIRST DAY IN THE CITY.

Out in early morning upon the housetop I saw the sun rise from beyond the Jordan. After a delicious breakfast of eggs, bread, honey, and several kinds of fruit, we started, with a guide, for the Church of the Holy Sepulcher. Fronting it is a neatly paved square, reached from the street by descending a flight of worn stone stairs. This area is usually thronged with Syrians, Abyssinians, Armenians, Greeks, Copts, and Turks, as well as Europeans. Monks and tradesmen also frequent the place daily to sell amulets and cheap relics. The Holy Sepulcher is open to all religionists except the Jews. These, with an intolerance unpardonable, are excluded. There is little doubt but that the "new tomb" of Joseph of Arimathea was in this mountainous eminence. It was so designated in the first, and confirmed by the fathers of later centuries. The magnificent dome of the Church of the Holy Sepulcher has been erected directly over this white-marble sarcophagus under which is the veritable rock-hewn "tomb." Near the sepulcher is a marble slab on which it is said they anointed the body of Jesus; and to the east of it is a small door, requiring a stooping posture to enter, made, in all probability, to harmonize with St. John's account, "And, as she wept, she stooped down, and looked into the sepulcher." About the tomb and the altar are gifts of precious stones, wreaths of pearls and diamonds, from the Christian sovereigns of Europe, and lamps of gold and silver kept continually burning. These, glittering with the smoke of the incense, the perfume of spices, and the attar of roses, induced in us a strange, weird sensation. Silently we said, " Jesus and the poor ; Jesus and the beggar by the wayside ; Jesus, once treading the winepress alone, without 'where to lay his head,' now a *god* with a costly, garnished sepulcher, and the poor of the nineteenth century begging, starving, dying !" Jesus was genuine: Christianity is a sham.

The crucifixion upon Calvary, the stone of anointing, the burial sepulcher, and other holy places, to say nothing of the Greek, Latin, Armenian, and Coptic departments of worship, are all included under the roof of the Church of the Holy Sepulcher. Mount Calvary, within a stone's-throw of the sepulcher, is reached by climbing a flight of eighteen stone steps, introducing us into a richly decorated chapel. In this chapel is quite a rock with a hole therein, said to have received the foot of the cross; and a tablet, showing where the "mother of Jesus stood" during her son's agony. Descending a rugged stone stairway, we entered the Chapel of St. Helena, mother of Constantine; where, three hundred years after the crucifixion, it is pretended were found the "three crosses" in a state of perfect preservation.

It is claimed that the Armenian Church covers the site where John was beheaded; and close by they pointed us to Adam's grave, and a picture of his skull. They also showed where the cock stood and "crowed three times" before Peter's denial; showed us the Judgment Hall; the place where Jesus, leaning against the wall when weary, made an indentation in the rock; the spot where he fell under the cross, calling upon Simon of Cyrene; the place where they scourged him; the cleft in the rock, made when he yielded up the ghost; and, what is more, they identified the exact locality where the angel stood that appeared to the Maries. Further, they pointed to the tomb of Melchisedec, the palace of Herod, the place where Stephen was stoned, the house of Dives, the dilapidated stone shanty of Lazarus, and the prints of Jesus' footsteps where he stood when confounding the "doctors of the law."

Naturally incredulous, the fixing of these localities with such cool precision disgusted me. Tradition and superstition are the handmaids of ignorance. The truth is, the most imaginative genius can not reconstruct Jerusalem as Jesus saw it, and Josephus and other Jewish writers describe it. The demon of war, crimsoning its streets, too often sacked the city. It has been burned, built, and rebuilt. The localities of towers and tombs, pools and sepulchers, therefore, are mostly hypothetical; and yet the general topographical outlines of the city and immediate country are as clearly marked as they are ineffaceable.

"THE WALL, AND THE GATES THEREOI."

The present wall, with its five gates, surrounding Jerusalem, is about two and a half miles in length; and portions of it evidently occupy the line of the ancient *first wall*. Some fifteen feet thick, and from twenty-five to forty feet high according to the location of the ground, this wall has salient angles, square towers, battlements, and a breastwork running around upon the top, furnishing a fine promenade for tourists. Standing upon the topmost stones, and surveying the scenery, we were shown a horizontally projecting column upon which Mohammed is to "stand when he comes to judge the world." It was interesting to examine the excavations of Capt. Warren, who, commencing some fifty yards outside the walls, pushed a shaft under them, discovering the foundations of the *old Temple*, the pillars and arches of which are marvels.

Visiting the gate that is called "Beautiful," and then passing out of St. Stephen's Gate, we descended the steep hillside to the vale of Kedron, just by the Valley of Jehoshaphat. No water flows along the bed of the Kedron, save during the rainy season. Previous to beginning the ascent of Mount Olives, we come to the garden of Gethsemane, a pleasant bit of level ground about fifty yards square, surrounded by a high wall, and containing, besides several old, scraggy olive-trees, some flowering shrubs, plants, and semi-tropical flowers, carefully cared for by Latin monks. Over this "Garden of Agony," Greek and Romish monks, fired with rivalry and jealousies, have not only wrangled, not only fought with their tongues, but they have several times actually come to blows and bloodshed. Turkish officials, in the name of the *Allah* of the prophet, were compelled to interfere. Behold how these Christians "love one another"!

THE MOUNT OF OLIVES.

Though the stones were rough and rolling, the nimbleness of our Arab steeds made us feel safe while climbing up the steep hillsides of Mount Olives from the Garden of Gethsemane. Jesus and the apostles must have often left the passing imprints of their bare feet along this winding way. Upon the summit we had reached, is a miserable. dirty village, whose dark-hued inhabitants greatly resemble, both in dress and appearance, the Mussulmans of India. The women, sitting at the doors of their low stone houses, partially covered their faces as we passed by; and the children chased us, calling for money as a matter of right, rather than charity. Upon the top of this uneven mount, guides, showing the impress of a large foot legibly stamped upon the face of a stone, declare that the indentation was there made when " Jesus ascended to heaven." Saying nothing of the unnaturalness of the imprint, the alleged ascension was not from Mount Olives, but from Bethany. Accordingly, the Evangelist Luke says, " Jesus led out his disciples as far as Bethany, and blessed them ; and, while he blessed them, he was parted from them, and carried up into heaven."

> " 'Peace I leave with you !'   From days departed
>   Floats down the blessing, simple and serene,
> Which to his followers, few and fearful-hearted,
>   With yearning love, thus spake the Nazarene, —
>   'Peace I leave with you !' "

CHAPTER XXVI.

> " The panting pilgrim's heart is filled
> With holiest themes divine,
> When first he sees the lilies gild
> The fields of Palestine."

JERUSALEM, literally the city of peace, built and destroyed, buried and resurrected, was plundered by the Egyptian conqueror Shashak; besieged and taken by Nebuchadnezzar, king of Babylon; robbed by Syrian kings from the north; subjected, with all Judea, to Roman rule 63 B.C.; destroyed by Titus; devastated by crusaders; and savagely sacked by the Saracens in the seventh century. Standing on Mount Olives, perhaps near where John leaned upon Jesus' bosom, and reflecting upon the above historical events, while an Arab lad was gathering some olive-branches as evergreen symbols of the angel-song " Peace on earth," my thought flashed backward o'er the waste of nearly twenty centuries, to the occasion that called forth Jesus' plaintively tearful appeal to his kinsmen. As a psychometrist knowing the murderous persecutions of the past, and as a seer foreseeing the future of the city of the prophets, he wept, saying, —

" O Jerusalem, Jerusalem ! thou that killest the prophets, and stonest them which are sent unto thee ! how often would I have gathered thy children together, even as a hen gathereth her chickens under her wings, and ye would not! Behold, your house is left unto you desolate. For I say unto you, Ye shall not see me henceforth, till ye shall say, Blessed is he that cometh in the name of the Lord."

As the summit of Olives is some three hundred feet highei than Jerusalem, the prospect, especially from the Bethany side, is magnificent. Eastward nearly twenty miles are the Jordan and the Dead Sea: the surface of the latter is said to be the lowest point of water upon the face of the globe, being one thousand three hundred and twelve feet lower than the Mediterranean Sea.

Travelers accustomed to the wide distances of America are astonished to find how near together nestle the Palestinian cities, so famous in the Scriptures. Bethlehem is but six miles south from Jerusalem ; while Bethany, the place with which are associated many of the sweetest and tenderest memories of Jesus, is but two or three miles from the city. It was from Bethany, then embowered in olive and palm, acacia, fig, and pomegranate, that the Nazarene commenced his triumphal march over the rising hills on which " much people that were come to the feast, when they heard that Jesus was coming to Jerusalem, took branches of palm-trees, and went forth to meet him, and cried, Hosanna ! "

Monks here show the cave-like grave from which Lazarus, who had fallen into a deep, unconscious trance having the appearance of death, was raised. Deep and damp, it was reached by several descending steps. Naturally skeptical touching " sacred spots," we did not care to enter. Here in Bethany lived Martha and Mary, whom Jesus so loved.

" BUT DID JESUS EXIST ? "

It is too late in the day of historical erudition to raise such an inquiry. Intelligent spirits without exception, — so far as I am aware, — thinkers and *savants* in all countries, admit that Jesus lived and taught, was persecuted, and martyred upon Calvary. Gerald Massey, in commencing his lecture upon the " Birth, Life, and Marvels of Jesus Christ," in Music Hall, Boston, Jan. 18, said, —

" The question of the real *personal existence* of the Man is settled for me by the references to *Jesus* in the Talmud, where we learn that he was with his teacher, Rabbi Joshua, in Egypt, and that he wrote a MS. there which he brought into Palestine. This MS. was well known to the rabbis; and I doubt not it contained the kernel of his teachings, fragments of which have floated down to us in the Gospels."

Aaron Knight, one of my spirit teachers, assured me, several years since, that from conversing with the apostolic John, and other ancient spirits, he had learned that Jesus, between the years of twelve and thirty, visited Assyria, Egypt, and Persia, there studying spiritual science. In consonance with this, " The London Human Nature " of 1872 (published by James Burns) has a picture (through the artistic mediumship of Mr. Duguid) *of*, and a communication *from*, the Persian spirit who on earth was the traveling companion of Jesus during his pilgrimage into Persia and India. The narration is thrillingly interesting.

While in Jerusalem, we visited a learned and venerable rabbi, to ascertain what the Talmud said of Jesus. He kindly read and translated for us, and also loaned us for the day a portion of the translation. From this " Talmudic pile " we gathered the facts that the *Mishna*, or repetition of the law, relating to governments, laws, customs, and events, transpiring long before and after the Christian era, contained the opinions of one hundred and thirty learned rabbis. The compilation of this was finished in A. D. 190, and is consid·ered by the Jews in all Oriental lands as divine. Certain comments annexed to the Hebrew text of the Mishna constitute the work known as the " Jerusalem Talmud." But the Neziken of the Mishna in one of its seventy-four sections (Order IV. chap. 10) while treating of the Sanhedrim, or great Senate and House of Judgment at Jerusalem, makes special mention of Jesus of Nazareth, — his " indifference to the law of Moses," his " pretended miracles," his

" stubborn waywardness," his "kingly ambition," and " repeated blasphemies." These testimonies are befitting *addenda* to " Jesus : Myth, Man, or God ? " *

THE MOSQUE OF OMAR.

It is common for Arabian and Indian Mussulmans, after visiting Mecca, sacred to the birth of Mohammed, and Medina, holy because holding the ashes of Araby's apostle, to visit Jerusalem, praying in the Mosque of Omar. This famous edifice, as an architectural structure, is unique, massive, and eminently rich in consecrated antiquities. Its overshadow-ing dome, its porcelain, blue enamel, crimson canopies, elaborately gilded texts from the Koran, and weird shrines of the patriarch, give the building a grand and imposing appearance. Mohammedans, ever hating Christian leather, require "infidels" from the West to enter their temples of worship with bared feet, or in slippers presented at the vestibule. But as workmen, last autumn, were repairing this mosque, — the crown of Mount Moriah, and original site of Solomon's Temple, — we were allowed to enter well shod ; when our guide, recounting the old and silly myth, pointed to the " stone," the rock of *El Sakara*, a large, irregular, limestone rock surrounded by an iron railing, and said to be "miraculously suspended." Passing by (without a thought) the loadstone suspension, this is declared to be the rock upon which Abraham sacrificed the " ram," the one that Jacob used for a " pillow," and the one, say Mussulmans, from which Mohammed made his miraculous flight to heaven upon his celestial steed *Barak ;* and, as proof, they point to the marks of the horse's hoofs in the rock.

This mosque has parted with much of its past splendor. Ibn Asákir saw it in the twelfth century. Then it was a

* This volume referred to by Mr. Peebles, "*Jesus: Myth, Man, or God ?* " giving the historical evidences of Jesus' existence, as well as drawing damaging comparisons between the results of sectarian Christianity, and the moral effects of the "heathen philosophy" so called, is for sale at the "Banner of Light" office.— ED. BANNER OF LIGHT.

building of beautiful proportions, having fifty doors, six
hundred marble pillars, fifteen domes, four minarets, and
three hundred and eighty-five chains, sustaining five thousand lamps.   Not until 1856 were Jews and Christians
allowed to enter this mosque.   Mohammedans believe that
angels keep nightly watch about the lofty dome, bringing
with them, to breathe, the air of Paradise.

THE JEWS' WAILING-PLACE.

Admitting, which seems reasonable, that the present
western wall, and a portion of the northern wall circling Jerusalem, occupy the very line of the *ancient first wall*, it is perfectly natural that Eastern Jews should meet at the base
of the wall upon the west side to weep and wail over
stones there placed before Herod's time.   Though there are
some present each day, Friday is the great wailing-day.
Assembled, —

The rabbi begins, "On account of the Temple which
has been destroyed, and the glory which has departed" —

" *We sit here and weep.*"

"Because our prophets and holy men have been slain,
because Jerusalem is a desolation, and because our Messiah
long promised has not come" —

" *We sit here lonely weeping and praying.*"

Both sexes were present.   The aged women, bowing,
sighed and wept; young maidens bathed the hallowed walls
in their tears; old men tottered up to the stones, prayers
trembling on their lips; while others wailed aloud as though
their hearts would break.   Seeing them made my soul sad.
And oh! how I wanted to tell them, Messiah has already
come.   Your Messiah, like the kingdom of God, is within
you; while the Christ-spirit has been coming during all the
cycling ages!   This locality along the outer wall may well
be termed "the Jews' wailing-place."

IN HELL AS PROPHESIED.

Leaving the close-communion Calvinistic craft while my cheeks were yet crimson, and hair flaxen, the clergyman, in a rage over my irrepressible infidelity, told me I would "go to hell." And it was true, — infinitely truer than *his* Sunday preaching, for I went, *yes*, went to hell; and that, too, while seeking Jesus, or, rather, his footpaths round about Jerusalem. After passing for half an hour under a scorching sun along the brow of Mount Zion, dotted with here and there an olive-tree, I suddenly found myself in the Valley of Hinnom, *Gehenna*, Hell; the place referred to in Mark ix. 45, 46, —

"And, if thy foot offend thee, cut it off : it is better for thee to enter halt into life, than having two feet to be cast into hell, into the fire that never shall be quenched ; where their worm dieth not, and the fire is not quenched."

This Valley of Hinnom, on the south-east side of Jerusalem, is nearly one mile and a half in length; and in ancient times there was an image here standing dedicated to Moloch, to which idolatrous Jews offered human sacrifices, even their own children. After King Josiah had partially purged the land of idolatry, this valley became the common receptacle of rubbish from the city, and of the dead bodies of notorious criminals, upon which festering filth worms reveled. And to stifle the stench, and prevent pestilential diseases, a fire was there kept continually burning; hence this place of fire, or hell-fire. The term Gehenna (Hell), composed of two Hebrew words, *Gee*, a valley, and *Hinnom*, the name of the man who once owned it, was used by Jesus figuratively to describe a state of deep, conscious misery. I do not agree with Theodore Parker that "Jesus taught the eternity of future punishment." The whole drift of his moral teachings and parables is against such a conclusion. True, he employed the phrase, "*The fire that shall never be quenched;* " but he used it in the limited sense of the Orientals.   Strabo the geographer, treating of the Parthenon, a temple at Athens, says, " In this was the inextinguishable or unquenchable lamp," and yet this lamp was quenched ages since.   Josephus, speaking of a festival of the Jews, writes, " Every one brought fuel for the fire of the altar, which continued always unquenchable; " and yet the fire was long ago quenched, with altar and temple in ruins.   So in this valley of Hinnom, — this Gehenna-*Hell* of the New Testament, — the grass in spring-time is green, and the flowers bloom; olive and fig trees bear their fruit; while near by bubbles the Pool of Siloam.   Hell, theologians to the contrary, is more a condition than a locality.

BETHESDA'S POOL AND MEDICINES.

This Pool of Bethesda, literally the " house of mercy," pointed out as within the city, near St. Stephen's Gate, is thus spiritually referred to in John's Gospel : —

" Now, there is at Jerusalem by the sheep-market a pool, which is called, in the Hebrew tongue, Bethesda, having five porches. . . .

" And an angel went down at a certain season into the pool, and troubled the water: whosoever then first after the troubling of the water stepped in was made whole of whatsoever disease he had."

There are strange traditions connected with this pool.   In Old-Testament times David, walking upon the housetop, saw the beautiful Bathsheba, wife of Uriah the Hittite, bathing in Bethesda's limpid waters.   And this "man after God's own heart," being touched with the infirmity of " affectional freedom," sent messengers, and " took her." The remainder of the story need not be told.   This reservoir of sanative waters was " troubled," that is, magnetized by an angel, or band of spiritual presences, something as certain modern media will, by holding, so " trouble " a goblet of water that the color will change, and medicinal properties be imparted.   The spirit-world is, in a measure, made up of the invisible essences of roots, plants, and minerals. Divine physicians know their uses. When the angels spiritually magnetized Bethesda's waters, the "blind, halt, and withered" stepped in, and were healed. Give intelligent spirits the conditions, and I dare set no bounds to their power. Intermittent springs, pools, and reservoirs, owing to earthquakes and other frequent convulsions of nature in tropical climates, often spasmodically rise and fall, and occasionally for ever cease to flow. September last, Bethesda was a dirty, sunken cesspool, with simply a show of shallow, turbid water.

THE DATE OF THE CRUCIFIXION.

A London critic has recently given Disraeli the Israelite, and present leader of the Tory party in Parliament, a terrible flagellation for the chronological blunder of putting the crucifixion in the reign of Augustus Cæsar, when the event transpired in the twentieth year of the reign of the Emperor Tiberius, son-in-law and successor of Augustus Cæsar. Herr Kaib, the great German *savant*, in a lately published work, shows that

"There was a total eclipse of the moon concomitantly with the earthquake that occurred when Julius Cæsar was assassinated on the 15th of March, B.C. He has also calculated the Jewish calendar to A. D. 41; and the result of his researches fully confirms the facts recorded by the Evangelists of the wonderful physical events that accompanied the crucifixion. Astronomical calculations prove, without a shadow of doubt, that on the fourteenth day of the Jewish month Nisan (April 6) there was a total eclipse of the sun, which was accompanied in all probability by the earthquake, 'when the veil of the temple was rent from the top to the bottom, and the earth did quake, and the rock rent' (Matt. xxxii. 51); while St. Luke describes the eclipse in these words: 'And it was the sixth hour (noon); and there was a darkness over all the land till the ninth hour (three o'clock P. M.), and the sun was darkened' (Luke xxi. 44).

"This mode of reckoning corresponds perfectly with the result of another calculation our author made by reckoning backward from the great total eclipse of April, 1818, allowing for the difference between the old and new style; which also gives April 6 as the date of the new moon in the year A. D. 31. As the vernal equinox of the year fell on March 25, and the Jews ate their Easter lamb, and celebrated their *Frib Passoh*, or feast of the passover, on the following new moon, it is clear April 6 was identified with Nisan 14 of the Jewish calendar, which moreover was on Friday, the *Paraskevee*, or day of preparation for the sabbath; and this agrees with the Hebrew Talmud. Thus by the united testimony of astronomy, archæology, traditional and biblical history, there can be but little doubt that the date of the crucifixion was April 6, A. D. 31."

Jesus, the Syrian seer, a radical reformer and divine teacher, died a martyr to the sublime principles he taught, — died with a prayer of forgiveness trembling upon his quivering lips. May we not say with the Revelator, " Worthy the Lamb "?

" THE STAR OF BETHLEHEM."

" The star in the east took its place in the choir ;
  While the seraphs sang alto, the angels sang air;
  They sang, and the cadence is lingering still, —
  ' Be our peace evermore to the *men of good will.*' "

As melody marries the words of a song, so truth marries the cycling ages. The priest officiating at the altar is history, — the issue, wisdom. But was this Bethlehem star a new star? Was it a comet? Was it a transient meteor? Was the brilliancy caused by planets in conjunction? Was it an atmospheric luminosity? Was it an angel assuming an astral appearance? Or was it a sudden stellar eruption similar to that witnessed by Tycho Brahe in 1572, when a star appeared suddenly, and increased to such an astonishing magnitude that it was visible at noon, maintaining much of its splendor for seventeen months? The French Academician, Alphonse De Lamartine, said that —

" Chinese astronomers, whose observations are noted for their accuracy, and extend back thousands of years, record that a bright comet did appear in the year 4 B.C., and remain visible seventy days during the vernal equinox. This is a curious fact, and it corroborates the assertion made by most chronologers, that the nativity occurred four years before the time usually assigned to it; so that we should now be in A. D. 1878, instead of 1874."

Though accepting the *fact* of the star on that auspicious evening, we utterly repudiate the theories of both astronomers and miracle-believers. Those philosophers and astronomers who saw the star were, according to Matthew, " wise men from the East," — *Magi;* and the term " Magi," from *Mag* in the Pehlvi language, implies a mystic, a visionist, a dreamer of dreams. Pliny and Ptolemy mentions *Arabi* as synonymous with *Magi.* Accordingly the more learned of the second century believed that the Magi who brought the offerings of " frankincense and myrrh " came from Southern Arabia, where these productions abound. But, whether they came from Arabia or Persia, those " wise men " were media gifted with clairvoyance ; and the star was a brilliant psychological presentation guiding them to the birthplace of him who, when mediumistically developed, spiritually educated, and baptized of the Christ, " went about doing good."

BETHLEHEM THE BIRTHPLACE OF JESUS.

Biblical commentators to the contrary, it is of little consequence whether the Nazarene was born in a peasant's house, a cave, or a dismal grotto. Along the Nile in Egypt they build of mud, but in Syria of stone; a limestone rock underlying, if not overtopping, most of the country. Bethlehem, a city of six thousand inhabitants, built of stone, has many houses hewn in the rocks, cave-like. It stands upon a hill, the sides of which are terraced with vineyards. The suburbs are bleak and wild. As whole, the city is more tidy and cleanly, however, than most of the Syrian villages.

Reaching Bethlehem about noon, we hurried to the Church of the Nativity, said to have been constructed over the cave-stable in which Jesus was born. The edifice is shaped like a cross, and was erected A. D. 325 by the Empress Helena. We rested and lunched in the Latin convent. The monks were very kind, and their rooms cozy and quiet. These Franciscan monks entertain travelers free of charge,

— a common practice in the East. At one o'clock we saw these monks feed a flock of poor children gratis. It was a beautiful sight; and in our soul we said, *Heaven bless these Roman-Catholic monks!* The country surrounding Bethlehem is full of interest. It was around these hills that the youthful David learned to make the lute and the harp. Here were the border-lands of Boaz; here Ruth gleaned the barley-fields; here was the wilderness of Judea, in which John preached repentance; here were the plains where shepherds were abiding when they heard the angel-song of " Peace on earth; " and here, too, was born Jesus, the Shiloh of Israel, and the " Desire of all nations."

When crossing these unfenced " shepherd hills," so called, said our spirit-friends, in Jesus' time, we noticed flocks feeding on a dry, hay-like substance, and shepherds watching them. Observing and meditating upon this, I thought of the hymn, — the *fugue* my mother used to sing in those sunny days of a New-England childhood, —

> " While shepherds watched their flocks by night,
>   All seated on the ground,
>   The angel of the Lord came down,
>   And glory shone around."

Oh the lingering melody of that mother's voice! its tender echoes can never die away from my soul. Further reflection brought to memory the sweet lines of our Quaker Whittier : —

> " Lo! Bethlehem's hill-site before me is seen,
>   With the mountains around, and the valleys between;
>   There rested the shepherds of Judah, and there
>   The song of the angels rose sweet in the air.
>
>   I tread where the twelve in their wayfaring trod;
>   I stand where they stood with the chosen of God, —
>   Where his blessings were heard, and his lessons were taught;
>   Where the blind were restored, and the healing was wrought.

Oh, here with his flock the sad Wanderer came!
These hills he toiled over in grief are the same;
The founts where he drank by the wayside still flow;
And the same airs are blowing which breathed on his brow."

WHY DID NOT CONTEMPORARY GREEKS AND ROMANS REFER TO JESUS?

This inquiry has little force. Why did not contemporary Hindoo historians choose to notice the presence of Alexander the Great in India? Why do prominent European writers deny the existence of the Grecian Pythagoras; alleging, among other reasons, that the name is traceable to the Sanscrit *Pitha-gura*, the schoolmaster? Why did not Homer, the contemporary of Solomon, make mention of him or of the Hebrews? Why do the writings of Thales, Solon, Democritus, Plato, Herodotus, Xenophon, and others, contain no references whatever to the Jews? Do such omissions prove the non-existence of patriarchs and prophets? It should be remembered that those were not the eras of a world-wide toleration and appreciation, nor of special telegrams and morning newspapers.

Saviors are fated to non-recognition by their fellows. Prophets have never had where to lay their heads. The proud and the erudite do not notice them. Thorns leave crimson kisses upon their pale foreheads. Jesus "the Galilean" was of this number. Neither rabbi nor Roman helped him to "bear the cross." But Greek and Roman writers of the second century make direct mention of him and the "superstitious vagaries" of the Christians. Historians of the coming century may deign to make records of the present exponents of the Spiritual philosophy.

SOLOMON'S POOLS.

These, by the winding road we went, are ten miles from Jerusalem. The place is called El Burak. The dilapidated old castle here standing was built upon Masonic principles.

The two pillars, the arch, the breastplate, the trowel, and the star inclosed in the circle, are plainly visible. The construction of these three gigantic pools, or cisterns, is ascribed to Solomon. If he was not the builder, who was? The one farthest east is six hundred feet in length, two hundred in width, and fifty feet deep. The proudest man-of-war that ever plowed the ocean might float thereon. The first of these pools is fed from a living fountain. During the rainy season the upper pool, overflowing, fills the others. The water from these immense reservoirs, carried through an underground aqueduct around the hills a little to the east of Bethlehem to Jerusalem, and used originally in the various services of the sanctuary, is at present used by the Mohammedans about the Mosque of Omar, who bathe their hands and faces before worshiping.

FROM JERUSALEM TO THE JORDAN.

Rising early from a good night's rest upon Mount Zion, breakfasting upon eggs, bread, grapes, figs, and honey, — *minus* the locusts, — and finding our sheik, and guide Selim, well armed, the muleteers and tenting apparatus in readiness, we were speedily in the saddle, wending our way through the vale of Kedron, by the tomb of Zechariah, the tomb of St. James, and the battered tomb of Absalom, which to this day, when the Jew, passing, especially upon a funeral occasion, picks up and hurls a stone thereat, exclaiming, "Cursed be the son who disobeys the father's commands!" The hills in this vicinity are literally honeycombed with graves and old tombs.

Reaching a rugged eminence a little distance from the city, Mr. Knight, a spirit-friend, spoke to Dr. Dunn's clair-audient ear, saying, "Along that valley to the right, Jesus and his disciples used to come into the city from Bethlehem; . . . and farther, on that palm-crowned hill, lived a warm personal friend of Jesus, with whom he frequently tarried over night." Spirits of the apostolic age, accompanying directed us to such localities as were yet magnetically aflame with ancient marvels. Not a spoken word of Jesus was lost; not a touch dies away into nothingness; the universe knows no annihilation. To this, psychometry is a living witness. While Mr. Knight was conversing with us, this passage flashed upon my mind like a sunbeam: —

"Did not our hearts burn within us while he talked with us by the way, and while he opened to us the scriptures?" (Luke xxiv. 32.)

MAR SABA AND THE DEAD SEA.

Journeying Jordan-ward, we met crowds, with their heavily-laden donkeys and camels, on their way to Jerusalem. The morrow was market-day. Syrian women still bear burdens upon their heads. Late in the afternoon we came to our tenting-place in a grassless, shrubless valley, rimmed around with sharply-defined hills. Near us was *Mar Saba*, a weird convent castle. No pen-picture can do justice to this Oriental edifice, with adjoining gorges, perpendicular cliffs, and rock-hewn chambers, where monks nightly mouth their midnight prayers. Within this half-martial, half-churchal structure are not only numerous small chapels, covered with old pictures and Greek inscriptions, but St. Saba's sepulcher, and a vault filled with fourteen thousand skulls of martyred monks.

The country is indescribably rough, ragged, and mountainous; the results of terrible convulsions are everywhere visible. Repairing to our tent-apartment from Mar Saba, just at dark, an Arab lad, nearly naked, brought us specimens of bituminous rock; it seemed filled with a species of petroleum. These dark, dismal, pitchy cliffs, with the bitumen, sulphur, niter, and phosphoric stones found in all this region, account for the plains of fire, or the destruction of the "five cities of the plain," — Sodom, Gomorrah, Admah, Zeboim, and Zoar, — upon purely natural principles. Having seen burning Ætna, stood upon sulphurous Vesuvius, walked upon Solfatara's cooled yet tremulous crater, as well

as utterly extinct volcanoes in different countries, I discover
no satisfactory evidences that the Dead Sea was once the
crater of an extinct volcano: rather should I consider it
originally a fresh-water lake. But, reflecting upon the millions of years that have rolled into the abysmal past since
the beginning of earth's mighty geological upheavings, who
dare define conditions, or fix bounds to ancient rivers, seas
or oceans? Immutable law governs all things. Explorers,
as well as roaming Arabs, tell us that along the southern
extremity of the Dead Sea are several bubbling hot springs.

Notwithstanding the nasal music, the multitude of fleas,
and the doleful shriek of night-birds, we slept comfortably
well in our tottering tent, guarded by sheiks and their
heavily-armed attendants.

Tuesday morning, Aug. 26, four o'clock found us approaching the Dead Sea upon the north, near the entrance of
the Jordan. It was yet starlight. Never did the stars
appear so brilliant. We felt the presence of spirits. It is
cool and comfortable traveling at this hour, even in half-
tropical Palestine. Riding our jaded horses to another
frowning summit, we caught a full view of this memorable
sea. Its crystal waves, lying tremulously at our feet, were
bathed in the sun, now rising gorgeously over the brown
hills of Moab. The Dead Sea, resembling externally a beautiful American lake, is some seventy miles in length, and
from three to twenty in width. Its waters presenting a sil
very, transparent appearance, are a little bitter, and salt even
beyond the ocean. They act something like alum in the
mouth, and cayenne in the eye. Birds sail over its blue
depths; while rank shrubbery, graceful reeds, and flowering
plants, grow down to the very sands upon the brink. If
there are no abrasions upon the skin, bathing in the Dead
Sea is exquisitely delicious. Owing to its great specific
gravity, twelve hundred, — distilled water being one thousand, — effort to remain upon the surface is needless, sinking impossible. Coming out from our swimming excursion

in these clear yet bitter, briny waters, there was a saline crystallization upon the beard, and an irritable, uncomfortable feeling upon the cuticle, till, galloping away over the plains six miles, we bathed in the soft, rippling waters of the Jordan.

> " On Jordan's stormy banks I stand,
>   And cast a wistful eye "

to *America*, — the noblest, grandest country in the world.

> " Breathes there the man with soul so dead,
>   Who never to himself hath said, —
>   ' This is my own, my native land ' ?
>   Whose heart hath ne'er within him burned,
>   As home his footsteps he hath turned
>   From wandering on a foreign strand ? "

What changes in this country since the time of the apostles! There's now a railway from Joppa to Jerusalem, owned mostly by the French. Its speed is fifteen miles per hour. It is but three hours from Joppa, now called Jaffa, to the once city of King David. Thirty years ago there was not a wheeled vehicle in Palestine. Jerusalem has one good hotel — " The New Hotel." Within the walls of the city are nearly 50,000, and about 28,000 of these are Jews. These are rapidly increasing in number. Soon the cry may be realized " Jerusalem for the Jews ! "

CHAPTER XXVII.

PRESENT GOSPELS.

ALL countries have had their inspired chieftains, all dispensations their prophets, and all recurring cycles their apostles. Many evangelists besides those of the New Testament have written gospels, — good messages of peace, love, and "good will to men."

It is perfectly natural that Rénan, while traveling in Palestine, should exclaim, " I have before my eyes a fifth Gospel, mutilated, but still legible."

Though the Ganges is sacred to the Hindoo, the Nile to the Egyptian, and the Jordan to the Christian, the liberal and the more intelligent of this century, rising above the special into the beautiful border-lands of the universal, see in every flowing stream a Jordan, in every sunny vale a Kedron, in every day a sabbath day, in every soul a temple for prayer, in every tomb a forthcoming Savior, in every healthy country a Mount of Transfiguration, and in every heart an altar of religious devotion, where the incense of aspiration is, or *should* be, kept continually burning.

WHY JESUS WAS BAPTIZED IN THE JORDAN.

All the Oriental religions had their regenerating rites. Egyptians were washed from their iniquities in the Nile. Upon sarcophagi and hieroglyphical scrolls Osiris is represented pouring water upon candidates in a kneeling position. The Avesta ceremonials of the Persians abound in directions for baptismal ceremonies. Even proud Romans practiced the rite ; and accordingly Juvenal criticised and satirized them for seeking to wash away their sins by " dipping their heads thrice in the flowing Tiber." Jesus, a Palestinian Jew, born subject to the law of Moses, must needs be circumcised and baptized for the washing-away of sin according to the Israel-itish understanding of ordinances in that era. But if Jesus was not consciously imperfect, was not a sinner, why should he submit to baptism by water ? Matthew says, " Then went out to him Jerusalem, and all Judea, and all the region round about Jordan, and were baptized of him in Jordan, confessing their sins ; " while Mark assures us that " John preached the baptism of repentance for the remission of sins." And John baptized Jesus in the Jordan. There-fore, as baptism was understood to be the " washing-away of sin," it is clear that Jesus was considered a sinner. Noth-ing upon theological grounds could be more absurd than the baptism of a *saint !*

Jesus, conscious of his imperfections, said, " Call not thou me good." The New Testament further declares that Jesus " learned obedience by the things he suffered," that he was " made perfect through suffering," and that he was called the " first begotten from the dead ; " but how begot-ten from the dead unless *himself* once dead in trespasses and sins ?

After Jesus confessed, and was baptized, — the water being a symbol of purification, — the " heavens were opened," and the Christ-spirit from the heaven of the Christ-angels descended upon him, and a voice came saying, " This is my beloved Son, in whom I am well pleased." Now we have Jesus Christ " our exemplar," Jesus Christ standing upon the basis of eternal principles, Jesus Christ the anointed and illumined, ministering the tenderest sympathy and love. Those parables are inimitable ; the Sermon upon the Mount stands out unparalleled ; while that pleading prayer upon the cross, breathing forgiveness toward murderers, proves the Nazarene divine.

JORDAN'S SOURCE AND SCENERY.

The Jordan of the Evangelists, originating at the base of snowy Hermon, passes through the Galilean lake ; through a rich valley-strip of land southward some two hundred miles ; through shaded banks of willow, sycamore, and such reeds as were shaken by the wind when the mediumistic John there stood baptizing *Him* who afterwards baptized with the Christ-spirit; and finally falls quite precipitously into those crystal depths of brine and bitumen, the Dead Sea. Though vineyards, balsam-gardens, and palm-forests have disappeared ; though the climate is bleaker, and the face of the country considerably altered, — still this saline sea, with river and mountain, sufficiently mark these Meccas of biblical history.

Easily fording the Jordan, we should call it in America an ordinary stream, nothing more. Tasting, I found the water soft, of an agreeable flavor, and great limpidity. Drinking freely, it wanted but one quality, — *coolness*. After quenching our thirst, cutting canes, gathering specimens, wading, bathing, and splashing in the waters, we lunched in the cooling shadows of rose-laurels and junipers, probably the same species of juniper as that under which Elijah sat when the angel came, and touched him (1 Kings xix. 4).

WHAT SPIRITS SAID OF JORDAN AND JERICHO.

Accompanying us in this wild region were exalted spirits who lived in the Nazarenean period, — royal souls then, angels now. These assured us that, during the past twenty centuries, rightly denominated a cycle, terrific convulsions had left their footprints upon the face of all that country known as Assyria. The Jordan itself is a much smaller stream now than then. Anciently it had two series of banks, one of which was annually overflowed from the melting of Hermon's and Lebanon's snows with the heavy rains of the winter season. The channel, deepening, especially near the

Dead Sea, has also changed its course. This the old bottom-land gravel-beds abundantly demonstrate. Portions of these flat lands have at the present time an exceedingly rich soil; and it only requires industry, irrigation, and cultivation to make the plains of the Lower Jordan fruitful as the orange-gardens of Sharon.

Dr. Thomson, after thoroughly exploring the whole Judean country, says: —

"Thus treated, and subjected to the science and the modern mechanical appliances in agriculture, the valley of the Jordan could sustain half a million of inhabitants. Cotton, rice, sugar-cane, indigo, and nearly every other valuable product for the use of man, would flourish most luxuriantly. There were, in fact, sugar-plantations here long before America was discovered; and it is quite possible that this plant was taken from this very spot to Tripoli, and thence to Spain by the crusaders, from whence it was carried to the West Indies. Those edifices to the west of 'Ain es Sultan are the remains of ancient sugar-mills, and are still called Towahin es Sukkar."

Near sundown, pitching our tent Aug. 27, adjoining Rihi, a village of squalid Arabs, we sat down for journal-writing and reflection. · Squads of curious Arabs continually prowled about our camp. These Bedouin-tenting denizens of the desert are coarse, rough, and often high-handed robbers. Many shades darker than the same class on the mountains, they subsist largely upon plunder, as do gypsies in some portions of the East.

JERICHO AND THE GOOD SAMARITAN.

Early rising is both commendable and healthy. The morning of Aug. 28, five o'clock, found us in the saddle approaching Jericho, anciently called the city of palm-trees; but the last palm, that a generation since stood by the old tower, a solitary sentinel, fell at last, and not a vestige of the date-palm now appears in the vicinity. Riding over lines of ancient walls, feet-worn pavements, mounds, fallen aqueducts and arches, bits of brick, and moldering piles, a

feeling of sadness brooded over my entire being. Is it possible that this was the magnificent Jericho of antiquity ? —
the Old-Testament Jericho, whose walls fell before those
echoing ram's-horn blasts sounded by seven mediumistic
priests ; the Jericho that many times saw the weary Nazarene on his way from the Jordan up to Jerusalem ; the
Jericho that takes in the great fountain of *'Ain es Sultan*,
and so famous in religious memory as connected with the
parable of the " Good Samaritan," and the lesson of universal brotherhood ? Is this teaching practiced by either Spiritualists or secularists ? Is there simplicity, confidence, purity,
peace, and brotherhood in the ranks of fashionable Christians ? Why, Christianity has become the synonym of pride,
fashion, plunder, persecution, and war! When the blood of
seventy thousand Mohammedans by the hands of crusading
Christians had crimsoned the streets of Jerusalem, the
prayerful murderers, in the name of religion, went and kissed
the cold stone that covered the tomb of him termed " The
Prince of peace ! " Hate of Christian priests for philosophers kept the Roman Emperor Julian with the old Pagan
religions. " Ere I leave the worship of the gods," said he,
" let me see a better state of society emanating from Chris
tian teachings."

RETURNING TO JERUSALEM.

Our spirit-friend Mr. Knight — referring, as we passed
along, to Jesus' aptitudes at teaching from nature, and then
commenting upon the sheep and the goats, the barren fig-
tree, the lilies of the field, and other Nazarenean illustrations
— said that twenty centuries had wrought marvelous changes
upon the face of Palestine. Volcanic countries were ever
liable to sudden commotions. The topographical, climatic,
and electric conditions were *all* considerably different. Something like two thousand years constituted a cycle ; and a
cycle had passed since the later Hebrew seers and poets,
standing upon the mount of vision, foretold the desolation

that should come. The causes were then in operation. All prophecy, however, is within the realm of causation.

Poetically speaking, Syria was once a land flowing with milk and honey. Its undulating valleys rejoiced in waving fields of corn; its crystal streams were bordered with palms and roses; its mountains were covered with olives, figs, mulberries, pomegranates, and clustering vines; and its rocky cliffs with grazing flocks and herds.

The present population of Palestine, estimated at two hundred thousand, is scattered over mountains dotted with mingled masses of rocks and ruins. It seems impossible that this country, now under the sultan's rule, once sustained three millions of prosperous people. And yet it is evident that there have been great natural and desolating convulsions since the days of Hillel, Philo, Josephus, and Jesus. Agricultural pursuits were abandoned for war, denuding mountains of their woody vestures, and hills of their figs, olives, and grazing herds. Shortly after the crucifixion, the country was wasted by famine, cursed by civil dissensions and foreign wars instigated by ambition and a merciless cupidity.

But we are again approaching the city so holy to Jews, Christians, and Mohammedans, —,the seventeen times besieged, rebuilt, and re-ruined Jerusalem, which to-day is little more than a gathering of rival bishops, ecclesiastics, monks, artisans, and traders, selling relics, and supplying the temporal wants of religious pilgrims, who thither flock to see the magnificent sepulcher and costly shrines dedicated to an inspired reformer, — a reformer who, when on earth, was considered by arrogant Pharisees as a wandering, sabbath-breaking, blaspheming, false " prophet of Galilee." Draining the cup of sorrow, drinking to the dregs the chalice of agony, he sadly said, " The foxes have holes, and the birds of the air have nests; but the Son of man hath not where to lay his head."

EXPLORING PALESTINE.

Why not, in a broad cosmopolitan spirit, explore Palestine, Tyre, Troy, and the once peopled isles of the ocean?

In 1848 Lieut. Lynch was duly authorized by our Government to go down the Jordan from Galilee, through the windings of that river to the Dead Sea. Capt. Warren's excavations in Jerusalem, and discoveries relating to ancient localities, entrances to Solomon's Temple, subterranean passages, winding aqueducts, wells, tanks, canals cut in solid rock, pottery, weights, seals, gems, and inscriptions in the Phœnician characters, and historical sites mentioned by Josephus, are exceedingly valuable to archæologists.

Prof. Palmer of Cambridge, and Mr. Drake, have recently explored the country lying between the peninsula of Sinai and Palestine, — desert of the Exodus, — in which the "Israelites wandered forty years." The country was covered with a brown, parched herbage. The route was interesting from the discovery of ruins, mounds, fortresses, and localities retaining the names they had in the days of David.

The American Steever's Expedition reached Beirût in 1873. Mr. Paine there discovered important Greek inscriptions. In March they went to Edom and Moab. Here was found the celebrated Moabite stone, shedding more light upon the invention of our alphabet than any thing yet discovered. The learned Dr. Deutsh said, "It illustrates to a hitherto unheard-of degree the origin and history of the art of alphabetic and syllabic writing as we possess that priceless inheritance." The purpose of this company is to determine traditionary places, discover inscriptions, secure relics, and make an accurate map of this whole Syrian country. Besides the usual surveys, they also take astronomical observations. They have already discovered the famous Mount Nebo and Mount Pisgah. Those who have read "The Book of Moab" will be deeply interested to know what they say about Zoa of Pentapolis memory. It is to be hoped that this expedition, considering the growing demands of science, will not be used in the furtherance of sectarian interests. When will our American Congress furnish funds to equip expeditions to unearth the treasures hidden in the mounds of the south-west, to penetrate the non-explored ruins of Yucatan, and the dust-buried temples of Peru?

NON-PRACTICABILITY OF REFORMERS.

Apollonius, the rival of the Nazarene, was a mediumistic " mendicant;" Cleanthes was a " vagrant;" Jesus "impracticable." *These* are the frisky judgments of pert, mole-eyed men. Seen from the slough of selfishness, and measured by a miser's standard, Jesus was decidedly impracticable. Listen : " Lay not up for yourselves treasures on earth." " When thou makest a dinner or supper, call not thy friends, thy brethren, thy kinsmen, nor rich neighbors to the feast, but call the poor, the maimed, the lame, and the blind." Nothing to a vain externalist could be more unnatural, nothing more egregiously impracticable to fashionable, Pharisaic worldlings.

The beautiful hymn of Cleanthes to Jupiter, from which Paul quoted this to the Athenians, " *For we are also his offspring*," will live on the page of poesy for ever. And yet poor, kind-hearted Cleanthes, who gratuitously taught philosophy and religion, was, upon the complaint of an envious and pompous Greek, brought before the tribunal of Arcophagus, and charged with having no visible means of support. Shadow-days have their compensations : justice is ultimately done. The moral teachings of Jesus, and Cleanthes' hymn, are in literature immortal; while the names and memories of their persecutors are rotting to nothingness in a resurrectionless oblivion.

CHAPTER XXVIII.

THE Grecian Plato was the prince of philosophers; the Syrian Jesus, of inspired religionists. What a vivid contrast of birth, education, and country, these celebrated chieftains present to the rational thinker! Plato was well born, his mother a descendant of Solon. Among his ancestors were several erudite and wise Athenians.

His birth occurred in the palmiest period of the most distinguished country of antiquity. His education was the best that Athens could afford. Neither body nor mind was neglected. Muscle, imagination, taste, and reason were equally cultivated. While yet a youth he became a disciple of Socrates, meeting the most brilliant spirits of the age. That splendid yet extravagant genius, Alcibiades, the solid, clear-headed Xenophon, the keen, sophistical Protagoras, the logical and philosophical Crito, and other eminent scholars and statesmen, could but educe all that was divinest in man. The very air of classic Athens seemed to breathe the genius of art, science, and poetry; while the wit of Aristophanes, and the tragedy of Euripides, moved the masses as do the winds the forest-trees. Then Plato traveled, studying under Euclid at Megara, under Theodorus at Cyrene, under the Pythagoreans at Tarentum, and under the Hierophants and Egyptian priests twelve years at Heliopolis. He ate but once a day, or, if the second time, very sparingly, abstaining from animal food. He maintained great equanimity of spirit, and lived a celibate life. Returning to his native country, laden with the intellectual riches of the East, he opened an academy at Athens, in the Gardens of Colonus, where he lived in contact with the greatest men of the period, and died at a ripe old age, leaving a school of thinkers and orators to perpetuate his philosophy. Clad now in the shining vestures of immortality, he walks a royal soul in the republic of the gods.

Jesus was born a peasant. Mary was good and pure-minded. Joseph was a country carpenter. Judea, geographically insignificant, and numerically small, was at this time in a condition of political and religious decadence. The whole land had nothing to inspire faith. Its shekinah was eclipsed, its prophets dumb, and its very memories like the embalmed mummies of Mizraim. An alien race sat upon the Syrian throne. A Roman official presided in the judgment-hall. Roman soldiers paraded the streets, Roman officers levied and collected the taxes, and Roman coins circulated in the markets. The Jews at this period were narrow, selfish, proud. Hatred of Gentiles was a virtue ; help for suffering foreigners, little better than a crime. Religion was a form ; fasts fashionable ; and a broad cosmopolitan charity unknown.

Jesus lacked early culture. John and James were scholars. Though uneducated in dialectics and the classics, Jesus was nevertheless clairvoyant, clairaudient, and marvelously intuitional. Accompanied by a legion of heavenly angels, he stood above human laws, a law unto himself, unique, emotional, incomparable. The schools of the rabbis being but conservatories of traditions, Jesus, inspired by his spirit-guides, traveled in foreign countries, Egypt, Assyria, Persia, studying the mysteries of the seers, and listening to the voices of ascended gods. He sat at the feet of religious mystics, Magi, and gymnosophists ; Plato, at the feet of orators and logicians. Jesus, whose daily psalm was love, whose touch was a blessing, and presence a benediction, cultivated the sympathetic, the self-denying, the *religious faculties;* but Plato the perceptive and the philosophical. Centuries have rolled into the abysmal past. Now millions march under the banner of the cross, made memorable by the martyrdom of that religious enthusiast and radical Palestinian reformer. The once thorn-crowned Jesus Christ is now companioned with those celestial angels, the presence of which make radiant the kingdom of God. The pre-eminent greatness of Jesus consisted in his fine harmonial organization; in a constant overshadowing of angelic influences; in the depth of his spirituality and love; in the keenness of his moral perceptions; in the expansiveness and warmth of his sympathies; in his unshadowed sincerity of heart; in his deep schooling into the spiritual gifts of Essenian circles and Egyptian mysteries; in his soul-pervading spirit of obedience to the mandates of *right* manifest in himself; in his unwearied, self-forgetting, self-sacrificing devotion to the welfare of universal humanity, and his perfect trust in God. *

CHRISTIAN TEACHINGS BEFORE THE TIME OF JESUS CHRIST.

The patriarch Abraham, when returning from the " slaughter of the kings," convicted of the sin of war, met Melchisedec, King of Salem, priest of the most high God, and received his blessing. Abraham, conscious of the superiority of this so-considered " heathen " King of Salem, King of Peace, paid tithes, giving him at once " a tenth of all." But " who was Melchisedec? " Why, he was the king of some contiguous nation, the peace-king of Salem, the baptized of Christ; in a word, a Christian. This Christ-spirit, or Christ-principle, is truly " without father or mother, without descent, having neither beginning of days nor end of life, a continually abiding priest."

There were Christians in those pre-historic periods, Christians in golden ages past, Christians long before the

Old Testament patriarchs traversed the plains of Shinar, and Christians who spoke the ancient and mellifluous Sanscrit. Many of the most genuine and self-sacrificing Christians on earth to-day are Brahmans and Buddhists. All great souls, under whatever skies, and in whatever period of antiquity, baptized by the Christ-spirit of peace, purity, and love, and illumined by the divine reason, were Christians.

Dean Milman admits that

"If we were to glean from the later Jewish writings, from the beautiful aphorisms of other Oriental nations which we can not fairly trace to Christian sources, and from the Platonic and Stoic philosophy, their more striking precepts, we might find, perhaps, a counterpart to almost all the moral sayings of Jesus." *

Bigandet, the Roman Catholic bishop of Ramatha, and apostolic vicar of Ava and Pegu, says, —

"There are many moral precepts equally commanded, and enforced in common, by both the Buddhist and Christian creeds. It will not be deemed rash to assert that most of the *moral truths* prescribed by the gospel are to be met with in the Buddhistic Scriptures. . . . In reading the particulars of the life of the last Buddha, Guatama, it is impossible not to feel reminded of many circumstances relating to our Saviour's life, such as it has been sketched out by the Evangelists."†

St. Augustine, treating of the origin of Christianity, affirms that —

"The thing itself, which is now called the *Christian religion*, really was known to the ancients, nor was wanting at any time from the beginning of the human race, until the time when Christ came in the flesh; from whence the true religion, which had previously existed, began to be called *Christian;* and this in our day is called the Christian religion, not as having been wanting in former times, but having in latter times received its name."

* Dean Milman, Hist. Christianity, B. 1. c. iv. § 3.
† Bigandet, Life of Buddha, p. 494.

The Emperior Hadrian, writing to Servianus, while visit
ing Alexandria, and referring to the religion of the old
Egyptians, assures us that —

" The worshipers of Serapis are also Christians; for I find that the
priests devoted to him call themselves the bishops of Christ."

Clemens Alexandrinus, so eminent in the early Church,
admitted that —

" Those who lived according to the true *Logos* were really Christians,
though they have been thought to be atheists, as Socrates and Heraclitus
among the Greeks."

The Rev. Dr. Cumming of London, in his discourse upon
the " Citizens of the New Jerusalem," says, —

" It is a mistake to suppose that Christianity began only eighteen
hundred years ago: it began nearly six thousand years ago: it was
preached amid the wrecks of Eden."

The Rev. Dr. Peabody (Unitarian) pertinently asks, —

" If the truths of Christianity are intuitive and self-evident, how is it
that they formed no part of any man's consciousness till the advent of
Christ ? "

The learned Baboo Keshub Chunder Sen, whom I had
met several times both in London and Calcutta, said in a
discourse just previous to leaving England for India, —

" The Hindoo, therefore, who believes in God, is a Christian. If
purity, truth, and self-denial are Christian virtues, then Christianity is
everywhere where these virtues are to be found, without regard to
whether the possessors are called Christians, Hindoos, or Mohammedans.
Hence it comes that many Hindoos are far better Christians than many
who call themselves so. The result of my visit is, I came as a Hindoo,
I return a confirmed Hindoo. I have not accepted one doctrine which
did not previously exist in my mind."

This rational position lifts the Christianity of the ages out
of the slough of sect, out of the realm of the partial, and

places it upon the basic foundation of the universal. Seen from this sublime altitude, all true Spiritualists are Christians, recognizing the evangelist's affirmation, that "Christ had a glory with the Father before the world was;" and, furthermore, that "Christ is the chief among ten thousand, and the one altogether lovely."

THE MEDITERRANEAN AND ITS ISLANDS.

The sapphire waves of the Mediterranean, rippling under cloudless skies in star-lit hours, lift the thoughts to the "isles of the blest." A shade deeper than the sky, the islands that stud these waters called to mind early readings of the East.

Rhodes, — "Laudabant alii claram Rhodon," as Horace sings, the sunny Rhodes of which Pliny records that the Rhodians never lived a day without seeing the sun; and Scio, that may have been the birthplace of Homer as well as any other of the nine cities that contend for the honor, — these, and other isles, gladdened my vision.

In Cyprus, held by Egyptians and Iranians before the time of Greece, excavators have recently discovered a colossal statue of Hercules, holding before him a lion. It was found at the old town of Amathus, said to have been colonized by the Phœnicians.

We anchored off Syra, a beautiful isle, set in a sea smooth and green as polished malachite. Here was born Pherecydes, one of the oldest Greek writers.

Rhodes will remain ever connected with the Knights of St. John, and the Colossus, one of the seven wonders of the world. Overthrown by an earthquake, it remained where it fell for over nine hundred years; ultimately it was cut up for old metal, and borne away by the Mohammedans. Its size was doubtless greatly exaggerated by Greek visitors. This island has much to interest antiquarians. Syracuse, founded in 734 by the Corinthians under Archias, upon the ruins of an ancient Phœnician settlement, is all aglow with

classical memories.   It was the most extensive of the
Hellenic cities.   Strabo states that it was twenty-one miles
in circumference.   Connected with its history were such men
as Æschylus, Pindar, Epicharnius, Thrasybulus, Dionysius,
Demosthenes, and Archimedes, slain by a soldier who did
not know his value either as mathematician or philosopher.

The modern Greeks, peopling these islands, have the reputation of being the worst exaggerators on earth.   They
are generally tall, having fine complexions, sharp noses, and
still sharper eyes.   Their perceptive are much larger than
their reflective brain-organs.   Like the Jews, and not very
unlike Americans, money is their god.   On deck are
a few Nubians, dark as night; Syrians, with Jewish visages;
several Cretans; one Arab trader, tall, thin, and withered;
and two or three Armenians, who are more European in
their characteristics.   The strange garments of these people
are more diversified than their complexions.   To a traveling pilgrim, how frail and fickle seem fashions!   Who
are those that summer and winter under the fez, the turban,
or pointed hood, under those flowing trousers, embroidered
vests, red sashes, and multiformed cloaks, sacks, and robes?
What are their aspirations and life employments?   These
are the practical questions that throng the mind.   They are
brothers of Oriental lands, brothers with the same beating, pulsing hearts as ours, and destined to the same immortality.

SMYRNA.

" And unto the angel of the church in Smyrna write, These things
saith the first and the last, which was dead, and is alive:

I know thy works, and tribulation and poverty. . . .

Behold, the Devil shall cast some of you into prison that ye may be tried.

Fear none of those things which thou shalt suffer: but be thou faithful
unto death, and I will give thee a crown of life. — JOHN THE REVELATOR.

Smyrna, golden with the memories of early Christian
teachings, sits to-day like a queen upon the border-lands of
the Orient.

Our entrance into the broad, beautiful bay was just before sunset. The city lies at the very extremity, and partly upon the hill-side to the right, as you approach the shore. The site of ancient, historic Smyrna was on the left, at the foot of the mountains, and some little distance from the modern. Earthquakes have effected serious changes in much of the topography of this country. The Mediterranean at this and other points is continually receding.

Excepting Constantinople, Smyrna is the most important commercial city in the Turkish Empire. Though sending large quantities of opium yearly to the United States, most of its export trade is carried on with Great Britain, consisting of cotton, carpets, wool, fruits, and opium. This latter article is raised extensively in the back country, and brought in upon camels for exportation, after inspection. How, in what way, is so much of it used in America?

Passing the Greek church, a modern structure, the Armenian houses, and a drove of burdened camels, to the suburbs of the city, I commenced ascending the hill towards the old castle, accompanied by a dragoman. It was nearly noon when I reached the tomb of Polycarp, the ancient Smyrnian bishop, the good Christian martyr, the acquaintance and fervent admirer of the Apostle John. This tomb, held semi-sacred by both Mohammedans and Christians, overlooks the one hundred and fifty thousand souls that constitute the present city of Smyrna.

Every thing in this country — cloths, fruits, potatoes, vinegar, firewood — is bought and sold by the pound. The figs and grapes of Smyrna are famous for size, quality, and abundance. It seemingly adds to the exquisite flavor of olives, oranges, and figs, to pluck them fresh from the trees. This I was privileged to do in several fields and gardens in Smyrna and the Grecian Isles. Doubtless the best figs never see America.

There are a number of prominent Spiritualists in Smyrna. Among the most active are C. Constant and M. E. H. Rossi

Calling at Mr. Constant's palatial residence, in front of which is a beautiful garden fringed with fig, lemon, and orange trees, we were, after taking our seat upon a most inviting divan, treated to a cup of Turkish coffee, fruits, and delicious preserves. This is the Oriental custom. Everywhere in the East, hospitality is as profuse as commendable.

The Smyrnian bazaars, though much inferior, are very similar to those in Constantinople. One Turkish city typifies all others, — dirt, filth, decay, narrow streets, and a mixed population. How sad that such a profusion of fruitage, that such a clear atmosphere and sunny sky, should look down upon so much stagnant, dozing shiftlessness! When Americans have peopled the prairies and the broad millions of the Far West, they may safely turn their eyes towards Asia Minor, and the over-estimated desert-lands of the Orient.

CLIMATE AND COSTUMES.

The Smyrnians, like multitudes in the East, seem to live out of doors. The warm climate invites to a free and easy life. They eat but little meat, subsisting almost entirely upon vegetables and fruits. Dining at the hospitable home of Consul Smithers, there came upon the table, after soup, fish, and other courses, seedless sultana raisins, different varieties of nuts, grapes, pomegranates, figs, apricots, and delicious oranges. Asia Minor is certainly the paradise of fruits. The variety of costumes renders a walk in the streets exceedingly interesting. With the national Greek or Albanian, the costume consists of a high fez, with a long blue tassel, red jacket with open sleeves, and richly embroidered; shirt with wide and flowing sleeves; a leathern belt, with a pouch; short pantaloons and white fustanella. The Turkish costume is somewhat similar, only they wear short, wide trousers, dark-colored jackets, and shoes with buckles. The fez is almost universal. The old style of turban is seen only engraved upon tombstones, or worn on the heads of old men in the back country. Some of the young Turks wear the French style of hats. The Persians wear tall, pyramidal-shaped turbans ; and all wind sashes around their waists. Strangers generally engage a " cavasse," — that is, a sort of Turkish guide, having a certain police power. Going back into the country, these are necessary, as there are Greek brigands lurking in the mountains. The " cavasse," clothed in full authority, doffs a tall Turkish fez, sack-legged trousers, mock jewelry, flowing mantle lined with fur, a belt with three pistols, several knives and dirks, and a sword dangling by his side. One far away from the city is in doubt which to most fear, — the guide, or the mountain brigands. Nothing, for a time, more attracted my attention off in the country from Smyrna, than the camels, — patient, faithful creatures! Sometimes there were hundreds in a train, each following the other, led by a lazy Turk astride a donkey, and all heavily burdened with cotton, madder-root, olive-oil in goat-skins, opium, figs, and other products from the interior. The caravans farther east are more extensive, and exceedingly profitable in their line of traffic.

EPHESUS, AND THE APOSTLE JOHN.

" Unto the angel of the church of Ephesus write, These things saith he that holdeth the seven stars in his right hand, who walketh in the midst of the seven golden candlesticks :

" I know thy works, and thy labor, and thy patience, and how thou canst not bear them which are evil : and how thou hast tried them which say they are apostles, and are not, and hast found them liars.

" Thou hatest the deeds of the Nicolaitanes, which I also hate. . . .

" To the angel of the church in Thyatira write, . . . I have a few things against thee, because thou sufferest that woman Jezebel, which calleth herself a prophetess, to teach and to seduce my servants. . . .

" Him that overcometh will I make a pillar in the temple of my God, and he shall go no more out: and I will write upon him the name of my God, and the name of the city of my God, which is New Jerusalem, which cometh down out of heaven from God : and I will write upon him my new name.

" And I will give him the morning star." — JOHN THE REVELATOR

Sailing up the Mediterranean I saw Samos, — literally "sea-shore height." This island, at an early period of history, was a powerful member of the Ionic Confederacy. Pythagoras left it, to travel in foreign countries, under the government of Polycrates. A future view of this classic isle from St. Paul's prison and Mount Prion, around which was grouped ancient Ephesus, famed as the seat of the most eminent of the old Asian churches, was very fine. Not far distant was the beautiful island of Cos, with its mountainous peaks, vine-clad hillsides, and pleasant-appearing homes, embowered in evergreen foliage. And there peered above the horizon Patmos, sainted Patmos, seat of John's visions and revelations. Banished from the world's bustle, and frequently in the "spirit on the Lord's Day," he became the recipient of truths and illuminations that streamed in glory down through all the sunrise hours of the Christian dispensation. .

Determined to see the ruins of this old Ionian city, Ephesus, once noted for its commercial prosperity, for its stadium, theaters, and Temple of Diana, as well as for the place where the Apostle John spent his last years, I left Smyrna Nov. 7, 1870.* It was sixty miles distant to Isaalouke, a disagreeable Arab town.

The English own this railway. An hour's ride on wretched horses dropped us down with a party of pilgrims to the rim of the Ephesian ruins. The original city was evidently built around the base of Mount Prion. Crumbling remnants of custom-house and ware-houses are yet visible. But the Mediterranean waters have so receded, that bay, harbor, and landing have given place to a broad basin covered with grasses and weeds, through which winds a small serpentine stream. The employees of J. T. Wood were putting down shafts between Prion and St. John's

---

* Descriptions in this volume relating to Smyrna, Ephesus, Constantinople, Rome, Naples, Pompeii, Herculaneum, &c., are taken from notes made during a previous visit to Europe, Turkey, and Asia Minor.

Church, in search of Diana's Temple, which was in process of completion when Alexander passed into Asia, 335 B.C. This temple was erected to succeed the one set on fire the night of Alexander's birth, 356 B.C. The labors of Mr. Wood were crowned with success; and portions of those magnificent columns may now be seen in the British Museum, with the gods and goddesses of that period, beautifully modeled and chiseled.

THE APOSTLE'S BURIAL-PLACE.

A pilgrim under a scorching Asian sky, resting, I leaned upon one of the pillars that Christian and Moslem tradition unite in declaring marks the Apostle John's tomb. It was a consecrated hour. While standing by his tomb, on the verge of Mount Prion, looking down upon the marbled seats of the Ephesian theater, — relic of Hellenic glory, — with my feet pressing the soil that once pillowed the mortal remains of the " disciple that Jesus loved," ere their removal to Rome, no painter could transfix to canvas, no poet conceive suitable words to express, my soul's deep emotions. The inspiration was from the upper kingdoms of holiness; the baptism was from heaven; the robe was woven by the white fingers of immortals; while on the golden scroll was inscribed, ' *The first cycle is ending: the winnowing angels are already in the heavens. Earth has no secrets. What of thy stewardship? Who is ready to be revealed? Who, who shall abide this second coming? Who has overcome? Who is entitled to the mystical name and the white stone? Gird on thine armor anew, and teach in trumpet tones that the pure in heart, the pure in spirit only, can feast upon the saving fruitage that burdens the tree of Paradise.*"

From the summit of Mount Prion, the Isle of Samos may be distinctly seen. Gazing at this in the distance, and nearer to the winding course of the little Cayster towards the sea, at the scattered remnants of temples, marble fragments, broken friezes, and relics of every description,

I could not help recalling the prophetic warning of John, in the Book of Revelation, "I will come unto thee quickly, and will remove thy candlestick out of its place, except thou repent" (Rev. ii. 5).

It is generally admitted that the Apostle John lived to one hundred and four years of age; and all we know of his later days is linked with Ephesus, — accurately described by Herodotus, Pausanius, Pliny, and others, — outside the records of the Church fathers. It is not known how long St. John resided in this portion of Asia: suffice it, that his memory still lingers here, enshrined even in the Turkish name of the squalid village about two miles from the ruins of the old Ephesian city, "*Ayasolouke*," which is a corruption of the Greek "*Agios Theologos*," the holy theologian, the name universally given to this apostle in the Oriental Church.

The mosque here, which is magnificent, even though in partial ruin, was undoubtedly an ancient Christian church, probably the identical one which the Emperor Justinian built on the site of an older and smaller one, dedicated in honor of St. John, who at Ephesus trained the disciples Polycarp, Ignatius, and Papius to preserve and disseminate apostolic doctrines in Smyrna and other cities of Asia. In the erection of this church edifice by Justinian, upon the spot where the venerable apostle preached in his declining years, were employed the marbles of Diana's temple. Visiting these scenes, Asian cities, and churchal ruins, strengthens my belief in the existence of Jesus, the general authenticity of the Gospels, and the profound love-riches of John's Epistles. It is the land of inspiration, of prophecy, and of spiritual gifts. Even the skeptical Gibbon, writing of the "seven churches in Asia," virtually admits the fulfillment of the apocalyptic visions. (Gibbon's "Decline and Fall," chap. lxiv.)

Eusebius and others tell us of the profound reverence that all the early believers in the doctrines of Jesus had for this aged and loving saint, who sorrowed with Christ in the garden, stood by him at the cross, received in charge Mary the mother of Jesus, and clairvoyantly beheld him ascend to the homes of the angels. This sentence from his pen will live for ever: "God is love." When he had become too weak and infirm to walk to the old primitive church edifice in Ephesus, his admirers, taking him in their arms, would bear him thither; and then, with trembling voice, he could only say, "Little children, love ye one another." These and other well-attested historic recollections, rushing upon my mind, lift me on to the Mount of Transfiguration.

The sun of the New Testament epistles is John, — the sainted John, that lovingly leaned upon Jesus' bosom. In youth he was my ideal man. To-day he is that angel in heaven whom I most love. Not Arabia, then, nor Palestine, but classic Ephesus, is my Mecca.

The poet Joaquin Miller sings thus of the "Last Supper:" —

"Ah! soft was their song as the waves are
That fall in low, musical moans;
And sad, I should say, as the winds are
That blow by the white gravestones.

What sang they? What sweet song of Zion,
With Christ in their midst like a crown?
While here sat Saint Peter, the lion;
And there, like a lamb, with head down, —

Sat Saint John, with his silken and raven
Rich hair on his shoulders, and eyes
Lifting up to the faces unshaven
Like a sensitive child in surprise.

CHAPTER XXIX.

THE ancient cities of Ionia were wonderfully well situated for the growth of commercial prosperity. The Greeks of to-day have superior talents for finance, and all else that relates to sharpness and downright persistency. They cherish ardent expectations of becoming some day the masters of the Mediterranean. To this end, with an eye on Constantinople, they are busy in devising schemes for the more complete consolidation of their empire. For acuteness, shrewdness, and exaggeration, they are said to excel any people in the world. It is a common saying in Levantine cities, " He lies like a Greek."

The modern Greeks are handsome. They step quick, are gay and airy, have clear complexions, classical faces, fine frames, and a noble carriage, that constantly excites increasing admiration. Their national costume, a seeming blending of Scotch and Turkish, is quite indescribable, though, on the whole, decidedly Oriental. They are fond of heavy cloaks, long gaiters, close-fitting trousers, fancy colors, and *all* picturesque effects. Proud of their past history, they delight to remind the citizens of the Occident that the greatest man the Teutons ever had tells us, " The sun of Homer shines upon us still ; " and another eminent man of the Anglo-Saxon race informs us that " it is Plato's tongue the civilized world is even now speaking, and Plato's landmarks that fix the boundaries of the different provinces of art and science." During the past forty years the Greeks have built over three thousand villages, fifty towns, and ten capitals. In Athens, in all the isles of the Archipelago, where the Greeks have either a governmental foothold or influence, strenuous efforts are being made to revive the written language of the country, — the old Hellenic. The Greek language they now use bears far more resemblance to ancient Greek, than does the present Italian to Latin. The periodicals printed in Athens to-day may be read with perfect ease by such scholars as are well acquainted with the Greek of Xenophon and other classical writers of that period. The Greeks and Turks are implacable enemies all through the East. In the Levantine cities, each reside in their own quarters. If they mingle, it is for trade and traffic. Both need to learn that " in Christ Jesus," — that is, the Christ-principle of brotherhood, — " there is neither Jew nor Greek," but all are heirs of a common Father's care and inheritance. " God," said the apostle, " is no respecter of persons."

CONSTANTINOPLE.

It was in the gray of early morning that we sailed calmly along the Dardanelles. Oh the glory of that October morning! The ideal becomes the real. The sun now colors the eastern sky with gold. Rising, it tips and turns the minarets to fire. The buildings, the vessels, the mosques, are all illuminated. Surely we may exclaim with Byron, —

" ' Tis the clime of the East, 'tis the land of the sun."

If Genoa has been called the proud, and Naples the beautiful, Constantinople may rightly claim for herself the title of magnificent. Seated in gardens upon one of seven hills, it is not strange that Constantine should have desired to move the capital of the Roman Empire to the site occupied by the imperial city. No soul alive to the beautiful in nature, or the exquisite in art, could fail of admiring its lofty and imposing position, its domes, its minarets, its sheltering groves of cypress, its hills in the distance, now crimsoning into the sear of autumn, and the blue waters that lie at the feet of these Moslem splendors. The Golden Horn is all that pen painters have pictured it. The Sea of Marmora is deep and beautiful. Hardly a ripple danced upon its surface during our passage over its crystal depths. What a magnificent harbor it would make, with Constantinople for the central capital of Europe, Asia, and Africa !

How rich in historic association is this city crowned with mosques ! Belisarius sailed from here into Africa, and along the Italian coast, while Justinian in 553 was erecting the present St. Sophia. On the opposite Asian shore, at Scutari, the Persians, after their conquests in Egypt and Syria, sat for a dozen years threatening the city. Here Tartars, Turks, and Croats first planted their unwelcome footsteps in Europe, inspiring the beginning of those fearful crusades. The first passed through Constantinople in 1097, Alexis reigning. About the year 1200, Baldwin conquered the city; and in the fourteenth century the Ottomans in Asia Minor laid the foundations of the empire that now extends so far into Europe. In 1453 Mohammed II. entered this Christian city in great triumph, and transformed it as if by magic into a Moslem capital. It is said by the historian, that, entering the gates, he steered straight for St. Sophia, to discover the priests who were hiding in the cathedral. They having escaped by a subterranean passage, he hacked off the head of the brazen serpent with his sword, to manifest his hate of images, and all forms of idolatry.

WALKS IN THE CITY.

How true of this great cosmopolitan city of a million souls or more, that " distance lends enchantment to the view " ! On the deck of the ship in the harbor, the gigantic tower at Pera, the flotilla upon the Golden Horn, the Bosphorus with its suburban villages, the palaces of the sultan, the archite‿tural effects of the mosques shooting up like marble pillars, the dark plumes of the cypresses, the peopled hill sides upon the Asian coast, and the stately, massive hospital, scene of Florence Nightingale's noble, womanly work during the Crimean war, thrilled my soul with intense delight.   But landing, and seeing the ruin, the filth, the dogs in the streets, the mixture of races, the crowded, dirty bazaars, our poetry speedily chilled to rigid prose.   Surely, —

> " Things are not what they seem."

Decline and decay characterize the sluggish Turkish nation.   A deathly torpor has seized its vitals.   It is truly the " sick man " of the Orient.   Russia wants the vast domain. England and France say, " Hands off!"   Germany and the central nations of Europe, think it well to maintain the balance of power as it is.   May not the modernized phase of Turkish theology have something to do with this stupor?   The Moslems are *fatalists*.   One article of their faith reads thus : * —

> " It is God who fixes the will of man, and he is therefore not free in his actions.   There does not really exist any difference between good and evil; for all is reduced to unity, and God is the real author of the acts of mankind."

" The old Turk residing in the interior of the empire," said Mr. Brown, secretary of the American Legation, "is a very different man from these modern Turks that linger around the capital.   The former wears his full trousers and flowing robes, surmounts his head with the old-fashioned turban, winds his shawl or girdle around his waist, carries his pipes and pistols, prays to Allah five times a day, and, despising trick, treachery, and duplicity, is sincere and truthful."

In point of honesty, truthfulness, and self-respect, nearly all travelers unite in saying that the Mussulmans of the Orient are superior to Christians, — the Christian masses of

* See J. P. Brown's Derv., p. 11.

Italy, Spain, Russia, or even England. "Behold the cres-
cent!" say the Mohammedans: "see how it has triumphed
over the cross. Is not *Allah* great?" For nearly twelve centuries Mohammed and the Koran have held the religious and
political destinies of the East; and at this hour Islamism is
rapidly extending in Northern Asia, Central Africa, and along
the borders of the Caspian Sea, affirming there is "*one God,
and Mohammed is his apostle!*"

TURKISH HOSPITALITY.

It requires little physical labor to live in these Eastern
countries. Hills and plains are burdened with fruits. The
climate invites the people to out-of-door life, which cheapens
home, and renders them content with slovenly and ill-fur-
nished accommodations.

The Turks are justly famed for their hospitality. Entering one of their low, flat-roofed houses in the country, they
immediately bring a cup of coffee, and exclaim with great
earnestness, "My father is your slave, my mother your
bondwoman, my wife your servant: my home is yours, — *all*
I have is yours." This, of course, is Eastern, and to some
degree figurative ; but they really mean by it generosity and
hospitality. Besides the dragoman and donkey, it costs little
or nothing to travel in Asia Minor.

Expenses, however, are increasing each year. Europeans
are teaching the Orientals shrewdness and selfishness.

LANGUAGE. — SOCIAL CUSTOMS. — WORSHIP.

The Turkish language is made up of some two parts Arabic, one Persian, one Tartar, and the remainder from the
Turkistan dialect, a difficult language to learn. The Arabic,
a magnificent language, is termed by linguists the Latin of
the East; the Turkish is compared to the French ; and the
Persian to the Italian, liquid and flowing.

The Turk never eats with his wife. "*Man was first made,
then woman,*" says Paul. This the Mohammedan quotes as

glibly as the Christian minister produces other passages from this apostle to bear against woman.

No good Mohammedan touches swine's flesh, or wines of any kind : these alcoholic drinks he terms " fire-draughts of hell." If you reprove them for polygamy, they, at once refer you to the practices of Abraham, Jacob, Solomon, and other biblical characters praised by Christians.

The government of Turkey is an absolute monarchy. The sultan's will is law. He is the supreme head of the Mohammedan faith. These Mohammedans believe that the Koran came direct from heaven, through the Angel Gabriel, and that divine inspirations came to Mohammed from Allah the same as in past times to Jesus and Moses.

I visited a large number of mosques.

Taking off the shoes before entering is expected and demanded. The imams (priests), facing Mecca, lead in the prayers to the one God, — Allah. Their sermons are highly moral, explaining the Koran, and its relation to the Old and New Testaments. Mohammed, though permitting a plurality of wives in imitation of the Hebrew patriarchs, recommended but one.

Extravagance is thinning the ranks of the harems. Few Turks care to support more than one wife to display her richly-colored garments in the bazaars. Though silks, satins, and fine plain merino cloths, are worn, the Levantine women, as well as those of the extreme East, are as fond of gay trimmings as they are of their ease. French styles are rapidly creeping into all Turkish countries.

The muezzin's calls sound from the minarets of the mosques five times a day, — at the break of morning, at twelve o'clock, at two hours before sundown, at the going-down of the sun, and again two hours after sunset. We recollect ascending the minaret of a mosque, that, like most of the ancient structures of the East, had long passed its age of beauty. The Oriental coloring had faded ; the pavements were sunken, and the mosaics crumbling, and dropping from the wall. Still the lofty hight, the majesty of the columns, the immense dome, deeply impressed us, and will other beholders for centuries to come. It was near the hour of twelve. Soon the muezzin came out from near the summit of the minaret, summoning to prayer in these words: "*Allah akbar, Allah akbar, La illah il Allah, Mohammed resoul Allah, Allah akbar.*" (God is great. There is no God but God, and Mohammed is the prophet of God. Come to prayer; come to security and peace. God is most great: there is no God but God.) They intone these prayer words of invitation in a plaintive, half-singing style, often varying them to suit the occasion. In the morning they usually cry, "Awake, awake and pray. It is better to pray than to sleep. There is but one God, Allah." At noon the piteous, pleading voice falls upon them, "God is great; the world is wicked. Come to prayer. There is but one God, Allah the merciful."

It is almost an absolute impossibility to convert a Mohammedan to evangelical Christianity. They can not subscribe to the Trinity; can not comprehend how Jesus Christ can be "very God," and yet the "Son of God;" can not understand how Jesus existed before his mother, and is of the same age as his Father. It is not quite plain to us!

TURKISH WOMEN.

Polygamy, or any form of "social freedom" involving promiscuity, is a practical hell in any country. Envies and jealousies abound. The caliphs have for weary years maintained more or less eunuchs as attendants in their harems.

The general characteristics of Turkish women may be best studied on Moslem festival-days.

They are not so really dressed as draped in a flowing robe, over which hangs a loose mantle, nearly covering the lower portion of their trousers. Their feet are small, and show very distinctly while walking. Over their yellow slippers they wear an ugly-looking overshoe, which they slip off when going into a mosque to worship. Indulging in the luxuries of the Turkish bath, they have the appearance of being exceedingly neat. Notwithstanding their veils, and professed seclusion from society, there is no difficulty in seeing them or their faces. Their features are generally small and delicate. Their veils are made of very transparent muslin, covering all but the eyes and upper portions of their neatly-painted cheeks. As a rule it is safe to infer this: the more symmetrical and beautiful the features, the more thin and gauze-like the veil.

The time was when the facial veils of Turkish ladies were really opaque: now, unless the woman is exceedingly lean and ugly, they are as thin as those through which the blushes of American brides may be seen, really enhancing the beauty they pretend to conceal.

Silly vanity is seen in all countries.

Though these women's eyes are hazel and handsome, they sparkle with no great life-purpose; their motions in walking are ungraceful; their figures resemble bundles of foreign drapery; and they are said by those who know them the most intimately to be exceedingly ignorant, helpless, insipid, and shiftless. Since polygamy is the rule, since they are the slaves of men's pleasures and passions, what otherwise could be expected? And these wives, these women, are to be *future mothers.*

As the Turk, who can have many wives, can have but *one* mother, the sultan's mother is virtually queen. The mistress of the treasury is next in honor to the queen, filling an intermediate place between the sultan and women of the harem. The Turks are very fond of the blonde Circassians. Purchasing them is now forbidden.

MOHAMMEDAN DERVISHES.

What Shakers and Quakers are to evangelical Christians, dancing dervishes are to Mohammedans. They believe in Allah, and in present inspirations and revelations. The elders are seers and celibates. Their lodges are retired homes. Their worship is unique ; their so-called dancing being more properly whirling. The healing dervishes, reducing themselves physically by subsisting upon two and three olives a day, perform the most remarkable deeds during their holy month of Ramazan. We saw them form their circle for the healing of the sick. When prepared by gesticulation, whirling motions, chants, and prayers, the sheiks, that is the elders, — healed by touch, by the use of "Mohammed's brass hand," and by treading, literally *treading*, in this state of ecstasy, upon the crippled limbs and diseased bodies of the sick, some of which were infants. If disease were located in the eyes, throat, or brain, they pathetized them. The Crown Prince of Prussia stood by our side "unshod," after the Mohammedan custom, while witnessing the healings, and the magnetic and instrumental feats, of this primitive people in their consecrated room.

Through my interpreter, who spoke Arabic and Syriac, as well as Turkish and English, I held long conversations with the sheiks concerning the origin of their orders, their worship, their visions, their knowledge of the spirit-world, and their gifts of healing.

SPIRITUALISM IN TURKEY.

There are excellent mediums and many Spiritualists in Constantinople. During the winter season they hold regular circles in Pera, the European part of the city. Writing and trance are the usual forms of manifestation. These spirits, with a few exceptions, teach re-incarnation. Invited, we addressed the Spiritualists in the hall of the *Chambre de Commerce*. The attention they gave, and the interest they manifested, were truly inspiring.

The Hon. John P. Brown, connected with the legation, and a thirty-years' resident of Turkey, I found to be a firm Spiritualist. In a letter written to the "Universe," he said, —

"Many Moslems also fully believe in a power or faculty of the spirit of man to see, behold, or have an intuitive perception of, things invisible by the ordinary organs of sight. This assertion they sustain by the frequent examples of individuals having the most correct and exact knowledge of events occurring at a vast distance from them, — of visions in which they behold, like pictures passing before their eyes, scenes of which they have never had any previous knowledge or perception. . . . These Turkish Spiritualists are always people of well-known purity and virtue, animated with the highest degree of benevolence, and deeply interested in the spiritual welfare of others. This belief is often acted upon and exercised in such a manner by others as to lead some persons to suppose that Spiritualism and animal magnetism are one and the same thing; for the pious Moslem believes that he can effect cures, or at least give relief from bodily sufferings, by prayer, and the imposing of his hands on the invalid."

TURKISH CHARACTERISTICS.

Human nature is naturally good, yet subject to the influences of environment. While there are good Turks — good in spite of their sectarian ecclesiasticism — the majority of them, especially in cities and populous centres, are ignorant, selfish, bigoted and fanatical, hating both Hindoos and Christians. They are slave-holders, polygamists and fatalists, believing in the Calvinism of predestination.

Appointed by Gen. Grant U. S. Consul in 1869 to a post in Asiatic Turkey, I write what I know. Seeing and living in a given nationality is knowing. The stale story tossed about by atheistic jesters, that parcels and property left by the street-side or by shop-windows are perfectly safe in Turkish cities as "there are no Christians near," is as silly and spongy as it is false. No baser thieves live than the thieves of Mohammedan countries. No one having lived in Turkey, or traveled extensively in Northern India or Africa, will dispute this statement; they are zealots and delight in war; their motto is "down with the infidel"; their recent Armenian butcheries reveal their real characteristics. Hindoos infinitely prefer English to Mohammedan rule.

CHAPTER XXX.

ATHENS.

> "Dream on sweet souls in purpling seas
> Till we reach the land of Pericles."

In life's golden time, when listening to the academic dec-
lamations of students upon the heroism of the ancient
Greeks, we dreamed of treading the shores of the classic
land, — land once pre-eminent in poetry, philosophy, painting, and the fine arts, and whose republics voiced the heaven-
winged words of equality and freedom. But the Greeks of
to-day are ancient Greeks no more. Civilizations move in
cycles and epicycles. The Grecian mind has been tending
downwards for full two thousand years. Its present glory
consists of its ancient ruins. A wizard hand, grayed and
grim, ever points backward to lost arts, lost grandeur!

Do we not remember Byron, whose lamp of life faded
under the Grecian skies he so enthusiastically loved ? How
musical his lines ! —

> "Know ye the land where the cypress and myrtle
> Are emblems of deeds that are done in their clime, —
> Where the rage of the vulture, the love of the turtle,
> Now melt into sorrow, now madden to crime ?
>
> .   .   .   .
> 'Tis the *clime* of the *East*, — tis the land of the *Sun :*
> Can he smile on such deeds as his children have done ? "

Piræus is the prominent port of Greece. Athens is five
miles distant from this landing. There is a railroad. But
here, *here*, is the once classic city.

Never can we forget our sensations when casting a first glance at the Acropolis. Passing up the Propillion, or grand entrance, we had a fine view of Mars Hill, where Paul preached the "Unknown God" to the Athenians. Two massive pillars of the Temple of Bacchus are still standing. There was a subterranean passage leading from this temple of mystic rites into the vast amphitheater. The Temple of Minerva and the Temple of the Winds are nearly piles of ruin. The Temple of the Muses, nine figures of choicest marble, must have been very beautiful. To the right of the Acropolis, massive and stately, is the Temple of Jupiter Olympus, many of whose proud columns, having defied the storms and devastating forces of time, remain as standing signals of architectural splendor and perfection. England has rifled some of these old temples to supply its museums with models for modern sculptors and artists.

Among the most celebrated of the ancient oracles was Delphos. Princes and philosophers flocked thither for consultations. Upon the hights of Mount Parnassus stood the magnificent Temple of Apollo; while at the foot was the spring of Castalia. Of this fountain, the Pythia, or priestess, drank; and in its crystal waters she bathed before invoking the presence of the gods. Then clothing herself in white, emblem of purity, she was magnetized by spirits, and spoke under their influence.

Nestling near the base of Mars Hill is the prison-cave where superstitious Greeks confined that ancient Grecian philosopher and Spiritualist, Socrates. The coarsely constructed iron gate, nearly wasted away, is still shown the traveler. The dingy, chalky apartment seemed cut into the side of the hill, — a gloomy den to converse with a Crito and an Alcibiades. Greece and Judea awarded to their inspired teachers crosses and hemlock-draughts. Such was gratitude. Have the times, only in methods, materially changed?

It was our purpose to have visited the plains of Marathon; the ruins of Corinth; the isle of Salamis, memorable for the great battle in which the Persian fleet of Xerxes was defeated by the Greeks 480 B.C.; and Eleusis, which introduced the famous Eleusinian mysteries into Athens as early as 1356 B.C.; but brigandage presented a formidable obstacle. Political outlaws are a perpetual scourge to the country. The government, though practically absolute, fails to institute and perpetuate law and order. In sorrow we turn from modern to ancient Greece.

NAPLES.

The Bay of Naples lifts the soul in thought to such shimmering seas as are said to dot the summer-land scenery of angel realms. The city itself, crescent-formed, is backed by an amphitheater of hills and mountains, the rocky slopes of which are covered with sunny villas, and sprinkled with orange and lemon, with fig and oleander. Fanned by invigorating sea-breezes, and walled in the distance by the Apennines, Naples sits a very queen upon the edge of crystal waters, unrivaled for the beauty of her situation.

The streets are paved with lava, and in the winter season thronged with strangers. Traveling the narrow sidewalks, one feels continually cramped, and sighs for the roomy promenades of prairie cities in the West.

Terraced toward St. Elmo, some of the houses seem clinging to rocky cliffs. Certain streets actually lie hundreds of feet above their immediate neighbors. The dearth of fresh, handsome buildings, and modern works of art, creates a soul-longing, for which the magnificent discovery of Herculaneum and Pompeii, with their matchless treasures of antiquity, only in some measure compensate. The narrow, dingy streets, the high, palace-shaped, yet badly constructed dwelling-houses, with huge iron gates in front, flat roofs, and balconies projecting from nearly every window; the never-ceasing noise, the interminable rattling of wheels during the hours of day and night; the insolent importunities of carriage-drivers, with hordes of pitiable beggars combining the most cringing manners with malicious attempts and devices at extortion, — all present a life-picture any thing but attractive.

GARIBALDI AND THE MONKS.

Standing in the Palace Square one day with Signor Damiani, he pointed us to the balcony from which Garibaldi, in 1860, uttered this stirring sentence to an immense multitude : —

"*Brothers*, believe me, the greatest foe to freedom, the greatest enemy of Italy, is the Pope of Rome."

This liberator of the people, Garibaldi, drove into Naples, Sept. 6, in an open carriage, directly past the fortified barracks of the Carmine, where soldiers were still holding out for Francis II. Not a hair of his head was harmed. Victor Emmanuel offered to make him a duke, and give him a large pension. He declined the dukeship, declined all honors, only caring to see Italy free, united, and happy.

Moping, brown-garbed, barefooted monks, a class of men that neither work nor wash, are as thick in Naples and the adjoining country as office-seekers in Washington. Italy was a clover-field for gowned monks, and a veritable paradise for priests, till Garibaldi, a few years since, partially aroused the people from their dream of submission. Thank God! say students and the young Italians of to-day, the number of these churchal orders is lessening each year Many of these monks literally live by begging. Lifting their greasy caps, and exposing their shaved heads, they plead by the wayside for a penny. Beggars and priests are the products of Roman Catholic Italy. Papal Rome is the hub of this ecclesiastic wheel.

Out of between twenty and thirty millions of Italians, hardly seven millions can read and write! The bare statement of such a *fact*, in connection with the stupid ignorance and wretched beggary of the middle and lower classes, is of itself a scathing condemnation of Roman-Catholicism. I had the honor of being present at the Anti-Council, or *Congress of Free-Thinkers*, called by Count Ricciardi, a Neapolitan deputy in Parliament, at Naples, on Dec. 8, 1869, the day on which was convoked the Council of the Vatican.

Noble and high-minded as was this body of men, the police, interfering, dispersed the delegates. They met afterwards in secret. The Pope shorn of his temporal power, speech is now free in Naples.

THE MUSEUM IN NAPLES.

This massive building, commenced in 1587 as a university, was finally adapted by Ferdinand I., in 1790, to a museum. Enriched with Etruscan vases, papyrus manuscripts, and Egyptian antiquities, as well as recently excavated treasures from Pompeii and Herculaneum, it is one of the most interesting museums in the world. The library contains about two hundred and fifty thousand volumes, and nearly three thousand manuscripts, some of which date to the eighth and tenth centuries. What interested us more intensely was the antiquities found in Herculaneum and Pompeii, buried for nearly two thousand years. The surgical implements, agricultural implements, ear-rings, brooches, chains, combs, gold lace, and ornaments of every kind, show clearly to what a high state of civilization the Pompeiians had attained before the Christian era. Not only these, but loaves of *bread* with the baker's name thereon stamped, honeycomb, grains, fruits, eggs, bottles of oil and wine hermetically sealed by the Vesuvius eruption of 79, are now exhibited in a wonderful state of preservation in this museum. In the Royal Library attached to this building are more than seventeen hundred papyri found in Herculaneum. These, with nearly as many found in Pompeii, are being unrolled and deciphered, preparatory to publication.

POMPEII AND HERCULANEUM.

Cinder-shingled Vesuvius buried these cities on the 24th of August in the year 79 of the Christian era. Their origin is lost in the misty regions of mythology. They were prosperous and famous more than two thousand years since. Livy speaks of their harbors as " magnificent naval stations." Fifty years before the advent of the Nazarene, the geographer Strabo praised the excellence of Pompeii's grain and oils. Roman patricians had embellished adjoining landscapes with splendid villas. Marius, Pompey, and Cæsar had residences in these cities.

Here, too, Cicero had a charming villa. He speaks of its beauty in a letter to Atticus, associating it with Tusculum. Pliny, the naturalist, was in charge of the Roman fleet stationed at Misenum when the catastrophe transpired. Striving to save others, he lost his life. To the younger Pliny are we indebted for a most graphic description of the scene. Ruthless as was this destruction, an index finger pointed to a compensation; for, if Vesuvius destroyed, it also shielded and preserved. Beautiful are the paintings and statues *lapilli*-entombed for nearly two thousand years. The excavations were commenced in 1748. During the exhumations, about one thousand bodies have been found, and with them papyrus, coins, cups, keys, necklaces, bracelets, rings, seals, engraved gems, beautiful lamps, gauzy fabrics, and even well-preserved blonde hair.

Pompeii is now almost completely unearthed. The resurrection is quite perfect. It was good for me to be there. Walking its Roman-paved streets, I felt introduced to the citizens and customs of an ancient civilization. And yet Pliny characterized this period as the age of " dying art," — dying as compared with those artists, Apelles and Protogenes, living nearly five hundred centuries earlier. Pompeii and Herculaneum are bridges spanning the gap of centuries, and holding together as with a golden link two civilizations. Studying the wisdom of the ancients compels us to recognize the spiritual unity of the race, that grand central truth around which the moral world revolves.

ITALIAN CHURCHES.

The real pride of Italy is her relics and churches. They are certainly rich in the artistic work of the masters. These paintings excite the most lively feelings of taste and fancy, as well as intensify reflections of a deeper nature, connected with the illustrious of past centuries. Still for devotional purposes they do not compete with the Gothic structures of Northern Europe. Churches exhibit national character. Floods of sunbeams through stained glass, mosaic pavements, variegated pillars, costly ornaments, priestly robes, smoking incense, airs that breathe of gayety, and   .

> "Light quirks of music, broken and uneven,
> That waft the soul upon a jig to heaven," —

are among the indispensables of joyous, impressional Italians. Italy's church-edifices to-day are absolutely magnificent; but with the decline of Roman-Catholicism, and the increase of knowledge, they will gradually assume the Protestant type, ultimating into elegant places of resort for educational purposes and scientific lectures.

ROME.

And this is Rome, — proud, seven-hilled Rome! The principal street is Corso. To the left of the Pincian Hill is the Tiber, rolling along its muddy tide as in old historic periods. Not far from its banks is the column of Trajan, and also that of Marcus Aurelius Antoninus one hundred and twenty-two feet high, and crowned with a statue of St. Paul; while there rises the dome of the Pantheon, and the cupolas and towers of costly churches. On the other bank of the Tiber, just over the bridge, is the massive tower of Hadrian's Mausoleum, or Castle of St. Angelo ; and, beyond, the grand old

Palace of the Vatican, from whence have gone edicts shaking kingdoms, and making crowned heads tremble.

The population of the Eternal City is about one hundred and eighty-five thousand. Of this number, nearly ten thousand are ecclesiastics of some kind. Only think, — one to every eighteen of the people! The streets are thronged with cardinals in scarlet, priests in shining black, and barefooted monks in hideous brown.

On Christmas Day, 1869, there were seven hundred and sixty-five church dignitaries in the city, connected with the Ecumenical Council. Of these, there were fifty-five cardinals, eleven patriarchs, six hundred and forty-seven primates, archbishops, and bishops, six abbots, twenty-one mitred abbots, and twenty-eight generals of monastic orders.

Never will the scene fade from our memory, of standing, and seeing these seven or eight hundred fathers of the Church reverently bow, and kiss the brazen toe of that ugly-visaged, speechless statue of Jupiter, *christened St. Peter.* Around Peter's tomb lamps are kept perpetually burning. Devout visitors to the Vatican, from America even, frequently kiss the genuine, though elegantly slippered, toe of the pope. The act is said to symbolize obedience and submission. The kisses of the faithful have worn the cold foot of the bronze statue of St. Peter to the thinness almost of a knife's edge. Praying and kissing continually abound in St. Peter's, while without the templed walls beggars are pleading for crusts of bread.

WANDERINGS IN THE ETERNAL CITY.

Rome must be judged by its own standard. It can not be compared with other great cities. It has no commerce, no manufactures, no enterprise, — *nothing* of what is considered essential to life in London or New York. It is the home of Popery, the center of a Judaized Christianity; and hence its very life is death, —·the "second death," so difficult of resurrection.

Roman manufactures consist of ecclesiastic bulls, edicts, commentaries, and creeds; of mosaics, cameos, scarfs, and copies of pictures. She imports her cloths, cottons, railway materials, cutlery, china, carriages, and military weapons. Teeming with the accumulated treasures of ages, she encouragingly allows her destitute children to be assisted by infidel foreigners, whose heretical books she confiscates, and whose souls she consigns — or would, had she the power — to eternal torments.

The Pantheon is one of the best preserved monumental buildings of this ancient city. On the day of our visit, the Piazza was dirty, and crowded with market-women. Rome would do well to wash her devotees. The edifice has sixteen columns of granite; each surmounted by a frieze and entablature, containing an inscription, which informs us that this "heathen temple" was founded by Agrippa, the friend of Augustus, 27 years B.C.

The Coliseum is considered the greatest wonder of Rome. Its magnitude surpassed all my previous conceptions. The circumference of its area is over one-third of a mile. It has four stories, each of a different order, — the Doric, Ionic, Corinthian, and the Composite, — terminating by a parapet. It is estimated that it would comfortably seat ninety thousand people. Masses of stones have been taken from these ruins to build palaces in the modern city; and yet the structure is so immense, their absence is hardly noticeable. The Coliseum and Forum should be seen by moonlight, say travelers. Midnight hours might throw a mysterious drapery around these ruins, concealing their imperfections, and hightening their grandeur; still I am sufficiently practical to prefer sunlight and daylight. The Coliseum was commenced in A.D. 72, by Vespasian, and completed eight years after by Titus. Much of the work was done by captive Jews. The opening festival scene, say historians, lasted a hundred days. Almost two thousand years has it stood a monument to Roman enterprise and muscular barbarity

And yet recent excavations reveal pavements, marble statues, and finely finished granite columns, thirty feet below the level of the arena. Evidently there was a previous building of massive dimensions on this site, the constructors of which were pre-historic.

ST. PETER'S AND THE BEGGARS.

The first sight of this most gorgeous of earthly temples strikes the traveler with a sense of unspeakable grandeur. This increases with each succeeding visit, till you stand under the firmament of marble, and cast your eye along the richly-ornamented nave, along the statue-lined transepts, and up into that circling vault, — that wondrous dome, supported by four piers, each 284 feet in periphery, and then you feast upon the fullness of its magnificence. The building stands on a slight acclivity in the north-western corner of the city. It is built in the form of a Latin cross, the nave being in length 607 feet, and the transept 444 feet. The east front is 395 feet wide, and 160 feet high; whilst the pillars composing it are each 88 feet high, and 8¼ in diameter. The hight of the dome, from the pavement to the top of the cross, is 448 feet. In front of the church there is a large piazza. The church occupies the place of Nero's circus, and is erected on the spot where St. Peter was martyred. It occupied a period of one hundred and seventy-six years in building, and required three hundred and sixty years to perfect it. It cost ten million pounds; it covers eight English acres; and is kept in repair at a cost of six thousand three hundred pounds per annum.

Raphael's "Transfiguration" is in the Vatican. The great master put his soul into this production. It was his last work; and, while executing it, he seems to have been conscious of standing upon the very verge of the summer-land. He died before finishing it, at the early age of thirty-seven years. After the departure of this great master-painter, the "Transfiguration" was suspended over his corpse. He now ranks a star in the art-galleries of heaven.

But who are these? Why such a troop of beggars at oui heels? Is this not a Christian city? Does not the vicegerent of Christ here reside? Did not Peter and Paul here preach? Was there not a special epistle addressed to the *Romans?* Did not Jesus command his followers to sell what they had, and give it to the poor, and follow him? Is this the fruit of nearly two thousand years of Christian teaching and practice? When among the heathen Indians of the great north-west, with the Congressional committee, I saw little begging; but here, near the feet of the *visible Christ*, Pius IX., I am surrounded by filth, beggars, and rags, or the scarlet of cardinals. While working for the downfall of Antichrist, my constant prayer is, " Thy kingdom come, and thy will be done on earth as it is in heaven."

Just under the shade of Pincian Hill, in a magnificent park, musical from flowing fountains, and dotted with palms and flowering-plants from the tropics, I took leave of Prince George de Solms, the personal kindnesses of whom I can never forget. Rome, its ruins and relics, its glory and its shame, I leave with the prayer of faith. If the pope has been pronounced "infallible," his temporal power is gone forever. Roman-Catholicism is waning in Europe; and Rome, city of the Cæsars, is dreaming of a resurrection.

FLORENCE.

Southern Europe is grim with the ghosts of dead cities. Florence, the glory of the middle ages, and formerly capital of Tuscany, is built in the form of a pentagon. Its population is something over one hundred and thirty thousand. This city was for a season the scene of the brave yet fiery Savonarola's labors. A kind of second Calvin, he was called the Catholic reformer of Florence. The pope trembled under his thunderbolts. Through the city flows the Arno. The suburban eminences are crowned with charming villas interspersed with clumps of olive-trees. These grow in such luxuriance that they called out one of Ariosto's sweetest songs.

Just out of this city, under cypress-trees shading a plain brown-marble monument, reposes all that is mortal of one who, not only in America, but in all enlightened lands, lives on earth immortal. The slab has only this: —

THEODORE PARKER.

BORN AT LEXINGTON, MASS., U. S. A., AUG. 24, 1810.
DIED AT FLORENCE, MAY 10, 1860.

Standing by the grave of this man, who was too broad for a sect, and too noble for a priest, strange and deep emotions thrilled my being's center; and I was proud that I had personally known him in life. Near by is the monument of Elizabeth Barrett Browning with simply the plain initials, "E. B. B." The inscription, exceedingly unassuming, seems a veritable prophecy from herself in these lines: —

> " A stone above my heart and head,
> But no name written on the stone."

Among other distinguished Italians, I here met Girolamo Parisi, the editor and publisher of the "Aurora," a well-conducted periodical, printed in Florence, and devoted to Spiritualism, psychology, phrenology, and moral philosophy. Its pages are rich in sound, substantial teachings. In doctrine, it accepts the re-incarnation system of the French school.

Happy were the hours I spent in the society of Baron Kirkup. Encircled by distinguished men of rank, having a massive library of books treating of magic and the unsystematized philosophy of the mystics, and being a practical mesmerist withal, the baron was brought into the fold of Spiritualism over eighteen years since; and he has never shrunk from a frank avowal of his principles. His daughter is the principal medium he consults. Some of the manifestations he has witnessed are absolutely astounding.

Our poet Longfellow, attending a séance at Baron Kirk-up's residence, avowed himself a believer in the present ministry of angels.

Appreciating the baron's labors in the restoration of the painting of Dante, there was conferred upon him by royal decree, *La Corona d' Italia.* He had previously been " knighted " by Victor **Emmanuel.**

Spiritism is a fact, and so acknowledged by psychic research societies and the most erudite men of the age. It is a fact freighted with many frauds and fraudulent mediums. Let them be exposed — all of them be exposed. Let the tares be pulled up and cast into the fire. I repeat, let them be exposed, whether fraudulent mediums or fraudulent Christians in pulpits wearing the livery of Heaven. In this matter we are a unit, dear brethren.

But as the heavens are higher than the earth, so is Spiritualism higher than Spiritism. Spiritualism is a truth, and all truth is immortal, " I am the way and the truth and the life," said the Christ of Nazareth. Spiritualism is also a religion and a philosophy. It is the complement of primitive Christianity and the antidote to materialism.

CHAPTER XXXI.

EUROPE AND ITS CITIES.

ORIENTAL life has a never-ending charm ; the charm of beauty, of tropical freshness, and perpetual summer. Humboldt declares in his "Cosmos," that a man once residing in the spice-lands of the palm and the banana, the cactus and the orange, can never be content to live again in the colder latitudes.

We reached this Austrian city, Trieste, the 15th of September. The cholera was prevalent, and the American consul absent in Vienna. Next to Naples, the harbor of Trieste is the most beautiful in Europe. The city is eminently commercial. Italian is the language most spoken. Nearly all nationalities may be seen in Trieste. The Greeks retain their turbans and flowing robes. Dark-haired, black-eyed Italians do the shop-keeping. Occasionally a German blonde threads the streets. The wealthier class of citizens reside in beautiful villas high up the mountain-side, and a little north of the city.

Leon Favre, the Consul-General of France, and a devoted Spiritualist, resides in Trieste. Unfortunately he was absent. Happy were the hours we spent with this gentleman and scholar, several years since, in Paris.

Signor G. Parisi, another eminent Spiritualist, whom we first saw in Florence, meeting us in the street, embraced us with a love paternal and fraternal. It is as customary in Southern Europe for men to embrace and kiss as for women. " Greet ye one another with a holy kiss " (2 Cor. xiii. 12).

Capt. Richard Burton, noted in literature, known as a visitor to Mohammed's tomb, and a traveler in Africa, is the British consul in this city. So far as the captain has any religious bias, it is towards Spiritualism. If he visits America next season, we may accompany him on a tour to Yucatan, and various ruins in South America.

VENICE, QUEEN OF THE ADRIATIC.

" I heard in Venice sweet Tasso's song,
By stately gondola borne along."

This is decidedly an odd city, a city built upon over a hundred little islands, a city with canals for streets. Only think of being taken from the depot, and rowed about the city in search of a hotel ; think of seeing front-doors open on to the water ; think of the queer taste that could select such a site for a city. Byron's ecstasies over Venice puzzle us.

The Venetian Republic elected its first doge, or president, A.D. 697. Its armies ultimately conquered the Genoese. The hundred Catholic churches of Venice, though rich in paintings, look interiorly dark and gloomy ; the streets are narrow and tortuous ; the marbled palaces are grayed and grim ; and the " gay gondoliers," who propel those four thousand licensed gondolas, are very much like other men that work for money. By a Venetian law dating back three hundred years, the gondolas are painted black. This gives them a hearse-like appearance. The aristocratic classes have their palaces on the Grand Canal, and keep their gondolas as our wealthier citizens keep their carriages. The city has three hundred and seventy-eight arched bridges of either iron or marble, and high enough for the passage of gondolas under them.

To religionists, St Mark's Cathedral is the charmed center ; to poets and sentimentalists, the Bridge of Sighs, rendered famous in Byron's " Childe Harold," —

" I stood in Venice, on the Bridge of Sighs,
A palace and a prison on each hand."

The hundred old palaces gracing the Grand Canal are named after their founders. Many of them are magnificent even in decline. By paying a small fee, the doctor and self were permitted to stroll through one of these splendid palaces, so unique, so rich in furniture and paintings, golden mirrors, and specimens of antiquity. Venice boasts the largest painting in the world. Venetian ladies, going to church, wear veils upon their heads. They are exquisite singers. Guides and gondoliers show the house from which Desdemona eloped with the Moor, and the residence of Shylock, who dealt so mercilessly with the Merchant of Venice. Enough of fiction : give us facts.

MILAN.

Northern Italy is transcendently beautiful. Most of the distance from Venice through Verona to Milan presents a continuous scene of luxuriant vegetation. The fortified towns, the chain of mountains on our right, terraced with vineyards, the lovely Lake of Garda linking Italy to Austria, and the irrigated lawns and landscapes, made our soul all the day sunny with gladness. Milan, considering the state of civilization and progress, is evidently the finest city in Italy, and the best-paved city in Europe. It is walled, with the gradings, gardens, and ornamental shrubbery so arranged that it seems surrounded with a park. The center of attraction to strangers is the world-renowned cathedral, a full description of which is impossible. To be appreciated it must be seen. Built in the form of a Latin cross, its length is four hundred and ninety feet, and its breadth one hundred and eighty feet. Its rich marble tracery, its forest of spires, its seven thousand statues, its aisles, pillars, and lofty arches, present a wilderness of magnificence absolutely indescribable. From the summit the Alps, with Mont Blanc in the blue distance, are clearly visible. As a monument of elegant and costly architecture, it must for ages stand unrivaled; and yet it is but a pygmy compared with St. Peter's at Rome.

PARIS AND THE COMMUNE.

Our route from Milan lay through Turin and Mont Cenis. Does not this Alpine tunnel — marvel of enterprise and engineering — prophesy of tunneling the English Channel? Paris, proudest city of Europe! Previous visits to the French capital under Napoleon only fanned the desire to see it since the Prussian victories, and the reign of that Commune which raised its spiteful hand against palaces, monuments, works of art, and rare old libraries, — a Commune that madly fired its own city! Strange way to actualize the grand theories of "liberty, fraternity, and equality," by obliterating all evidences of former genius and culture!

Arriving at Paris in early morning, the first glance showed no signs of the war, nor of Communistic vandalism. A longer stroll lifted the veil, and revealed the reality. The Tuileries, Hotel de Ville, Chateau du Palais-Royal, the Louvre, the library of the Louvre, and hundreds of other buildings, were either fired or burned to ashes. Men and women of the baser sort vied with each other in scattering petroleum and mineral oils. Parisians proved themselves worse enemies of France than Prussians.

The Hotel de Ville was famous not less for its antiquity and architectural beauties than for having been the place where the mayor of Paris handed the tricolor cockade to good King Louis XVI.; where they arrested Robespierre July 27, 1794; and where the festival was held of the marriage of Napoleon I. with Marie Louise.

The pen that writes of Paris between the 18th of March and the 28th of May, 1871, should, to correspond with the scenes, be dipped in blood. Barbarians have burned cities, and annihilated the books and art-treasures they could not understand. But the Commune outdid this, destroying indiscriminately museums, libraries, and granaries. The burning of Paris was discussed and openly decided upon in the councils of the Commune. The decree was published in "The Official Journal." Rigault, Billivray, *et al.*, spent their leisure with their mistresses; while even Pascha! Grousset, appointed delegate for foreign affairs, gave himself up with other leaders to bacchanalian excesses. While shouting, "Down with the house of Thiers, and confiscate his property," decrees went forth, "Use petroleum," "Repeal all law," "Fire the churches," "Suppress the newspapers," "Abolish marriages;" and all this in the name of *liberty, fraternity, freedom,* — "social freedom," *par excellence!*

Doubtless the Thiers government was in some respects oppressive; but did this justify the atrocities of the Commune? Burning a barn to kill a weasel, demolishing a costly edifice to get rid of a wasp's nest under the eaves, would be a ranting diabolism paralleled only in folly by French Communism.

Excepting Flourens, the leading members of the Commune seemed inflated with ambition; inspired with the love of money and pleasure, wine and women.

The Franco-Prussian war, and the Commune, quite effectually paralyzed Spiritualism. It is now re-gathering its scattered forces. At Mrs. Hollis's séance, held in the apartments of Mrs. Mary J. Holmes, near the Champs-Elysées, I had the pleasure of meeting that gifted author, Victor Hugo. He wept like a child when receiving a communication from a loved friend in spirit-life.

ILLEGITIMATE CHILDREN.

Official returns from Parisian hospitals last year showed, that, of the births in the city, fifteen thousand three hundred and sixty-six were illegitimate. Boxes called *tours* are established in various parts of Paris, each of which revolves upon a pivot, and, on a bell being rung, is turned around by the proper person inside, to receive the child that may have been deposited. No attempts are made to ascertain the parents. These children never know a father's care, a mother's love. Nurses are secured from the country.

The suburban villas of Paris send into the foundling hospitals annually over four thousand of these illegitimate children, a large portion of which are received by the *Hospice des Enfants Assistés*, founded in 1640. Virtually twenty thousand illegitimate children, abandoned by their parents, plead yearly in Paris for paternal recognition, and maternal tenderness, — plead in vain. This is the legitimate outcome of French socialism.

GOETHE AND BARON GULDENSTUBBE.

Neither genius nor true greatness can be entirely disconnected from angel ministrations. Poets, philosophers, all, are inspired of the gods. The following, from "Lewes's Life of Goethe," refers to the poet's last hours : —

"The next morning he [Goethe] tried to walk a little up and down the room, but after a turn he found himself too feeble to continue. Reseating himself in an easy chair, he chatted cheerfully with Ottilia on the approaching spring, which would be sure to restore him. He had no idea of his end being so near. It was now observed that his thoughts began to wander incoherently. ' See,' he exclaimed, ' the lovely woman's head — with black curls — in splendid colors — a dark background !' Presently he saw a piece of paper on the floor, and asked how they could leave Schiller's letters so carelessly lying about. Then he slept softly, and, awakening, asked for the sketches he had just seen. They were sketches in a dream."

An eminent professor, intimately connected to Goethe's family, refers to noises, whistling sounds, and voices, heard near the close of this great man's life. These are his words : —

"It seemed as if, in a less frequented part of the house, a door either unknown, or long forgotten, slowly opened, creaking on its rusty hinges. Then a beautiful female spirit-figure appeared, bearing a lamp burning with a light-blue flame; her features were surrounded by a halo of glory. She gazed calmly upon the the terror-stricken witnesses, sang a few stanzas of some angelic melody, and then disappeared ; the door, closing behind her, presenting the same sealed appearance as before. In solemn silence the observers retraced their footsteps to the chamber of mourning, and there learned that the spirit had returned to God, who gave it. The last words audible were, "More light!'"

When in Paris the first time, guest of Mr. Gledstanes, the French Consul Leon Favre accompanied me to the residence of the Swedish Baron Louis Guldenstubbe. This gentleman, a distinguished Spiritualist, was related to a Scandinavian family of great renown. "Two of his ancestors, Knights of the Order of the Grand Templars, and of the same name, were burned alive in 1309, in company with Jacques de Molay, by order of Pope Clement the Fifth."

If it be true, as is sometimes asserted, that the country of one's birth and hereditary descent are not without influence upon mediumistic qualities, the baron was favored in both these respects. The mother who gave him birth in the country of Swedenborg, the mystic Scandinavia, prone to Spiritual belief, early initiated him in this kind of reading. When quite young he was remarkable for presentiments and visions.

He published several volumes relating to his researches in the science of positive and experimental pneumatology, besides a deeply interesting contribution upon "direct spirit writing." Both himself and sister were mediums. The baron recently passed to spirit-life, esteemed highest by those who knew him best.

ALL CITIES REPUDIATED.

As wens and warts to human bodies, so are cities to a country. Unnatural, they are the cesspools of crime, competition, and avarice. While Nature has lavished her gifts with prodigal hand, men should make community-villas, and gardens of hill and dale, each and all earning their bread by honest toil. Rome, grim and grand, unites the dead past and living present. The Papal Church is the most logical of any. It has an infallible God, an infallible Lord Jesus, an infallible Church, an infallible Douay Bible, and an infal-

lible Pope; and all communicants have to do is, to attend
mass, confess their sins, pay their priests, and go to glory!

Threading the streets of Naples, and the suburban villages,
one wonders how six hundred thousand inhabitants can here
live. Lazzaroni are thick as flies around pools. Jews, Quakers, and Shakers take care of their own poor. Lyons, the
Lowell of France, is alive with silk manufactories. Paris is
handsome and proud, showy and sinful. Berlin is rich in
historic and artistic attractions. The cathedrals are open
at all hours of the day in these cities. On their feet-worn
floors, prince and peasant meet as equals. Gardens in European cities and hamlets are enjoyed by the people as by the
proprietors. Visitors do not presume to meddle with plant
or flower. The citizens generally are better mannered and
more polished than in America. Our caste is based upon
wealth. Our boasted individuality has degenerated into a
selfish rascality. Our laws punish little, and pardon great
criminals. New-York City only a year since had sixty thousand children of school age that had never been inside a
schoolroom. American self-conceit and English caste are
both abominable. As nations they are antichrist.

GRAND OLD LONDON.

Crossing the English Channel from France to Dover, a
few hours through the fertile fields of Merry England
brought us to the heart of London, the city of cities, with a
population almost equal to that of the whole State of New
York. Individuals may drive twenty miles in a straight
line upon any one of London's diameters. The seven parks
have been termed, not inaptly, the lungs of London. They
lie chiefly at the West End. The Richmond Park, owned by
the crown, has two thousand two hundred acres, and is
eight miles in circumference. Hyde Park claims four hundred acres. Victoria Park, named in honor of the Queen, is
comparatively new, but exceedingly beautiful with lake and
pleasure boats. The Parliament Buildings, Gothic in form,

and covering over seven acres, are as queer as magnificent, Westminster Abbey, venerable structure where have taken place all the coronations since Edward the Confessor, is visited more for a sight at the tombs of Shakspeare, Milton, Addison, Campbell, Dickens, and other distinguished authors, than for worship. Crystal Palace, embracing several hundred acres, with broad avenues, extensive gardens, floral embellishments, and within the building statues, paintings, and unique marvels, presents rare attractions. Madame Tussaud's wax-works are not as admirable as have been represented. The Tower of London is stern and gloomy, — the traditions repulsive. In one of these towers is a large iron cage, containing a collection of jewels estimated at twenty million dollars. The great Koh-i-noor diamond is among this collection. " The crown of her Majesty Queen Victoria is a cap of purple velvet, inclosed in hoops of silver, surrounded by a ball and cross, all of which are resplendent with diamonds. In the center of the cross is the ' inestimable sapphire,' and in front of the crown is the heart-shaped ruby said to have been worn by the Black Prince."

Remembering the teaching, " Lay not up for yourselves treasures on earth," why not dispose of those jewels and diamonds at once, using the proceeds to procure homes for the homeless, and bread for orphans?

The British Museum is an institution of itself. Blessings upon all old book-shops! English parsons think Oxford the mother of the best English. Americans quote Boston as authority. The English excel in justice, simplicity of faith, and solid friendship; Americans in tact, originality, and audacity. The Latin race is bad at colonizing; but, wherever Englishmen go, they create a new England. Their individuality, like the sponge, excels in absorbing. Their houses are their castles. I admire the English.

The English have more German characteristics than we. In their travels they go to Germany, Italy, or the East. Americans rush to Paris. A gulf separates the working

people of England from the nobility. The latter clutch
dead bones to knock the life out from progressive souls.
And, further, boasting of a titled ancestry, they search at
the roots of trees for fruits, — *such* fruits as burden only the
topmost branches. Though the Nile has many mouths,
it has no discoverable head. A privileged few own nearly
all the soil. These have yet to learn that legitimate production is the only basis of ownership. What men by faithful toil make to grow or produce is theirs, and nothing more.
There's a tendency in London and throughout England to
co-operation and a practical communism.

THE SPIRITUAL OUTLOOK.

Belief often blossoms out into knowledge. Traveling westward as a missionary, I circumnavigated the globe, and know
the world to be round. Progress is the key-word of all nationalities, and Spiritualism God's witness of a future existence, in the Pacific Isles, and all portions of the Orient, as in
the Occident. Believe me, it was joy unbounded almost,
after this last, perplexing voyage, to be dropped down in .
London, to walk familiar streets, look into friendly faces,
clasp cordial hands, listen to the ringing accents of good solid
English, and receive such a cordial public reception at the
fine Florence Hotel under the supervision of Mr. J. J. Morse.

English Unitarianism is icy, arrogant and cultured. Orthodox theology is a spent force. Spiritualism is a living
gospel power; and the English are making rapid strides in
the dissemination of its heavenly principles. I could but
exclaim, How changed since James Burns and self strolled
through London's labyrinthine streets in search of the Cavendish Rooms, to commence a series of Sunday meetings!
Competent editors, erudite essayists, eloquent speakers, and
superior mediums for demonstrating the reality of the phenomena are now *all* doing substantial work upon the temple
of truth. I was the first Spiritualist lecturer in London.

Books, journals, Spiritualist literature of all kinds and gradations, are rapidly increasing in England and the British Empire. Under this head, the most unique, and the most wonderful too, in some directions, are a series of books by ——, entitled the "Book of God," "Book of Enoch," "Apocalypse," &c. For acquaintance with Brahmanism, Buddhism, and other Oriental religions, together with research into the mysteries of the East, these volumes stand quite unrivaled.

SUGGESTIONS TO TRAVELERS.

As a tourist, have some higher purpose than mere pleasure.

"O happiness! our being's end and aim,"

though good poetry, is wretched philosophy. Happiness should be no man's "aim." It would be the quintessence of selfishness.

While packing your trunk (*one* is enough), store away in your soul's silent chambers a choice stock of good temper and patient forbearance. Passports are no longer necessary, even in Turkey or Egypt. In case of accident or trouble, however, they might be convenient for identification. Take as little clothing as possible; it is cheaper in most countries than America. Guide-books are indispensable; while guides are often a pestilence and a prey. The Bank of England is best known in the East; but a "circular letter of credit" from any responsible house in New York or Boston is negotiable in the prominent cities of foreign countries. If there should be any difficulty, our consuls will remedy it. In the Asiatic cities secure, for sleeping, an uppermost room: you will find better air, and less fleas.

Fire-arms of all kinds should be left at home: it is generally the most cowardly that carry them. Dogs fight because they are dogs. Few men are sufficiently brave to run, rather than fight. That Miltonian war in heaven was a myth; and all fighting is anti-Christian. The cost of travel depends altogether upon tourists. Bating the beggars, and the to-be-expected fleecing of travelers, the average hotel charges are much cheaper in some parts of Europe, and equally as cheap in Asia, as America.

SUNRISE AROUND THE WORLD.

It is no marvel that sun-worship was once common in the East, nor that modern Parsees look upon the sun as the symbol of universal light, the divine Intelligence of the universe. How true that, in the modified language of another, the "morning dawns on the isles of the Pacific, where the palm-grove, the coral-reef, and the lagoon are to be seen. Westward it moves, irradiating at once Australia and Japan, the gold-diggings of the Briton, and the summer gardens of the Tycoon. Next Java seas and Chinese waters reflect the morn; the one studded with spicy isles, the other teeming with ships of antique form. On it goes, lighting up the populous cities of China, the shrines of Siam, and the temples of Burmah, until the tops of the Himalayas reflect the first rays of coming day. Brighter grows the light upon its lasting snows, and wide it spreads on either hand, o'er ocean's waves and Tartar land,

'O'er many an ancient river,
O'er many a palmy plain,'

until jungle and city, deep defile and Hindoo temple, are flooded with the light of day. Onward still it moves, over Afghanistan and Persia, until the snows of Ararat are suffused with a crimson glow. Brighter grows the light, until surrounding seas reflect the day, until the camel's shadow is projected on the sand, and the mosque and the minaret are revealed on Zion's Hill. Onward still it advances in ceaseless march, illumining the classic shores of the Mediterranean, and spreading far away to Caffre hut and Lapland burrow; embracing at once Zambesi and Nile valleys, Grecian isles, and Russian steppes. At length the Alps are all aglow, and the shadows of night chased from the valleys. Darkness retires from the scene, and reveals the rolling Rhine, the plains of France, and the hills of Spain. The British Isles, too, are all in view, — the greensward of England, and Scotia's rugged strand. Having lighted up the Old World, westward it moves to seek a New. The waves of the Atlantic are irradiated from pole to pole. Ten thousand sails mirrored on the deep, or rocked by the tempest, reflect the day. A New World comes in view, from the shores of the Amazon to Labrador; wide savannas, emerald isles, populous cities, mighty rivers, and pine-clad hills, embrace the day. On marches the morn over fertile plains and dark primeval forests, over the banks of the Amazon, the windings of the Mississippi, the network of railways, and the waters of the great lakes, until beyond green savanna and rolling prairie it glows on the snows of the Andes, and the tops of the Rocky Mountains, where the condor trims his plumage, and the grizzly bear skulks to his lair. Down the mountain-side it pours, until Chilian cities and Californian sands are mirrored in the waters of the Pacific. Again its march is o'er the deep, until, amid the beauteous isles where day began, it resumes its glorious course of sunrise round the world."

TRAVEL EDUCATIONAL.

Travel is a school of trial; and traversing Oriental lands requires considerable pluck, perseverance, and determination. Though passing through diverse experiences, though subjected to strange mixtures of diet; though often sweltering in torrid climes; though scattering Spiritualistic literature among missionaries and mandarins, Brahmans and Buddhists; though resorting to donkeys, camels, and elephants in the line of locomotion, as well as sedan-chairs, palanquins, railways, and ill-ventilated steamers, still we met — thanks to God and ministering spirits — with no serious disaster by land or sea. And, further, if we except custom-

house annoyances, and the begging proclivities of pariahs
and other lower classes in the East, all the races and tribes
with whom we had to do, Maoris and Malays, Hindoos and
Arabs, treated us with considerations of kindness and good
will.

Sitting quietly now in my library-room, and retrospecting
the year and a half's absence consumed in this round-the-
world pilgrimage, it seems hardly possible that I've seen the
black aborigines of Australia, and the tattooed Maoris of
New Zealand; that I've witnessed the Hindoos burning
their dead, and Persians praying in their fire-temples; that
I've gazed upon the frowning peak of Mount Sinai, and
stood upon the summit of Cheops; that I've conversed upon
antiquity and religious subjects with Chinamen in Canton,
Brahmans in Bengal, Parsees in Bombay, Arabs in Arabia,
descendants of Pyramid-builders in Cairo, and learned rabbis in Jerusalem; that I've seen Greece in her shattered
splendor, Albania with its castled crags, the Cyclades with
their mantling traditions, and the Alps impearled and capped
in crystal. Ceylon, too, in all its glory.

The Spiritual séance that we held upon Mount Zion, in
Jerusalem, when ancient spirits that personally knew Jesus
after the "days of Herod the king" came and conversed
with us, was to me the most consecrated hour of life. It
was the door, the very gate to heaven, and *that* ajar! The
particulars and preparations for the séance, with the teachings, the inquiries, and responses, will be written out in the
future. The time is not yet. We are living in the Second
Coming, the continuous coming of Christ, a coming in
judgment, in "power and great glory!"

As midnight hours are lighted by starry hosts; as grasses
and grains, fruits and yellowing harvests, first freshen, then
come to maturity through the warmth and light of the sun,
so comes the soul's salvation through Christ. "We are
saved by his life" (Rom. v. 10). Christianity — that is,
the Christ-principles enunciated by Jesus Christ — stands

upon an imperishable basis. With its everlasting arms of tenderness, it infolds the world, and pours forth a crystal flood of love as boundless as inexhaustible.

It is difficult to realize that I've been in Bethlehem, walked in the Garden of Gethsemane, stood upon Mount Olives, bathed in the Jordan, breathed the air that fanned the serene face of Jesus when weary from travel under the burning skies of Palestine, looked thoughtfully upon the same hills and valleys clothed in Syrian spring-time with imperial lilies, and had the same images daguerreotyped upon my brain that impressed the sensitive soul of the " man of sorrows," — the teacher sent from God.

As the voyage of mortal life must end some time, so must the record of these travels. If those who have followed me have been edified, and morally benefited, then am I satisfied. The " greatest word," said Confucius, " is ' reciprocity.' " Writing in haste, we may have committed some minor errors, or expressed opinions without sufficient research ; but the endeavor has been to treat the subjects referred to candidly, bringing to our aid the most reliable information, and *all* to impart correct ideas of the millions peopling the East.

Though each nation has its individuality, and each zone its peculiar attractions ; though there are choicer antiquities, and more classical lands ; though there are sunnier skies, and tropical fruits mellowing in one eternal summer, — still I admire my native land. And yet standing upon the mount of vision, illumined by the principles of the Spiritual philosophy, I know no rich, no poor, no Asia, no America, no caste, no country ; but *one divine humanity*, resting upon the beating, loving bosom of God.

CHAPTER XXXII.

> Bright is the world to-day!
> But there are souls void of celestial fire,
> Benumbed to apathy, who in the mire
>   Have fallen by the way.
> Shall I not rouse them to behold the light?

IT was no more true in Bishop Heber's day than now, that "spicy breezes blow soft o'er Ceylon's Isle." I reached Colombo, the Capitol of Ceylon, from Australia, April 5, 1897, and stopped at the Grand Oriental Hotel, near the landing. But brief was my stay, as Mr. P. de Abrew, a cultured Buddhist gentleman called, and, accompanying him, I was taken in a *rickshaw*, a tidy, two-wheeled little carriage drawn by a Tamil coolie, to the Musaeus school for Buddhist girls. This is a splendid brick building in the cinnamon gardens. The school is conducted by Mrs. Maria M. Higgins, formerly a resident of Washington, D. C. Much of the financial prosperity of this school is due to the generosity of Wilton Hack, Esq., of Western Australia. It was a pleasure to me to wedge a brick into this magnificent structure dedicated to the education of Buddhist girls, many of whom were orphans. Here I was a guest — feeling at home. Mr. Abrew donated the land for this school-building, surrounded by tropical shrubbery and semi-shaded by evergreen, bread-fruit and cocoanut palms. If I could say but one impressive word to Ceylon, Burmah and India, that word should be education.

Be it said in honor of Col. H. S. Olcott, a noted American writer and author whom I well knew a quarter of a century since, that he has organized over one hundred schools in Ceylon for elementary instruction in English, for the propagation of the higher education and for the elucidation of the doctrines of Buddhism. Sectarian missionaries are not deeply in love with the Colonel, nor his Theosophical Buddhism.

It was in Chittendon, Vt., the home of the Eddy mediums, that I first met Col. Olcott. Madame Blavatsky was there also ; both flaming Spiritualists known as "investigators." Though a Theosophist now, he has never ruthlessly smitten the rock, Spiritualism, from whence he was hewn. All true Theosophists are Spiritualists, and very many Spiritualists are Theosophists. The phenomena of both demonstrate a future existence ; and they both toil to overthrow superstition, bigotry, Athanasian and Calvinistic creeds, and to usher in the reign of reason and the acknowledged brotherhood of all the races.

Upon introducing me to an audience of Priests and Buddhist students for an address in the Ananda College, Colombo, Col. Olcott very appreciatingly said : " It was Dr. Peebles' book of ' Buddhism and Christianity Face to Face,' published after his first tour around the world, that gave me an introduction to the Buddhist High Priest, Sumangala ; ultimating later, in my visit to, and subsequent educational work, upon the island." Often do we write wiser than we know. No good thought dies — no truth perishes.

CEYLON'S CHARACTERISTICS.

This lovely island in remote antiquity was called in Sanskrit, *Lanka*, and seems to have been first mentioned in that famous Hindoo poem, " Ramayana." Its length from north to south is less than 300 miles. It has an area of something over 25,000 square miles, and may well be called the gem of the sea and the pearl of the ocean.

Ceylon was doubtless peopled in a later period from India,

the legends of antiquity testifying that at one time the island was accessible from India by land at low water. In the Singhalese we plainly see a blending of two or more races, the majority coming from northern India, bringing with them the Sanskrit; while the Tamils came from South India. Colombo, the capital, has a population of about 130,000, a mixture of Singhalese, Hindoos, Parsees, Arabs, Afghans and other races, clad in almost every costume conceivable.

The lowest race, the Rock Veddahs of the island, are nearly extinct. They do not live or build houses in trees as has been reported, but they live in grass-made huts and caves. They are very shy of civilized people. They use only the bow and the arrow to kill their game. They eat bats, rats and lizards ; roast wild pigs and monkeys are equally considered by them the choicest delicacies. The Valley Veddahs are a higher class, yet very low in the moral scale. They intermarry. These aborigines will soon fade away in consonance with the law — the survival of the fittest.

Saturday, April 10th. Called in the morning upon the United States Consul. His wife is a Singhalese. In the afternoon went to a Buddhist funeral. The deceased was a young lady connected with the higher classes. The cemetery was about one mile from the Musaeus school. There was a very large concourse of people, and among them, twenty-three Buddhist priests clad in their yellow robes. The mourners followed the corpse borne by friends to within some thirty yards of the grave, when they stopped and commenced weeping, mourning, groaning and agonizing in a most pitiable manner. When ! Oh, when ! will mortals learn to differentiate the body from the risen and immortal soul? A corpse is only a lifeless shape of disorganizing putridity — a deserted shell — a vacated house to be speedily burned.

The grave was rimmed around a foot or more with beautiful flowers on each side. The priests upon reaching the grave formed a circle around it, holding in their hands many yards of soft white muslin, a portion of it resting upon the metal-

Megettuwatte, the Controversialist.

lic coffin, glittering like silver under shimmering sunbeams. Then the high priest offered prayers in the ancient Pali, the other priests responding. Then followed chants — chantings of life, of death and the consolations of the future. Perfumed sacred water was poured into all of the priests' hands, and two earthen bowls of water were broken at the head and foot of the grave, symbolizing as the water poured out, the release of the spirit from the broken, buried body. Several of the priests as well as Col. Olcott made short speeches. The friends of the deceased filled up the grave with their ungloved hands and covered it with flowers. All Buddhist priests are cremated ; while the masses both cremate and bury.

Sunday, 12th, went with Mr. de Abrew and the Musaeus school teachers out to the Kotahena temple — the temple of Migettuwatte, the famous preacher and debater. Standing in his pulpit just outside of the unique, yet gorgeous temple, in which the image of Buddah, twenty-seven feet in length, lies reclining on the right side with a circled aureola of golden rays around his head, such as we see around the heads of Christian saints and martyrs, I tried to picture to myself the discussion that this Buddhist priest Migettuwatte held with the Rev. Mr. Silva, upon the comparative merits of Buddhism and Christianity. It was the consensus of opinion that the Rev. Silva was signally routed. The priest was the best scholar and far the most eloquent. The alleged miracles connected with Buddhism are almost infinitely more numerous and astounding than those connected with Christianity. Why, when Buddha made his reported third visit to Adams Peak in Ceylon, he left his footprint upon the rock — and it remains unto this day.

TEMPLES IN ROCKS.

Accompanied by a Singhalese youth, I went out to *Aluxihára*, meaning dwelling-place of monks. It was at Matalé, the terminus of the railway leading from Colombo up through

Kandy. It was some three miles from the station to this famous rock temple. We rode in springless bullock carts, drawn by large hump-shouldered bullocks. They go on a good trot. We passed many poor-looking, palm-thatched cottages ; saw natives by their huts, eating their dried fish and rice with their fingers ; jogged along by vacated coffee-tree plantations and rice paddies. Now we have passed the gate from the main road, and following the winding way, we are at the foot of the great rock temple, the crevices of which shelter a million bats. Here is what corresponds to a church edifice cut into an immense granite boulder, the workmanship of which would do honor to the sculptors of ancient Greece. In this stone temple of worship is a massive image of Buddha, with a sevenfold rainbowed circle around his head. The walls are covered with old religious carvings and paintings of Buddha's conflicts with demons, of his fast friend Ananda, of many saints and their temptations by demons. There were several priests in this stone temple and they kindly showed us the nine points of bending and bowing in Buddhistic worship. On the highest point of this rock is the legendary imprint of Buddha's foot, fully six feet in length.

ANURADHAPURA.

Ceylon abounds in buried cities and ruins, some of which are pre-historic. Among these are remnants of antiquity near the Aluxihara temple at Dambulla. But these pale away into insignificance compared with those at Anuradhapura and vicinity. Approaching, you first see the so-called brazen palace, which is a " vast collection of monolithic granite pillars 1,600 in number, standing about 12 feet out of the ground, and arranged in lines of 40 each way. The corner pillars are massive in size. They were probably all " coated with chunam and covered with copper." The foundations of this palace were laid by King Dutugemunu in the second century, B. C., and supported a building nine stories in height, containing 1,000 dormitories for priests and some other apartments. These were the palmy days of Buddhism. The roof of this magnificent monastery was of brass, the walls, says the native historian, were embellished and resplendent with gems, the great hall was supported on golden pillars resting on lions; in the centre was an ivory throne, with a golden sun and a silver moon on either side, and above all gleamed and glittered the imperial " Chatta," the white canopy of dominion and peace. This monastery was reconstructed and reduced to seven stories in height in the year 140 B. C.   Just south of the brazen palace is the "sacred " road along which the pilgrims have come for over two thousand years with their offerings to the shrine of their religion. The offerings are mostly flowers and gifts for the poor. Near this road is the celebrated *Bo-tree*, the oldest historical tree in the world. It was planted 245 years before Christ, and accordingly is now 2,130 years old. This tree, though bearing no fruit, has a very beautiful foliage. The tree is considered sacred, because under it in India, Gautama sat when he attained Buddha-hood. The chronicles of this tree are considered authentic, all dynasties considering it sacred. It is surrounded by a grove of palms. The leaves that fall from it are highly esteemed as relics by the thousands of pilgrims who come here to worship during the full moons of June and July. All about are figures of Buddha, monolithic pillars, medicine baths, dagobas, statues leaning or fallen, ponderous cisterns, ancient shrines crumbling with the weight of weary centuries, and costly carved ascetic cells — clustering acres upon acres of ruins, revealing the ancient grandeur and glory of Ceylon.

THE ANTIQUITY OF CIVILIZATION.

There are written characters in Ceylon antedating the Pali and the most ancient Sanskrit. Professor Sayce is forced to admit that the language spoken in Chaldea was the parent of the Egyptian, proving that a high state of civilization prevailed in that region three thousand years before the date assigned by Archbishop Usher to the Mosaic so-called creation of the world. Pity be to our Bible worshippers!

In the Nippur explorations there has been found a library containing no fewer than thirty thousand clay tablets, these records having been inscribed nearly five thousand years ago, and Professor Hilprecht, who has been engaged in deciphering these enduring records, declares that he can no longer "hesitate to date the founding of the temple of Bel and the first settlement in Nippur somewhere between 6000 and 7000 B. C., possibly even earlier." Sargon and his son, Naram Sin, can be shown to have reigned in Babylon as far back as 3800 B. C., and these two monarchs, it is now proved, "come at the end of a long preceding historical period," and their annals "have been verified by contemporaneous documents"; so that "henceforward, Sargon and Naram Sin, instead of belonging to the gray dawn of time, must be regarded as representatives of the golden age of Babylonian history." There is valid evidence to show that "the temple of Mul-lil (in the city of Nippur) must have been founded at least as early as 6000 B. C."; and it is impossible to say how far back in the history of the world later discoveries may carry us. It is now clear, however, that "for unnumbered ages Babylonia had been the centre of culture for the whole of Western Asia, and that at times it had been the political centre of Western Asia as well." These tablets elucidate the history of the world eight and ten thousand years ago.

"The American expedition," says Professor Schlesinger, "was fortunate enough to exhume the library at Nippur, and the thirty-two thousand tablets have gone to the United States. The nature of the collection may be inferred from the following list of its contents: Syllabarias, letters, chronological lists, historical fragments, astronomical and religious texts, building inscriptions, votive tablets, inventories, tax lists, plans of estates, contracts, etc."

A Buddhist Priest.

PECULIARITIES OF BUDDHIST PRIESTS.

The Buddhism of Ceylon is not in perfect accord with the Buddhism of Japan and China, although they agree in what may be denominated the essentials. Before a Buddhist student can be ordained he must go before the chief priest and twenty elders, all robed in white garments, and answer the following questions:

1. Are you afflicted with leprosy, ulcers, cutaneous eruptions, consumption, or possessed with demons?

2. Are you free from the bonds of slavery? Are you involved in debt? Have you obtained the consent of your parents? Have you completed your twentieth year? Are you provided with a cup and a priestly garment?

If answered in the affirmative, then his hair is shaven off, his body perfumed with sandal powder and other delicious odors.

Priests dress in yellow robes — a cloth around their loins to the ankles, and another of deep yellow, several yards long, thrown over their left shoulders and reaching nearly to the ground. Generally they wear no shoes; a very few wear sandals. They shave each other. They take no money for services. They live by alms-asking. Their feet are handsome and their eyes expressive and bright. They are celibates. They eat but twice a day. It is considered great merit to feed or give to a priest. They bless the giver.

The Buddhists' Sundays are governed by the moon, hence they assemble four times a month, or at the moon's changes, for religious instructions. They have one yearly season of devotion that corresponds somewhat to Lent. This lasts three months, the priests leaving their temples and going among the people preaching the gospel of Lord Buddha.

In all temples there are one or more images of Buddha. Lights are kept burning. They also burn incense upon certain occasions, sprinkle holy water and tinkle a little bell.

Generally a Buddhist priest has a palm-leaf fan in his

hand. In traveling he must not see more than the length of a bullock before him. Gazing about is considered irreligious. No priest must sit privately on a seat with a woman secluded from sight. He must not address a woman in more than five or six sentences without an intelligent witness present. Every fifteen days the priests assemble for a lecture from the High Priest. Their rules of discipline are rigid. For drunkenness, eating at night, sleeping on high beds, accepting gold or silver, wearing jewelry, or using perfumes, they are liable to discipline, and, if persisted in, expulsion.

A priest never bows to persons, as he is supposed to be superior to man. Priests never worship the gods; but when they preach they invite the gods to listen. Many of them understand medicine as taught in their Pali books. No one must sit on a higher seat in a congregation than the priest. He sits while preaching, the people standing. Buddhists have no fixed creed. The northern and southern sections of Buddhism agree in all essentials.

KANDY, RUMBUKKANNA AND THE JUNGLE.

It is seventy miles from Colombo to Kandy, the old capital of the Kandian kings. This city of twenty-five thousand inhabitants is half embowered in tropical foliage, and surrounded by evergreen hills, mirrored in an artificial lake. Its famous Dalada Temple was built to hold Buddha's tooth — a sham tooth, as every scientist and pathologist knows. Adams Peak may be seen from the Kandian Hills; while the fine sanitarium of Neura Eiliya, nearly three thousand feet above the level of the sea, is only fifty miles distant. This is a noted resort of the rich man and the artist, the sick, the lame and the lazy. The climate here is not only temperate but cool and bracing.

Left Kandy for Rumbukkanna on the 16th, to meet Col. Olcott, who was to address a school by a noted temple out in the jungle. When the colonel reached the station there was a crowd awaiting him. When he alighted the people shouted and the elephants were made to kneel down, then rise up and trumpet in his honor. A Singhalese crowd followed him to the Government Rest House, where I was breakfasting. In the mean time deputations came in from districts ten and fifteen miles distant. They met in front of our hotel, a motley crowd, and entertained us with native music — I think they called it music, certainly it was noise. Mr. Subasinnah, a gentlemanly Singhalese, brought his Buddhist Sunday-school class before us, the calisthenic and gymnastic exercises of which very much resembled the children's progressive lyceums of America. These native children, though brown-skinned, are bright, active and handsome. The exercises at the Government House concluded, with their accompaniaments of flags waving, tom-toms, hand-drums and devil-dancings, the full procession was formed for a five miles' march into the jungle. I was dumped into a seatless, springless bullock-cart with the colonel and three Buddhist priests. The packing was too close for comfort. We move on, led by waving banners, elephants and donkeys, now over a hill, now under a decorated arch, now through a grove of wild cocoanut-trees, devil-dancers with jingling bells upon their ankles before, devil-dancers behind and cheering all along the line. No artist could have transferred this scene to canvas.

MOUNTED UPON AN ELEPHANT.

Weary of the jolting, uncushioned cart, it was gravely proposed that I take refuge upon the largest of the elephants in line. It was agreed to. He was a monster of an animal. Lying down, as commanded by his owner, I mounted him with some native assistance. Already was he burdened with five passengers all riding astride — no houdah! The march continues. We are in the thick of the jungle. The elephantine movements of this great animal were only comparable to a steamer rocking, struggling in a howling monsoon. It was soon a question of bullock-cart or elephant, which? Sitting astride his nearly square back and fearing there might possibly be two of me soon, I dismounted, and betook myself to the cart again!

Here we are now at an old, gorgeously-decorated temple out in the jungle. Met at the door-way and blessed by the priests, we passed on and out into an emerald-carpeted field, where, under the waving boughs of a majestic Bo-tree there had been erected a platform festooned with wreaths and flowers of seemingly a thousand hues. There was an audience before us of some two or three thousand. All were sitting. The scene was entrancing. Col. Olcott, at his best, delivered an eloquent address upon education, brotherhood and the beauties of ethical Buddhism. It was loudly cheered. To make practical his address, the colonel drank from a bowl of water brought to him by one of the lowest caste persons present, to show the true, fraternal spirit of Buddhism.

What do you say? — caste among the Buddhists, when one of the first teachings of Guatama Buddha was, " Down with caste ! " But remember that Ceylon was conquered by the Hindoos, who introduced and enforced the caste system, the remnants of which have not yet been exterminated.

Introduced by Colonel Olcott as an old American friend of his, imbued with the ethics of Buddhism, the brotherhood of man and all humanitarian reforms, I addressed this great mass-meeting of Buddhists upon the schools, manners, customs and religions of America, and never did I address a more quiet or appreciative audience. The meeting was continued till the next morning, two Buddhist priests preaching and chanting alternately all the long night. Asiatics are anxious to know the truth.

On our way back to Rambukkanna, near evening-time, we were overtaken by a terrific thunder-storm, the rain pouring in torrents and leaking down through our palm-thatched bullock-cart; one of the bullocks balked; one of the rude vehicles upset ; another broke down because of the flooded road-way. Oh, the times and terrors of these pilgrims! Dripping, hungry and weary, we felt like singing :

"Our crosses are many, our crowns are few."

THE PRINCE-PRIEST.

Seldom does royalty become humility. Seldom do princes assume the garb of beggars and go about doing good. In a palm-embowered suburb of Colombo is the temple of the prince-priest of Siam. He speaks fine English. He shrinks from no argument with missionaries. He is very social and wears his Buddhistic robe of yellow very gracefully. A prince, a scholar, an ambassador to St. James and nearly half the courts of Europe, he had seen enough of the folly, deception, illusion and hollowness of the world; and coming to the conclusion that he was a soul, he renounced the world — the world and its illusions, and became a Buddhist monk. He is now calm, serene, happy — consecrating his life to the diffusion of Buddhism, to doing good, to begging of the rich to give to the poor!

TEAS OF CHINA AND CEYLON.

"Which are the preferable teas" is a common inquiry — "those of China, or of Ceylon?" The coffee plantations of the Ceylonese have been largely supplanted by tea-plants and shrubs, owing to a disease among the coffee trees. Tea-raising is very profitable in the warm, humid climate of Ceylon. The tea-plant would grow ten or fifteen feet high if left to itself; but the shrubs are kept clipped down to within one and two feet from the ground. Only the young and tenderest top leaves are picked. Poor Tamil coolie women do the most of the picking. A large basket is suspended upon their backs, and the leaves are nipped off and tossed behind them into these baskets. Their only dress is a loin-cloth. They sweat profusely. The manufacturing establishments for preparing, drying, sorting and boxing interested me

deeply. Many are the processes, one of which is the fer-
mentation of the moist tea leaves ; another is passing them
over and through a copper screen ; another is the stirring
with the coolie's hands while drying ; another is the stamping them down (when dried) in boxes and chests by the
Tamil coolie boys' bare, perspiring feet. At the Matale
manufactory the tea leaves ready for sorting and packing
were scattered over the floor, half an inch deep in some
places, with half-naked, barefooted, feet-sweating coolies
treading around in them, soon to be steeped and sipped as
a delicious beverage by Western nations. Tea leaves as a
drink are useless, expensive, astringing, stimulating and
medicinal. Theine is used as a medicine. Paris has a large
hospital for old, nervously broken-down tea-topers. "Which
of the Oriental teas, then, is the best ? " The answer is, those
that are the least injurious, unhealthy, dirty and nasty. Take
your choice, and tan your stomachs with theine ! O ye tea-
toper slaves of the nineteenth century!

THE KING OF SIAM IN CEYLON.

As fate or fortune would have it, I was in this evergreen
isle of temples and spices when the Siamese King on his
way to the Queen's Jubilee visited Ceylon. Great preparations were made for his reception. Through the kindness of
my old-time friend whom I first met at the " Eddy mediums,"
in Vermont, and who stands very high among the Buddhists
of Ceylon and the Brahmins of India for the impetus he has
given to education and free thought, Col. Henry S. Olcott,
I was secured a seat within the magnificently decorated pavil-
ion (by paying ten rupees) only a few feet from the king's
chair. He walked up under the handsomely trimmed and
flowered-covered arch with the strutting English officials,
dressed in a plain, American-like suit. No sword, sash or
epaulettes, not even a finger ring. Sensible king, said I.
Conducted to his chair upon the platform, amid the music of
Buddhist priests' chanting, he performed some religious cere-

monies, received addresses and replied to them in both Pali and English.

I had a pleasant five minutes' chat with him in the queen's house. Upon leaving, and telling him that I was travelling around the world gathering materials for a book, he most courteously said: " If you come to my country I will give you every facility for collecting such materials."

The king is a genial, sunny-faced gentleman of, say, forty years of age, with not a bit of swell or starch about him. He is as popular in his kingdom as was President Lincoln in America. Educated in London and Paris, he speaks fine English, is straight as an arrow, yellow-skinned and exceedingly affable.

ASOKA BUDDHISM AND CHRISTIANITY.

What relation does Buddhism bear to Christianity? is an ever-recurring question. The numerous inscriptions of King Asoka, who, reigning over forty years, died at the ripe old age of eighty, 223 B. C., unquestionably was the best and the wisest of the old Indian sovereigns. The inscriptions of his time — a Bible on rocks — are affording a rich harvest for archeologists and antiquarians. Some of Asoka's edicts remain to this day chisel-imprinted on pillared rocks and in old stone caves. Explorers and archeologists have just discovered among the ruins of Rampuwar two Asoka pillars, nearly imbedded in soil and sand, one of which contained important inscriptions.

These inscriptions, in either Sanskrit or Pali, have been largely copied and translated. Some few were too defaced to be clearly read. The translations relating to governmental commands, with moral and religious advice to both Brahmins and Buddhists, are of a most interesting character. No interpolations can here be charged. Defying the cankering tooth of time, these inscriptions are genuine.

WHAT IS THEIR MORAL IMPORT?

They breathe the spirit of toleration to unbelievers and brotherly love to all. Buddhists have never persecuted for religious opinion's sake. In this, Buddhism puts Christianity to shame. These Asoka edicts prohibited the sacrifice of animals either for food or for religious ceremonies. They ordered shade-trees and fruit-trees to be plánted along the great thoroughfares, and wells to be dug along such and such distances to quench the thirst of travelers along the highways. They enjoined obedience to parents, respect and reverence to the aged, kindness to animals, frequent bathings, and forbearance to all other religions. Query — How much has the world advanced ethically since the Buddhistic era of Asoka?

WHAT IS THE HISTORIC IMPORT OF THESE EDICTS?

Much, very much! To use the language of Hon. P. C. Chatterẏii, judge of the High Court, Calcutta, author of " Asoka and His Edicts," " this Indian king, fired with the missionary spirit, sent missionaries to preach the doctrines and moral precepts of Buddhism to all the civilized nations of the West. Egypt, Syria, Cyrene, Epirus and Macedon were visited by them, as the thirteenth rock inscription edict shows. The Western kings with whom Asoka made treaties were Antiochus of Syria, Ptolemy of Egypt, Margus of Cyrene, Antigonus of Macedon and Alexander of Epirus. These kings, over 200 years before Christ, permitted Buddhists to preach and teach in their countries, the fruits of which appeared in the rise of the Therapeutæ of Egypt, the Essenes in Syria and Palestine, and the Neo-Zoroastrians and Neo-Pythagoreans — all of whom were Buddhists under different names. Thus the teachings of Buddha were carried to the remotest corners of the ancient civilized world." And so Judaism and Buddhism formed the menstruum — the religious and ethical soil out of which grew primitive Christianity. In this there was no miracle.

Many of the rock edicts of Asoka, chronological, ethical and religious, are still standing, and can be seen by any one who will take the trouble to visit them. They have not been revised and re-revised by priests, like the Christians' Bible.

Already thirty-nine of these edicts have been discovered and translated. Some have partially perished by the corroding action of time. Others were defaced by the vandal Mohammedans. Arabs by descent, wherever they conquered they destroyed temples, inscriptions and manuscripts. They forced their religion by the sword. When conquering Northern India they compelled thousands upon thousands of old men to submit to circumcision. They are to-day fanatics, bigots, fatalists and polygamists. True, there are good men among them — good in spite of their Islamism. I write what I know, for as a United States Consul I lived among them for years and know them thoroughly. They are the Jews — the baser sort of warlike Jews — of Asia and Africa.

Explorers and archeologists expect to find, in the near future, more of these Asoka edicts in Afghanistan, and the countries north of the present India, that this Buddhist king once governed. Just recently they found and deciphered one of these inscriptions in Mysore. And so, step by step, the long half-hidden past is yielding up its treasures ; and, being resurrected into the living present, solving many of the knotty problems of history.

Those wishing to know the genius, status and progress of Buddhism should procure Col. H. H. Olcott's " Buddhist Catechism," the thirty-third edition of which, approved by the High Priest Sumangala of Ceylon, has just been published. In the suburbs of Colombo I visited the temple and stood in the pulpit where Priest Mitteguttawate used to preach, and whose discussion with the Rev. de Silva formed the foundation of my book on " Buddhism and Christianity Face to Face."

BUDDHISM AS IT IS.

Theology, in an ecclesiastical sense, bears little or no relation to the life and teachings of Guatama Buddha. Buddhism is benign and ethical, rather than dogmatic. It is based upon four " noble truths," so called :

1. The existence of suffering.
2. The cause of this suffering.
3. The cessation of suffering.
4. The eightfold path that leads to the cessation of suffering.

This eightfold path consists of these steps upward : 1, a right comprehension of life ; 2, right and high aspirations ; 3, right and appropriate speech; 4, upright moral conduct; 5, a befitting way of earning a livelihood ; 6, endeavor in doing good ; 7, intellectuality to enlighten others, and, 8, purity of life.

Birth, say Buddhists, is suffering, old age is suffering, disease is suffering, and death is suffering. The causes of this suffering are desire, selfishness, lust. This seeking for happiness, this craving for worldly enjoyment, this struggling for satisfaction, for power, for fame — in brief, this heart-clamoring for existence. It is these selfish lusts for worldly gratification that lead to and necessitate incarnation after incarnation back into human bodies.

Those who wisely enter the path and persistently follow it make an end of sin — an end of suffering, and so avoid re-births back into mortality.

This is the formula in which those Buddhists take refuge who follow the path by practising the precepts of Lord Buddha :

"I take my refuge in the Buddha.—[The Enlightened One.]
I take my refuge in the Dharma. — [The pure religion.]
I take my refuge in the Sangha." — [The Buddhist Church.]

There are, say Buddhist priests, three sins of the body, four sins of the tongue, and three sins of the mind. " The sins of the body are murder, theft and adultery; of the tongue, lying, slander, abuse and gossip; of the mind, envy, hatred and error."

The ten commandments condensed are —

I. — Kill not, but have regard for all life.

II. — Steal not, neither rob, but help every one to have the fruits of his labors.

III. — Abstain from impurity, and lead lives of chastity.

IV. — Lie not, but be truthful. Speak the truth fearlessly, yet in a loving heart.

V. — Invent not evil reports, neither repeat them. Carp not, but look for the good in your fellow-beings.

VI. — Swear not, but speak with propriety and dignity.

VII. — Waste not your time in idle gossip, but speak words of wisdom or keep silent.

VIII. — Covet not, nor envy, but rejoice at the good fortune of others.

IX. — Cleanse your heart of malice, and cherish no hatred, not even against your enemies.

X. — Free your mind from ignorance, practise kindness and seek to learn the truth — these lead to life eternal.

Further quoting from the Maha-Bodhi publication, the seven jewels of the law which united form the bright diadem of Nirvana are purity, calmness, comprehension, love, wisdom, perfection and divine enlightenment.

The most prominent priest of Ceylon is High Priest Welligama, Shri Sumangala. He is a most genial and courteous old man, delighting to aid one in solving the knottiest problems connected with Buddhism. There is a revival of Buddhism in Ceylon and other Oriental countries. Some of her monks are afire with the missionary spirit. Already H. Dharmapala, Secretary of the Maha-Bodi Society, is in America teaching that gospel of gentleness and mercy that distinguishes Buddhism from other Oriental religions.

Buddhism and Brahminism are becoming better understood continually by the Western world. The exponents of each are also on better terms. Hence that progressive Hindoo, P. C. Moozomdar, in an address delivered last year in

Galle, Ceylon, said: "I do not ask you, my Buddhistic friends, to forsake Buddhism, but to give it a new spirit and bring it under a new dispensation. There must in the future be a new Hinduism, a new Islamism, a new Christianity, and a new Buddhism, that all these religions may mix and mingle to form one universal fresh progressive religious dispensation, wherein all sects may behold what is best in their own faiths, and above all behold the eternal countenance of the Giver and Father of all truth, all goodness and all humanity."

CHAPTER XXXIII.

THE INDIA OF TO-DAY.

" Afar down I see the Infinite Past ;
   I know I was even there.
   I waited unseen and always, and slept through the lethargic mist,
   And took my time, and took no hurt from the fetid carbon.
   Long I was hugged close — long and long.
   Immense have been the preparations for me,
   Faithful and friendly the arms that have helped me ;
   Cycles ferried my cradle, rowing and rowing like cheerful boatmen.
   For room to me stars kept aside in their own rings ;
   They sent influences to look after what was to hold me.
   Before I was born out of my mother, generations guided me.
   My embryo has never been torpid, nothing could overlay it,
   For it the nebula cohered to an orb,
   The long slow strata were piled to rest it on,
   Vast vegetables gave it sustenance,
   Monstrous sauroids transported it in their mouths and deposited it with care.
   All forces have been steadily employed to complete and delight me :
   Now I stand upon this spot with my soul.
   I am soul."

" WHICH is the finest country in the world ? "   " Which
would you prefer to live in ? " are the ever-recurring questions that I have to answer.   The matchless Max Müller in
his " What can India Teach Us ? " says: " If I were to
look over the whole world to find out the country most
richly endowed with all the wealth, power and beauty that
nature can bestow — in some parts a very paradise on earth
— I should point to India.   If I were asked under what sky
the human mind has most fully developed some of its choicest gifts, has most deeply pondered on the greatest problems

of life, and has found solutions of some of them which well deserve the attention even of those who have studied Plato and Kant — I should point to India. . . . But I am thinking of India as it was, two thousand, it may be three thousand, years ago."

Nations, empires rise and fall like the waves of the ocean. Of this fact, India is a standing demonstration. The India of the present, famine-scourged and plague-stricken, was the poorest country I saw during my travels. "The English," say these struggling millions, "have by taxation and bad legislation squeezed the financial life out of us. We are helpless in the hands of a giant."

British India, including the French, Portuguese and other settlements, numbers about three hundred millions. The southern regions of this immense country are intensely hot a portion of the season ; but in the northern elevated regions the climate is temperate. Here, and especially in Southern India, there are three seasons : the hot, the rainy, and the partially temperate. I was there this last season in June, at the beginning of the rainy season. The missionaries had fled to the mountains.

During the southwest monsoons the rains fall in torrents on the western coast; while the northeast monsoons bring rain to the eastern portion of the country. If the monsoons fail to bring rain, famine is sure to follow. Rain-falls in the Deccan are about 20 inches, Madras 52 inches ; while up on the Khasia hills there is an average of 610 inches per year. Trees and vegetation in this country are unrivalled in variety, richness and beauty. It is not strange that there were originally tree-worshippers in this land of eternal verdure.

RELIGIONS AND LANGUAGES OF INDIA.

This country is so extensive that a description of one portion will not always fit that of another — hence the seeming contradictions of travelers.

Hindooism with its different gods is professed by something like three-fourths of the population. Jainism, a compound of Brahmanism and Buddhism, and numbering five million, abounds mostly in Western India. The Jains had a representative to the World's Parliament of Religions in Chicago. The Brahmins, the Orthodox Brahmins, had no representative. No Brahmin priest can leave India without losing caste.

About one-sixth of the people of India are Mohammedans. They are far the most numerous in the northern part of India. When conquering a portion of India they destroyed the sacred books of the Hindoos and demolished some of their most magnificent temples. Arabs in origin, they are religious bigots, zealots, fatalists, polygamists and political vandals.

The sect of Manaks live on the banks of the Satlaj and number about two millions. They are declining.

The Parsees, descendants of the fire-worshippers of Persia, and believers in Zoroaster, are found mostly on the western coast of India and especially in the regions of Bombay.

There is a sect in Southern India called Jacobite Christians ; possibly a million of Roman Catholics, mostly on the Malabar coast, descendants of Syrian Christians ; and in all something like five hundred thousand Protestant Christians in all India. It is safe to say that Christianity, notwithstanding its immense financial expenditures, has scarcely produced a ripple upon the religious consciousness of India.

There are as many as thirty languages spoken in India. These branch out into many mixed dialects. Ancient Hindoo settlers in this country — the Aryans — introduced the Sanskrit. The Assam, Nepal, Kashmir and others are derived from the Sanskrit. There is a revival of the study of the ancient Sanskrit at the present time in India; and the same may be said of the English. Every Hindoo boy of ordinary intelligence is anxious to learn the English tongue, hoping for employment and better pay.

The languages of Southern India are grouped under the

name of the Dravidian. This was the language of the original inhabitants. The Tamil, Telegu and the Kanarese, spoken generally in Madras and through the Madras Presidency, are outputs from the Dravidian. The Gondi is spoken by a rude tribe called Gondes, in Central India. The Snidi and the Kach tongues come largely from the Persian and the Arabic. The Pushtu is the language of the Afghans in India. The Tamil is spoken through almost the entire country south of Madras. The Dravidians were a darker-skinned people than the Aryans. Babel is the proper word to apply to the languages of India. A dozen different interpreters are necessary in traveling through this vast country.

About three-fourths of the population of India are subjects of the British Crown. There are several feudatory States under British protection, paying tribute; and there are three Independent States : Nepal, Bhutan and Sikkim. The more intelligent people of India everywhere from the cool mountains north to the torrid heat of the south are politically restless. They have aspirations for more liberty, and for national unity, with the privileges of self-government.

THE MADRAS PRESIDENCY.

Madras, the largest city in Southern India, has a population of five hundred thousand. The government buildings are grand and imposing. Under their shadow is the most abject poverty. The city with its suburbs extends nearly nine miles along the coast. It has no good harbor. Certain lines of steamers do not stop during the monsoon months. Blacktown, the crowded portion, is within the old city walls. One of the main roads leading out of the city conducts one to Saint Thomas Mount, where, according to tradition, St. Thomas, the Apostle of India, preached, and, later, was martyred. Being one of a party from Adyar, we richly enjoyed a visit to this historic mountain.

Riding down from Adyar, through the city, and especially through Blacktown, one sees women working side by side with the men, toiling upon the roads, digging post-holes, clearing away street-filth, shoveling up newly dropped cow chips, and doing all kinds of the lowest drudgery. In another portion of the city you see milk-and-water carriers with great jars suspended from an elastic bow over the shoulders ; men dressing their hair, cleansing their ears, cutting their toe-nails, scouring their teeth, rubbing their bodies with oil, or being shaved, before everybody's gaze. The bathing in the tanks, of men, women and children, the washing, by pounding the garments across great stones, the half-naked bodies and uncovered heads of over one-half of the native population, the entirely naked children and the bullock carts, where the driver sits on a projection between the heads of the little hump-shouldered animals — all present a living and most interesting, if not uplifting panorama, to the American traveler.

BURIED FAKIRS.

If the dormouse can go into a torpid, lethargic and seemingly lifeless state for the winter, if the common housefly can hibernate for several months, why may not man ? Both noted Englishmen and Hindoos assured me that certain persons, first hypnotized and prepared, had been buried for months — dead to the world — and then resurrected to their health and their homes. These people are called Fakirs.

Few have not heard of the Lahore fakir who, as recorded by Dr. W. L. McGregor (surgeon in the English army) in his history of the India Sikhs, was buried in a coffin-like box some two months, and then revived upon being exposed to the air. The history lies before me. The affair was verified by other physicians who speak of the "suspension of respiration, digestion and assimilation while in this trance." "It is well known," says Dr. McGregor, "that native Hindoos can train themselves to go without food for a long time, that they can refrain a while from breathing and can put themselves into a death-like trance, in which, as in cases of asphyxia, both respiration and circulation cease for a time."

This fakir was born in Kunkul, a place famous for fakir
phenomena. He declared that his trance sleep was delightful. He was about forty years of age. One of the gentlemen who witnessed this burial feat is still living in Lahore.
The place was well guarded, so as to admit of no imposition
or fraud. " Outside of the whole," says Dr. McGregor, " there
was placed a line of sentries, so that no one could approach
the building. The strictest watch was kept for sixty days
and sixty nights. At the expiration of the time the Maharajah, his grandson, several of his sidars, General Ventura,
Captain Wade and myself proceeded to disinter the fakir.
The box was unlocked, opened, the white sheet removed,
the wax taken from his nose, mouth and ears, and warm
water poured upon his head — when his pulse began to beat,
and his lungs to expand. Soon he became conscious. This
and similar cases are well authenticated by physicians,
Maharajahs, English officers and others of the highest re-
spectability."

Asking for the philosophy of this, the reply was: the
body is only a bit of machinery that the *Atma*, the inmost
soul, manipulates and runs. And under proper conditions it
can leave its tenement returning to it at will.

THE YOGI THAT I LAST SAW.

Hearsay incites to investigation, while seeing is knowing.

Accompanied by Dr. English and Mr. Kneudson, of Adyar,
with two intelligent Brahminical interpreters, the one the
president of the Hindoo Triplicane Society, to which I had
previously lectured, we rode down through Madras and on
through Blacktown, out into a retired suburb to see a famous
Yogi. He had been a traveling Swami Yogi for ten years ;
but for twenty years he had sat in this mud-walled hut, back
from the wayside, connected with which was neither chim-
ney nor window. He keeps a fire or light of some kind constantly burning. Conducted by our Brahminical friends, and
stooping, we entered the low doorway and squatted down,

Yogi Meditation.

there being in his hermitage neither chairs nor seats. The Yogi approached us with a pan of ashes, sprinkling them upon our foreheads. The ashes were from the burning of dried cow chips. The Yogi's feet and lower limbs were naked. There was a string of indescribables around his neck and the turbaned hood partly concealed the matted hair and ashes upon his head. The close, smoky atmosphere was almost insufferable. The surroundings were dreary enough to delight a den of demons.

This Yogi eats but one meal a day, and that is rice with a little milk. He looked lean, pinched and skinny. All of the fixings in his hermitage were smoky, sooty, dirty, repulsive. He talked glibly with the interpreter about the teachings of the Vedas, the Upanishads and other Hindoo literature, but gave no proof of telepathy, clairvoyance, levitation, psychic phenomena or of any approach towards the Supreme Soul.

The Yoga state is called Samadhi, and in this state it is said that fire will not burn, water will not drown, nor will a . deadly cobra bite Yogis. I should think not — if they are all as lazy and dirty as this one.

Sitting in this old Yogi's hut, I felt like saying : " Push an opening up through this thatched roof and let in God's fresh air and sunlight ; go and wash yourself ; go and put on some nice clean garments ; eat at least two good meals a day ; stand up straight instead of squatting on the ground like a toad ; work six or eight hours each day at some useful manual labor, and the rest of the time, if you so choose, meditate, and repeat Om, the ' word of glory.' "

The India of three thousand years ago is not the India of to-day. India with its magnificent Vedanta philosophy — almost the equivalent of the Spiritual philosophy in America, has been on the decline for a thousand years, or longer. During its fading glories it has been the great hatching maw of metaphysical monstrosities, such as this : " the age of. Brahma, or one hundred of his divine years must equal 311,040,000,000,000 of our mortal years." Buddhism is considered by the philosophically inclined infinitely preferable to Hinduism.

Colonel Olcott went to India a firm believer in the occult powers of the Yogis. He has been in India over seventeen years. In his search for Yogis, he found, so he said in one of his addresses, "only a crowd of painted imposters who masquerade as Sadhus, to cheat the charitable, and secretly give loose to their beastly natures."

THE HINDOO SWAMI VIVEKANANDA.

Americans are sensationalists, say the phlegmatic-inclined Germans. They are certainly fond of new toys if labeled foreign. It greatly amused the Theosophists and the cultured Brahmins of India, as well as interested myself to see how Unitarians, Universalists, Free-thinkers and some Spiritualists got wild over this Swami, "the great Hindoo Brahmin," who, by the way, was not a Brahmin ; and, further, he cannot become a Brahmin except through death and re-birth into a Brahmin family. His real name is Norendra Nath Dutt. His father is a lawyer in Calcutta. And this Swami Vivekananda, otherwise the sensational Mr. Nath Dutt, was educated at the Church of Scotland Institution, and studied law for a time. He attended the Brahmo churches, acted upon the stage at the residence of B. K. C. Sen. Babu P. C. Mozoomdar in his life of Chunder Sen, says, "Mr. Dutt was introduced to me as the Paramhansa, great devotee of Dakshineshwar. He discoursed in a sort of half-delirious state, becoming now and then quite unconscious." This shows him to have been a Spiritualist medium.

It was in 1889 that Mr. Dutt with several other Bengalese, agreed to become Sannyasis, wandering Hindoo monks. The old original Sannyasi were supposed to abandon all worldly concerns, and to depend upon alms for support. They were ascetics. Some smeared their heads with ashes. Others, until the British police interfered, went entirely naked ; . . . But Mr. Dutt, believing in progression, founded a sort of new

order, one more gay and festive.   His early asceticism failed
to follow him to England and America.

His Oriental garb of orange, crimson girdle, turbaned head,
and gorgeous outfit generally, though unauthorized, if I am
credibly informed by his order of monkhood, would with his
fluent English naturally attract crowds in America.   Ascetics
of his school abjure beef, wine and all animal food.   Their
food is generally rice and one meal a day.   What the
Swami's diet was in America I do not know.   The word
Swami, by the way, means Lord.   The " Calcutta Indian
Mirror," writing of Mr. Dutt, *alias* Swami Vivekananda,
says: "We have no objections to the publication of such
American panegyrics on the Sannyasi, but since he came to
us to act on the stage of the Nava-Vindavan theatre, or
sang in one of the Bramo Somajes of this city, we know him
so well, that no amount of newspaper writing could throw
any new light on our estimate of his character."

THE SWAMI AND THE YOGA PHILOSOPHY.

There has just fallen into my hands away here in India, a
new book by this Swami Vivekananda, entitled " Rajah
Yoga ; or, lectures on the Yoga Philosophy."   Heartily do I
wish that my American countrymen could hear some of the
learned pundit's criticisms of this book.   Any honorable
author in writing of a philosophy would include both
theory and practice.   What practical Yogaism is you will
see presently.

The Yoga philosophy is attributed to Patanjali, and Yoga
originally meant " the suppression of the transformation of
the thinking principle "; but now it has come to mean union,
teaching how the human soul may attain union with the
Supreme Soul.   This Hindoo Swami in treating of the
" Yoga philosophy " — a massive bundle of metaphysical
non-demonstrable propositions and archaic assertions — wittily
skipped through it and over it, picking out the plums and
quoting some of the aphorisms with comments.   The work

was shrewdly, cunningly, takingly done. This book looks
well, reads well, and is chiefly valuable for its omissions of
the Yoga practice, the ridiculous Yoga postures and the
filthiness connected with it.

YOGA POSTURES AND PRACTICE.

The "Hartha Dipika," in describing the proper place for a
Yoga location, says a cave, a dwelling, or small monastery in
an out-of-the-way place, not larger than a cube of six feet,
will do. The cell or mattrilla should have a small door,
and no window; it should be free from holes, cavities and
inequalities. Of the eighty-four postures that Yogis must
assume, the following are among the more important:

In this Yoga cave or hut, the right foot should be placed
on the left thigh and the left foot on the right thigh; the
hands should be crossed and the two great toes should be
firmly held thereby; the chin should be bent down on the
chest, and in this posture the eyes should be directed to the
tip of the nose. This is called Padmassana, the lotus posture.

Hold the great toes with the hands and draw them to the
ears as in drawing a bow-string. Look at a point between
the eyebrows and cut off the inspiration and expiration of
the breath as far as possible.

Other postures, according to Manibal and R. C. Bose, consist in the mixing of the prana with the apana, the lower
breath; inhaling at the left nostril, and letting the breath out
at the right nostril.

Some of these Yogis had long nails and matted hair; some
gazed at the sun, like the one I saw in Benares; some went
naked; some gazed for days, months and years at the "navel-
wheel of the body"; some inhaled smoke; some ate grass,
leaves and cow's dejecta (see Col. Olcott's "Asceticism," p.
3), and others still posed on one foot. But enough! There is
evidently no danger, notwithstanding the Swami's eloquence,
of Spiritualists accepting the Yoga philosophy, or engaging

Hindoo Penance.

in Yoga postures to come into union with the Supreme Soul.

The noted author, J. Murdock, of Madras, in criticising the Swami's lectures upon the Yoga philosophy, quotes from him the following passage relating to God:

" Starting from some fungus, some very minute, microscopic bubble, and all the time drawing from that infinite storehouse of energy, the form is changed slowly and slowly, until, in course of time it becomes a plant, then an animal, then man, ultimately God " (page 42).

This may be Yoga philosophy, but it is not reason, science, or common-sense.

SPIRITUALISM IN INDIA.

Though there is no organization in India under the distinctive name of Spiritualism, yet if Spiritualism means conscious communion with the so-called dead, then the Hindoos have been Spiritualists for ages. Their old religious books abound in converse with Devas (Sanskrit), celestial beings — invisible beings also good and bad, and with Pitris (Sanskrit) departed ancestors. These latter they propitiate. A Hindoo pundit informed me only a few days since that all Hindoos believe that the invisible spaces are nearly filled with different gradations of spirits, one class, connected with our solar system, being estimated at 330,000,000,000. These spirits as well as the stars are believed to exercise mighty potencies in influencing human beings.

Throughout the whole of the Sanskrit literature, from the Vedas to the Puranas, mention is made and that frequently of Bhutas, Pretas, Pitris, Devas, Pisachas — the invisible spirits of Hindoo ancestors. India's sacred books speak of their abodes, describe their distinctions and general characteristics — their power, their obsessing influences and how to avert their control by mantras, or invocations.

Swami Vivekananda, made a hero of at some of the Spiritualist camp-meetings in America, said to the Rev. Mr. Flagg, of New York, that — " Our Hindoo ancestors all be-

lieved in spirit return and spirit converse ; and they continue
to believe that they are our unseen helpers. . . . Spiritualism
like the Yoga philosophy is very old in India." He attended
Mrs. Williams's materializing séances in New York, and
expressed great delight at the privilege; under date of
March 11, 1895, he wrote her : " I shall soon have a class on
the Spiritualistic basis of the Hindoo religion, and I shall be
highly pleased to have you one of my class."

Brahmins generally oppose Spiritualism in the English
and American sense of the word. They do not discrimi-
nate between or differentiate Spiritualism from Spiritism
with its concomitant obsessions. The stock in trade of
Spiritism, the equivalent almost of Pitrisism, is phenomena ;
while the basic foundation of Spiritualism is Spirit — pure,
changeless, infinite Spirit. Spiritualism is the direct antithesis of materialism, and it incites to the study of man's
intellectual, moral and spiritual nature — to the psychic
forces that influence sensitives; and it encourages the
development of the spiritual in man, as well as demon-
strates a future progressive existence. Spiritualism is the
foe of bigotry, persecution, superstition and sectarian Christianity. Certain Theosophists have been instrumental, I
fear, in leading many thoughtful and cultured Hindoos
astray, touching the merits and moral grandeur of Spiritualism. The aims of Theosophy and Spiritualism are one
and the same — the uplifting of humanity.

THE ADYAR MANSION.

Adyar is the head-centre of Theosophy. " Are you a
Theosophist, doctor? " Yes, if allowed to define Theosophy
for myself.

The real loyal Theosophical society, founded by Madame
Blavatsky and Col. Olcott, is located at Adyar, five miles
from Madras, on the river Adyar near its entrance into the
ocean. The Adyar building is palatial in appearance and
Oriental in style. A portion of this unique, palace-like

structure is three stories high, the lower portion of the front part supported by pillars is all open, with a raised rostrum for lectures, receptions and a general reading-room.

Sitting and reading or musing, I frequently saw little squirrels, toads and lizards hopping or playfully running across the marble floor. No one disturbed them, so they had become both trusting and friendly. There are twenty-five acres connected with this Theosophical Mecca, planted and decorated with bread-fruit, mango and other trees of richest foliage. The house, half-buried in climbing, ever-blooming vines, facing the river, has doors wide and ponderous. The windows are exceedingly large and uncanny. The rooms are capacious with high ceilings. The floorings are stone or marble upon which rest heavy pillars, and the walls are hung with the shields of the different Theosophical branches in all lands. The library is absolutely massive, containing many very valuable, unpublished manuscripts. The shrine is located directly in rear of the lower library, and in which are paintings of some of the Mahatmas, the existence of which is not yet fully settled.

Adyar is not only restful, inviting to study and medita-tation; but, the centre of Theosophical culture, research and authority for the enlightened Theosophic world. Happy were the days and weeks that I spent in this palace of books, companioned with Col. Olcott, the only living founder of modern Theosophy!

CAN EUROPEANS AND AMERICANS LIVE IN INDIA?

Emphatically, Yes! if they behave themselves and even decently obey nature's divine laws.

India is not antagonistic, either from a physical or moral point of view to the European races. True, if men go there and drink liquors, walk the streets at late hours, and dive into dens of dissipation as too many of them do, their health fails. Only a miracle could make it otherwise.

If young soldiers going from England to India become

the victims of disease — a loathsome disease, the fault is
their own, and should not be accounted to the hot climate,
but rather to the heated passions of animal-flesh-eating civilization.   People have been theologically taught so long to
lay their personal sins to climate, to poor old Adam in the
garden, or to some other cowardly palliating device, and
then, that the consequences of their sins can be blotted out
by belief in the blood and merits of the Lord Jesus, that
their addled brains whirl and swing, doubtingly, between
Eden and Calvary.   Christians, and especially missionaries,
rising above creeds and Calvinistic confessions, should teach
Oriental nations — if anything — that the universe is governed by immutable laws, cause and effect; and if they violate nature's laws, they must suffer the consequences, regardless of any Adam, Krishna, or Jesus.

English women and American missionary women also, who,
when in their native countries walked a good deal, and on
their feet superintended and took a part in their household
work, when reaching India, drop down too often into a
pitiable indolence.   They employ a small army of servants.
They take no exercise except to go down a stairway for their
meals and step into a barouche for an evening's drive.   They
do their shopping from the carriage, or sitting in a chair —
in brief, they are literally lazy !   And laziness tends to ill-
ness, for which India's climate is held responsible.

It is said also by a class of pessimists, that the children
of Europeans deteriorating in India, must be returned to
their native countries, early, or early as possible for recupera-
tion.   This is not only misleading, but physiologically unjust,
untrue.   If English, Indian-born children were relieved of an
abnormal hot-bed existence — if they were properly bathed,
dieted, lightly clothed and properly educated in the laws of
hygiene, their shoulders would broaden and their cheeks red-
den with the crimson blush of health.

English soldiers transferred to India, gratifying their lower
propensities, feasting upon the corpses of cows, sheep and

hogs boiled or broiled, and, washing down the half-cooked, half-masticated flesh of the above-named dead animals with strong coffee or brandy and soda, sow to the whirlwind of disease and death. They reap what they sow. This is *Karma*. It is not the hot, debilitating climate of India, but their depraved conduct that so early kills them.

WHAT THE HINDOOS SAY OF THEIR CLIMATE.

A prominent India journal says : —

" If the natives of our country led such lives as do the English and even many of the missionaries, they, too, would deteriorate. It is accepted as an axiom that Europeans born in the country and reared here, as well as Eurasians, are steadily deteriorating from the stamina and vigor of the original stock. A greater error could not be fulminated. The finest specimens of manhood physically, are represented by Europeans who have been in the country for three generations. Among the Eurasians, splendid specimens of physical manhood can be shown. Of course, city-bred men are always inferior to those who are country bred, and so it is in India. . . . If it was generally known that Europeans can live as safely and as healthily in India as in any part of Europe, that is, if they live sensibly and hygieni- cally, many Europeans would settle in India and invest capital, for India is a grand country. The resources of India awaiting development are im- mensely great. European enterprise, European capital, would make India a magnificent country. Crude materials are lying throughout the length and breadth of the land, awaiting capital and intelligent enterprise, to turn them into manufactures yielding handsome returns. It is necessary for India's welfare that the truth regarding the Indian climate should be gen- erally known."

IS THERE MUCH LEPROSY IN INDIA ?

Not very much. It is not as prevalent as it is in China, Singapore, or the Sandwich Islands. In Ceylon, I employed a leprous Kandian youth to write for me, that because of his leprosy had been dismissed from Government Service. I had no fear of the disease. If contagious at all, it is only feebly so. It was after nine years of continuous contact with lepers that Father Damien of Honolulu memory died. Very few women are lepers. It is the general opinion of physicians that syphilitic persons, upon exposure for a certain period,

are more apt to have the disease than the otherwise
healthy. The period of incubation of the disease is placed
from three to twenty years. Often a husband may have it
for nearly a lifetime and none others of the family. Hered-
ity is a certainty, however, and yet it sometimes skips one
and two generations. A young and very intelligent Hindoo
of Madras, upon whose person the sluggish swellings had just
appeared and who consulted me, said that his grandfathers on
both sides had succumbed to the disease, but there was not a
vestige of its appearance in either of his parents. The eti-
ology of this disease is at best but poorly understood; still,
it is certain that a syphilitic soil contains just the qualities
that if the leprous bacillus be introduced, it will develop
this terrible disease.

Many Oriental lands are yet but partially explored and
geographically mapped. On my second tour around the
world, I spent some time in poor half-unknown Cambodia.
Here, one of the hospital physicians at the Capital informed me that there " were many lepers in the country;
but the people neither avoid, nor refuse to eat with them,
nor even to sleep with them." Dr. Coltman writes that the
reason of this was that because the "ruler of the country in
one instance was a leper, and the people ceased, on this
account, to feel dislike to it." Leprosy is not painful. Often
the first symptom is a numbness of the part attacked. In
Northern China there is no segregation of the leper class.
They are seen mixing about among the healthy, buying, selling and in no way deprived of their freedom.

It is a mistake to say that leprosy is an incurable disease.
But neither calomel, iron, quinine, strychnia, cod-liver oil,
nor the mineral acids will cure it. The remedy lies in the
use of grains, vegetables and fruits for foods, pure, distilled
water, pure air, medicated steam baths, and massage with
the touch of the magnetic hand. Medically speaking, one of
the best constitutional alterative tonics is the syrup of the
iodide of iron in small doses. Dr. Cantlie uses the ointment

of Unna, composed of chrysarobin five per cent., salicylic acid two per cent., and ichthyol five per cent. When used on the face it should be much reduced.

Dr. Coltman says : " I have used an ointment of carbonate of zinc for the ulcerative process. I have also used with good success hydrarg. ammoniat, zinc oxid and plumbi acet. made into an ointment with cosmoline." But, besides keeping the excretory organs active, diet, steaming, rubbing — massage is indispensable. Let no leper despair of a cure.

INDIA'S PROGRESS UNDER BRITISH RULE.

Child marriage constitutes one of the dark spots to-day on the fair face of India. I will not describe it. It will not well bear description, from either a physiological or social standpoint. It is quite possible that Mrs. Dr. Ryder has greatly magnified its mischief. Brahmins and intelligent Hindoos unitedly so affirm. But, be this as it may, it is certain that she does not care to have her book circulated in India — the very place where it should be circulated, if just and critically authentic in statement.

Suttee, the self-immolation of the widow by burning alive upon the same funeral pyre of the dead husband, was popular and considered justifiable in India for hundreds of years. Priests justified and encouraged it as they did hundreds of other superstitions. The sources of priestly revenues in nearly all lands are superstitions and donations. Priests are the temple beggars.

Brahminical writers of the agone centuries asserted that widow-burning was authorized by their sacred books; but deeper researches by more competent Sanskrit scholars, discovered no authority either in the Vedas or Manu for the murderous practice. Akbar, so far as his rule extended, partially prohibited it in the sixteenth century.

The burning of widows was very prevalent in India long after the East India Company came into power. This Company tried to prohibit it, by forbidding it unless voluntary on the part of the widow. This did not materially diminish the number burned, "for in the twelve years between 1815 and 1826, there were 7,154 officially reported in Bengal alone."

In the year 1829, Gov. Bentinck enacted a law, declaring all aid, assistance or participation in any act of suttee, to be murder and punishable with death. The Brahmin priests denounced this law with great vengeance as interfering with their religion. Priests, always conservative, lag behind prophets and people. Rammohun Roy, be it said to his credit, discouraged and preached against the suttee practice. He was an inspired Hindoo, as was Chunder Sen.

Superstitions necessarily decline before the march of science and culture. The sacredness of the Ganges as a river for penances, immersions, swearing by, and for the depositing of those of the dead not burned, is going out of date with many other old-time superstitions.

Once I counted, in years agone, four dead, decaying human bodies floating on the placid Ganges, while taking a boat-ride before sunrise, down along the river by Benares, city of sacred shrines and temples, in several of which were kept and religiously cuddled — if not worshipped — elephants, bulls and monkeys. The Palestinian Nazarene said, "God is Spirit, and they that worship Him, should worship Him in Spirit and in Truth."

Caste, if anything of the kind is admissible, should be based upon intelligence and moral worth and not upon blood as in Britain, nor upon sordid wealth as in America. Social caste initiated and instituted in the East by a scheming priesthood, is at best a scourge, a pretension, a vile moral pest. It cannot long stand before railways and the sturdy tread of science. Already it is softening, broadening, among the more enlightened of the Indians. Brotherhood as taught in the Vedas — as taught by the Hebrew prophets and later by Spiritualists and Theosophists — is becoming an inspiring watchword in India's progress. One

of Lord Buddha's first teachings was — " down with caste !
as death levels all, so a true and holy life must equalize all."
Unwisely flattering the caste Hindoos, Mrs. Besant (a recent
outgrowth from materialism) half apologized for the Indian
caste system in her published lectures. It was neither western nor womanly. Our real friends do not flatter us. It is
the lame that require crutches, and the egregiously bad that
need apologizing for and bolstering up with honeyed words.
Another travailing birth of Mrs. Besant up out of archaic
legends, Upanishad mysticisms, impossible miracles and
incarnated monstrosities christened gods, into the golden
sunshine of Spiritualism — that divine Spiritualism whose
corner-stone is Spirit — pure, boundless, changeless — O
infinite Spirit, and she will find rest for her weary, wandering feet — rest within the templed gates of the true " wisdom
religion," Spiritualism, that Spiritualism which implies spirit
meditations, spirit communications (not with invented
" shells "), but with our loved in the higher spheres of intelligence, and the leading of a calm, serene, spiritual life.

SLAVERY IN INDIA.

Not only previous to English rule had the plague, famines
and devastating wars prevailed among the Maharajah, rajahs
and tribal kings and chiefs, but slavery, recognized alike by
Hindu and Mahomedan law, was perpetrated " in India by
the four unfailing sources of birth, war, debt, and famine."

" On the British acquisition of the country, slavery of a firm type existed
everywhere, chiefly in the form of domestic servitude and agricultural bondage. The early English manuscript records refer to it without any hint
of blame and simply as an existing fact. What is to be done with a boat-
load of slaves which had got into the hands of the police? what is to be
done about recruits who have enlisted in one of our battalions, but are
reclaimed by the local landholder as his slaves ? what is to be done with a
deceased nobleman's retainers, ' the majority of whom are slaves?'
Those were the commonplace questions to which slavery as an accepted
institution gave rise in the last century. As late as 1841 the Commission-
ers are said to have found in a single tract over two hundred landholders

each in possession of two thousand slaves. Their report shows that the number of slaves varied in different districts from one-sixth to one-half of the entire population. Sir Bartle Frere estimated, if we remember rightly, that there were *nine million* slaves in India in 1843.

"The Maratha misrule in Orissa, for example, led to horrors scarcely less terrible than those of the 'middle passage.' The Ganjam records disclose miserable gangs of peasantry who had been shipped from Orissa for sale in Southern India. The frail crafts that carried them were often driven ashore on the Madras coast. Wretched, footsore parties, rescued by the compassion of our officers, were passed northwards from one British factory to another, till they reached the Orissa frontier, leaving a trail of their sick and dying along the route. A proclamation by the Madras Government against this abuse of the system proved in the last century ineffectual. The whole system is so completely forgotten that the local annalist remarks, 'But for the original papers which I here cite in support of my statements, its existence at any time would now be denied.'

"Two chief sources of the slave population were the enslavement of families for debt and the sale of women and children during famine. It must be remembered that local scarcities, often deepening into famine, were almost of yearly occurrence in India before British roads broke down the isolation of districts. Such scarcities acted as a constant cause of the sale of women and children. In 1769–70 a native officer indicated the severity of the Bengal famine by the fact that buyers of children could no longer be found. In 1790 the peasants in the Maratha district of Cuttack gave themselves and their families away for food. During the famine of 1813 half the free population in the district of Agra was reported to have disappeared, a boy being sold for a single meal. In the scarcity following the floods of 1834 children were hawked about the streets of Calcutta. Male adults, women, boys and girls had their regular market rates — girls fetching four to ten times the price of boys, according to their good looks. The sale of his family formed a normal resource of the peasant during famine.

"So deeply rooted was slavery in the customs of rural India that the first British attempts at interference proved vain. After earlier measures against the importation of slaves by sea, a local order in 1820 forbade the actual sale of slaves in the districts which we had conquered from the Peshwa; a legislative enactment in 1827 required that such sales, to be valid, must be duly registered before a magistrate. The *status* of slavery was clearly recognized and Lord William Bentinck's effort in 1834 to liberate the slaves who passed to the British Government among the other chattels of the Raja of Coorg obtained but partial success. Of 1,115 slaves thus set free, only thirty families took to cultivation on their own account and 250 accepted service under peasant proprietors. Hereditary thraldom had worked so deeply into the minds of the rest that they re-entered of their free will the class of bondsmen and 'were treated exactly as if they had remained slaves, many of them destroying their certificates of freedom.'

"The Indian law of 1843 is sometimes spoken of as an Abolition Act and it is inferred that slavery could have had little vitality in India because the Act aroused no overt resistance. As a matter of fact, when the law was first proposed, even after the Parliamentary report and with the powerful advocacy of Mr. Bird's minute, it met with such opposition that it was laid aside. It was only the accident of the whole power of the Government passing into Mr. Bird's hands, while Lord Ellenborough was playing the stage-conqueror in Northern India, that enabled the Act to be passed. Nor did the Act venture to abolish in express terms the *status* of slavery in India. It refused the aid of the Civil Courts to enforce the sales of slaves or to enforce rights of property in them, or to dispossess holders of property on the plea of its having been derived from a slave. The Act also made offences against slaves punishable by the criminal law as if committed against free persons. The great wars from which the Company had just emerged and the new wars on which it was about to enter, left little leisure for internal politics. But economic causes were at work against the old-world slavery of India, and the people were slowly prepared for its total prohibition by the Penal Code of 1860. Forty years elapsed between the local executive order against slave sales in 1820 and the time at which the British-Indian Government ventured to make slave dealing in India a criminal offence."

The above from the " Weekly Times," Feb. 19, 1897, with previous liberal and confirmatory quotations from Hindoo journals, very clearly proves that India was by no means a paradise previous to British rule. That she has always ruled wisely and beneficently, I neither affirm nor believe. My convictions are to the contrary. Too well do I know of the brusque, overbearing and almost brutal characteristics of certain English officials in the East.

Seemingly strangers to the fact that themselves and the Hindoos are of one original stock, the Aryans, they seem blind to the nobler instincts of fraternity, and half-dead to that sweet spirit of gentleness and tenderness that becomes such a professedly high degree of civilization. Queen Victoria is as deservedly as decidedly popular in India. Her

officials are not. It is the feeling with multitudes of the
natives that English rule partakes largely of despotism and
tyranny over the masses that have little or no means of re-
dress — no Parliamentary voice. Deprived, they say, of the
" ballot — of home rule — of fire-arms and other inalienable
rights, we are taxed down to the verge of starvation."

The English having abolished the suttee practice and slavery, they should now grapple with and ultimately abolish the
child-marriage system. Very many Hindoos are already opposed to it, realizing that true marriage — the life-long union
of two loving souls can be arranged and should be consum-
mated only by the intelligent and the reflecting involved in
the union. Love is the soil, subsoil and cement of marriage. And Hindoo parents might just as well eat or drink
for their children as to love for them, and marriage without
love is only another name for lust, and lust leads to social
death. It has been said by certain fanatics that puberty
prompts to speedy marriage and " nature must not be med-
dled with." Then do not cut the nails, trim the hair, clothe
the body, fell the forests, nor pull the weeds from your garden. Down on all such rubbish and moral rottenness!
Woman is not physiologically mature till twenty-two or four
years of age, and man some two years later. Maturity, health
and wisdom are the indicators of marriage. Infantile betrothals and child-marriages are abominations to be abrogated.

BRITAIN AND INDIA FACE TO FACE.

Never before in the annals of time have two great civilizations, differing so widely, been brought face to face. The
struggle for supremacy commenced years ago. It continues.
It is the struggle of the mad north-lands against the milder-
mannered and warmer south-lands — the struggle of physical
force and push, against a quiet and more restful intelligence
— stern materialism against a mystic Spiritualism — physics
against metaphysics, and science, an ever-changing science
against myth and religious tradition.

A scholarly Brahmin recently wrote as follows in the " Madras Mail " :

" That Hindoo life is now being deeply affected by contact with the Western civilization and the ideas which Western education aided by the railway, the telegraph and the telephone brings, goes without saying, and it can hardly be doubted that though it may not be entirely replaced by European civilization, it will in the end be considerably modified by it. There are many among us who deplore the fact that the good old institutions should now, under the influence of these new ideas, be in danger of destruction or alteration. In the case of some this feeling is to be explained by the tendency which is found to exist at all times and in all countries, to admire the past and to regard all change as deterioration. But there are others who think that the civilization of the West has not on the whole contributed to the happiness of a nation, that while it has certainly led to the production of immense wealth, it has also brought about a selfish, sordid spirit and much misery, and that under it, the difference between him who hath and him who hath not is getting more and more accentuated. It is urged that in the unrestricted competition which forms a very essential feature of this civilization, the rich man is getting richer and the poor man poorer, and that in the struggle between capital and labor the latter necessarily gets worsted, with the result that side by side with the accumulation of large wealth in the hands of a few, you have a very large portion of the community in an abject state of poverty and utterly at the mercy of the moneyed classes."

Speaking in general terms, India, one of the grandest countries on earth, rich in soils, rivers and forests, summering under an eternal sun, peopled with intelligent Aryan millions, among whom are men of the deepest research, profoundest thought, exalted attainments and aspirational desires for political freedom, the development of their fatherland, the physical, mental and moral welfare of their countrymen — and yet is stricken with famine, with the plague, burdened with a merciless taxation and staggering under an ever-accumulating, unbearable load of poverty. God and good angels lift the cloud and hasten the day of India's redemption.

Hindoo life is pre-eminently village life. Though toiling off on farming-lands during the day they flock into the villages at night-time. This great country is not dotted with farmhouses and school-houses as in America. And yet the Hindoo, whether of the higher or lower caste, is exceedingly anxious for an education. Brahmins are naturally great students. There are schools in some localities for even the pariahs. Col. Olcott established one of this character near Adyar. Tennyson and Carlyle, Emerson, Darwin and Wallace are well-known among the higher classes of India. American literature, too, is rapidly finding its way into the more distant villages away out from the crowded cities. Many of these people prefer Longfellow ; prefer, I cannot tell why, American to English works of history, poetry and medicine. Last month I received five letters from Madras, Tinnevelly, Lahore and Madura, asking for American journals and books treating of science, history and Spiritualism.

Just as I was leaving Madras last May, a Hindoo journalist handed me quite a pamphlet entitled "Chromopathy," a sort of a compilation from the works of my erudite fellow-countryman, Dr. E. D. Babbitt, author of "Principles of Light and Color," "Human Culture and Cure," "Religion as Revealed in the Material and Spiritual Universe," etc., all or which are scholarly, up-to-date works, with visions of the beyond — works of deepest research and broadest range of thought as touching originality, science and philosophy — life, health and immortality.

These books and others treating of sunlight, massage, electricity and the finer forces generally, together with the instruments used by the doctor in treating and curing diseases, may be obtained by writing Dr. E. D. Babbitt, 253 South Broadway, Los Angeles, Cal.

CHAPTER XXXIV.

"Tell me, I cried, O prophet,
Thou shade of the mighty past —
What of the truth in the future?
Is its horoscope yet cast?"

IN the gray of antiquity, Solon, a Grecian sage, buckled on his sandals and traveled afar into Egypt in search of truth — and while he traveled he also taught. There are no higher aims in life than teaching and being taught.

Learned Brahmins of to-day often travel the length and breadth of India, teaching as they go. These are not fakirs, but Sanskrit-versed sages. If they — if any Brahmin goes into a foreign country to settle, or as a traveler eating the foods of foreigners he forfeits his caste. Hindooism in some of its phases was represented at the " World's Parliament of Religions," but Orthodox Brahminism was not. No true Brahmin presumes to leave India, nor will he till caste dies out into the better, broader faith of brotherhood.

The Arjuna of Lahore, writes as follows of a traveling sage : —

During the last week Lahore had the good fortune of seeing a man who might rightly be considered a model of the ancient Hindu and a worthy inspirer of the rising generation of the modern Hindus. Mr. D. Subba Rao belongs to a very respectable family of Maharatta Brahmans now residing at Madura, Southern India. Being an elderly gentleman, he has given up his home and family, wife and children, and is traveling all over India visiting the national sacred shrines and coming into personal contact with the intellectual lights of the Native India of to-day. Like many of his countrymen (the Madrasis), he has an extraordinary command over the English language; in fact he uses it so simply, correctly, eloquently and without a show of effort, that one cannot but admire. His simple mode of living, his noble features, his high thinking, his wealth of experience, his intellectual strength to deal with and speak extempore on almost all the subjects of human concern, do not demand but command respect from any educated person who has some interest in the intellectual advancement of his countrymen. And over and above all this he is a master of some of the occult sciences of divination, Phrenology, Physiognomy, Psychology, Palmistry, moles, etc., and not at least, *Mantra Shastra*. He holds a considerable lot of autograph letters, photographs, medals, rewards, and other tokens of regard from the highest men of India, intellectually and politically. . . . His secular qualities not less than his occult acquirements, have given him a very remarkable and unique position in the life of the modern India, as he is in possession of the most private secrets of, as well as the public information about the leading natives of India and not only of their present and past state but even of their future! He is a great scholar and he is very fond of examining every character in the light of his divine art. Those who have had the occasion of examining him in it must have been agreeably startled at his proficiency in spiritual gifts; he told us of a *mole* which was on a private part of the body of the present writer, a knowledge of which must have been impossible to an ordinary mortal! We wish him every success in his patriotic ambitions.

Such a man traveling in America would be considered a Spiritual medium, although it would not be thought a very high phase of mediumship to be pointing out "moles" on the body.

Continental, English, and American Spiritualism and Spiritualists were shamefully misrepresented in India a number of years ago by Madame Blavatsky and some of her biologized subordinates. The future will rectify all this; for

"Ever the truth comes uppermost,
And ever is justice done."

R. B. J. Sukharam, Gadgil, L. L. B., a Hindoo of some attainments, informs us that the "Pishachas spoken of in their sacred books refer to gross, depraved human souls, which, after the death of their bodies, are earth-chained as a result of their utter lack of Spirituality and purity. It is these disembodied human beings that do the communicating with the living." He further informs us that, according to the Hindoo belief, "very selfish men, men of mere intellectual endowments, who lack Spiritual intuitions, may become pishachas equally with the vicious — pishachas being the returning souls of demon men." He continues: "In this invisible state, the soul, being deprived of the means of enjoyment through its own physical body, is perpetually tormented by hunger, appetite and other bodily desires, and can have only vicarious joys by approaching within the aura, or by entering into the living physical bodies of others, or by absorbing the subtilest essences of the depraved and the oblations offered for their own sake."

Not all pishachas can enter the "living human bodies of others; and none can enter the body of a holy man — an ascetic." "Hindoo funeral ceremonies, from the first to the eleventh and twelfth days after a person's death, are little more than methods to prevent the hungry earth-bound soul from becoming a pishacha. If the pishacha, or deceased friend, begins to manifest itself, there are special ceremonies, called *pishacha-machini*, intended to emancipate this soul from the state of desire."

Indians, as do Christian sectarists, regard all influences from the spirit-world as abnormal and dangerous. Religious ecclesiastics always connect such manifestations with the devil, or with the demons of the under-world; while Hindoos generally consider the return of spirits, especially if occurring in their own families, as a great misfortune; and yet, singular as it may seem, they make scarcely an effort to study hypnotism, psychic vibration, will-force or the trance, but, crying pitris, pishachas, obsession, they rush wildly off to the priests in some of their temples to have the spirit-intruder expelled. And, probably from experience, these priestly adepts are vastly more expert in exorcisms than the Christian missionaries.

Often did I witness, while traversing India, their rude methods of dispossessing the obsessed. Not only did I see camphor and various gums burned, but women beaten to "drive the devil out." In obsessional cases, decision of character, a positive will and a high soul purpose are invariably more successful than uncouth figures and the muttering of priestly mantras. And this — all this is an admission of the fact, the stubborn fact of Spiritualism. But is it not dangerous? Yes, much as the fire is that may burn homes and cities — much as water is that may flood the streets and the fields. What then? Shall the fires that cook our food be forever quenched? and shall rains no more fall upon our grasses and groves? Shall love, because not differentiated from lust, and so abused, be crushed out of humanity's great sympathetic soul? How disgracefully pitiable this chop-logic of the semi-idiot and the bigot!

The great Swedish seer, Swedenborg, truthfully taught that the heavens and the hells, the upper and lower kingdoms of conscious intelligences, are all open to the different races of earth. And, whether admitting or not, we are all, through the finer forces and the laws of vibration, influenced by the unseen auras, by the thoughts and the spirit intelligences of those that dwell in the invisible spheres about us.

Phenomenal Spiritualism, old as antiquity, is a fact; and all history and all sacred books confirm the fact. It is the antithesis of a hopeless, dreamless materialism. It is God's living witness of a future conscious existence. Religious Spiritualism is a fact *plus* truth — Divine truth — that touches, and transfigures the soul into the divine image. And this Spiritualism, already cosmopolitan, is on earth to stay in some form and under some name; and all the combined potencies of superstition and bigotry, of hells and devils cannot drive the blessed truth of angel ministries out of human hearts and souls. It is as firmly rooted there as is the intuitive conviction of immortality itself.

Leaving Ceylon again, April 23, for India, crossing the

Old Hindoo Temple.

narrow strip of waters, ever rough in the monsoon seasons, with no decent harbor for landing, I reached Tuticorrin the next day, seeing a gathered conglomeration of Indians in their primitive type of naturalness. The railway station was crowded with these poor pariahs from drought-smitten districts, excitedly chatting and clinging to their bundles, waiting to ship for Colombo, then pursuing their way back to the great Ceylonese tea-plantations.

It was nearly night when we reached Madura, a city of eighty thousand, and originally a great religious capital, old as ancient Jerusalem, or Rome in her palmiest period. Here resided that once powerful monarch Tirumai Nayak. And here may be seen a magnificent temple, covering an area of over fourteen acres, unique as ancient — that the vandal Mohammedans failed to destroy. Making little mention of its images, its lighted altars, its sacred elephants, its gold-leaf covered gods, with its hall of a thousand pillars — the whole structure is weird, grand, gorgeous and peculiarly Oriental. Some of the architecture is absolutely exquisite. Once Madura was the center of great learning and political influence. "It was," says a noted English writer, "the seat of a university long before Cambridge or Oxford had come into existence, a university which united in itself the functions of an academy and a royal society of letters, which dispensed fame to poets and conferred immortality on works of genius."

Strange as it may seem, Brahma has no temples in India, and receives no worship. Gods have their day and die away into oblivion. Madura is a great center of Saivaite worship, each worshipper bearing upon his forehead three horizontal paint-lines; while the Vishnuites have one straight line of paste or paint drawn down the forehead to the nose. Others have different marks to symbolize the sect to which they belong; the Brahmin wearing his three-plied string over his shoulder. Exceedingly pleasant are my memories of several cultured Brahmins in this city, and also of a distinguished Parsee physician — all Theosophists. Fortunate is the traveler that meets such friends and courteous guides along life's checkered pilgrimage. . . .

On Monday evening, May 4, I lectured before the Hindoo Triplicane Literary Society of Madras. It was decidedly a learned audience, the majority being graduates of the Madras Presidency College. This institution has nearly two thousand students. It faces the ocean. Passing it one day in a carriage I observed many of the students out under the tamarind and orange trees engaged in their studies. Such energy can scarcely fail of being crowned with success. Leaving the carriage I went over to the Vishnu Temple, musical in one department with chantings in the Tamil and responses by the priests. On the outside of the temple I saw the elephant belonging to it, and the great uncouth several-storied car, decorated with gods and religious devices, and drawn around the square enclosing the tank on festival days. It requires probably a thousand people to draw this car. Music precedes the march and flowers are sometimes thrown under the wheels — but enthusiastic worshippers do not thrust themselves under these ponderous wheels to be crushed, as missionaries have falsely reported in Christian lands.

Madame Blavatsky in her will requested that the anniversary of her death be kept by readings from the Bhagavad Gita and from Arnold's "Light of Asia," with appropriate addresses. It is called the White Lotus Anniversary, and was punctually kept in Adyar. The platform was tastefully ornamented with palms and tropical foliage. An empty chair was placed upon the platform decorated with white lotus blossoms. The pillars in the rear of this palatial building were trimmed with tropical foliage shaded by waving palms. Pundits read from the Bhavagad Gita in Sanskrit. Colonel Olcott, myself, and several Brahmin Theosophists delivered short addresses. Whatever be said of Madame Blavatsky's eccentricities and wilderness of writings not always carefully thought out, nor logically presented, nor positions proven, she was nevertheless a wonderful woman — a marvellous, inspirational and materializing medium! What a pity that one so active and talented should now be imprisoned (Mrs. Besant being authority) in the physical body of a dark-skinned Hindoo boy. Candidly I think her the freed and deserving subject of a higher and far nobler destiny.

THE PLAGUE.

Under some name the plague during past centuries has swept millions into eternity. Especially may this be said of India and China. Other countries have been similarly smitten. It is not difficult for the educated physician to divine the causes of this disease, which should have been called the glandular plague, rather than "bubonic."

Briefly summed up, the causes were dirt, dampness and germ fungi. This plague-epidemic, as was generally conceded by the Bombay press, attacked the rats first. These live and thrive best in low, dark, underground places. Multitudes not only died with this disease, but they soon carried the infectious germs along their dark, hidden runways to old tiled or palm-thatched shanties, but in time to the better residences. The rats died first because nearer the damp, filthy soil-surface. It is positively certain that filth and dampness were the chief determining factors in each local outbreak. Cleanliness, pure air, hygenic foods, in a word, sanitation methods will readily destroy the mad depredations of the plague.

Personally I have a deep interest in everything that tends to the physical, mental and spiritual upbuilding of India's thronging millions. Naturally, as the needle to the pole, do my fraternal affections flow out to the Aryan Indians far over the seas. Keeping you in remembrance, oh, Brahmins, I ever clasp you to my heart!

Standing upon the mount of vision I see still farther — see that there are ties between us which we share in common with all the world. To say, with Terence, "Humani nihil a me alienum puto," is to repeat a truth, confirmed by the ripest experience, and to which modern science attaches the profoundest significance. The superstitions and politics, the

aspirations and the glories of the Brahminized races are not
without their analogies in our midst to-day.   May the international blending of the Occident and the Orient prove a joy
and a blessing to each and all.

Pilgrim as I am — afloat on the ocean of being as we all are,
circumstances affect us, and unseen powers a great cloud o
witnesses, influence us.   We did not choose our birth-land, nor
time of coming into this objective existence ; nor the government under which we would be born.   Fate and forces beyond our control placed us here.   And all is well !   Regardless of color, clime or nationality, humanity has a common
origin, a common pulse-beat, a common heart-throb and a
common uplooking towards a gloriously progressive immortality.   One God, one life-influx, one law, one brotherhood,
and ultimately one destiny for all human intelligences.

CHAPTER XXXV.

THE MEDITERRANEAN SEA. — EGYPT AND ANTIQUITY.

> Whatever disappointment may befall me
> In plans or pleasures in this world of doubt,
> I know that life at worst can but delay me,
> But no malicious fate has power to stay me
> From that grand journey on the Great Life route.

JUNE 11, and homeward bound, we are now steaming and struggling along in the Indian Ocean in a terrific monsoon. For nearly two days the rain poured down in torrents, lightnings flashed, thunders howled and the winds reached the rapidity of a furiously-rushing land cyclone. It was really a fearful clash of the elements for a time. The steamer " Aden " that I originally designed to take passage on, succumbed to the storm on the Arabian coast and went down with nearly her entire crew.

Our stop at Aden, Arabia, was brief — but none too brief, considering that we could only see a unique village squat in the sand with barren hills and mountains rising up in the background. One poor forlorn-looking Arab approached our steamer in a rickety boat with ostrich plumes for sale. None purchased. It is scarcely safe to clasp too closely Ishmael's hand. The blood of Palmer, linguist and scientist, still cries from Araby's sands.

June 14; the days are lengthening. We enter the narrow passageway to the Red Sea. The heat, as usual here, is pitilessly oppressive. The passengers, mostly English, have their daily game of cricket. Some pitch quoits; others smoke

and play cards, two Roman Catholic priests joining them.
The Southern Cross now hangs upon the horizon's verge afar
down in the southwest skies — and the North star is rising
higher and higher each night.

A cricket player, from overheating the blood yesterday,
died this morning of apoplexy. He, the shell, the tent that
he dwelt in, will be buried in the sea to-morrow morning —
the fifth sea-burial since leaving Ceylon. Another passenger,
our ship doctor informs me, is dangerously ill with inflammation of the stomach. What are the causes? doubtless, excessive eating: fruit, coffee and biscuits at 7 A. M.; regular
breakfast at 9 A. M.; lunch at 1 P. M.; dinner at 6 P. M.;
and supper at 9 o'clock in the evening. Besides these five
meals, tea and cakes are served at 3 o'clock P. M. — and
people have indigestion and inflammation of the stomach.
Quite likely, and quite deservedly! Few die from starvation, many from gormandizing.

CITY OF SUEZ.

This is an old, dull, Egyptian town, constituted principally
of a Custom House and a cluster of ordinary buildings. The
real city is a little distance from here, and far from being
imposing. The street people seemed poor, and many of them
were suffering from sand-caused sore eyes. The Suez Canal
is about ninety miles in length. It is not wide enough for
two steamers to pass, or move along abreast. Financially,
this canal has proved a marvellous success. What of the
proposed Nicaragua Canal? Will it be built — and with
American capital?

We are at Port Said to-day, the largest coaling station in
the world. Here is where the steamers enter the Mediterranean Sea.

Egypt has changed little since my previous visit. Her
pedestals and pyramids defy the bony finger of Time. In
Ceylon, as before mentioned, I met the exiled Arabi Pasha.
He was charged with a military revolt, demanding from the

Khedive an immediate change of ministry and the increase of the army to eighteen thousand. The Khedive yielded. Arabi rapidly became popular, owing to his strong dislike to Europeans. He soon defied the authority of the Khedive, and became, practically, military dictator. English and French fleets were sent to put down the rebellion. Arabi's army was defeated at Tel-el-Kebis, and Cairo was occupied. Arabi Pasha was tried, convicted and banished to Ceylon, where, as a political exile, he continues to pine for his native land. His residence is upon the side of a mountain in the suburbs of Kanda. He receives a small yearly annuity. One encouraging word from England would return this old patriot to his native country, that his bones might sleep with those of his kindred — but Briton is dumb.

SLAVERY IN AFRICA.

The Koran justifies slavery. And African Mohammedans, originally from Arabia, persist in buying, selling, hunting and holding the black men of Africa in slavery. Nations more enlightened than Arabs have encouraged slave-holding. It was as early as 1620 that Africans were purchased by selfish men to labor in America as slaves. Even " eminent Christian ministers (see Rev. Blyden's " Negro Race," page 33) held negroes in bondage." William Penn, the Quaker, though very kind to the Indians, held, at one time in his life, slaves. Rev. George Whitfield and President Edwards, author of several standard works on Theology, were slaveholders. The British Government brought these slaves in her merchant ships to America. For a number of years Africans were shipped to North America as cattle and sold. Preachers not only held and worked slaves, but the Right Rev. William Meade, bishop of the diocese of Virginia, published a book in defence of slavery. Here's an extract (page 35) : " Almighty God has been pleased to make you slaves, and give you nothing but labor and poverty in this world, which you are obliged to submit to, as it is his will that it

should be so. Your bodies, you know, are not your own.
They are at the disposal of those you belong to," etc. Bishop
Ives taught that slavery was right, saying that when "Ones-
imus ran away from his master, Paul sent him back with a
letter." So the "man of to-day ought to send runaway slaves
back to their masters." These were the teachings of many
bishops and priests as late as the year 1840.

The Bishop of Abyssinia published a letter in the "London
Times," just after the Queen's jubilee, defending the right
and justice of slavery in Zanzibar, over which the English
hold a sort of a protectorate. The above references to slavery
remind me that when, in 1854, I was preaching universal salvation by grace, universal salvation anyhow, in Baltimore, Mr.
Ironmonger, one of the deacons of my church, took a slave-
girl, seven-tenths white, as security for a debt. The demand
not being met, this nearly white slave-girl was put upon the
slave-market block and sold to the highest bidder. My re-
proofs to the deacon, together with the further facts that I
had become a Spiritualist, that I circulated Fremont anti-
slavery tracts in the congregation, and recommended Horace
Greely's "New York Tribune," raised such a political and
religious cyclone that I was quite in danger of my life. The
party of "plug-uglys" was active in those days, especially
by night. Soon I resigned, yet preached two months after
my resignation. The society, upon my leaving, voted resolutions of love and confidence, and pronounced me both a "devoted pastor" and a "Christian gentleman." The resolutions I still retain. From this time, freed from creeds and
all churchianic conventionalities, my real success in life
began.

THE GRANDEUR OF ANTIQUITY.

Journeying in the East and studying the civilizations of
explored, unearthed antiquity, the inquiry still is, which
country was first in what we denominate a great civilization,
Babylon, China, India, or Egypt? Authorities still differ.

The erection of the great pyramids, which so many writers regard as an indication of the highly civilized state of Egypt at the time of their erection, is, in fact, a striking proof that before this period the nation had made very considerable progress in the arts and sciences. The people who built the pyramids had already long since fallen from their highest civilization. The origin of our sciences and many moral precepts still taught by the wisdom of nations is found recorded on the papyri and on the bas-reliefs of the monuments of upper Egypt; while many a dogma on which existing religions are based may be traced to its original form in the documents discovered in the tombs of Thebes and Abydos.

The Egyptians were a race of builders, as the pyramids testify, and they built with a resolve for permanence which has never since been approached. Upon the walls of their edifices they inscribed their annals. Here, in characters as sharp in outline and as vivid in color as on the day they were engraved and painted, we find the record of their creed, their exploits, their manners and customs. But the key to the ancient writings had been lost, and until within the last 100 years the records were inscrutable. With the discovery of the Rosetta stone in 1799 the secrets of the Egyptian writers were unlocked to us. Rosetta is forty-four miles northeast of Alexandria, with which it is connected by a railway.

We are now able to read what the ancient Egyptians wrote, but we cannot say we wholly comprehend it. The genius of this wonderful people was wholly foreign to our own. Kings were garbed as deities and demigods; history was sheathed in myth and allegory, and involved in symbol and metaphor. The fundamental maxim of Egyptian philosophy seems to have been this: "Mortal existence is brief; beyond death lies the only true life; man's duty is to make ready for it." The earliest inscriptions are perhaps 7,000 years old, in the era of the second Egyptian dynasty. From the third dynasty, about 3700 B. C., direct writings abound.

The translation of the heiroglyphic and cuneiform inscriptions of Egypt and Mesopotamia has already thrown a broad light upon the half-told stories of the early peopling of the valleys of the Nile and Euphrates, and as additional historic relics are being constantly brought to view, and there seems to be no limit to the deciphering capacity of minds schooled in the subtleties of translation, still stranger developments in the future may be confidently expected. These discoveries have not only exposed the errors of written history in referring to events, conditions and individual character, but they have brought into prominence great political powers and dynasties, feared and respected before Nineveh or Babylon appeared and known heretofore only as unimportant dependencies.

The earliest and greatest of these nations unrecognized by history were the people of Akkad. They were of the Turanean stock, and their original home was in the uplands of Armenia, and northward where, some

6,000 years or more before the Christian era, they attained a high civilization. They invented the cuneiform letters used in Babylonia and Assyria, and were far advanced in the arts when they spread over Chaldea and the Mesopotamian basin. There, mingling with the Semite races, they created the great empire of Babylonia, and in time lost their distinctive character by imparting it to the Assyrio Semitic races with whom they were thrown in contact.

It has also been discovered that the Hittites were for centuries a warlike and conquering race, rulers over a large empire embracing many different peoples, and not only vastly superior to the Hebrews in martial powers, but capable of successfully coping with the military strength of Egypt or Babylonia. The Old Testament speaks of the Hittites. It is supposed that the Israelites, semi-barbarous, knew of but a small colony of the race occupying lands south of Palestine. At the height of their power the empire of the Hittites extended over Northern Syria and the whole of Asia Minor, with a fortified capital on the Euphrates. To the north it stretched to the Black Sea, and its southern capital was on the Arontes, the principal river of Syria. The Hittites were also of Turanean or Tartar stock, and were finally subjugated by the Assyrians 717 B. C.

Concerning the erroneous manner in which history has dealt with the characters of many of the prominent actors in the past, we will give but a single example — that of Sardanapalus. It is now shown upon the tablets that he was far from being the weak and sensual sovereign described by the poets. It is in clearest proof, on the contrary, that he was the most powerful and enlightened monarch of his time, distinguished alike for energy, sagacity and appreciation of art and literature. He founded a library and school of learning " for the instruction of the people of Nineveh," as expressed by the tablets. " The discovery of this storehouse of national records," says the author, " almost compensates the literary world for the loss of the Alexandrian Library." As he was the grandson of Sennacherib, " the Assyrian " who, as told by Byron, " came down like a wolf on the fold," and the flower of whose army was destroyed by the Lord, we will mention, in conclusion, that the cuneiform records make no reference to that event, although they tell the story of the return of Sennacherib to Assyria with " 200,000 captive Hebrews and other Syrians " in his train." [1]

MALTA.

On the Mediterranean several days we reach Malta, a city

[1] Those who wish to pursue exhaustive studies of the recent explorations at Nippur and through the regions of ancient Babylon should procure the two large volumes of J. P. Peters, Ph.D., Sc.D., D.D., just from the press of Putman & Sons. price $5.00. They contain a mint of information.

standing upon a limestone rock, built largely of rocks and into rocks. The dust is intolerable, the few trees and shrubbery live by irrigation. Goats have the right of way, as do dogs in Constantinople. The guides that I had to do with in this little City by the Sea were either robbers, liars, or beggars; and yet, they were eminently religious, belonging to the Roman Catholic Church. The priests here stalk through the streets in their long black robes, the head-gearing being a queer three-cornered cocked hat. Their conspicuous presence is repulsive. Conducted to the Governor's palace I found him a most courteous gentleman, taking pleasure in showing me the beautiful paintings of the Grand Masters of the Knights of Malta — being a Knight myself they interested me most intensely. In ancient times, this island was occupied by the Phœnicians, and now by the English. It has had, upon the whole, a most remarkable history, being held at different times, by Phœnicians, Cathagenians, Greeks, Romans, Arabs. The footprints of each may be traced to-day in varied ruins. The Romans, while here, constructed and dedicated a magnificent Temple to Apollo, some of the scattered pillars still remaining. It is recorded that St. Paul was shipwrecked here, A. D. 58. The bay bears his name. The Maltese language is composed largely of the Arabic.

Old residents here informed me that the climate was uniform and delightful, being quite a health-resort in wintertime. The soil back from the seashore is sufficiently fertile to produce two crops a year. The summer sets in about the first of June, and the hottest days are tempered by the north and northwesterly winds. Rains in wintertime are frequent.

While the ghastly chapel of bones repelled me, and the Capuchins' Convent, where several skeletons of deceased monks are placed in niches, dressed in the ecclesiastical robes they wore during their church-life, disgusted me, I richly enjoyed the catacombs — these underground excavations consisting of long, dreary passages, out of the walls of which were cut sepulchral niches for men, women and children.

Some of the bones seem almost perfect, but they crumble to dust at the first touch. Abela, Ciantar, Gart-Said, and other historians inform us that these catacombs were dug into the rocks by the early Christians to avoid the fierce persecutions of the pagans. Recent discoveries of picture paintings, sculpture and inscriptions, confirm this opinion.

MUSING ON THE MEDITERRANEAN.

Sea captains and sailors are neither misers nor bigots. The seas lengthen the golden chains of friendship, enlarge human nature and widen the horizon of faith and fraternal sympathy.

Yesterday, June 18th, we halted in our voyage at Brindisi, under Government regulations. All passengers from India were obliged to go through the farce of a medical examination. No symptoms of the bubonic plague were seen or scented.

At sea again! The Mediterranean waters are smooth as polished glass — too placid for a rippling wave or silvery crest. In the hazy distance Mount Etna lifts its volcanic head. Looking down upon it are Sicily's burning skies. Scientists are not united yet as to cause of volcanoes. Opinions and theories concerning these internal fires are not demonstrations.

June 20th — another burial at sea to-day — a woman long crushed with a brutal, drunken husband. They were Welsh, with a family of three small children. He had been seen to beat this poor consumptive woman aboard the steamer. Her sickness had excited the deepest sympathy of the passengers — and the husband's long years of abuse, when intoxicated, had broken her spirit, wrecked her happiness and hurried her to a grave down among the green seaweeds of the ocean. These people made a mistake in their marriage. And now, why should legal enactments have compelled these parties to continue this mistake till " death did them part "? — compel them to continue the mistake, increasing the population of the world the meantime, with poor, illy-begotten and pitiable possibilities of humanity, to later fill jails, poorhouses, or penitentiaries?

Love is not lust. A forced "love," a forced continuance in a loveless marriage, a forced increase of children, and forced injuries in married life, mental or physical, may be legal and respectable; but they are, nevertheless, degrading and damning to posterity. Does not the power, in intelligent persons, to make a contract, imply the moral right to unmake it? Are human contracts infallible and eternal? If the parties themselves cannot amicably adjust their matrimonial differences, let parents and friends be called, constituting a friendly court of family advisers; if this does not succeed, let the matter be referred to a board of arbitration, the parties mutually selecting the arbitrators — if this fails appeal to the court of equity. Do anything, almost, rather than live in a marriage-hell of suspicion, of jealousy, of inharmony, of incompatibility, of drunkenness, peopling the world with mental dwarfs and blood-thirsty criminals. Love is of God — and that only is love which is clean, pure, unselfish — and that only is law which is based upon the immutable principles of right and justice, and which conduces to the highest good and happiness of its subjects.

THE QUEEN'S JUBILEE.

June 22, 1897. Off from the coast of Portugal, once a country famous for discovery, and rich in gold; but now poor. And Spain, also, once proud and immensely rich from Inca and Aztec robberies, but now comparatively poor and seldom noticed in the international affairs of Europe. The law of eternal justice exercises sooner or later judgment in the earth.

Our passengers celebrated the Queen's Jubilee by a great dinner and a shipboard dance in the evening. The Captain's response to the principal toast was painfully incoherent; its chief virtue being its brevity. He ought to read Emerson, Holmes and Longfellow, and then sit a student at the feet of Gladstone, before further attempting public speaking. The

toast was drank to a ringing " God Save the Queen." The
speeches all were sufficiently British and self-congratulatory
to arouse German ire and Italian anger. These nationalities
aboard not only showed their displeasure in several ways, but
openly expressed delight — that while England had largely
lost her former prestige, Russia now wielded the dominating
sceptre of influence over the Continent and all through the
great East. Greece and Turkey were discussed with considerable acrimony, in connection with the slaughter of a hundred thousand Armenians by the great assassin of the nineteenth century, the Sultan of Turkey.

Considering that I was the only American passenger, I was
asked, half in jest, I at first thought, to respond to a toast involving international commerce. I did so, deprecating war
and recommending universal arbitration. I further assured
my fellow-passengers of America's good-will towards England
and her colonies, and that I took very great pleasure in the
jubilee celebration, not from any special admiration of the
Queens and Kings constituting the unhappy reigning families
of Europe — the Czar traveling in an iron-clad car from fear
of assassination — but from the higher, diviner consideration,
that humanity is one. Some of these crowns were already
worm-eaten and tottering. The trend of the world's thought
was towards governments by the people and for the people —
governments in which brains rather than blood should rule.

Queen Victoria as a woman, as a mother, as a royal-souled
grandmother, as a discreet and honored widow, as the reigning Empress not only of India and millions of English-speaking people, but of portions of Africa and other countries, and
whose sceptre is the symbol of civilization — calls forth my
profoundest admiration. Oh, that there were more enthroned
women in the world!

As a physician and hygienist, I further honor the Queen
for ordering each autumn American apples and graham grits;
for having kept a clean court; for having, from her own
bosom, nursed her babes; for never having painted nor pow-

dered her face; for never having worn corsets nor peaked-toed shoes; nor followed the Paris fashions of French demi-mondes, as do many giddy, light-headed women of both England and America. Hail, all hail, then, to Queen Victoria!

A London writer says : —

" Imagine what it must be for this old lady, this venerable grandmother drawn slowly along in her little wicker carriage by a mild, docile donkey, to be able to say ' My son, will, one day, doubtless reign over the United Kingdom; my grandson is the German Emperor and King of Prussia; one of my granddaughters is Empress of all the Russias; I have a son who reigns over the modest Duchy of Saxe-Coburg Gotha; one of my daughters was Empress of Germany; one of my grandsons is Grand Duke of Hesse; I have granddaughters who will reign over Roumania and Greece; the King of Belgium and the King of Portugal are my cousins; the whole of Germany is filled with my descendants and their connections and, leaving out of consideration some few Catholic dynasties, there exists not one Royal house on the earth that does not look towards me as the venerable grandmother, the source of that perennial stream of Majesties and High-nesses.'

" In truth, this simple enumeration has in it something dazzling and the pages of the ' Almanach de Gotha ' have a brilliancy that is almost blinding when one views, stepping out of them, this long procession of the powerful of the earth all coming on this jubilee occasion to bow the knee before the daughter of the House of Hanover and render her homage as the typical Sovereign of this century."

IN LONDON.

Gladly leaving the steamer this day, July 26th, I press the soil and the streets of London for the seventh time. London is the city of cities, the Mecca to which all civilization and culture naturally flock; and, by common consent, it is the best governed city in the world. Beginning with the British Museum, I confess to a profound admiration of it and its people; never forgetting, however, my Scotch ancestry.

Millions from the Continent and the far-away Orient, having witnessed the Jubilee exercises, are now on their winding ways homeward bound. If some are financially the worse for

their journeyings and for partaking of the festivities with
unavoidable discomforts, they are the wiser also.   Experience
is often a very expensive school.   Moral justice, merciless in
penalties to physical law, will not loosen its grip till the
uttermost farthing is paid.

"What wilt thou have," said Emerson; "pay for it and
take it." Do not complain; do not worry; what is legiti-
mately your own you will ultimately get.   What is not your
own by the divine law of right, if you get, you will lose, and
the loss can never be quite regained.   The vicarious atonement is, at best, but a clumsy misfit to partially rectify an
archaic blunder — a bit of buttonhole theology to shield vil-
lains from justice and comfort the lazy — a foul blot upon
the back chapter of Christendom.   Jesus did not die for
Socrates or Plato; did not die and "pay it all"; *all* the
debts for anybody.   No, *no* — each and all must pay their
own debts, cultivate their own corn-fields, chew their own
bread and butter, earn their own heaven!   I would sooner
have Jesus masticate my food for me than to have him atone
for, and pay by his blood, my passage to heaven.   How mean
any decent saint would feel to enter the New Jerusalem upon
the merits of some one else!   "Work out your own salvation," was a command of Paul — and a very commendable
command.

THE TYRANNY OF FASHION.

Fashion is comparatively headless and heartless.   It is also
a merciless tyrant.   To follow its freaks is to die the death,
not of the true and the noble, but the early death of the
unwisely wicked.   Oriental people do not become bald-
headed.   Among other reasons is this, they do not wear the
hard, stiff hat.

Remembering well my first visit to London, over thirty
years ago, and a dinner given me by Benjamin Coleman, a
very estimable man and pioneer Spiritualist, I recall as among
the guests present William Howitt, the noted author, and
other distinguished gentlemen.   Our theme of conversation

was Spiritualism and its progress in all enlightened countries. When about leaving, Mr. Coleman, handing me my easy-going, soft hat, said, in a kindly undertone, "You will have to change this to a regulation hat; all gentlemen with us wear the tall, silk hat." It crimsoned my face for a moment, but, rallying, I replied, "Hats are made for the protection and comfort of heads. They do not grow, but heads do." Independent, and possibly perverse by nature, I clung to my comfortable felt. In the meantime, English heads have grown. The following extracts are from the "London Times," July issue : —

Lord Ronald Gower, in a second letter to *The Times* on this subject, says that he does not for a moment hope for a sudden cessation of the tall hat; but if men of sense and good taste would only have the courage to cease to appear in London in the tall hat and in its place wear some simple, soft and sensible hat, then we might hope to see the bright day when the tall hat would only be worn by mutes and bagmen, scarecrows, and fossilized old fogies.

"Thomas Bowler" writes from Brighton, saying the high chimney-pot hat, he is thankful to say, is almost a thing of the past in that enlightened borough, although it is still adhered to by a few Sunday cockneys and ultra-Sabbatarians. It has been almost displaced by the round or the short soft hat, which, if not more graceful, is far more comfortable.

"A Man about Town" says that "Gracchus" may take heart of grace, for since last jubilee the young of all classes have abjured the tall top hat. In our most frequented thoroughfares on any Sunday night not one per cent. of the crowds of middle-class men will be found wearing a silk hat. The "Johnnies," too, of the Upper Ten and the lords are also rapidly emancipating themselves, for in the Park or Piccadilly they now usually disport themselves in soft, or straw hats. Those who declare that only a tall hat can be worn above a frock coat seem quite oblivious of the regulation dress for a naval officer — viz., frock-coat and cap. Fancy the captain of an ironclad appearing on duty in a chimney-pot, stove-pipe hat.

"Equal rights, equal duties, special privileges to none,
Are the only grand attainments that ever can be won."

LONDON.

There is not, there could not be, but one London. It is a world in and of itself; a living sample of an inextinguishable identity; a compact unity in diversity. Its population, though decidedly English, is, to a certain extent, a conglomeration of all races, tribes and tongues. One may drive twenty miles in a straight course across any of London's diameters. And never have I seen more obliging shopkeepers, more polite policemen, or real genuine gentlemen than in this great mammoth city. The English, while more cautious and conservative, are also more fixed and substantial than Americans. This is everywhere manifest in the solidity of their institutions and in their massive architecture. Every bridge, every archway seems to have been built for eternity. A Briton's house is his castle, once invited into it, and ever afterwards you have a substantial friend.

Arriving in London on a Saturday, I repaired quickly to the Florence House, kept by Mr. J. J. and Miss Florence Morse, where I found every possible comfort as well as handclasps warm with friendship. Mr. J. J. Morse is one of the most energetic workers as well as strong pillars in the temple of English Spiritualism. Sunday evening, expecting to be unrecognized, I quietly slipped into the Cavendish Hall, where I had lectured some thirty years ago, to listen to Mrs. E. W. Wallis, announced to answer questions under spirit control. Her work was done admirably and satisfactorily. She was frequently cheered. My old friend, Thomas Everitt, occupied the chair. Mrs. Everitt's mediumship is still afire with demonstrations of immortality. This same evening I met Mr. and Mrs. Watson of Jamestown, N. Y., Mr. and Mrs. Hill and Mrs. Cadwalleder of Philadelphia, Pa., and other Americans. What a contrast in appearance, this audience, with those I had so recently addressed in Ceylon and India!

The week following my arrival in the city, Mr. and Mrs. J. J. Morse, opening their commodious parlors, decorated and festooned for the occasion, gave me a splendid reception. The rooms were packed and among them many of my old friends, such as the Everitts, the Tebbses and many others. Mr. Morse presided. Miss Florence Morse and other musicians gave us excellent music. Addresses were made by the Rev. John Page Hopps, Mrs. Watson, Mrs. Cadwalleder, Mr. Everitt and several others. A choice collation was served of coffee, cake, ice-cream and fruits. It was a most enjoyable season. Lecturing a Sunday evening in the Cavendish Hall by invitation of E. Dawson Rogers, the very able editor of "London Light," I met J. Enmore Jones and others of my old and highly-esteemed friends. All pure friendships are eternal. Mrs. Watson supplied the Cavendish Society a Sunday evening later. She is a very clear and attractive speaker and, what is more, a most admirable woman.

Invited to Glasgow and other places to lecture, I greatly desired to go, but home associations were calling, urging me back to my native land. Life is only another word for activity. For myself there seems to be no rest this side the crystal river of death.

> I paced, with restless feet, the shores of time,
> With fever'd brow and aching heart. 'And when
> I gazed across the vast expanse outspread
> And pondered o'er what it might mean, a voice
> Came from the bosom of th' eternal deep,
> And, answering my silent pray'r, it said
> "Thus art *thou,* mortal — moving on and on
> From Infinite to endless Infinite,
> In constant, ever-fluctuating, flow."

Frequently asked, Is there any advantage in traveling under the auspices of Thomas Cook and Son? I have to say decidedly — *there is!* The traveler gets better service and cheaper hotel rates, and then, Cook and Son's agents in all the civilized countries of the world are polite and courteously attentive. They meet you at the Custom Houses of the various ports and assist in the examination of your luggage. They see to your getting the proper interpreters and give you gratuitously all needed advice concerning side routes and seasons of the year best adapted to different climates of the East. Heartily do I wish that I could speak as flatteringly of the P. & O. line of steamers, but I cannot. Often, though you have first-class tickets, you get only second-class attention. They thrust three or four into a cabin and allow them to half suffocate if the weather is a little stormy. The stewards are often unaccommodating and the bell-boys often take their own time to respond, and yet they expect regular " tips." They employ cheap Hindoo deck labor, because these poor coolies will work for a song. Take passage by the Orient, a competing line, or by almost any French or German steamer, and you will get better table fare and far more attention from servants.

Human life is a pilgrimage, a pacing-ground for experiences. Along the way are smiles and tears, sunshine and shadow — life and death.

"I think of death as some delightful journey
   That I shall take when all my tasks are done.
Though life has given me a heaping measure
Of all best gifts and many a cup of pleasure,
   Still better things await me farther on.

"This little earth is such a narrow planet,
   The distances beyond it so supreme,
I have no doubt that all the mighty spaces
Between us and the stars are filled with faces
   More beautiful than any artist's dream.

"I know that I shall surely behold them,
   When from this waiting-room my soul has soared —
Earth is a wayside station, where we wander,
Until from out the silent darkness yonder,
   Death swings his lantern, and cries ' *All aboard !* '

"I think death's train sweeps through the solar system
   And passes suns and moons that dwarf our own,
And close beside us we shall find our dearest,
The spirit friends on earth we held the nearest,
   And in the shining distance Love's white throne."

Works of J. M. Peebles.

Immortality,

And our employments hereafter, with what a hundred spirits, good and evil, say of their dwelling-places. Cloth $1.00; paper 50 cts.; postage 15 cts.

Seers of the Ages.

Ancient, Mediæval and Modern Spiritualism. This volume, nearly 500 pages, traces the phenomena of Spiritualism down through all the ages. Price $1.50; postage 12 cts.

Magic.

One of the series of lectures delivered by Dr. Peebles before the medical class of the College of Science in San Francisco. Price 10 cts.

Critical Review

Of Rev. Dr. P. E. Kipp's Sunday night Sermons against Spiritualism. Price 15 cts.

Hell.

A critical review of Rev. Dr. P. E. Kipp's sermon upon "What and Where is Hell?" Price 10 cts.

How to Live a Century,

And grow old gracefully. 109 pages. Price 52 cents.

The First General Epistle

Of Dr. Peebles to the preachers and members of the "Anti-Spiritualistic Convention." Price 5 cts.

Spiritual Harp.

A collection of vocal music for the choir, congregation and social circles. Cloth $2.00; full gilt $3.00; six copies $10; 12 copies $19, postage 14 cts.

Spiritualism Defined and Defended.

Being an introductory lecture delivered in the Temperance Hall, Melbourne, Australia. Price 10 cts.

The Soul;

And its Pre-existent State. Is Re-incarnation True? Price 10 cts.

Ingersollism or Christianity, Which?

Price 15 cts.

The Third Journey Around the World,

Studying nations, races and their religions, in search of truth. Describes the Brahmins, Buddhists, Parsees, Fakirs, Magicians, Child Marriage, Theosophy, The Plague, The Famine, etc. Price $1.50.

How Not to Die; Immortality on Earth.

Now ready for the press; 200 pages. Price 50 cts. For sale at the "Banner of Light" office, Boston, Mass.

The Pro and Con of Spiritualism.

Dr. Henry A. Hart *versus* Dr. J. M. Peebles. 20 pages. Price 10 cents.